Classical Political Economy

Classical Political Economy

Primitive Accumulation and the Social Division of Labor

MICHAEL PERELMAN

ROWMAN & ALLANHELD Publishers
FRANCES PINTER (Publishers) Ltd., London

ROWMAN & ALLANHELD

Published in the United States in 1984
by Rowman & Allanheld, Publishers
(A division of Littlefield, Adams & Company)
81 Adams Drive, Totowa, New Jersey 07512

Library of Congress Cataloging in Publication Data

Perelman, Michael.
   Classical political economy.

   Bibliography: p.
   Includes index.
   1. Classical school of economics—History.
2. Economics—History. 3. Division of labor—History.
4. Capitalism—History. I. Title. II. Title: Primitive
accumulation and the social division of labor.
HB94.P47   1983   330.15′3   83–13976
ISBN 0–86598–095–0

Published in Great Britain in 1983 by Frances Pinter (Publishers)
5 Dryden Street, London WC2

British Library Cataloguing in Publication Data

Perelman, Michael
   Classical political economy.
   1. Economic history—18th century   2. Economic
history—19th century
   I. Title
   330.9′04   HC54

   ISBN 0–86187–321–1

83 84 85/ 10 9 8 7 6 5 4 3 2 1

Printed in the United States of America

Contents

Preface

In the development of a theory, the invisible of a visible field is not generally *anything whatever* outside and foreign to the visible defined by that field. The invisible is defined by the visible as its *invisible, its forbidden vision:* the invisible is not therefore simply what is outside the visible (to return to the spatial metaphor), the outer darkness of exclusion—but the *inner darkness of exclusion,* inside the visible itself. . . .

Louis Althusser, "From Capital to Marx's Philosophy," p. 26

This book is novel in three major respects. First, it addresses the question of what determines the social division of labor, the division of society into independent firms and industries. Second, it develops the theoretical implications of primitive accumulation. Third, it offers a significantly different interpretation of classical political economy, demonstrating that this school of thought supported the process of primitive accumulation.

This book may be controversial because it contradicts the commonly accepted theory that classical political economy offered its unconditional support for laissez faire. I question the relative importance of the almost universally admired Adam Smith and make the case that Smith and the other classical authors attempted to promote the process of primitive accumulation.

Classical political economy presents an imposing facade. For more than two centuries, its professed adherents have been grinding out texts to demonstrate how a market generates forces that provide the most efficient method for organizing production. The concept of primitive accumulation —that is, the process of depriving people of their means of producing for themselves—seems far removed from the literature of classical political economy. For the most part, even Marxists accept classical political economy at face value. Adam Smith, David Ricardo, and the others are assumed to be uncompromising advocates of laissez faire. In fact, these authors engaged in a subterfuge. While publicly promoting laissez faire as an ideology that would give capital absolute freedom of action, it also called for intervention of one sort or another to coerce people to do things that they would not otherwise do. Specifically, classical political economy encouraged policies that would hinder people's ability to produce for their own needs.

Perhaps because so much of what the classical economists wrote about traditional systems of agricultural production was divorced from their seemingly more timeless remarks about pure theory, such portions of their works have been passed over in haste by later readers. Although this aspect of classical political economy might not have seemed to fall outside the core of their work, a distinct pattern of antagonism to small-scale producers emerges.

I found this observation to be of interest, but it seemed extraneous to my main line of research at the time, concerning the social division of labor. I had originally intended to restrict my research to the very simple question: What does it mean that the economy is divided into an assortment of industries and firms?

I began this work with the conviction that in the realm of theory, progress is made by asking unasked questions. The simpler the question, the more instructive the exercise. I turned to the classical political economists for guidance. After all, their works were created during an unparalleled development of the social division of labor.

I was surprised to learn that classical political economists paid almost no attention to the theory of the social division of labor. Adam Smith offered a detailed description of the social division of labor in his famous pin factory, but he did not bother to extend his discussion to the next question: What does it mean that society is partitioned in such a way that the pin industry purchases its metals or fuels instead of producing them itself? How does such an arrangement originate? Could such changes in the pattern of industries make a difference in an economy even if technology were held constant?

These questions then led me to ask why so little discussion was devoted to such questions. Might not this silence have something to reveal? Following this line of investigation, I looked at what classical political economy had to say about the peasantry and self-sufficient agriculturalists. In general, classical political economy favored the separation of industrial and agricultural pursuits. Its efforts to throttle small-scale agricultural producers were, in fact, a method of manipulating the social division of labor. Much of this discussion touched on what we now call "primitive accumulation."

Nonetheless, the classical political economists generally maintained their silence regarding this matter when discussing matters of pure economic theory. The subject of the social division of labor cropped up only when the market proved itself incapable of engaging the rural population fast enough to satisfy the theoreticians of the market. This strategy was embodied in a crude proto-Marxian model of primitive accumulation. The basic lesson of this model is that nonmarket forces might be required to speed up the process of capitalist assimilation in the countryside. Although laissez-faire policies were preferred in classical political economy, non-market forces were deemed acceptable when the market would not lead to the desired result. When seen in this light, I discovered that most of the classical political economists expressed positions diametrically opposed to the theories usually credited to them. This discovery led me to give a substantially new reading to the history of classical political economy.

I have also begun to apply the same procedure in analyzing Marxist theory and neoclassical theory. The results of this inquiry will appear in two subsequent volumes. Here, too, my work has demonstrated to me that my initial question leads to a substantial re-evaluation of the received doctrine.

Before turning to the main body of this work, I wish to append a caveat. In studying the shadows cast by the classics, we must keep in mind that such images have fewer dimensions than the object under study. They may also be deformed. The classical political economists wrote from the comfortable heights of elevated social position. Working-class organization was interpreted as mere disorder. Because of this insensitivity, a work such as this is necessarily unbalanced. Much attention is given to the efforts of capital to control labor, but little is devoted to the reverse. Thus, I leave the reader with the responsibility of estimating the actual balance of forces.

The preparation of this manuscript would have been impossible without the help of Blanche Perelman. Her careful editing for both logical flow and content were invaluable in preparing this manuscript.

Introduction:
Dark Designs

> In order to develop the laws of bourgeoise economy . . . it is not necessary to write the *real history of the relations of production.* But the correct observation and deduction of these laws . . . always leads to primary equations . . . which point toward a past lying behind the system. These indications . . . then offer the key to understanding the past—a work in its own right.
>
> Karl Marx, *Grundrisse,* pp. 460–61

On Reading Classical Political Economy

Classical political economy is the product of a stormy period that was distinguished by the emergence of capitalist social relations. The momentous changes of the time left their mark on the pages of classical political economy. In this sense, classical political economy can be compared to solar eclipses: We have always been fascinated by this rare celestial phenomenon, since it was once thought to serve as a warning of epochal changes. Classical political economy may be read in much the same fashion. The titans of political economy were thought to have been able to see over the heads of their contemporaries into the future. Their theories foreshadowed coming changes in the structure of society. Thus we turn to the classics again and again.

Classical political economy is not always read in this manner. Sometimes reviews of the past are merely used to reinforce the views of the present.

Some readers find anticipations of later technical refinements, such as the theory of utility maximization or the law of diminishing returns. Others use the classics to put their contemporaries in an unfavorable light. Keynes, for example, contrasted the good common-sense of the mercantilists with the irrelevant elegance of Professor Pigou. Still other readers are attracted to the classics' emphasis on dynamics, growth, or capital accumulation. In all these readings, the classics appear to act as a polestar by which we can fix our bearings.

In reality, the classics are not a fixed body in space, but a heterogeneous body of literature written over a period of about one hundred years. If fixity appears, it is the result of a uniform reading. Yes, disputes flare up, but the same pattern roughly holds according to the conventional reading. Classical political economy is almost universally held to orbit around a point somewhere between Adam Smith and David Ricardo. Some hold it to be closer to one or the other, but in general we find consensus.

I propose a new reading of classical political economy. In this cosmology, the center is nearer to Sir James Steuart and Edward Gibbon Wakefield. From this perspective, Adam Smith looks less like the sun than a moon, a lesser body whose light is largely reflected from other sources.

This rereading of classical political economy suggests significant insight into the history of a body of literature that is reread with interest today. I believe that it offers much more. Classical political economy, for all its heterogeneity, did manage to compress much of the varied experience of its day into a compact body of literature that reflects the history of relations of production.

Unlike a solar eclipse, which was superstitiously interpreted as a sign of things to come, classical political economy was a conscious attempt to understand the emerging forces of capitalism. Even when the classical political economists comprehended their own subject imperfectly, their intuition led them to express important insights of which they may have been only vaguely, if at all, aware. I mean this last statement in the same sense that a psychologist might detect an important revelation in a seemingly offhand remark of a patient. In fact, since some of these disclosures might entail unwelcome conclusions, the patient might be more likely to let them come to light in unguarded moments.

Given this perspective, the study of classical political economy can be an effective approach to the study of the history of relations of production. In effect, we can look at the eclipse of precapitalist production relations in much the same fashion that we were taught to watch a solar eclipse as children: punch a small hole in a piece of paper held above another piece. The dark design that appears on the lower paper is a shadow of the eclipse, albeit with some refraction. Both phenomena, the planetary configuration millions of miles away and the social changes a century or more in the past, reflect important forces which still shape our lives. Even when we are reduced to studying them as shadows, the attempt is still worth the effort.

When we study the world of early capitalism through the classical political economists, the pattern of their work begins to conform to a consistent design. These writings consistently supported positions which would work to harness small-scale agricultural producers to the interest of capital. Those who lived by self-provisioning cast a shadow across the pages of classical political economy, a shadow which had previously gone unnoticed. This shadow of an all but forgotten way of life led me to discover a different project of classical political economy, one that contradicted the standard interpretation of the literature. Although political economy did not neglect market forces when they led to an outcome favorable to capital, it was by no means unalterably wedded to the market. When small-scale producers refused to supply enough labor to satisfy capital, classical political economy promoted measures to further primitive accumulation.

Since classical political economy was so willing to promote primitive accumulation, we might expect to find a continuing interest in manipulating the social division of labor. My own investigation of modern agriculture suggests to me that such an expectation will not go unfulfilled (see Perelman 1981), yet this subject remains almost entirely unexplored.

The paucity of studies on the social division of labor is not altogether surprising. Neoclassical theory begins with an assumption that the economy is already divided into a given set of industries. Theoretically, of course, these can be rearranged, as in the example of an industry that disappears because of vertical integration (see Perelman 1981a). In terms of abstract neoclassical theory, an economy may be operating perfectly efficiently given one social division of labor, yet may be able to reach a higher level if the social division of labor were changed. Yet neoclassical economics has given no thought to the forces that might cause the social division of labor to change. In addition, Marx also failed to give sufficient attention to the theoretical niceties of the social division of labor in one respect: He treated constant capital as a macroeconomic category that could be aggregated over an entire economy. That position is not necessarily correct. A new social division of labor can alter the total amount of constant capital even if technology is held constant (see Perelman 1981a).

Summary

Chapter 1 deals with the history and theory of primitive accumulation. Most discussions of primitive accumulation address the subject as a shorthand expression for describing the brutality of the initial burst of capitalism. In contrast, this chapter makes the case for treating primitive accumulation as a theoretical concept that is essential in analyzing the ongoing process of capitalist accumulation. It shows that classical political economy had an implicit proto-marxian theory of primitive accumulation. In addition, it discusses the pattern of practical measures that altered the social division of labor to the detriment of independent and small-scale producers.

Chapter 2 details the relationship between early classical political economy and the rural population with an eye to the efforts to create a capitalistic social division of labor. It demonstrates the continual importance that classical political economy placed on the process of primitive accumulation.

Chapter 3 concentrates on the important work of Sir James Steuart, by far the most interesting and the most incisive theorist of primitive accumulation and the social division of labor prior to Marx. Besides seeing the implications of primitive accumulation more clearly than the other classical political economists, Steuart stood alone in his willingness to write openly and honestly about the subject. This characteristic explains the comparative obscurity of his reputation.

Chapter 4 continues the analysis of the relationship of classical political economy and primitive accumulation into the age of David Ricardo and Thomas Robert Malthus. By reading their works in terms of their relationship to political economy, we discover a different interpretation of classical political economy than what is normally given to that literature. This chapter demonstrates that despite the adherence to the doctrines of laissez faire in theory, classical political economy maintained a strong interest in promoting policies that furthered primitive accumulation.

Chapter 5 is devoted exclusively to Adam Smith. Smith attempted to develop an alternative to Steuart. According to Smithian theory, the social division of labor would evolve in a satisfactory manner without recourse to outside intervention. This chapter demonstrates that even Smith's celebrated discussion of the invisible hand was developed as a means of avoiding the challenge that primitive accumulation posed for his system. By showing that the social division of labor would evolve without recourse to outside intervention, Smith had hoped to put the question of primitive accumulation to rest. Although Smith's theory was accepted as such, practice continued in a different manner. In fact, Smith himself advocated practices that were not in accordance with his theory.

Chapter 6 continues the study of Smithian theory and practice by comparing Smith with his friend Benjamin Franklin. This genial American was a man of practice rather than theory, yet his practical analysis greatly influenced the theory of his day. Franklin's role is especially important with respect to Adam Smith, since Smith based much of his theory on the experience of the Colonies. Although Smith made great use of the colonial experience, the colonials did not take him nearly as seriously as the English did. The reason is not hard to fathom. In harnessing the story of the Colonies to his ideological cart, Smith did not do justice to the actual situation in the Colonies. By tracing his analysis of the Colonies, this chapter delves deeper into the manner in which Smith purposely obscured the nature of the social division of labor.

Chapter 7 investigates the reaction against Smith beginning with the relatively unknown work of Robert Gourlay and the development of his ideas by the practical school of Edward Gibbon Wakefield, the systemic colonizer who stressed that the social division of labor should be organized for the purpose of capitalist development. It concludes with an analysis of John Rae.

Chapter 8 discusses the commonality between Smith and such later revolutionary leaders as Mao and Lenin.

chapter 1

Primitive Accumulation

Primitive accumulation plays approximately the same role in political economy as original sin does in theology.

Marx, *Capital,* vol. 1, p. 873

Introduction

The seemingly Marxian expression "primitive accumulation" began with Adam Smith's notion that "the accumulation of stock must, in the nature of things, be previous to the division of labour" (Smith 1937, p. 260). Marx translated the term *previous* as *ürsprunglich* (Marx and Engels 1973; 33: 741), a word which Marx's English translators rendered as *primitive.*

Smith's theory was odd, to say the least. The division of labor is to be found throughout history. It exists even in animal societies (see Morely 1954). Yet Smith would have us believe that the division of labor had to wait for the accumulation of stock. Such an idea is patently false. In no way can we interpret the division of labor in an anthill or a beehive as a consequence of *stock,* Smith's code work for capital.

Marx rejected Smith's otherworldly conception of previous accumulation. To distance himself from Smith, he prefixed the perjorative *so-called* to the title of the final part of the first volume of *Capital,* which was devoted to the study of primitive accumulation. The contrast between Smith's scanty treatment of previous accumulation and Marx's extensive documentation of the subject is striking. Where Smith scrupulously avoided any analysis of social relations, Marx produced an elaborate study of the connection between the development of capitalistic social relations and the so-called primitive accumulation.

The massive array of historical material found in Part 8 of the first volume of *Capital* suggests that Marx faulted Smith for being insufficiently historical. In addition, Marx chastised Mikhailovsky for his suprahistorical treatment of primitive accumulation, in which Russia's future was mechanically extrapolated from Marx's analysis of the European experience of primitive accumulation (Letter to the Editorial Board of the *Otechestvenniye Zapitski* in Marx and Engels 1975, pp. 291–94).

In spite of the importance Marx put on situating theory in its proper historical context, he seems to have also charged Smith with being excessively historical, since he attempted to explain the present existence of class by reference to a mythical past.

Marx's reference to original sin cited at the head of this section indicates how a theory can be criticized for both too much and too little historical emphasis. That theological doctrine, which rests on a slender historical foundation, is used to explain the misfortunes that people suffer today. Thus it has been challenged both because it turns attention away from the present to the past and because our knowledge of that past is open to serious questions. Such an attack from two sides could easily take on a Hegelian turn. In fact, it did.[1] This material is worth citing in detail:

> The conditions which form its point of departure in production —[then] the condition that the capitalist, in order to posit himself as capital, must bring values into circulation which he created with his own labour—or by some other means, excepting only already avail able, previous wage labour—belongs among the antediluvian conditions of capital, belongs to its *historic presuppositions*, which, precisely as such *historic* presuppositions, are past and gone, and hence belong to the *history of its formation*, but in no way to its *contemporary* history, i.e., not to the real system of the mode of production ruled by it. While e.g., the flight of serfs to the cities is one of the *historic* conditions and presuppositions of urbanism, it is not a *condition*, not a moment of the reality of developed cities but belongs rather to their *past* presuppositions, to the presuppositions of their becoming which are suspended in their being. The conditions and presuppositions of the *becoming*, or the arising, of capital presuppose precisely that it is not yet in being but merely in *becoming*; they therefore disappear as real capital arises, capital which itself, on the basis of its own reality, posits the conditions for its realization. [Marx 1974, pp. 459–60]

---

[1] Colletti singles out the following passage to indicate Marx's relationship to Hegel (Colletti 1979, p. 130).

In *Capital*, the same idea appears with a similar wording, except for the elimination of some of the more Hegelesque terminology (Marx 1977, p. 775). Taken very simply, Marx seems to have been suggesting the following line of reasoning: Originally the separation of workers from the means of production was an historical event necessary for the establishment of capitalism. Once capitalism had taken hold, the means of (re)producing this separation could be found in purely market forces that leave workers nothing more than the means of reproducing their own capacity for labor. This temporal cleavage between the moment of primitive accumulation and the era of capitalist accumulation appeals to our common sense; however, it is itself rather ahistorical. Marx's own treatment of primitive accumulation carried us through a process lasting several centuries.

Granted that primitive accumulation is a process, a further question arises: Why does this process, or at least Marx's treatment of it, stop so abruptly? Marx offered few examples of primitive accumulation that occurred in the nineteenth century except in the colonial lands. Was Smith correct after all in relegating primitive accumulation to the past—at least in the societies of advanced capitalism? Marx never answered this question affirmatively. In fact, he seems to have suggested a negative response. Since Part 8 follows the chapter entitled "The General Theory of Capitalist Accumulation," did Marx intend a dramatic break in his presentation? That he began the chapter in question with an overview of the theory of primitive accumulation suggests a continuity.

Was primitive accumulation, then, a part of the continuing process of capital accumulation? In his letter to the editorial board of *Otechestevenniye Zapitski*, mentioned above, Marx wrote:

> The chapter on primitive accumulation does not claim to do more than trace the path by which in Western Europe, the capitalist economy emerged from the womb of the feudal economic system. It therefore describes the historical process which by divorcing workers from their means of production converts them into wage workers. [Marx and Engels 1975, p. 293]

Marx's emphasis on the historical aspect of primitive accumulation was intended to diminish the importance of the chapter which he called "this historical sketch" (ibid.). The political intent of this posture was to denigrate the attempt of Mikhailovsky to use the chapter to convey the impression that Russia's future would be determined by the "inexorable laws" of capitalism (ibid.). Marx's letter is consistent with my interpretation that the importance of his work on primitive accumulation was not what it taught about backward societies, but about the most advanced societies.

Keep in mind that when Marx's study of primitive accumulation finally reached the subject of Edward Gibbon Wakefield, Marx did not qualify his appreciation of the father of modern colonial theory by limiting the importance of Wakefield to what his writing revealed about an earlier England, but to the England where Marx lived and worked (Marx 1977, p. 940; see also Marx 1853, p. 498). In spite of the presumptions of some recent authors to prove otherwise (see, for example, Foster-Carter 1978, esp. p. 229), Marx himself, referring to the institutions of Mexico, insisted that "[t]he nature of capital remains the same in its developed as in its undeveloped forms" (Marx 1976, p. 400n).

If the foregoing interpretation is correct, why was Marx not more explicit? The reason is to be found in the purpose of his exposition of primitive accumulation. Primitive accumulation was indeed a brutal experience, as we know by the time we have reached the end of the first volume of *Capital*. The workings of the laws of supply and demand are no less brutal than the arbitrary application of force and violence. Moreover, the laws of supply and demand are more effective. Thus we read:

> It is not enough that the conditions of labour are concentrated at one pole of society in the shape of capital, while at the other pole are grouped masses of men who have nothing to sell but their labour power. Nor is it enough that they are compelled to sell themselves voluntarily. The advance of capitalist production develops a working class which by education, tradition and habit looks upon the requirements of that mode of production as self-evident natural laws. The organization of the capitalist process of production, once it is fully developed, breaks down all resistance. The constant generation of a relative surplus population keeps the law of the supply and demand of labour, and therefore wages, within narrow limits which correspond to capital's valorization requirements. The silent compulsion of economic relations sets the seal on the domination of the capitalist over the worker. Direct extra-economic force is still of course used, but only in exceptional cases. In the ordinary run of things, the worker can be left to the "natural laws of production," i.e., it is possible to rely on his dependence on capital, which springs from the conditions of production themselves, and is guaranteed in perpetuity by them. It is otherwise during the historical genesis of capitalist production. The rising bourgeoisie needs the power of the state, and uses it to "regulate" wages, i.e., to force them into the limits suitable to make a profit, to lengthen the working day, and to keep the worker himself at his normal level of dependence. This is an essential aspect of so-called primitive accumulation. [Marx 1977, pp. 899–900]

In short, I believe that we can safely expect to discover that the process of primitive accumulation continues well into the epoch of classical political economy. Indeed, in England, as well as in the other countries of advanced capitalism, the conversion of small-scale farmers into proletarians continued throughout the nineteenth century and into the twentieth. This process involved more than the "silent compulsion" of market forces. The state, also, played a powerful role (for the United States, see Perelman 1977 and 1981).[2]

At one point, Marx vaguely alluded to the ongoing nature of primitive accumulation. In suggesting a connection between the nature of primitive accumulation and the centralization of capital which was taking place as a result of the workings of credit and the joint stock form of enterprise, Marx wrote:

> Success and failure both lead here to a centralization of capital, and thus to expropriation on the most enormous scale. Expropriation extends here from the direct producers to the smaller and the medium sized capitalists themselves. It is the point of departure for the capitalist mode of production [presumably referring to primitive accumulation]; its accomplishment is the goal of this production. In the last instance, it aims at the expropriation of the means of production from all individuals [thereby creating the organizational structure appropriate for socialism]. [Marx 1967; 3: 439]

In this sense, primitive accumulation is not merely an historical phenomenon. It continues even today. Its role may be quantitatively less important than the "silent compulsion of economic relations," but it continues nonetheless.

The theory of primitive accumulation can be extended further in space as well as in time. Primitive accumulation can occur in the city as well as in the countryside. Typically, the analysis of primitive accumulation is presented as the destruction of the peasant economy, the effect of which is to create capitalists on the one side and workers on the other. Indeed, on the eve of capitalism, when the majority of people were peasants or at least had some connection with farming, this emphasis was understandable. However, people directly provide for themselves in a multitude of ways other than the growing of food. Depriving them of other means of provision forces a dependence on the market in just the same fashion as restricting access to the means of food production. Let me use a contemporary example: Packing

---

[2] The state played a similar role even in precapitalist societies. For example, the tribute levied by the Danes in the twelfth century impelled Britain to monetize the economy (Sohn-Rethel 1978, p. 107).

people into crowded urban quarters leaves little space for doing the laundry.[3] Thus people become dependent upon commercial laundromats. Adding together the sum total of such expenditures amounts to a powerful pressure to obtain money. Frequently the response is to sell more labor to purchase the required goods and services.

We see the impact of such behavior reflected in the rising numbers of women in the labor force. Kolko calculates that the share of life years available for wage labor for the average adult has increased from 39 percent in 1900 to 44.4 percent in 1970, despite rising education, child labor laws, and a shorter work week (Kolko 1978, p. 267). At the same time, the ability of the average family to produce for its own needs has substantially diminished. The fast-foods industry is predicated on the difficulty of working at a job and performing a multitude of other chores in the same day.

In writing on the subject of primitive accumulation, Marx proposed the formula, "Accumulation of capital is . . . multiplication of the proletariat" (Marx 1977, p. 764). By this standard, we could interpret the restructuring of the life of a modern household as a contemporary variant of the process of primitive accumulation, whereby the mass of people working for wages has increased.[4] Thus wage labor and nonwage labor are linked. The analysis of the one category necessitates consideration of the other. As we shall see, their mutual interplay can best be comprehended by means of the concept of the social division of labor. In the case of our modern-day example, goods and services that were once produced within the household become commodities sold by commercial firms. This new arrangement is related, at least in part, to the ownership of the means of creating these goods and services in the household. Formally, the lack of ownership of a workspace for doing laundry is similar to the lack of ownership of the parcel of land on which a household once grew its own food. In either case, the denial of ownership to a particular means of production tends to create a change in the mix of wage and non-wage labor. In this sense, the concept of primitive accumulation is closely related to the concept of the social division of labor.

The classical political economists understood primitive accumulation as a means of radically altering the social division of labor. This new social division of labor was recognized as a precondition of the creation of a proletariat. The hopes and plans for manipulating the social division of labor were never discussed in a coherent fashion in the literature of classical political

---

[3] Paul Sweezy interprets Japan's huge entertainment sector as a partial result of the small living quarters of the people (see Sweezy 1980, p. 13).

[4] This idea should not be taken too literally. To do so risks doing violence to the concept of the proletariat.

economy. Such material is found in many scattered, and seemingly unrelated, sources. Yet, taken as a whole it presents a consistent program for primitive accumulation.

The classical theory of primitive accumulation can be expressed as a model. In some respects, it resembles a rude proto-marxian model stripped of the dialectic. In analyzing this model, keep in mind that Marx began by taking the categories of classical political economy as they were. By investigating them more fully, he was able to take these static, undialectical categories and invest them with a dynamic, dialectical quality. One can follow much the same procedure in the study of the classical theory of primitive accumulation.

Carrying out such an analysis, the classical theory of primitive accumulation has a twofold importance. First, it reveals a side of classical political economy that previously has gone unnoticed. Second, it teaches us to see primitive accumulation as an ongoing process. In this sense, the analysis of the classics has more to offer than much of what has since been written about the subject of primitive accumulation.

Most of the modern commentaries on primitive accumulation do not do it full justice. Primitive accumulation is relegated to the distant past, except perhaps in the colonial lands. Consequently, the relationship between workers and their means of production is implicitly assumed to be static.

To some extent, the deficiencies of the commentaries to which I allude may be understandable. At times, even Marx wrote of primitive accumulation with an air of finality and possibly even with a touch of Smithian mythology. For example, the first mention of the concept of primitive accumulation in *Capital* appears in Chapter 23 on "Simple Reproduction" (Marx 1977, p. 714). At this point, Marx had to address the question: How does the system come to be structured into capital and labor? Marx responded with the statement:

> *From our present standpoint* it therefore seems likely that the capitalist, *once upon a time*, became possessed of money by some form of primitive accumulation. [Marx 1977, p. 714; emphasis added]

His uncharacteristic "once upon a time," which sounded as unreal as Smith's history, was obviously provisional. The words "from our present viewpoint" also suggest that a more thorough analysis would be forthcoming. For reasons already discussed, the thoroughgoing analysis was never provided. Instead, we find only history. This history, however, can be integrated with an analysis of modern capitalism. To this end, we must carry the history of primitive accumulation through the epoch of classical political economy by connecting this concept with the social division of labor.

Commodity Production and the Social Division of Labor

> The foundation of every division of labour which has attained a certain
> level of development, and has been brought about by the exchange of
> commodities, is the separation of town from country. One might say
> that the whole history of society is summed up by this antithesis.
>
> Marx, *Capital,* vol. 1, p. 472

According to Marx, "The social division of labour . . . forms the foundation
for all commodity production" (Marx 1977, p. 471; see also Lenin 1974, p.
37, where the same idea is repeated twice). The social division of labor that
concerned Marx, as well as the majority of classical political economy, was
not the division of labor in Adam Smith's famous pin factory, where each
worker was assigned a specialized task. In fact, Marx even went so far as to
inform Engels that he wished to use *Capital* to show that "in the mechanical
workshops the *division of labor*, as it forms the basis of manufacturing and is
described by Adam Smith, does not exist" (Marx and Engels 1973; 30:
pp. 223–24).

As I have already mentioned, the category of the social division of labor
refers to the partitioning of the economy into entities that produce items
such as pins, iron and food, etc. The social division of labor thus encompasses
what contemporary economists call "industrial organization," although it is
broader in scope and not limited to commodity production.

As a starting point, let me refer to Joseph Lowe's *The Present State of England.* Therein we find the following passage:

> In London the class of shoemakers is divided, says Mr. Gray, into
> makers of shoes for men, shoes for women, shoes for children; also into
> boot-cutters, boot makers. Even tailors, though to the public each
> appears to do the whole of his business, are divided into makers of
> coats, waistcoats, breeches, gaitors. [Lowe 1823, p. 61]

In effect, Lowe suggested that the definition of an industry depended on the
nature of the commodities produced rather than on the apparent occupation
of workers. His emphasis on differentiation pointed the way toward the
modern literature, although in no way could he have foreseen the wide
diversity of modern commodities. A few decades ago, who would have
dreamed that contemporary consumers would be faced with a choice between the purchase of ready-baked bread, frozen dough, or even prebuttered
bread (see Lancaster 1966)? Faced with the complexity of this approach,
Triffen rejected the concept of an industry as a proper category for economics
(1940, p. 89).

In contrast, Marx's method would lead us to define an industry in terms
of the social relations of the commodity form. Neither the concept of an

industry nor that of a commodity is as straightforward as it might seem. Thus Marx's reluctance to trust appearances was stronger than Lowe's. Marx would not treat an object as a commodity merely because it would be recognizable as a waistcoat or a child's boot:

> Objects of utility become commodities only because they are the products of the labour of private individuals who work independently of each other. [These] producers do not come into social contact until they exchange the products of their labour. [1977, p. 165; see also 1967; 3: 880]

Marx explained this distinction in terms of the umbrella industry of the United States (1977, p. 476–77n). Prior to the Civil War, umbrella manufacturers were merely assemblers of the components of umbrellas.[5] Consequently, individual components such as umbrella handles were commodities. If the companies that produced the handles also assembled the umbrellas, then handles would no longer be commodities.

This question was raised in the United States Congress because of the turnover tax that was instituted during the Civil War. Marx concurred with the judgment of the Congress: "A thing is produced 'when it is made' and it is made when it is ready for sale" (ibid.). Thus an industry can exist only within the context of a network of social and market relations. Accordingly, Marx noted, "the market for . . . commodities develops through the social division of labour; the division of productive labours mutually transforms products into commodities, into equivalents for each other, making them mutually serve as markets" (1967; 3: 637).

An analysis of the social division of labor is admittedly complex. Ultimately, the social division of labor is dependent upon the social relations of production, but within certain limits it unfolds according to its own particular laws. Along these lines, Engels wrote to Conrad Schmidt in a letter dated 27 October 1890:

> Where there is division of labour on a social scale, the separate labour processes become independent of each other. In the last instance production is the decisive factor. But as soon as trade in products becomes independent of production proper, it has a movement of its own, which, although by and large governed by that of production, nevertheless in particulars and within this general dependence again follows laws of its own inherent in the nature of this new

---

[5] Stigler (1951) offers a similar example for the British gun industry.

factor; this movement has phases of its own and in turn reacts on the movement of production. [Marx and Engels 1975, p. 397]

Recent economic literature has concentrated upon the Smithian division of labor, and where it has touched upon the social division of labor, it has almost totally excluded considerations of the relations of production (see Marx 1977, p. 486). One partial exception is Friedrich von Hayek. In response to the "monetarists" who advocate a constant increase in the rate of monetary growth, Hayek argued that a changing social division of labor can alter the amount of monetary transactions involved in delivering the same final output to the market (Hayek 1932, pp. 61ff). Thus, for example, if the umbrella assemblers produce rather than purchase handles, then their cost of umbrella handles would no longer include the markup on handles, but only enough funds to pay for the costs of handle production. The transfer of handles to the assembler accounts to "internal barter" (ibid., p. 60).

The typical neglect of the social division of labor has left a serious gap in modern economic theory (see Marx 1977, p. 486). Earlier, Carl Rodbertus, for example, had argued that a proper analysis of the basic categories of national economy was inconceivable without the prior notion of a social division of labor, whereas Smith's division of labor brings one no further than the analysis of individualistic behavior (Rodbertus 1899, pp. 93–109). Thus Smith's method is inadequate. The social division of labor must be seen within the context of capital in general. Unfortunately, such a perspective has rarely been adopted.

Smith's analysis of the division of labor has another shortcoming. It treats the division of labor as the result of voluntary actions of people. My object is to bend the rod the other way. I will emphasize that the social division of labor is intimately bound up with struggle between classes.

In a sense, this perspective is not new. Harry Braverman (1974) has taught us to see the close relationship between coercion and the social division of labor. In his work, this relationship could be traced to the increasing control of the labor process due to the separation of mental and manual labor. In effect, workers came to be deprived of a portion of the means of production —the productivity attributable to their skills—by virtue of a restructuring of the labor process.

At the time of emergent capitalism, the creation of a new social division of labor involved a more direct expropriation of the lower strata of society than the deskilling Braverman described. It was closely associated with the historical phenomenon of primitive accumulation. In fact, we can equate primitive accumulation with what Engels called "great division of labour between the masses discharging simple manual labour and the few privileged persons directing labour" (1894, p. 217). The classical political economists, from Petty in the late seventeenth century to John Stuart Mill in the mid-nineteenth century, were keenly interested in organizing this unfolding of the social division of labor.

The idea that political economists would take an active interest in the social division of labor might sound odd to many modern-day students of political economy. The very idea of organizing a social division of labor appears to fly in the face of the general understanding of classical political economy; however, this appearance is illusory. In fact, they even conceived of policy in terms of a social division of labor on a world scale. For example, consider Nassau Senior's attack on the Corn Laws. He warned that if the English persisted in protecting their market from food imports, countries such as the United States and Germany would turn to industrial pursuits (see Senior 1841; McCulloch 1841, p. 10, cited in Fay 1932, pp. 86–87; and Hilton 1977, pp. 115, 184, and 280). To open British markets to the free importation of grain would serve to safeguard English industrial hegemony by inducing potential competitors to specialize in the production of raw materials.

Friedrich List, writing from the German perspective in the same year as Senior, agreed with the latter about the impact of free trade. List believed that free trade would permanently condemn Germany to the subordinate role of agricultural supplier to England. He accused the English of going to great lengths to maintain Germany as a vassal of England. He added that the English were notorious for the largesse they bestowed upon German free-traders, including political economists (List 1841, pp. 7–8).

Lucille Brockway (1979) has shown us the extent to which even seemingly innocent scientific activities were actually part of a concerted effort to organize a social division of world labor. Should we believe that only the political economists were unaware of such matters? Brockway's study details the role of plant explorers in the evolution of the world capitalist system. The adventures of Darwin and the other British botanists might seem far afield at first glance, but they had a vital mission to play. Latin America was blessed with perhaps the most important set of exotic genetic resources then known to the world. Tapping them was made expensive because of the low population density of that continent. Two choices were open to the British: Either rubber or chinchona would be grown in Latin America with scarce domestic or imported labor—an expensive proposition—or such crops had to be grown elsewhere.[6]

The latter option was more desirable, but one matter stood in the way. The

---

[6] In 1774, Samuel Johnson asked, "Why does any nation want what it might have? Why are spices not transplanted to [the British colonies] in America? Why does tea continue to be brought from China" (Johnson 1774, p. 61)?

British did not own the means of propagating such crops. This technicality did not deter them. They simply refused to recognize any proprietary rights of the people or even of the rulers of these peripheral lands. The plant explorers were charged with obtaining the plants by any means possible in order that they could be bred for production in the colonies of British Asia. By and large, they succeeded. The plants were smuggled out of Latin America, as well as the tea cuttings from China, were simply taken without any compensation—a primitive accumulation of biological resources. Two years later, Adam Smith wondered about the complex social division of labor required to produce a woolen coat:

> How much commerce and navigation . . ., how many ship-builders, sailors, sail-makers, rope-makers, must have been employed in order to bring together the different drugs made use of by the dyer, which often come from the remotest corners of the world. [Smith 1937, p. 11]

Significantly, Smith neglected to consider the labor of those who grew the plants. The conscience of the British, however, was little troubled by such considerations. To complete the circle, impoverished Indians were brought to labor in the plantations of Malaysia, Ceylon, and Mauritius, as well as in the British plantations in the Western Hemisphere. This reorganization of the world economy was an important element in England's industrial growth. As List wrote:

> One can establish a rule that the more a nation is richer and more powerful, the more that it exports manufactured products, the more it imports raw materials, and the more it consumes tropical commodities. [List 1841, p. 70]

The classical political economists surely understood such considerations. More to the point, like Marx, the majority of the early classical political economists recognized that the social division of labor was the foundation for commodity production. At first, the problem was to eliminate what, for want of a better term, is called the "natural economy" which "confront[ed] the requirements of capitalism at every turn with rigid barriers" which seemed unlikely to collapse on their own accord (Luxemburg 1968, p. 369). William Robertson, the Historian Royal of Scotland and leading figure in Edinburgh literary circles, in a work allegedly based on Smith's then unpublished *Lectures on Jurisprudence* (see Scott 1965, pp. 55–56), wrote concerning the prospects of naturally developing market relations:

> The wants of men, in the original and most simple state of society, are so few, and their desires so limited, that they rest contented with what they can add to these by their own rude industry. They have no

superfluities to dispose of, and few necessities that demand a supply. [Robertson 1769, p. 84]

Over time, according to Marx, with the active support of political economy, capital successfully:

> transformed the small peasants into wage-labourers, and their means of subsistence and of labour into material elements of capital.
> . . . Formerly, the peasant family produced means of subsistence and raw materials, which they themselves for the most part consumed. These raw materials and means of subsistence have now become commodities.[7] [Marx 1977, pp. 910–11]

This process was not a once and for all reshaping of the social labor process. As late as 1925, J. Russell Smith wrote about workers in the southern United States who disdained agricultural wage labor because they could "get an equal amount of food by going hunting, fishing or berrying—facts of profound influence in checking the development of manufacture" (Smith 1925, p. 381). Even now development studies return to this refrain. The World Bank report for Papua New Guinea reads:

> The prospects for improving traditional agriculture by adding cash crops or by diversifying subsistence production are difficult to assess. Characteristic of New Guinea's subsistence agriculture is its richness; over much of the country, nature's bounty produces enough to eat with relatively little effort. . . .
> Until enough subsistence farms have their life styles changed by the development of new consumption wants, the relative ease of producing traditional foods may discourage experimentation with new ones. [International Bank for Reconstruction and Development 1977, p. 43; partially cited in Payer 1982, pp. 218–219]

In this vein, Marx speculated that capital "conquers the domain of national production only very partially, and always rests on the handicrafts of the towns and the domestic subsidiary industries of the rural districts, which stand in the background as its basis" (1977, p. 911).

The ongoing process of subordinating the relatively self-sufficient household to the needs of capital was of strong practical concern for classical political economy. For example, Montifort Longfield, writing in 1833 from

---

[7] This transformation had already begun in part under the feudal mode of production. For example, hand mills were banned to make people dependent upon the mill belonging to the lord.

Ireland, where subsistence farming was still a force to be reckoned with, used the unwaged worker to close his system in much the same manner in which Ricardo used the concept of no-rent land. According to Longfield's formulation, the standard of living of the subsistence farmer sets the level of wages which, given the existing technology, determines the rate of profit (Longfield 1834, pp. 190–91; see also Earle and Hoffman 1980). Unfortunately, the crucial role of the subsistence sector was not more explicitly spelled out.

J. R. McCulloch also stumbled upon this relationship between the rate of profit and the subsistence sector (1854, p. 34). He observed that the degree of poverty among the peasantry determined the wage rate which, within the context of his Ricardian perspective, would have set the rate of profit, given the usual assumptions of his school. As was his practice, McCulloch, however, failed to translate his perceptive observation about the real world onto a theoretical level of analysis.

McCulloch was not alone in this respect. In spite of the intense concern with the subsistence sector, on an abstract level classical political economy was generally unwilling to recognize openly the antagonism between capital and the traditional economy. Instead, "political economy confuse[d] on principle, two different kinds of private property, one of which rests on the producer himself, and the other on the exploitation of the labour of others" (Marx 1977, p. 931). It conveniently forgot that the "latter is not only the direct antithesis of the former, but grows on the former's tomb and nowhere else" (Marx 1977, p. 931; see also Marx 1967; 2: 35).[8] Where political economy did come close to confronting this conflict, it appeared to be intentionally obscure. One partial exception was Senior, who chose to treat the matter as a cultural phenomenon, sneering at that "rude state of society [in which] every man possesses, and every man can manage, every sort of instrument" (1836, p. 74). In advocating a market economy based on a more complex social division of labor, he casually noted, "Indirect production is, in a great measure, the result of civilization" (1928, p. 133). Even after Senior's concept of indirect labor reappeared in BohmBawerk's elaborate theory of roundaboutness, it was presented in such a way that the social relations of that category were nowhere to be found (see BohmBawerk 1959: esp. p. 87). Nonetheless, Senior, for all his other deficiencies, deserves some modicum of credit for raising a concept parallel to the social division of labor to a level faintly approaching abstract theory.

---

8 For a reflection of this conflict in Japan, see Smith (1966, p. 75).

The Household as an Agent of Production

A full understanding of the social division of labor requires that the concept of the household be integrated into the theoretical analysis. Thus the social division of labor, as I shall use that category, will include all labor performed within the household. Because household labor is often ignored in analyzing commodity production, some explanation should be given for its inclusion.

Keep in mind that political economy began in an age in which the social division of labor was not very detailed. It would be an overstatement to describe the economic environment of the time as one in which "each individual household contains an entire economy, forming as it does an independent center of production" (Marx 1965, p. 79; 1977, p. 616n; 1852, p. 478; and Engels 1881, p. 460); however, such an image would not be very inaccurate. For example, we can turn to John Rae's description of life on the Canadian frontier during the nineteenth century to get a feel for the extent of the self-sufficiency of a typical farmstead (see Rae 1834, p. 57). Obviously, the people whom Rae described were not reliving the life of precapitalist England, but his description does convey a flavor of the self-sufficient household.

In particular, the households of precapitalist societies had no conception of cost accounting. Before capitalist production was fully developed, one could not locate a clear boundary separating those activities directed toward the production of commodities for sale on the market from those other activities performed to reproduce the household. For example, when seventeenth-century London bakers applied for an increase in the price of bread, they sent in an account of the weekly cost of a bakery including the baker, his wife, four paid journeymen, two apprentices, two maidservants, and three or four of the baker's children. The business, involving the production of thousands of loaves of bread, was carried on in the baker's own house. The care and feeding of the workers, along with the members of the baker's own family, were integral parts of the production process (see Laslett 1971, pp. 1–2; see also Kautsky 1899, p. 156; and Weber 1923, p. 172).

Similar arrangements among employer and employee continued well into the twentieth century in China and Japan (Moore 1951, p. 86). Commercial and domestic economies were also interwoven in the institution of boarding houses. Even in the United States during the late nineteenth century, nearly one-fifth of the working-class families studied by the Bureau of Labor took in boarders (Smuts 1959, p. 14; see also Harvey 1976, p. 282; and Stearns 1974, p. 416). Boarding was especially important for immigrant families. A 1908 study found that among the Slavs of Homestead, Pennsylvania, 43 percent took in boarders. In half of these families, boarders provided more than 25 percent of the total family income (Byington 1910, pp. 142–44; see also Jensen 1980, p. 20; and Greer 1979, p. 117).

As capitalism evolved, the cleavage between household production and commodity production became more and more pronounced. No longer was the production and consumption of use values emphasized within the household. Instead, an emphasis on exchange values became the order of the day. Working-class families began to specialize more in the sale of labor power to purchase commodities marketed by profit maximizing firms. This shift is clearly reflected in Tribe's history of farm management literature (Tribe 1978, Chapter 4; see also Marx 1967; 2: 134n). The development of capitalism depended upon the transformation of these independent household labor processes into a unified "social process" (Marx 1977, p. 453). This unification required that the relatively complete economic structure of the independent household be broken down in order that it would become dependent upon commodities that were in general produced with wage labor.

Within this transformed system, capital demanded that the household function as a factory (see Cairncross 1958, p. 17) for the production of workers, who "resemble[d] the component parts of the vast machines which they direct" (Senior 1841, p. 504). All other aspects of life were to be subordinated to this end (see Hammond and Hammond 1919, p. 6).

The adaptation of the family economy to the needs of capital was not always a painless process. "Each stage in industrial differentiation and specialization struck . . . at the family economy, disturbing customary relations between man and wife, parents and children, and differentiating more sharply between 'work' and 'life'" (Thompson 1963, p. 416). However, these changes were necessary.

Things consumed in the household were ultimately to serve for the production of labor power. In addition, the work performed in the household was also to contribute to the production of labor power. As Marx wrote, "From a social point of view, therefore, the working class, even when not directly engaged in the labour-process, is just as much an appendage of capital as the ordinary instruments of labour" (Marx 1977, p. 719). Consequently, "consumption is not simply a consumption of . . . material [or service], but rather consumption of consumption itself" (Marx 1974, p. 301). In this sense, capital succeeded in "transform[ing] . . . lifetime into labortime" (Marx 1977, p. 799).

The linkage between the production of commodities in the factory and labor power in the household proved to be a most profitable combination. The working class was left with the responsibility of exchanging its wages for its means of subsistence, then combining these commodities with household labor in order to renew its supply of labor power. Thus, beginning in the last decade of the eighteenth century:

> a barrage of pamphlets exhorted the working classes to . . . substitute vegetables, Indian corn, arrow-root, etc., for more expensive items in the budget. Simultaneously several pamphlets explored the means of relieving the burden of the high costs of provisions. Eden devoted almost forty pages of his study of the poor to the frugality of the north, and in 1806 Colquhoun promised that "a greater boon could not be conferred upon the labouring people, than a general circulation of the art of frugal cookery." [Smelser 1959, p. 351]

In Marx's words:

> The maintenance and reproduction of the working class remains a necessary condition for the reproduction of capital. But the capital may safely leave this to the workers' drives for self-preservation and propagation. [Marx 1977, p. 718; see also p. 1033]

This arrangement made for substantial economies. In the more explicit words of one forthright American manager:

> I regard my work-people just as I regard my machinery. . . . They must look out for themselves as I do for myself. When my machines get old and useless, I reject them and get new, and these people are part of my machinery. [cited in Ware 1924, p. 77]

Because of the savings associated with the self-maintenance of the human working machines, employers took an active interest in the most personal of acts of their employees. The welfare secretary of the American Iron and Steel Institute urged tutelage of the worker in the:

> regulation of his meals, the amount, the character and the mastication of them, the amount and character of drink, the hours of rest and sleep, the ventilation of rooms . . . washing of hands before meals, daily washing of feet, proper fitting of shoes, amount and kind of clothing, care of the eye, ear and nose, brushing of the teeth, and regularity of the bowel. [cited in Montgomery 1979, p. 40]

In the colonial lands, capitalists proved to be even more appreciative of the work done in the household. One colonial report recommended that:

> native labourers should be encouraged to return to their homes after the completion of the ordinary period of service. The maintenance of the system under which the mines are able to obtain unskilled labour at a rate less than ordinarily paid in industry depends upon this, for

otherwise the subsidiary means of subsistence would disappear and the labourer would tend to become a permanent resident . . . with increased requirements. [cited in Meillasoux 1972, p. 102; see also Deere 1976]

As a result of this sort of arrangement, the modern South African mining industry is free to pay a wage that its own management admits:

isn't sufficient to meet the needs of a man and his family unless it's augmented by earnings from a plot of land in the man's homeland. A family man from Johannesburg, for instance, couldn't live on what we pay. [Magubane 1979: pp. 116–17; see also p. 123]

This ability to leave labor with the responsibility to fend for itself, when wages are insufficient to support a family, is an immense boon to capital. Even when no outside income is required, the effort labor expends in organizing and arranging its own affairs relieves capital of much responsibility (Marx 1977, p. 1033). In fact, Smith, in his chapter on "Wages of Labour," suggested that this factor accounted for the superiority of wage labor relative to slavery (Smith 1937, p. 80; see also Marx 1977, p. 1033).[9]

Classical political economy did recognize the value of the services rendered by the household; however, that literature also excluded the household from all theoretical discussions. When classical political economists did address the process by which the household economy was being harnessed to the needs of capital, they almost always were engaged in discussions of very practical policy matters such as Irish politics or Poor Laws. This revealing discontinuity between the theoretical expressions and the practical applications of classical political economy becomes obvious once the household is understood to be an integral part of the system of commodity production. Unfortunately, the household is rarely treated adequately in this respect.

Early political economy was in fact rather brutal in its position with regard to the household economy. However, once it became confident that the

---

[9] However, this distinction should not be carried too far. Slaves also had to use their free time to grow food and perform other tasks (see Fraginals 1978; 1: 121, and Taussig 1979, p. 75). In fact, Hilton even suggests that European serfdom may have originated in the lands distributed to Roman slaves who were expected to feed themselves (Hilton 1978, p. 273). Many observers made much of the operational similarity between wage labor and slavery. For example, James Mill noted "What is the difference, in the case of a man, who operates by means of a labourer receiving wages (instead of by slaves)?. . . The only difference is, in the mode of purchasing" (1826, p. 219). Others accepted that slaves were different but that this difference worked to the advantage of slaves, who were thought to fare better than free workers (see Cunliffe 1979, pp. 7, 21). This idea finds an echo in *Time on the Cross* (Fogel and Engerman 1974).

household economy was so hobbled that it would fall in line with the needs of capital, it carefully revised its version of the history of the development of the social division of labor. Hence, the silence concerning that subject.

Modern economics has proven itself ill equipped to see through this falsification of economic history. In order to lend credibility to its theory built up around its central concept of utility maximization, it has conditioned itself to look upon the household as an agent of consumption (see Cairncross 1958). Marx correctly dismissed the relevance of any serious consideration of satisfaction as the basic category of analysis in studying the household: " The consumption of food by a beast of burden does not become any less a necessary aspect of the production process because the beast enjoys what it eats" (Marx 1977, p. 718).[10]

The political context of the neoclassical analysis of the household is instructive. Later, I shall show the hostility which classical political economy expressed against the household while self-provisioning was a serious barrier to the extension of the capitalist mode of production. Today, the household is no longer a serious threat. Its role as a producer is subordinated to capitalist commodity production. Within this framework, neoclassical theory describes the household in terms of individualistic utility maximization. Thus, neoclassical theory defends the status quo by arguing that capitalism serves the best interest of the household as a consumer (see Becker 1965). Accordingly, students are taught to apply the theoretical apparatus of utility maximization to explain such diverse phenomena as the extent of food waste, reading, sleeping, or even family size (Becker 1965, pp. 503, 509, and 513–14). In all fairness, I should note one partial exception, Alfred Marshall, who inserted a perceptive footnote in his *Principles*. After complaining that British and American housewives were not as accomplished in "making limited means go a less way . . . than the French housewife . . . not because they do not know how to buy, but they cannot produce as good finished commodities out of the raw material of inexpensive joints, vegetables, etc."[11] (see also

---

10 Nasssau Senior expressed a similar thought: "And in what does the consumption of food by a labourer differ from that of coals by a steam engine? Simply in that, that the laborer [sic] derives pleasure from what he consumes, and the steam engine does not" (Senior 1928; 1: 172).

11 Based on his experience in feeding both the Bavarian army and the inmates of the Bavarian poor houses, whose labor he turned to good profit, Count Rumford supposed that "the number of inhabitants who may be supported in any country upon its internal produce, depends almost as much upon the state of *the arts of cooking* as upon that of agriculture" (Rumford 1795, p. 179). Unfortunately, this gentleman's main contribution to the culinary arts was the substitution of water for food.

Stearns 1974, p. 18, and 1974a, p. 404 for parallel criticisms of British house-wives), Marshall suggested:

> Domestic economy is often spoken of as belonging to the science of consumption: but that is only half true. The greatest faults in domestic economy, among the sober portion of the Anglo-Saxon working classes . . . are faults of production rather than of consumption. [1927, p. 119][12]

Neoclassical economists should not be singled out for failing to see the relationship between circuits of production and consumption. Many Marxi-an theorists are not beyond reproach with respect to this subject. Although this failing is less frequent in more recent work, all too often Marxist works rely on a formal schema, in which precapitalistic formations are identified with the production of use values, in contrast to capitalism, in which production is simply treated as commodity production. This tendency seems to have misled some people into ignoring the role of household production. However, just as a factory combines living labor with other commodities (constant capital) in order to produce goods for sale, a working-class household also combines living labor with other commodities (variable capi-tal, or we might say whose value equals that of variable capital) to produce a salable product, labor power (see Rae 1834, p. 203, and Senior 1928, pt. iv, chap. 2, sec. 3).[13] Say extended this logic by defining a "full-grown man [as] an accumulated capital" equipped to earn profits (Say 1880, p. 333n). In this

---

12 Wicksteed (1910, p. 18) also made an allusion to women's productive work, but he was mostly concerned with their role in the allocation of resources. In *The Common Sense of Political Economy*, he went into great detail concerning the role of the *Materfamilias* shopping and doling out food. Later he did mention the example of stuffing a goose and schemes for getting boarders, but these examples occur within a long list including family prayers and the cultivation of general aesthetic tastes (ibid., p. 159). Even here, he was merely setting out to prove his subjectivist thesis that "the principle remains unchallenged that the marginal significance decreases as the volume of total satisfac-tion swells" (ibid.). The contrasting presentation of women's work in Marshall and Wicksteed does credit to the former.

13 Marx's expression is slightly different, but in keeping with the above formulation: "Labor-power itself is, above all else, the material of nature transposed into a human organism" (1977, p. 323n). Some misunderstanding might arise, however, because variable capital is often described as a value which workers receive, whereas constant capital frequently refers to the things which they use in the work place. In reality, the things brought into factories and households both enter by way of transactions.

The ancients were far more aware of the linkage between production for use within the household and labor power. For example, Steuart reminded his readers that Herodotus reckoned the cost of the pyramids in terms of carrots and onions (Steuart 1767; 1: 7).

respect, Marx correctly observed that "[a]lthough . . . the exchange of money for labourpower. . . does not as such enter into the immediate process of production, it does enter into the production of the relationship as a whole" (Marx 1977, p. 1006; see also pp. 717–18).

Thus we should interpret the household in terms of the contradictory general system of capitalist social relations, although such an effort is no easy matter. We can find within capitalist households the means of both mutual support and mutual oppression (Humphries 1976, and 1977; and Lazonick 1978).

As capitalism itself became more complex, so too did the demands put upon the household. The process of renewing the energies of workers is complicated by the particularly difficult stresses created by work and life in modern capitalist society (Aglietta 1979, p. 158; Gorz 1968, pp. 88ff). Attention has been drawn away from this phenomenon by the enormous number of household chores that have been taken over by commodities. Food has become processed and clothes ready-made, yet significant opposing tendencies have been less noticed. During the early twentieth century, certain branches of the industry have attempted to create new markets by discovering appliances which could revolutionize the productive potential of household labor. Their interest was to cause the "owner[s] or operator[s] of appliance[s] . . . to adapt [themselves] . . . to a transformation from a hand and craft technique over into a machine process" (cited in Ewen 1976, p. 164). For example, during the heyday of Taylorism, time and motion experts were also hired to design kitchens in order to bring capitalist work rhythms into the household (Ewen 1976, p. 166; see also Gideon 1948, pp. 512ff).

New social norms of consumption (see Aglietta 1979, pp. 159ff) were imposed to reinforce the "invisible threads" that bind labor to capital (Marx 1977, p. 719). Although Engels was correct in pointing to the relatively declining role of the family as an autonomous unit with the rise of capital (Engels 1891, pp. 191–92; see also Weber 1923, p. 94), we should be careful not to underestimate the continuing importance of the role of the household in modern capitalism, even though the specifics of this role have changed.

In spite of the labor-saving appearance of the modern household, those tasks which do remain within the realm of the household economy have frequently become much more demanding. Budgeting and shopping stand out as obvious examples (Walker and Woods 1976). In addition, commodities are sometimes complementary to household labor. For example, in the United States, laundering had been taken over by commercial enterprises by the twentieth century. With the introduction of the washing machine, many families began to do their own laundry either at home or at a laundromat

(Hartmann 1976).[14] Becker (1965, p. 508) describes a similar pattern for the history of shaving.

These examples suggest that the home may be becoming a center of commodity production once again. With the increasing importance of information processing, more businesses are economizing on costly urban office space by furnishing workers with home computer terminals. This system is beneficial to profits in other respects. Wages no longer have to cover the cost of commuting (see Vickers 1981). Moreover, the physical separation of workers reduces the risk that they might organize themselves.

In summary, as the household was forced to adapt itself to the demands of capitalist society, it underwent great changes. The examples Marx used to point out such forgetfulness suggest that he did not take this question lightly. He wrote of the common use of opiates for want of time for breast-feeding and described the consequences of leisure insufficient for families to learn to cook or sew (Marx 1977, fn. pp. 517–18). With biting irony he noted:

> [F]rom this we see how capital, for the purposes of its self valoriza-
> tion, has usurped the family labour necessary for consumption. This
> crisis [during the cotton famine which the English textile industry
> experienced during the American Civil War] was also utilized to teach
> sewing to the daughters of the workers. . . . An American revolution
> and a universal crisis were needed in order that working girls, who spin
> for the whole week, might learn to sew! [Marx 1977, pp. 517–18n]

Consequently, household production must be considered in conjunction with the social labor process in general. As Marx noted, although the "worker's productive consumption [the use of constant capital in the workplace] and his individual consumption are . . . totally distinct . . . , in the latter [activity] . . . he . . . performs . . . necessary vital productions outside the production process" (Marx 1977, p. 717). Classical political economists, however, formally dismissed activities performed in the household as "unproductive labor" because the gentry employed servants to do household labor; nonetheless, the "largest part of society, that is to say the working class, must incidentally perform this kind of labor for itself" (Marx 1971, pt. 3, p. 166).

The importance of this unpaid household labor is far from inconsequential. According to Cairncross, "the American worker has at his disposal a larger stock of capital at home than in the factory where he is employed" (Cairncross 1958, p. 17). In 1968, when the Gross National Product was $864 billion, the equivalent market value of the goods and services produced in the United States households was estimated to be $212 billion (see Burns

---

14 See also the parallel history of shaving in Becker (1965, p. 508).

1976, p. 22; Scitovsky 1976, pp. 86–89; 279–82; and Eisner 1979). The estimate by Nordhaus and Tobin that the ratio of nonmarket to market consumption increased from 3:5 in 1929 to 3:4 in 1965 suggests that perhaps the relative importance of household labor may, in fact, be increasing (Nordhaus and Tobin 1972, p. 518), although such estimates may well be biased by the exclusion of unreported business transactions (see Bowsher 1980).

Capital is not unmindful of the position of the household in the economy. Elsewhere I have used this sort of analysis to explain the unseen manner in which the changing social division of labor has furthered the accumulation process within the agricultural sector (Perelman 1981). Here I shall concentrate on showing the relationship between domestic production and the accumulation process especially as it is reflected in classical political economy. To further this exposition, I now turn to a simplified analysis of the structure of the labor process.

A Simple Schematic of the Social Labor Process

Recall Lenin's thesis about the social division of labor. This "foundation for all commodity production" was discreetly buried with the texts of pre-Marxian classical political economy. In unearthing this history, both petty commodity production and the feudal mode of production must be exhumed and the roots of capitalism exposed.

The reorientation of the household to the production of labor power did not come without a struggle on the part of the traditional economy. This conflict between capitalist production and household production (including simple commodity production) is clearly revealed in the works of classical political economy. This theory developed around the behavior of the typical working- class household which divides its day between working for wages and what we might call "household production." This term includes both self-provisioning and the production of food and some handicrafts for the market.

Although the household remains an essential element in the overall process of commodity production, one important feature distinguishes the household from capitalist enterprises: No value is assigned to that labor performed in the household for the purpose of producing use values. The value of labor power equals the value of variable capital which "consists materially of the means of subsistence of the labourers" (Marx 1967: p. 530). No account is taken of the amount of household labor which contributes to the reproduction of labor power (Marx 1977, pp. 659 and 983).[15] In other

---

[15] This equality is a first approximation. Just as prices and values for individual commodities may diverge in industrial production, so too can the value of labor power

words, the reproduction of a household entails the consumption of a certain quantity of food, shelter, clothing, and other articles of consumption. The value of the labor power sold by such a household will equal the total value of all these purchased inputs used in the reproduction of labor power. If the typical household were to begin to bake its own bread rather than purchase it, the labor of commercial bakers would no longer be counted into the value of its labor power. Thus the value of its services would fall by a corresponding amount, since the labor used to bake in the household does not enter into the value calculation. In contrast, when a firm reduces its consumption of constant capital by incorporating more of the productive process within its boundaries, the resulting increases in labor power required in the firm will add to the value of the commodity. Thus the value of the commodity it produces is reduced only if the total labor embodied in its production (constant plus variable capital) declines.

We can see this relationship more clearly in a simple diagram. Figure 1 shows a representation of the simplified system of commodity production in which the household does not appear as an agent of production. Constant capital (C) is combined with labor power (LP) to produce commodities (W) which go to replace the constant capital and variable capital (V) or are made available for capitalist consumption or accumulation, as shown by the arrow directed from W.

Figure 2 introduces the household as an agent of production. The labor time of the household is divided among household production (H) and commodity production, represented by the dimensions of V and S, where the latter letter stands for surplus value.

The aggregate working day is broken into the three segments: (1) the number of hours households devote to producing on their own account; (2) the number of hours in which they work for wages while producing those goods and services that they will purchase as commodities; and (3) the number of hours in which they work for wages while producing those goods and services which are bought by other classes. Assume that the second stretch of time is devoted to the production of necessities and the third to luxuries.

The classical model presumed that the standard of living for the workers was to be set at a normal subsistence level. Moreover, the level of technology

---

deviate from the commodities consumed within a working-class household. Such inequalities may arise as a result of the stage in the life cycle of a particular household. They may also be a consequence of an atypical pattern of consumption of some households. On the whole, such differences will wash out when we deal with averages of a large number of households.

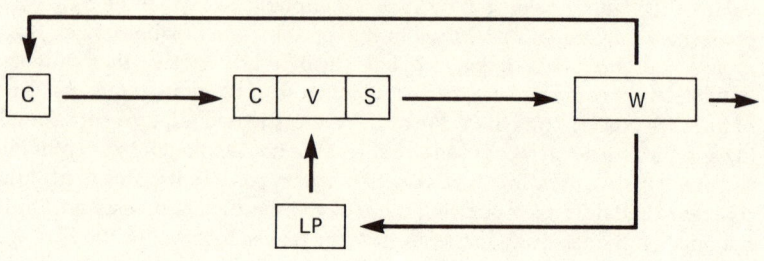

Figure 1
Simplified Production Process

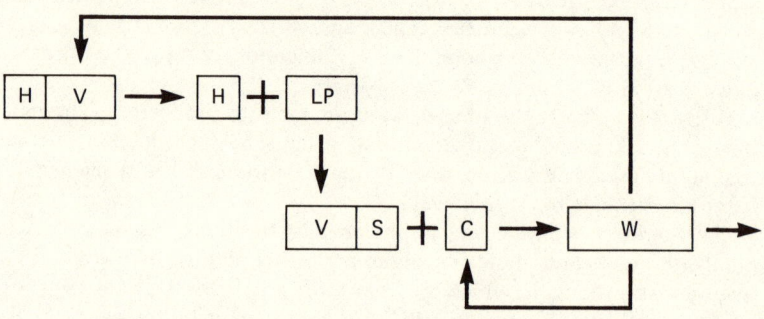

Figure 2
Production Processes With Households Included

that was applied within the household and within the firm was assumed to be equal, at least during the early stages of economic development. Now let us adopt a simplification often associated with Marx, which actually originated in classical political economy (see Senior 1836, p. 174): The aggregate of all households can be treated as a single entity. Assuming that all goods marketed by households are necessities, then all household production can be treated as equivalent to self-provisioning.

Now let us summarize this bare-bones model. The collective household sector works a fixed number of hours producing necessities. Since technology is the same whether or not an hour of work takes place in the household or within a capitalist firm, the total time devoted to producing necessities is also constant. Since the total working day is given, the number of hours used to produce luxuries is also fixed. Consequently, the only variable in the system is the division of time between the production of necessities in the household and the production of necessities while working for wages.

The more households produce their necessities on their own account, the less wages they will require to be able to achieve the normal standard of living. Although the time devoted to wage labor is variable, the time devoted to the production of luxuries is not. This feature is central to the model. Suppose that the normal working day is ten hours, of which five are devoted to the production of luxuries. In addition, suppose that households work for wages full time. Thus for each hour worked, the household sector receives wages to purchase commodities that require a half hour of labor to produce. Now let us change the conditions so that households work two and a half hours on their own account. Under this new assumption, households need only half as much wages. However, the amount of time devoted to luxuries does not decline. Consequently, for each hour spent working for wages, the household sector receives a payment equivalent to only one-third of an hour of labor.

This sort of reasoning was commonplace at the time. For example, most of those writers known as Ricardian socialists attempted to make empirical estimates of the ratio of paid to unpaid labor (see King 1981).

I maintain that much of classical political economy was built around a model such as I have described above. In addition, this model indeed does contain some essential truths about the society in which classical political economy found itself; and that much of the conflict between classes which occurred during that period can be understood in terms of this simple model.

The fundamental assumption to this model concerns the length of the working day. The full working day did not represent a universal condition of society, but rather an ideal that capital actively attempted to achieve. Because households were called upon to exchange much labor for a wage worth substantially less, they were loathe to engage in wage labor. They opted to withhold their labor, preferring to substitute leisure for the commodities that they might potentially purchase with wages. This model is fairly realistic for the early period of capitalism before capital had revolutionized the production process. In the initial stages of development:

> capital subordinates labour on the basis of the technical conditions within which labour has been carried on up to that point in history. It does not therefore directly change the mode of production. [Marx 1977, p. 425]

At that time, capital's control over the traditional producers remained only a "formal" control (Marx 1977, pp. 645 and 1019–38). The creation of surplus value depended upon capital's success in creating absolute surplus value by lengthening the working day. Thus we find a universal condemnation of all those who chose to remain true to their preindustrial ways.

In summary, households are part of the social labor process. The real work day does not necessarily cease once the worker has left the factory or the office—even though the greed for absolute surplus value can make capital oblivious to this fact. From what has been said thus far, we can conclude that such a changing composition of commodity production and household labor could have a significant effect on the rate of surplus value. Other things being equal, the more activities that could be transferred to the household, the higher the rate of surplus value. This point is crucial. The substitution of household work for work done for wages reduced the value of labor power, but this relationship must be qualified. In terms of the division of the working day between paid and unpaid labor, if the spinning and sewing were done in addition to the normal working day, then the amount of paid labor (V) could decrease, leaving an additional amount of time for the production of surplus value; however, even if the working day were to be shortened to compensate for the extra time spent in spinning or sewing, the number of unpaid hours of work (S) could remain unchanged. In that case, the ratio S:V would increase.[16]

Living in an era that has until recently been dominated by Keynesian economics, we immediately see further limitations to this formulation. Increasing variable capital increases the demand for commodities. Higher demand offers substantial advantages for capital. In addition, the more the labor process falls under the direct control of capital, the greater the likelihood of eventual technical change (see Marx 1977, p. 432). Despite these qualifications, the rate of surplus value will be increased by a greater reliance on household labor, other things being equal. This theoretical result reflects the practical concerns of classical political economy.

Classical Political Economy and the Labor Process

The classical model of primitive accumulation is very close to Marx's analysis of capitalist reproduction in the limited sense that it could be reworked into something more like what we find in *Capital* without violating any of its

---

[16] Note that if the process were carried to its limit, the value of variable capital would disappear, and with it wage labor. However, reality is not a linear phenomenon, but a dialectical one, which depends upon contradictory tendencies.

particulars. Nonetheless, I must emphasize that it is *not* Marx's model; it is too rigid, too undialectical. It is not Marx, but classical political economy.

Demonstrating that this model was an integral part of the program of classical economy casts doubt on the current fashion of reading the classics with an eye to showing their preoccupation with the maximizing behavior of individuals. In fact, classical political economy was, first and foremost, a study of the overall accumulation process.

In this respect, the effect of household production is extremely important from the point of view of capital, which profits from a high rate of surplus value. Adam Smith, for example, noted in passing that workers who farmed or gardened for themselves required less money for their own support (Smith 1937, pp. 116–17). This factor was not irrelevant in England, where gardens adjoining workers' cottages provided important supplements to the commodities purchased with wages (see Chambers and Mingay 1966, p. 134; Thompson 1963, pp. 214, 230, 269, and 276; Mantoux 1961, chap. 3; Hammond and Hammond 1919, pp. 3–5; and Engels 1845b, pp. 9–13).[17]

The British Board of Agriculture attempted to assist those who employed farm labor to benefit from a more self-sufficient labor force. It offered a gold medal "to each of the five persons, who shall, in the most satisfactory manner, prove, by experiment, the practicability of cottagers being enabled to keep one or two milch cows on the produce of the land cultivated with spade and hoe only" (cited in Sinclair 1803, p. 850). The Board did not intend to return to precapitalist subsistence farming. Its president, Sir John Sinclair, wanted the small farming to be operated under three principles (ibid., p. 851):

1. That a cottager shall raise, by his own labour, some of the most material articles of subsistence for himself and his family;
2. That he shall be enabled to supply the adjoining markets with the smaller agricultural productions; and
3. That both he and his family shall have it in their power to assist the neighboring farmers, at all seasons, almost equally as well as if they had no land in their occupation.

Sinclair had two objects in mind, both of which pertained to primitive accumulation. First, he thought that the provision of a small plot of land would make peasants accept enclosures more readily. Second, a glance at Sinclair's three points indicates that he thought that if small-scale farms could be properly proportioned, agricultural employers could profit from a

---

17 As late as the 1930s, Henry Ford required that his employees tend gardens; furthermore, a staff of inspectors kept his company informed about those who were remiss in their horticultural responsibilities (Sward 1972, pp. 228–29).

cheap labor force. Sinclair calculated that the cottagers would earn slightly more than half their income from wages. The rest was expected to come from their sales of agricultural produce. Moreover, in excess of one-third of their money wages was expected to return to the landed gentry in the form of rents paid for their tiny plots of land (ibid., p. 854). In many respects, Sinclair's vision had been put into practice. By the nineteenth century, the bulk of very small farmers were wage earners who supplemented their earnings with agricultural pursuits (see Wordie 1974 and Wells 1979). Small-scale farming and handicrafts reinforced each other. Alone, either form of production would be unable to withstand the competitive pressures from more modern methods of production (see Lenin 1898, p. 362; Marx and Engels 1895, p. 412). Combined, they displayed a remarkable resiliency (Marx 1967; 3: pp. 333–34; and Marx and Engels 1975, p. 412). Marx cited a Mr. W. Cooke, who was earlier a correspondent of the *London Times* at Shanghai and Canton, to demonstrate the savings of such an arrangement. According to Cook, British exports often had to be sold in China at prices that barely covered their freight (Marx 1858, p. 334; see also Smith 1978, p. 491 and Myers 1980, p. 151). What was true for China had at one time held in England and the other Western European nations (see Wieser 1927, pp. 287–88; see also Rodbertus 1851 and Marx 1963–71, Part 2, Chapter 8, Part 4).

Political economy formally recognized the advantages of such an arrangement very early. Sir James Steuart, for example, is typical of this attitude. Steuart, a vehement opponent of the self-sufficient household, allowed that many wage workers "prosecute their manufactures in the country, and avail themselves, at the same time, of small portions of land, proper for gardens, grass for cows, and even for producing certain kinds of fruits necessary for their own maintenance" (Steuart 1767; 3: 111). Here was the same technology that supported the household economy; yet in an entirely different context, it served to further the process of accumulation.

Steuart carefully differentiated this form of household production in terms of its social relations:

> This I do not consider as a species of farming. . . . Here the occupation of the inhabitants is principally directed towards the prosecution of their trades: agriculture is but a subaltern consideration, and will be carried on so far only as it occasions no great avocation from the main object. It will however have the effect to parcel out a small part of the lands into small possessions: a system admirably calculated for the improvement of a barren soil, and advantageous to the population, *when the spirit of industry is not thereby checked.* [Steuart 1767; 3: 111–12; see also Marx 1977, p. 911; emphasis added]

We get an even clearer reflection of the relationship between household labor and the rate of surplus value in an anonymous review of William Cobbett's *Cottage Industry*, a precursor of the contemporary books designed to teach families to produce their own food. After first distancing himself from the author's dangerous political views, the anonymous reviewer, either Francis Jeffrey or Henry Brougham (see Fetter 1953, p. 251), explained the particular advantage of inculcating a spirit of self-sufficiency among the working class:

> Let it be remembered, that after procuring raiment and shelter, almost the whole time and attention of the bulk of the people in every community, is of necessity devoted to the procuring of sustenance, that their comfort depends exactly on the greater or lesser degree of the abundance, and the better or worse quality in which this sustenance is obtained. Whatever therefore, by how little soever an addition, enables them to increase its quantity and mend its composition, brings a solid improvement to their condition and helps the great business of their whole lives. The points to which the book before us directs their attention, are of greater importance, because *no cultivation of the economy recommended can be attended without the counteracting check which follows close behind so many other improvements in the labour of the poor, a fall of their wages.* Whosoever should teach the reaper to do his work in half the time, would at the same time teach the farmer to give him half the wages, nay, a general practice of working farm work two or three hours extra would not increase his hire, but he will receive as much wages as if he industriously brews and bakes, and tends useful animals at by hours, as if he consumed these and his earnings together at the alehouse. [Anon. 1823, p. 119; emphasis added]

We could hardly hope for a more vivid expression of the logic of classical political economy. Although these words did not come from the pen of the most important luminaries of classical political economy, they did come from an editor of the *Edinburgh Review*, a position that made him a highly influential promoter of political economy (see Fetter 1957, p. 19).

Such people knew that the structure of domestic production was no trifling matter. The savings that household labor could offer could be quite substantial. Moreover, the reviewer presumed that the inevitable result would be a fall in the level of wages. An example of this principle is suggested by Steuart, who estimated that two days' earnings from spinning was required to nourish a Scottish spinner for a single day during the eighteenth century (Steuart 1767; 3: 304; see also Smith 1937, p. 117).

A woman recalling her youthful labors in an early nineteenth-century textile mill made a similar observation:

> For hitherto woman had always been a money-*saving*, rather than a money-earning, member of the community, and her labour could command but a small return. If she worked out as a servant, or help, wages were from fifty cents to one dollar a week; if she went from house to house by the day to spin and weave, or as a tailoress, she could get by seventy-five cents a week and her meals. As a teacher her services were not in demand, and nearly all the arts, the professions and even the trades and industries were closed to her. [Robinson 1898, p. 2]

Engels also took notice of the workings of the domestic system. He protested against the manner in which German capitalists profited from the ability "to deduct from the price of labour power that which the family earns from its own little garden or field" (Engels 1887, p. 301). Moreover, the ownership of a morsel of property served to reduce further the level of wages by restricting workers' mobility to areas within a short distance of their land (ibid., p. 301). In addition, the very poverty of groups like the Saxony hand weavers made them far less resistant to drawn-out struggles (Engels to Bernstein, 30 November 1881 in Marx and Engels 1973; 35: 237–38). Thus household production could be held responsible, at least in part, for the abyssmal poverty of the German worker (see, in contrast, Sismondi 1827, p. 230). In response to German conditions, Engels denounced gardening and domestic industries as "the most powerful lever of capitalist exploitation" (Marx and Engels 1975, pp. 358–59).

Engels was not antagonistic to domestic industries and household work as such. Although he was critical of the cultural deprivation of the traditional economy based on the combination of domestic industries and gardening (see Engels 1845, pp. 9–13), he recognized that this arrangement had earlier formed the basis for a modest prosperity (Engels 1887, p. 301; 1845, pp. 9–13). However, the impact of this form of work in his day was decidedly negative. To begin with, "the kitchen gardening and agriculture of the old rural hand weavers became the cause by virtue of which the struggle of the hand loom against the mechanical loom was everywhere so protracted and has not yet been fought to a conclusion in Germany" (Engels 1887, p. 301). His verdict seems also to be applicable to the case of Flanders. According to the recent testimony of Mendels, the influence of domestic industries was "perverse in the sense that it perpetuated the dismal pressures that had first induced its penetration into the countryside" (Mendels 1975, p. 203).

Of course, Engels did not mean that the elimination of the hand loom was an end in itself. His immediate concern was the political situation in Germany, where the unwillingness of many workers to abandon their house garden compelled them to accept employment in domestic industries long after mechanization had substantially devalued such labor. Not only were these workers reduced to a meager subsistence, but their competition dragged industrial workers down with them (Engels 1887, p. 300). Even when such peasant workers find employment in modern industry, they frequently refuse to identify with workers' struggles because they expect to become agriculturalists again in the near future (see Sabel 1982, pp. 102ff). German workers, according to Engels, were tolerating the intolerable, but he consoled himself that toleration would soon turn to rebellion as the pressures intensified.

While Engels opposed the reliance on domestic industries, both German capital and what he termed "bourgeois-social philanthropists" regarded "the introduction of new domestic industries as the sole remedy for all rural distress" (Engels 1887, pp. 304, 302). In other words, the opponents of capital called for a more rapid introduction of technologies associated with modern capitalism, while capital preferred more primitive methods.

Also, note the use of lumping together of domestic industries and household production during the next few paragraphs. We have followed Engels' practice in this matter. The two forms of production are, strictly speaking, quite different, although at certain points in European capitalist development workers have supported themselves to a great extent through a combination of both.

Engels' condemnation of household production is echoed by a modern day participant in that mode of production, the wife of an impoverished twentieth century Bolivian miner:

> [T]he miner is doubly exploited no? Because with such a small wage, the woman has to do much more in the home. And really that's unpaid work we're doing for the boss, isn't it? . . . The wage needed to pay us for what we do in the home, compared to the wages of a cook, a washerwoman, a babysitter, a servant, was much higher than what the men earned in the mine.[18] [Barrios de Chungra 1979, pp. 44–45]

---

[18] The reasoning expressed by this woman might be so obvious that it might appear to be without analytical content. Appearances in this case are misleading. Consider the case of Thomas C. Smith, a generally insightful student of Japanese agrarian development. He makes repeated reference to the complaints of higher wages paid to Japanese workers during the nineteenth century (see, e.g., Smith 1966, pp. 83, 110). Although he notes the loss of access to communal resources (p. 99) and the consequent need to purchase more from the market, he is unable to make the connection between the increase in variable capital and the decline in self-sufficiency (p. 144).

The case of domestic industry in Germany or housework in Bolivia illustrates how capital may benefit from a high degree of household self-sufficiency. Obviously, other considerations must also be taken into account. Engels noted the manner in which a resilient household economy impeded technical advances in Germany. We should note that in Japan, and to a lesser extent in Taiwan, the major force for development has been the manufacturing carried on during the spare time of the peasant household (see Smith 1966 and Chinn 1979). True, in these cases, the social relations of production were substantially different from those of the occidental peasant farmer (see Berque 1976); however, both Engels and Lenin saw much the same process taking place in their native lands (Engels 1887, p. 303; Lenin 1894, p. 317). For example, until after 1900 Belgian coal miners would take time off to tend their potato patches in what were called "potato strikes" (HenneauDepooter 1959, p. 117).

Household production, of course, is not an unmixed blessing for capital. Time spent in the household economy puts a limit on the number of hours available for wage labor. In England, for example, as capitalist farming came to depend more and more on specialized labor, spinning and weaving in the cottages was sometimes prohibited lest it interfere with the supply of agricultural labor (Ashton 1972, p. 115). In addition, the products of the household economy compete with commercially produced commodities. Thus a strong household economy tends to restrict capitalism to luxury markets (see Melotti 1977, p. 109). In this regard, Marx observed that "only the destruction of rural domestic industry can give the home market of a country the extension and stability which the capitalist mode of production requires" (Marx 1977, p. 911). For example, a nineteenth-century owner of a cotton spinning plant near Portland, Maine, was said to have had to charge nothing for a considerable time until people came to be dependent on his services (Anon. 1816, p. 62).

In conclusion, the preferred mix of household labor and wage labor will depend upon a complex calculus of class struggle within a given technological matrix. In this sense, the contrast between a Marxian analysis of household production and the classical model of the same phenomenon becomes readily apparent.

Another Look at Primitive Accumulation

In general, the pre-Marxian outlook on the household economy tended to be presented in terms of absolutes. At first, the primary concern was that workers had to be separated from their land. For example, the Board of Agriculture Report of Shropshire in 1794 noted that "the use of common land by labourers operates upon the mind as a sort of independence." Others observed that enclosure would ensure that "subordination of the lower ranks of society which in the present times is so much wanted" (cited in Mill 1967, p. 278; see also statements by Arthur Young and others in Thompson 1963, pp. 219–23). William Cobbett found much the same response when he attempted to offer each laborer an acre of wasteland on the condition that he would enclose it, cultivate it, and live on it: "Budd said, that to give the labourers a bit of land would make them 'sacy'; Chiddle said, that it would only make them breed 'more children'; and Steel said, it would make them demand 'higher wages'" (Cobbett 1831: i, p. 88). Marx cited a Dr. Hunter, who fretted, "A few acres to the cottage would make the labourers too independent" (Marx 1977, p. 881; see also Thompson 1963, p. 217). This sort of calculation is not unique to capitalism. A sixteenth-century Polish writer advised, "The peasant must have as much land as necessary so that in a good year a good worker need not buy bread" (cited in Kula 1976, p. 49).

According to one proponent of the nineteenth century enclosures:
The possession of a cow or two, with a hog, and a few geese, naturally exalts the peasant. . . . In sauntering after his cattle, he acquires a habit of indolence. Quarter, half, and occasionally whole days, are imperceptibly lost. Day labour becomes disgusting; the aversion increases by indulgence. And at length the sale of a half fed calf, or hog, furnishes the means of adding intemperance to idleness. [Billingsly 1798, p. 31 cited in Horn 1980, p. 52]

Wilkinson cites a farmer, writing of the pre-enclosure cottager, "some few excepted, if you offer them work they will tell you they must look up their sheep, cut furze, get their cow out of the pound, or perhaps say they must take their horse to be shod, that he may carry them to the horse race or a cricket match" (1964, p. 18).

In part, the separation of land and labor was achieved by means of the enclosures. One of the supporters of the enclosures, a farmer, John Arbuthnot, proposed that if "by converting the little farmers into a body of men who must work for others, more labor is produced, it is an advantage which the nation should wish for" (Arbuthnot 1773, p. 124, cited by Marx 1977, p. 888). Arbuthnot, at least, had the vision to see the potentially beneficial results of the creation of collective labor. Robert Wallace even understood the process in terms of the production of surplus and the creation of a more refined social division of labor:

[I]f the lands be divided into very unequal shares, and in general, may produce much more than will decently support those who cultivate them, the country may notwithstanding be well peopled, if the arts be encouraged, and the surplus above what would support the labourers of the ground be allotted for such as cultivate the arts and sciences. [Wallace 1809, p. 17]

Most observers contented themselves with seeing no farther than the consequence that the poor would be forced to "work everyday in the year" (cited in Hill 1967, p. 278). This result alone was enough to win the wholehearted support of the enclosures by the majority of the ruling classes.

Later, capital came to perceive the advantage of a little bit of land combined with wage labor.[19] A few samples of eighteenth-century recommendations on the appropriate degree of self-sufficiency suggest the prevailing attitudes on the subject. In 1800, the *Commercial and Agricultural Magazine* calculated that "a quarter of an acre will go a great way towards rendering the peasant independent of any assistance," but that a much larger area would cut into the amount of labor a worker was willing to supply (cited in Thompson 1963, pp. 219–20). Capital thus had to exert great care lest the worker become "a little gardener instead of a labourer" (cited in Chambers and Mingay 1966, p. 134).

Robert Gourlay, an associate of Arthur Young, made a similar point:

> The half acre of land is condescended upon as being such a quantity as any poor man could make the most of at his spare hours, and from which he could raise sufficient food for a cow, along with his liberty of pasturage on the common; but there are reasons which would make it politic and right to diminish both the extent of the common and the garden plot. A quarter of an acre is the proper size for a garden, and 25 instead of 50 acres of common would be quite sufficient.
>
> A rood of land, under good garden culture, will yield a great abundance of every kind of vegetable for a family, besides a little for a cow and pig. . . . It is not the intention to make labourers professional gardeners or farmers! It is intended to confine them to bare convenience. The bad effects of giving too much land to labourers was discovered more than thirty years ago, in the lowlands of Scotland. . . . the bad effects of the little potatoe farms in Ireland are well known; and nothing but dirt and misery is witnessed among the Crofters of the Highlands of Scotland. A tidy garden, with the right of turning out a

---

[19] These advantages are in a continual state of flux depending upon the existing social conditions. At one point, Marx seemed about to touch upon this matter. Unfortunately, he left it with the almost casual observation, "England is at certain epochs mainly a corn-growing country, at others mainly a cattle-growing country. These periods alternate, and the alternation is accompanied by fluctuations in the extent of peasant cultivation" (Marx 1977, p. 912).

cow in a small well-improved and very well-fenced field, would produce efforts of a very different kind indeed. [Gourlay 1822, pp. 145–46]

At a time when households were far more self-sufficient, emergent capital was quite clear, however, on how it should approach the household economy. It knew that to obtain surplus value, it had to extend the working day over and beyond the time necessary for the collective labor force to reproduce itself. To make this point clearer, think of a developed capitalist system. Assume that five hours would suffice to produce the commodities consumed by the collective labor force. Thus a ten-hour day in the factory would allow for five hours of surplus. Workers would be paid the equivalent of one hour worth of value for each two hours on the job. If the rate of surplus value were to be increased, the ratio would become even more unfavorable.

Suppose that in a society in which capitalist production were less evolved, only nine hours were spent in the place of employment. The tenth hour would be used within the household economy. Workers could retain the results of their tenth hour of labor, which, together with a wage equivalent to nine hours of labor, could offer them a standard of living identical to the workers who would spend the full ten hours engaged in wage labor. Under these circumstances, workers would be paid the equivalent of four hours of value for nine hours of work; in other words, one and a quarter hours of work would be required to earn the equivalent of one hour of value.

How realistic is this line of reasoning? As I mentioned before, it implicitly assumes that the productivity of labor in any given process is more or less equal in both the place of employment and the household. If the value of one hour of paid labor in the factory can exchange for a high enough quantity of use values, workers might be able to exchange the nine hours of labor for four hours of value, which could offer them the higher standard of living than that enjoyed by self-employed peasants. While this possibility may appear likely today, during the early days of capitalism, the technology frequently employed by capital was not significantly different from the traditional household techniques.

At other times, it may be argued that it was superior. The physiocrats estimated that the spade husbandry of the peasants returned 20 to 30 times as much grain as had been planted. Cultivation with the plow returned only six (Weulersse 1959, p. 154; see also O'Connor 1848). Mirabeau described the farmers of a suburb of Paris who earned about 28 pounds per year from a single acre of land (Weulersse 1910; 2: 317). According to William Pitt, market gardeners near populated areas were assessed 11 pounds, 7 shillings per acre (cited in Wordie 1974, p. 600). Obviously, they had to be able to pay this amount to continue to practice their trade. We should not mislead ourselves into believing that the proceeds from these operations were due merely to the higher price per unit. Their output was nothing short of phenomenal.

A Paris gardener, M. Ponce, produced more than 44 tons of vegetables per acre, not to mention 250 cubic yards of topsoil (see Kropotkin 1906, p. 220; 1899, pp. 62ff; and Ponce 1870, pp. 32–49; also see the estimates of the produce of an English market garden in Maitland 1804, p. 132). By contrast, in the United States contemporary commercial producers manage to harvest only 15 tons of onions or 8.6 tons per acre of tomatoes, the highest yielding vegetables (United States Department of Agriculture 1979). Other plants such as spinach or pepper only produce 4 or 5 tons per acre in the United States (ibid.).[20]

In conclusion, traditional household production remained a viable alternative to wage labor. Jean-Baptiste Say penned one of the clearest expressions of this logic in a letter to Robert Malthus:

> I shall not attempt to point out the parts of this picture which apply to your country, Sir. . . . But if social life [a term which Say used almost like the social division of labor] were a galley, in which after rowing with all their strength for sixteen hours out of the twenty-four, they might indeed be excused for disliking social life. . . . I maintain no other doctrine when I say that the utility of productions is no longer worth the productive services, at the rate at which we are compelled to pay for them. [Say 1821, pp. 50–51; see also Ricardo 1951–73; 8: 184]

Thus, according to the implicit model of classical political economy, capital faced a serious contradiction. On the one hand, a highly active household

---

[20] We tend to underestimate the relative efficiency of the household in certain spheres of activity. In fact, even in the United States today less abstract labor is required to produce some goods in the home than to provide them commercially. For example, the growing of vegetables may take less labor on a farm than in a household garden, but when account is taken of the complexities of the marketing system and the labor embodied in the farm inputs, the domestic technology may well turn out to be superior. Scott Burns estimates that an hour spent in growing vegetables can save a family an average of ten dollars per hour, considerably more than the typical wage rate (Burns 1979). John Jeavons, a pioneer in the application of the scientific method to gardening techniques, estimated that by 1982 he would be able to produce a complete diet on 2,800 square feet of marginal land with a daily effort of 28 minutes, not much more than would be required to shop for the food (see Taper 1979). True enough, not all families have access to garden plots, but other forms of household production may still be rational. Burns' earlier work (1976), although unscientific, is a useful catalogue of such examples.

economy raises the potential rate of surplus value. On the other hand, the extremity of the potential rate of surplus value causes workers to resist wage labor. Consider, for example, the experience of a Boer farmer in 1852: "I have asked Kaffirs . . . to enter my service, and they have asked whether I was made to suppose that they would go and work for me at 5s. per month, when by the sale of wood, and other articles they could obtain as much as they wanted" (cited in Magubane 1979, p. 75). In late nineteenth-century Nigeria, Acting Governor Denton applied much the same logic to argue for the continued reliance on slavery: "In much fear that they [the slaves] can find means of subsistence ready to hand without work they will cease to do anything in the way of cultivating the land as soon as the restrictions of domestic slavery are removed" (cited in Hopkins, p. 96).

The extent to which a high rate of surplus value intensifies the resistance to wage labor is impossible to measure precisely. Even where substantial differentials between household and capitalist technologies exist, such as in present day India, subsistence farmers do display remarkable reluctance to work outside the family plot (Bardhan 1973, p. 1380; Bardhan 1979). However, this phenomenon could also be explained by the well-known reluctance of workers in traditional economies to accept employment as wage labor even when it would raise their standard of living (see Pollard 1965, p. 191). Irish women, for example, were reported to have been willing to accept half the salary they could obtain in a factory if they could do the same work at home (Pollard 1965, p. 173). The case of the handloom weavers is even better known:

> The unwillingness of the hand-loom weavers to enter the mills and manufactories is well known to the whole trade. This arises from them having acquired habits which render the occupation in mills disgusting to them, on account of its uniformity and of the strictness of its discipline. They are unwilling to surrender their imaginary independence, and prefer being enslaved by poverty, to the confinement and unvarying routine of factory employment. [Kay 1835, cited in Pollard 1968, p. 111]

Comparisons are made even more complicated by the variability of earnings. Edmund Morgan observed that in colonial Virginia, people frequently preferred a more leisurely subsistence economy despite frequent bouts of hunger and malnutrition (Morgan 1975, pp. 64–65).

To sum up to this point, I have suggested that classical political economy put forth a theory which held that a greater degree of self-provisioning increases the rate of surplus value, other things being equal. This model was applied to analyze the practical problem of resistance to wage labor. Unlike the classics, I explained this model by means of an example of a hypothetical individual choosing whether or not to engage in wage labor. The classics, by contrast, were unconcerned about the theoretical niceties of individual maximizing behavior. They set out to change the conditions to which individuals would have to adjust.

This distinction is not inconsequential. Capitalism does not begin in department stores. Where self-provisioning meets a large fraction of the needs of a typical household, an individual worker is not likely to choose wage labor even if the rate of surplus value were not high. One set of workers could not specialize in the full-time production of shoes, clothing, or even food unless others would make a complementary choice to supply those goods which the former workers ceased to produce for themselves. I shall return to this problem later in discussing the work of Sir James Steuart. For now I need only mention that workers who would find themselves in such an environment produce so much for their own needs that the value of their labor power would be very low. Consequently, they would be less than eager to exchange their labor for wages.

Even if we accept that this structural impediment could be overcome in time, the classics were still unlikely to leave the fate of capitalism to the free choice of the workers. After all, the working class generally appeared irrational to the superior orders. All too often it failed to conform to the approved norms of the bourgeoisie. Even today, observers who presume that wage labor is the "natural" state of humanity are perplexed by the apparently irrational rejection of wage labor (Weber 1923, pp. 260–61; and Moore 1955, p. 162; see also Redford 1926, p. 19), but our numerical example demonstrates how this sort of behavior may be correct even with the narrowest bounds of economic calculation.

In short, capital was convinced that it had to take matters into its own hands in order to control the accumulation process. Consequently, the history of the recruitment of labor is an uninterrupted story of coercion either through the brute force of poverty or through more direct regulation which made impossible a continuation of the old ways (Moore 1951). After all, almost everyone close to the process, friend or foe of labor, agreed with Charles Hall's verdict, that "if they were not poor, they would not submit to employments" (Hall 1805, p. 144)—at least so long as their remuneration was held low enough to create substantial profits.

The Squeeze

Nor can I conceive a greater curse upon a body of people, than to be thrown upon a spot of land, where the productions for subsistence and

food were, in great measure, spontaneous, and the climate required or
admitted little care for raimant or covering.

> Forster, *An Inquiry into the Causes of the*
> *Present High Price of Provisions*, p. 10

Even though their standard of living may not have been particularly lavish,
the people of precapitalistic northern Europe, like most traditional people,
seemed to enjoy a great deal of free time (see Perelman 1977, chap. 18; and
Ashton 1972, p. 204). For example, Adam Smith explained the excellent
poetry of primitive cultures as a result of such leisure (Smith 1762–63, Lecture 21 January 1763). In English feudal society, for example, where the
gentry was powerful enough to extract on the order of 50 percent of the
peasants' produce (see Postan 1966, p. 603),[21] the common people still seem
to have been able to maintain innumerable holidays that punctuated the
tempo of work. Joan Thirsk estimates that about one-third of the year,
including Sundays, was spent in leisure (cited in Thomas 1964, p. 63). A
much more extravagant estimate was produced by Kautsky, who estimated
that 204 annual holidays were celebrated in medieval Lower Bavaria
(Kautsky 1899, p. 107).

Capital viewed holidays as a waste of potential working time. Thus political economy condemned the celebration of so many holidays (see Cantillon
1775, p. 95, or Senior 1831, p. 9). The suppression of the holidays was
accomplished by virtue of vigorous action on the part of the clergy (see Hill
1967, pp. 145–218; see also Marx 1977, p. 387). In France, Voltaire called for
the shifting of holidays to the following Sunday. Since Sunday would have
been a day of rest in any case, employers could enjoy forty additional
working days. This proposal caused the Abbé Baudeau to wonder about the
logic of intensifying work when the countryside was already burdened with
an excess population (Weulersse 1959, p. 28).[22] Of course, these changes in
the religious practices of Europe were not induced by a shortage of people,
but by their unwillingness to conform to the needs of capital.

Much more than the mere elimination of religious festivals was required

---

[21] The estimate of 50 percent would not hold for the entire period. In southern
France, for example, rents appear to have grown from about one-fourth of the field
in 1540 to one-half by 1665 (LeRoy Ladurie 1974, p. 117).

[22] The suppression of religious festivals must not be interpreted as an indication that
representatives of capital took working-class devotion lightly. In some rural districts
of nineteenth-century England, working in one's garden on the sabbath was punisha-
ble. Some workers were even imprisoned for this offense (Marx 1977, pp. 375–76n).
Piety, however, must also be placed in perspective. Thus the same worker might be
charged with breach of contract should he prefer to attend church on the sabbath
rather than report for work (Marx 1977, pp. 375–76n).

to mold labor to the requirements of the new mode of production. Even during the early period of the Industrial Revolution, on both sides of the Atlantic, many employers were forced to content themselves with the services of people who worked on their own farms during all but the slack periods of the agricultural cycle (Mantoux 1961, p. 70; and Diamond and Guilfoil 1973, p. 206). We hear, for example, a Quaker merchant during the Seven Years' War apologizing for a delayed shipment with the excuse: "Our sailors are so much out in harvest time" (George 1953, p. 44).[23] This bottleneck proved especially troublesome when the increasing capacity to weave cloth was unmatched by comparable progress in spinning, traditionally an agricultural sideline (see Smelser 1959, p. 65).

Over and above such inconveniences, capital had to conquer the household economy in order to be able to extract a greater mass of surplus value. The device to which capital resorted was not secret. Workers had to be deprived of their means of production.[24] Consequently, "we find on the market a set of buyers, possessed of land, machinery, raw materials, and the means of subsistence, all of them, save land, the *products* of *labour*, and on the other hand, a set of sellers who have nothing to sell except their labouring power, their working arms and brains" (Marx 1865, pp. 55–56).

Typically, the story of primitive accumulation is viewed against the backdrop of the enclosure movement; however, enclosures were also intimately associated with the agricultural revolution. Thus, opposition to the enclosures sometimes appears as the futile flailing away at the inevitable progress of human society.

Primitive Accumulation and the Game Laws

The game laws demonstrate that a broad set of forces affected primitive accumulation. In traditional societies, hunting was an important means of providing for oneself and one's family. For example, in his tour of the Scottish Highlands, Daniel Defoe discovered that "however mountainous and wild the country appeared, the people were extremely well furnished with provisions" (Defoe 1724–26, p. 666). Among the major sources of food, he noted "venison exceedingly plentiful, and at all seasons, young or old, which they kill with their guns whenever they find it" (ibid.).

---

[23] An executive for Levi-Strauss reports that this problem still troubles the textile industry. Roy Cavender, contractor manager and director of product integrity for the Sportswear Division complains, "Many times during the fall in farm areas, there is an increase in absenteeism due to crop harvest" (cited in Sabel 1982, p. 247).

[24] For a description of a later repetition of the same process on a world scale, see Luxemburg (1968, chap. 27).

Later visitors to Scotland fretted that hunting was a barrier to the expansion of wage labor. Thomas Pennant, a botanist, provides much valuable information about this subject in his *Tour in Scotland* (1771). Pennant was considered to be a sympathetic interpreter of Scottish society, more so than, say, Samuel Johnson, in spite of the harshness with which Pennant regarded those who used hunting rather than wage labor to supplement their livelihood (see Lascelles 1971, p. xviii).

Writing from a spot near Edinburgh, Pennant noted, "I was informed that labor [sic] is dear here . . . ; the common people not being yet got into a method of working, so do very little for wages" (Pennant 1772, p. 71). Once he reached the Highlands, he complained: "The manners of the native Highlanders may be expressed in these words: indolent to a high degree, unless roused to war, or any animating amusement" (ibid., p. 176).[25] The energy the Highlanders devoted to hunting contrasted unfavorably with their enthusiasm for wage labor:

> The inhabitants live very poorly. . . . The men are thin, but strong; idle and lazy, except when employed in the chace [sic], or anything that looks for amusement; and are content with their hard fare, and will not exert themselves farther than what they deem necessaries [sic]. [ibid., p. 115]

Here was the problem highlighted in the classical model of primitive accumulation. People preferred their leisure rather than the small value they could obtain from a long stint of wage labor. Pennant drew some hope from what he saw in the salmon fisheries on the beaches near Aberdeen, where the women carried their heavy loads of salmon in baskets which they hoisted onto their shoulders:

> and when they have sold their cargo and emptied their basket, (they) will replace part of it with stones: they go sixteen miles to sell or barter their fish; they are very fond of finery, and will load their fingers with trumpery rings, when they want both shoes and stockings. [ibid., p. 126]

One could only guess how many hours of their drudgery were exchanged for each hour of the jewelers craft.

Samuel Johnson offered another example of what was entailed by the transition from household production to commodity production. Traditional

---

25 Compare with Adam Smith's observation: "The life of a savage, when we take a distant view of it, seems to be a life of either profound indolence, or of great and astonishing adventures" (Smith 1755–56, p. 250; see also Rae 1834, p. 131).

Scottish brogues could be made at home in one hour. Commercially produced shoes sold for one-half crown (Johnson 1774, p. 50). According to Adam Smith's estimates of wage rates for labor in the vicinity of Edinburgh, where workers were undoubtably paid more than in the countryside, a person would have to work for three days to earn enough money to purchase a pair of shoes (Smith 1937, p. 75). Naturally, under such conditions, people would be reluctant to exchange their leisure for the advantage of commercially produced shoes.

Whatever restricted people's opportunity for self-provisioning met with Pennant's approval. He commended the practice of the Earl of Bute, whose "farms were possessed of a set of men, who carried on at the same time the profession of farming and fishing to the manifest injury of both. His lordship drew a line between these incongruent employs, and obliged each to carry on the business he [Bute] preferred, distinct from the other" (Pennant 1774, p. 160). Nonetheless, Pennant had no technical complaint to lodge against these poor husbandmen. He admitted that "in justice to the old farmers, notice must be taken of their skill in ploughing even in their rudest days, for the ridges were strait [sic], and the ground laid out in a manner that did them credit" (ibid.).

Pennant's concerns were not technical. He wanted a new system of dependency. Thus, he praised the management of the Breadalbane estate, where tenants could stay rent free "on the condition that they exercize some trade. [Consequently, Breadalbane] has got some as good workmen, in common trades, as any in his Majesty's kingdom" (Pennant 1772, p. 90). To establish such dependency, Pennant saw the need to restrict the possibility of hunting for one's own food.

In England, the game laws prohibited all but the nobility, which accounted for about one percent of the population, from hunting. This legislation was created with an important purpose: "The game laws were born out of a desire to enhance the status of country gentlemen in the bitter aftermath of the Civil War. Their message was that land was superior to money" (Munsche 1980, p. 164).

The framers of the game laws were quite clear about the hierarchy of class relationships they intended to promote. Not only were the wealthy bourgeoisie forbidden to hunt in spite of their wealth; the poor would also be cut off from a traditional means of support. In this vein, James Steuart, writing from Scotland, treated the suppression of hunting merely as "an augmentation of inland demand for agricultural commodities" (Steuart 1767; 1: 37). The preamble to the 1692 law was very specific about the relationship between the game laws and the poor:

Whereas great mischief do ensure by inferior tradesmen, appren-

tices, and other dissolute persons neglecting their trades and employments who follow hunting, fishing and other game to the ruin of
themselves and their neighbors, therefore, if any such person shall
presume to hunt, hawk, fish or fowl (unless in company of the master
of such apprentice duly qualified) he shall . . . be subject to the other
penalties. [William and Mary 3 and 4, chap. 23, reprinted in Chitty
1812; 1: 459–65; also cited in Ignatieff 1978, p. 26]

Although the game laws were often denounced as a vestige of feudalism, the
draconian period of the game laws coincided with the high point of classical
political economy. The Waltham Black Acts of 1722 were among the earliest
of the severe measures to punish poachers. This legislaton was devised at a
time when venison had become a great delicacy, perhaps because of the great
expanse of land required for raising a deer (see Thompson 1975, p. 30). The
penalties for taking smaller game were less severe until landowners began to
take measures to increase their quantity. During the first six decades of the
eighteenth century, only six acts were directed against poachers of small
game. During the next fifty-six years, thirty-three such laws were passed.
As a result, "[m]eat virtually disappeared from the tables of the rural poor"
(Deane and Coale 1965, p. 41).

By 1827, the Black Acts were repealed. In 1831, some more measures were
eliminated. Over the next two decades, still more of the controversial features were repealed (see Horn 1980, Chapter 6). Although Parliament did not
grant farmers the right to kill hares on their land without permission of the
landlord until 1880 (Munsche 1980 p. 157), the most intense application of
the game laws falls between 1776, when the *Wealth of Nations* was published,
and the 1840s, an interval often used to mark the age of classical political
economy.

The British game laws, the harshest in the world (see Engels 1845,
pp. 552–53), were applied with special ferocity. Poaching was taken so seriously that it was, upon occasion, even equated with treason. Some poachers
were actually executed for their crime under the famous Black Acts (Thompson 1975, p. 68) Long after people ceased to be hung for poaching, the law
still countenanced the equally harsh verdict of spring guns and man-traps set
to punish the unwary hunter (see Smith 1821, pp. 213–34). William Cobbett
complained:

> I saw divers copies of a hand-bill notifying an approaching public
> sale of farming stock . . . , and [on] one of these bills having been given
> to me, I saw that, amongst the farming stock were a fire-engine and
> several steel man-traps . . . . [D]ismal indeed were the times when

fire-engines and man-traps formed part of the implements of husbandry! [Cobbett 1831: i, pp. 122–23]

Until 1827, the courts held that these barbaric devices were legal according to the common law. They were eventually prohibited only because the deaths they inflicted on gamekeepers and children, rather than the injury of poachers. As Lord Suffield noted, "poachers are almost the only persons who escape being shot by spring guns" (Suffield 1825, cited in Munsche 1980, p. 72).

The game laws must be interpreted in the context of the changing nature of property rights. The early game laws grew out of the movement to cut large masses of the rural people from their traditional means of production (Thompson 1975, pp. 94, 99, 207 and 261). Specifically, these laws were a response to the refusal of the poor to accept the encroachments of the landlords (see Ignatieff 1978, p. 16). In Germany, the mere foraging for berries was deemed a crime (Marx 1842, pp. 234–35). Marx himself suggested that the harsh treatment meted out to those who illegally gathered wood in the forests was significant enough to have first drawn his attention to social problems (Marx 1970, pp. 19–20; and Marx and Engels 1973; 39: 466).

The impact of the game laws was substantial. Jefferson, for example, in a letter to James Madison, dated October 28, 1785, written in Fontainbleau, where the king hunted in the fall, noted the enormous land resources devoted to keeping game in France (Jefferson 1950–; 8: 681–83). Jefferson, to his credit, understood the importance of such uses of the land:

> In Europe the lands are either cultivated or locked up against the cultivator. Manufacture must therefore be resorted to of necessity, not of choice. [Jefferson 1787,p. 42; emphasis added]

During the early eighteenth century, the game laws were harsh and repressive, but they could also be tempered by the paternalistic obligations still expected of the gentry. Generally, those most in need could count upon some generosity from the superior orders; however, the social mores were changing.

Adam Smith seems to have been a major influence in changing life styles of the time. His lectures on *Belles Lettres and Rhetoric* appear indirectly to have initiated the craze for deep parks (Olwig and Olwig 1979, p. 19; Whitney 1924 and Smith 1762–63, Lecture, 21 January 1763). Later, he applauded the growing preference for more natural looking habitats: "It was some years ago the fashion to ornament a garden with yew and holly trees, clipped to the artificial shapes of pyramids, and columns, and vases. It is now the fashion to ridicule this task as unnatural" (Smith 1790a, p. 183; see also Comito

1971). Indeed, Smith's vision of a "natural" landscape was well suited to the world of the bourgeoisie.

This new way of life was reflected in the evolution of the definition of hospitality. A writer in the 1761 edition of the Annual Register noted that the aristocracy could "no longer affect an old-fashioned hospitality, or suffer the locust of the country to eat them up, while they keep open-house and dispense victuals and horns of beer to all comers" (cited in Munsche 1980, pp. 133–34). According to the same source, "genteel entertainment" with "French food and select company" became the style. The cuisine was always limited to French foods. A writer of 1815 noted that game was "an essential ingredient in every entertainment that has the slightest pretension to elegance" (cited in Munsche 1980, p. 22).

When the game laws did come up for discussion in Parliament during the late eighteenth century, the ruling strata adopted a curious position. Although hunting was an improper diversion for the poor, it was commended to the rich since hunting was regarded as an encouragement to agricultural production. The opportunity to hunt seemed to be the only means of bringing the wealthy into contact with their land (see Cobbett 1806–20; 32: 833ff; and Horn 1980, p. 172). Thus, the game laws may be seen as an embarrassing admission about the social value of the gentry.

By the nineteenth century, the game laws could no longer be justified by the prestige of the gentry, which had begun to decline in 1756, when Britain endured several military defeats during the outbreak of the Seven Years War. The public looked to a reinvigorated militia to renew civic virtue (Munsche 1980, p. 112). The feudal warrior, like the medieval artisan, was consigned to the past.

The future battles would be decided by ships and other fixed capital of warfare together with mobilization of broader segments of society. Bourgeois captains of the battlefield would run their operations with the same sort of equipment and personnel as bourgeois captains of industry (see Smith 1937, pp. 653–69; and Marx 1974, p. 109; and Marx to Engels, 25 September 1857, in Marx and Engels 1975, pp. 91–92). Within this conception of warfare, farmers acquainted with firearms would be invaluable. The gentry were asked if they valued their country as much as their partridges (Western 1965, p. 119).

In spite of his deference to feudal warriors, Sir James Steuart, as well as Adam Smith, were members of Poker Club, which was formed to support a Scotch militia (see Bell 1960 and Rendall 1978). Smith, who usually stressed the sloth and lethargy of rural workers, took a different position in discussing the need for free time for training the militia. In this context, he had to recognize that agricultural progress might have been bought at the expense of the rural workers: "Those improvements in husbandry . . . which the

progress of arts and manufactures necessarily introduces, leave the husbandman with as little leisure as the artificer" (Smith 1937, p. 659).

True, the game laws smacked of feudalism, so much so that Brian Inglis
claimed that they were the only oppressive part of the feudal system which
remained on the statute books (see Inglis 1971, p. 243). Even the astute Jacob
Viner seemed to hold the same opinion (Viner 1968, pp. 39–40). Indeed, the
law was often administered in a decidedly feudal style. The case of Richard
Dellers became a particularly famous example. On the basis of information
from his gamekeeper and a servant, The Duke of Buckingham convicted
Dellers. The Duke, presiding over the trial in his own drawing room, informed the unfortunate Dellers that if he uttered one impertinent word, he
would be taken to jail or the stocks (Munsche 1980, p. 76; see also Cobbett
1830; 1: pp. 191–93). Henry Brougham, speaking in 1828, when the Dellers
affair was still fresh in the mind of the British public, roared: "There is not
a worse constituted tribunal on the face of the earth, not even that of the
Turkish cadi, than that which summary convictions on the Game Laws
constantly take place; I mean a bench or a brace of sorting justices" (cited
in Munsche 1980, p. 76).

Although their origin of the game laws was indeed feudal, they evolved
with the changing class structure of British society. In the end, one of the
most hated institutions of feudalism, long remembered in legend for leading
Robin Hood onto a path of crime, became an important ingredient of capitalist development.

This change began when proponents of the rising bourgeoisie called for
reform of the game laws in the interest of substantial farmers and tenants.
Some thought that a compromise could be effected by appointing such
people as gamekeepers (Munsche 1980, p. 113). More frequently, the reform-
ers proposed that the property qualifications be lowered so that the middle
class could also have the right to hunt. Even the sympathetic Sydney Smith,
who wished "to preserve the lives of . . . the least worthy of God's creatures"
with a vigor equal to that which protected "the Christian partridge . . . the
immortal pheasant . . . the rational woodcock, or the accountable hare" (cited
in Auden 1956), could only see his way toward strengthening the property
rights of the wealthy landowners in order that game could be treated as any
other commodity (Smith 1819).

Although the barbarism of the existing game laws may have been somewhat of an embarrassment for the bourgeoisie (see Cobbett 1806–20; 32:
pp. 833ff; and Smith 1819), they did not wish to dampen its impact. John
Christian Curwin, the leading reformer of the late eighteenth century, asked
Parliament in 1796 to follow the lead of Russia by substituting the taxation
of game for the game laws. Such a tax was preferred because it "does away
with all necessity of restrictions, and puts it out of the power of persons who

might injure themselves and the public by misspending their time in pursuit of game" (cited in Cobbett 1806–20; 32: 836). His proposal did nothing to reduce the penalties for poaching. In fact, in some ways it would have made them even stronger.

Why would such violence be sanctioned by the law? According to Blackstone, "the only rational footing, upon which we can consider it a crime, is, that in low and indigent persons it promotes idleness and takes them away from their proper employments and callings" (Blackstone 1775; 4: 174–75). Pitt agreed (cited in Cobbett 1806–20; 32: 851). I know of only one seemingly dissenting voice: Adam Smith, the great master of capitalist apologetics. Adam Smith was perhaps unique among the major classical political economists in taking note of the game laws:

> There can be no reason in equity for this. . . . The reason they give is that the prohibition is made to prevent the lower sort of people from spending their time on such unprofitable employment; but the real reason is that they delight in hunting and the great inclination they have to screw all they can out of their hands. [Smith 1978, p. 24]

In a sense, Smith's words contained an ounce of truth. The practice of restricting self-provisioning predated capitalism. As Smith noted, feudal lords prohibited the use of hand mills to force people to use those of the lords (Smith 1978, p. 85). People were forbidden to do certain types of work in their homes to ensure the privileged positions of masters (see Weber 1923, p. 120). These instances notwithstanding, no class proved itself as effective in separating workers from their means of production as the bourgeoisie.

Smith may have been correct in his interpretation of the motives of the gentry, but like the rest of his class he said nothing and did nothing to lighten the imposition of the game laws on the poor. Moreover, when the western European nations extended their domination to the peripheral regions, they were quick to recognize the value of such arrangements. For example, in French Equitorial Africa the Mandja people were banned from hunting (Rodney 1974, p. 166). Since these people had almost no livestock, hunting provided their major source of meat. Thus the ban was an effective measure to force the Mandja to work on the French cotton plantations.

Eventually, the old game laws seemed to have served their purpose. New laws were constructed around the concept of private property instead of the exalted privileges of the gentry. Hunting preserves became a major source of income for the gentry (see Ross 1973, p. 249). The reformed game laws would allow bourgeois farmers of the middling sort to hunt on their own lands as freely as the gentry could on theirs. In this respect, the new laws appealed to Smith's sense of equity. Smith did not say that bourgeoisified game laws would give common workers the right to hunt. Such people would still be excluded. In short, Smith's humanistic words meant much less than they appeared to mean. The bourgois interpretation of equity was not necessarily in the interest of the lower classes. So long as the game laws were grounded in traditional rights, the gentry's claim to exclusive hunting rights was subject to some doubt. The poor could also appeal to certain traditions and ambiguities (see Blackstone 1775; 2:p. 410).

Parallel with the rise of classical political economy, the courts began to recognize game as a form of property. The taking of game was tantamount to an attack on property rights and thus had to be punished severely. Moreover, in the eyes of the gentry, the game laws were an essential bulwark of the social order. The lesson was not lost on either the gentry or the bourgoisie that one of the earliest acts of the French Revolution was the repeal of the game laws. A few months later, Horace Walpole, after noting the speed with which the French game laws were eliminated, confided to Lady Ossory:

> I never admired game-acts, but I do not wish to see guns in the hands of all the world, for there are other ferae naturae besides hares and partridges—and when all Europe is admiring and citing our constitution, I am for preserving it where it is. [Walpole 1789, p. 69, cited in Munsche 1980, p. 126]

Lord Milton made a similar point to Lord Kenyon in 1791:

> The Republican party has made the Game Laws the object of their abuse and detestation; in France, the instant they began to overturn the constitution and level all distinctions, these were the first they pulled down. It therefore seems to me that they should be most respectfully guarded. [cited in Munsche 1980, p. 127]

These fears were compounded by another dimension of the game laws. According to a good many people, hunting was an important means of imbuing the gentry with appropriate martial skills (see Steuart 1767; 1: 85). Many members of the ruling classes would have been reluctant to encourage the spread of such skills among a broader section of the populace. Blackstone, for example, in discussing the beneficial results of the game laws, wrote of "the prevention of popular insurrection and resistance to the government, by disarming the bulk of the people; which last is a reason oftener meant, than avowed, by makers of forest or game laws" (Blackstone 1775: ii, p. 412). Moreover, access to weapons was a major factor in determining the level of exploitation (see Pettengill 1981).

The game laws took on even more importance as the changing class relations in the countryside during the early nineteenth century led to more heated conflicts. Landlords' relations with tenants became more distant and more exploitative. Long-term leases became less common. Rental income was on the rise. Any good will was fast disappearing from the countryside. Cottagers were being eliminated. Full-time workers and servants were being replaced by casual labor. After the Napoleonic Wars, some 250,000–400,000 men were demobilized. Many of their traditional jobs in the countryside had been lost to threshing machines during the war (see Munsche 1980, p. 136).

The conviction rates indicate the intensification of class struggle in the countryside. In 1816, the first year for which national figures are available, 868 persons were imprisoned for game offenses; by 1820, the number had risen to 1467. In Wiltshire, the winter of 1812–13 saw eight committals under game laws. By the winter of 1817–18, the number had risen to 85. In Bedfordshire, seven people were imprisoned in 1813; 77 in 1819. By the first half of 1820s, 65 persons annually were imprisoned for infractions of the game laws. In Wiltshire, the average had risen to 92. In Wiltshire alone, more than 1300 persons were imprisoned under game laws in the fifteen years after Waterloo, more than twice the number for the previous fifty years (Munsche 1980, p. 138).

Even after the game laws were reformed in 1831, the numbers of convictions still continued their dramatic increase (Munsche 1980, p. 157). During the 1840s, in some rural counties, 30 and even 40 percent of all male convictions were for infractions of the game laws (Horn 1980, pp. 179–80).

The game laws had another dimension. The animals which were protected by the laws ravaged the nation's crops. Much of what the game left was trampled by hunters and their horses. A letter to the editor of the *London Magazine* in 1757 claimed:

> The present scarcity is owing to an evil, felt by the industrious husbandman, who has in many places in this kingdom, seen all his care, labour, and industry sacrificed to the caprice and humours of those who have set their affections so much on game. Numberless are the places and parishes of the kingdom which have had at least one third part of their wheat crop devoured and eat[en] up by hares. [Anon. 1757, p. 87]

A modern student of the game laws observed, "Pheasants, if anything, were more destructive" (Munsche 1980, p. 46). The destruction of crop by game was a very important phenomenon. In France, for example, on the eve of the revolution, the people were given the chance to express their concerns. In almost every case, the people of the countryside demonstrated their exasperation at the devastation caused by game and hunters (see Philipponeau 1956, p. 29, and Young 1794, p. 9). As mentioned above, one of the first acts of the revolutionary government was to repeal the game laws. At the time, Arthur Young noted, "One would think that every rusty gun in Provence is at work" (Young 1794, p. 9; see also pp. 441–42). The grievances of the English peasants were no doubt just as strong:

> Sportsmen, it was said, continually broke fences, beat down unharvested corn, trampled turnips, disturbed sheep 'big with lamb' and generally pursued game with little concern for the damage they caused. The quantity and volume of these complaints suggest that such conduct was common and deeply resented. [Munsche 1980, p. 45]

In the 1840s, an estimated quarter of the crops of Buckinghamshire were destroyed by game (Horn 1981, p. 179). On only one occasion, Parliament indicated an interest in this problem:

> [F]or most sportsmen, the season began with partridge shooting on the first of September . . . , but following the bad harvest in 1795 . . . ., [e]arly in 1796, Parliament voted to postpone the start of partridge shooting until the fourteenth of September. [Munsche 1980, p. 46]

This provision was repealed by the next year. The consequent loss of grain continued without comment from the ranks of political economists, whose keen vision rarely left any opportunity for increased productivity pass unnoticed. Adam Smith took some notice of a different aspect of the dissipation of resources associated with hunting. He complained that the "large tracts of land which belong to the crown [were] a mere waste and loss of country with respect both of population and produce" (Smith 1937, p. 776). His recommendation that such lands be sold seems to have been based on fiscal considerations alone. He was silent about the parallel misallocation of private land. Nonetheless, Smith deserves some credit for broaching the subject, since all other political economists failed to make any mention whatsover.

In fact, despite the widespread injuries inflicted by the game laws, political economy seems to have altogether ignored the implications of this legislation. For example, on the subject of transportation, the usual punishment inflicted on poachers, Frank Fetter, after noting the attendance and voting patterns of political economists in Parliament, observed, "transportation was not an issue in which many political economists were concerned" (Fetter 1980, p. 192).

Why should political economy have taken note of so much of the minutae of society, while remaining oblivious to the monstrous impact of the game laws? I maintain that this omission on its part in no way absolves them of any responsibility for the repression and destruction associated with the operation of the game laws. Silence in the face of such conditions amounted to an effective form of support. Before adopting such a position, consider the lively interest which political economy took in all matters pertaining to the functioning of the economy. Here was a law which created a substantial hardship for an enormous number of people. It allowed many workers to be incarcerated or transported. It condoned the destruction of valuable crops. Yet, when the laws were debated in Parliament in 1830, not one prominent spokesman of political economy called for their abolition. Instead, Robert Peel, whose family wealth had come from the employment of those who were leaving the land, cautioned Parliament not to act with undue haste:

> [W]e are apt to be too sanguine in our anticipations of advantages to be derived from a particular change. He was afraid that we overlooked the love of enterprise and amusement, which rendered the pursuit of game attractive to the common people. [Hansard, pp. 597–98]

The imagery of the nineteenth-century "enterprise and amusement," so admired by Peel and his class was described in detail by John Ruskin:

> Your ideal of human life then is, I think, that it should be passed in a pleasant undulating world, with iron and coal everywhere underneath it. On each pleasant bank of this world is to be a beautiful mansion, with two wings; and stables and coach horses; a moderately sized park; a large garden and hot houses; and pleasant carriage drives through the shrubberies. In this mansion are to live the favoured votaries of the Goddess: the English gentleman, with his gracious wife and his beautiful family; always able to have the boudoir and the jewels for the wife, and the beautiful ball dresses for the daughters, and hunters for the sons, and a shooting in the Highlands for himself. At the bottom of the bank, is to be the mill; not less than a quarter of a mile long, with a steam engine at each end, and two in the middle and a chimney three hundred feet high. In this mill are to be in constant employment from eight hundred to a thousand workers, who never drink, never strike, always go to church on Sunday, and always express themselves in respectful language. [Ruskin 1866, p. 61]

Not all of the bourgeoisie were able to realize this dream, but enough could that the landscape of the nation was transformed. According to Engels, for each acre of English common land brought into cultivation by means of enclosures, three acres of Scottish land were eventually transformed into deer parks (Engels 1894, p. 213; see also Marx 1977, pp. 892–95). Marx noted, "Everyone knows that there are no true forests in England. The deer in the parks are demure domestic cattle, as fat as London aldermen. Scotland is therefore the last refuge of the 'noble passion'" (1977, p. 892).

Marx's discussion of the deer parks is worth noting in one respect. It is the only reference in Part 8 that deals with the domestic economy of England after the era of classical political economy had been completed (Marx 1977, pp. 892–93). The conversion of forest into well-guarded deer parks represents the final extinguishing of the last flicker of the old feudal rights of the peasantry. In this sense, this discussion conforms to the narrow interpretation of primitive accumulation.

In contrast, the substitution of deer for sheep, also discussed by Marx in this same section, represents a restriction of the production of food or clothing, which is fully explicable in terms of supply and demand. If the gentry preferred to use their land for hunting, they were not directly attacking people. If wool or mutton became more expensive as a result, we cannot hold an individual culpable. Yet the effect is no less severe for the people who suffer.

I do not intend to push the definition of primitive accumulation that far. I only wish to include those cases which directly impact on a household's ability to produce for its own needs. The example of the deer parks does suggest how such primitive accumulation, in the broad sense, can occur without the arbitrary application of power.

Concluding Note on Political Economy and Poverty

Neither the game laws nor the other aspects of primitive accumulation won a prominent place in the annals of political economy. Classical political economy rarely directly addressed the question of poverty. As Adam Smith noted:

> The poor man goes out and comes in unheeded, and when in the midst of a crowd is in the same obscurity as if shut up in his own hovel. Those humble cares and painful attentions which occupy those in his situation, afford no amusement to the dissipated and the gay. They turn their eyes from him, or if the extremity of his distress forces them to look at him, it is only to spurn so disagreeable an object from among them. The fortunate and the proud wonder at the insolence of human wretchedness, that it should dare to present itself before them, and with the loathsome aspect of its misery presume to disturb the serenity of their happiness. [Smith 1759, p. 51]

Engels noted that the physical layout of Manchester was designed to protect the sensitivities of the bourgeoisie:

And the finest part of the arrangement is this, that the members of this money aristocracy can take the shortest road through the middle of all the labouring districts to their places of business without ever seeing that they are in the midst of the grimy misery that lurks to the right and the left. For the thoroughfares leading from the Exchange in all directions out of the city are lined, on both sides, with an almost unbroken series of shops, and so are kept in the hands of the middle and lower bourgeoisie, which out of self-interest, cares for a decent and cleanly external appearance. [Engels 1845b, p. 348]

Young people who dared to explore the hinterland of poverty within the city were sometimes drawn to the study of political economy in the false hope of finding an answer. For example, Alfred Marshall wrote:

I read Mill's *Political Economy* and got much excited about it. I had doubts as to the propriety of inequalities of *opportunity*, rather than of material comfort. Then, in my vacations I visited the poorest quarters of several cities and walked through one street after another, looking at the faces of the poorest people. Next, I resolved to make as thorough a study as I could of political economy. [cited in Keynes 1963, p. 137]

Jevons also expressed a curiosity about the "dark passages between the strand and the river" (see Black and Koenigkamp 1972, p. 17; see also Jevons 1972, p. 67). However, we have no record of either Jevons or Marshall continuing this interest in poverty once each had established himself as a mature economist. Since the bourgeoisie was generally spared a direct encounter with poverty in its daily life, it often first witnessed squalor on its visits to the Continent or to Ireland. There poverty was something foreign that confirmed the correctness of the British system. At home in England, one could expect the poor to keep themselves out of sight. When they dared to impose themselves, they evoked an angry reaction, just as Adam Smith had said.

This studied pose of ignorance did not mean a lack of awareness. In the study of the doctrines of classical political economy which follows, we shall see that political economy applied the classical theory of primitive accumulation with unerring accuracy. In every case classical political economy called for action with respect to self-provisioning that would maximize the production of surplus value.

chapter 2

A Great Beginning

[A] real state and a real government only arise when class distinctions are already present, when wealth and poverty are far advanced, and when a situation has arisen in which a large number of people can no longer satisfy their needs in the way in which they have been accustomed.

G. W. F. Hegel, *Lectures on the Philosophy of World History*, p. 168

Classical political economy was never willing to rely completely on the market to organize production. It called for measures to force those who engaged in self-provisioning to be integrated into the cash nexus. This chapter will demonstrate that this assertion holds true for William Petty, Richard Cantillon, the Physiocrats, and classical political economy in general. True, classical political economy did not treat self-provisioning as a theoretical category; however, the categories within which early classical political economy cast its theory did contain implicit judgments about nonmarket activities. This hostility to self-provisioning was camouflaged under a theoretical apparatus that denied legitimacy to all activity which did not conform to the norm of production by wage labor.

According to the famous Four Stages theory of Smith and Turgot, social development was bound up with the passage from hunting and gathering to animal husbandry, then agriculture, and finally commercial society (see Meek 1977b). This classical anticipation of Marx's theory of base and superstructure represented an undeniable advance in the understanding of the economy understood that once people could no longer grow their own food, they became dependent upon the market for their nourishment. Not surprisingly, almost all representatives of political economy agreed on the beneficial effects of high food prices (see Furniss 1965 and Wermel 1939, pp. 1–14, 17, 24). For example, Hume even went so far as to assert "'tis always observed, in years of scarcity, if it be not extreme, that the poor labour more, and really live better" (Hume 1752c, p. 357).

A further example is Francis Hutcheson—"the never to be forgotten Dr. Hutcheson" as he was described by his student, Adam Smith (letter from Smith to Dr. Archibald Davidson, 16 November 1787, reprinted in Mossner and Ross 1977, p. 309)— the same Francis Hutcheson whose *A Short Introduction to Moral Philosophy in Three Books* (1742) seems to have served as a model for the economic sections of Smith's Glasgow lectures (see Scott 1965, pp. 235, 240). A later work, his *System of Moral Philosophy*, exemplifies Dr. Hutcheson's contributions to that field of knowledge. After a few brief notes on the need to raise prices, Hutcheson mused:

> If a people have not acquired an habit of industry, the cheapness of all the necessaries of life encourages sloth. The best remedy is to raise the demand for all necessaries. . . . Sloth should be punished by temporary servitude at least. [Hutcheson 1755; 2: 318–19]

Indeed, temporary servitude at least. What else might the good doctor recommend to students of moral philosophy in the event that temporary servitude would prove inadequate in shunting people off to the work place? The three sentences in the citation were sufficiently related that Hutcheson did not even bother to separate them by beginning a new paragraph. No, primitive accumulation alone was not sufficient. As Hutcheson understood, the other blade of the scissors was the stern measures required to keep people from trying to survive outside of the system of waged labor.

Beginning with the Tudors, England enacted a series of stern measures designed to prevent peasants from drifting into vagrancy or falling back on degrading welfare systems (Marx 1974, p. 736, and 1977, p. 896).[1] Those who refused employment were subject to whipping or were branded with a red-hot iron (Mantoux 1961, p. 432). The attitude toward the poor was clearly reflected in the literature on the subject (see, for example, Hobbes 1651, chap. 30, p. 387). Writers of every persuasion shared an obsessional concern

---

[1] Similar statutes appear almost simultaneously during the early sixteenth century in England, the Low Countries, and Zurich (LeRoy Ladurie 1974, p. 137).

with the creation of a disciplined labor force (Furniss 1965; Appleby 1978).[2] Criminality as well as disease was charged to a want of discipline (Ignatieff 1978, pp. 61ff). By the late eighteenth century, even hospitals came to be regarded as a proper medium to instill discipline (see Ignatieff 1978, p. 61). One writer suggested that the footmen of the gentry could rise early to employ their idle hours making fishing nets along with "disbanded soldiers, poor prisoners, widows and orphans, all poor tradesmen, artificers, and labourers, their wives, children, and servants" (Puckle 1700; 2: 380, cited in Appleby 1976, p. 501). Townsend argued that each waking moment could be put to good use. He hoped that in the evenings when farm workers return from threshing or from plough, "they might card, they might spin, or they might knit" (Townsend 1786, p. 442). No source of labor was overlooked. William Temple argued for the addition of four-year-old children to this labor force. Not to be outdone, John Locke called for the commencement of work at the ripe age of three (Furniss 1965, pp. 114–15). By 1724, Daniel Defoe was delighted to discover that so much progress had taken place that the children of Norwich were already earning their bread by the age of four or five (Defoe 1724–26, p. 86; see also p. 493).

Others called for new institutional arrangements to maintain a steadily increasing flow of wage labor. Fletcher of Saltoun recommended perpetual slavery as the appropriate fate of those who would fail to respond to less harsh measures to integrate them into the labor force (see Marx 1977, p. 882). Hutcheson, as we have seen, followed suit. Always the idealist, Bishop Berkeley preferred that such slavery be limited to "a certain term of years" (Berkeley 1740, p. 456). In a movement that Michael Foucault has termed "the great confinement," institutions were founded to indiscriminately take charge of the sick, the criminal, and the poor (Foucault 1965, pp. 38–65). The purpose was not to better the conditions of the inmates, but rather to force them to contribute more to the national wealth.

As the workings of capitalism came to be better understood, the appeal of formal slavery diminished. The same results could be achieved by maintaining the working class in a continual state of deprivation. Patrick Colquhoun, a London police magistrate, noted:

> Poverty is that state or condition in society where the individual has no surplus labour in store, or, in other words, no property or means of subsistence but what is derived from the constant exercise of industry. *Poverty is, therefore, a most necessary and indispensable ingredient in society . . . . It is the source of wealth, since without poverty there could be no labour.* [cited in Hollis 1973, p. 321; emphasis added]

---

[2] For a less harsh selection, see Wiles (1968).

This bourgeois preference for "the silent compulsion of economic relations" was understandable. Consider the wisdom of the Reverend Townsend, writing as "A Well-Wisher to Mankind":

> [Direct] legal constraint [to labour] . . . is attended with too much trouble, violence, and noise, . . . whereas hunger is not only a peaceable, silent, unremitted pressure, but as the most natural motive to industry, it calls forth the most powerful exertions. Hunger will tame the fiercest animals, it will teach decency and civility, obedience and subjugation to the most brutish, the most obstinate, and the most perverse. [Townsend 1786, p. 404–7]

Unfortunately, capital could not rely on "silent compulsion" until the structure of capitalism had begun to take form. Prior to that time, it had to take action to shape society according to the logic of accumulation. Classical political economy was coy about the importance of these institutional changes. It covered itself with a flurry of rhetoric about natural liberties. On closer examination, we find that the notion of the system of natural liberties was considerably more flexible than it appeared. Let us turn once again to Francis Hutcheson, who taught Adam Smith about the virtue of natural liberty. In a work that served as a model to Smith's own lectures, he wrote:

> It is the one great design of civil laws to strengthen by political sanctions the several laws of nature. . . . The populace needs to be taught, and engaged by laws, into the best methods of managing their own affairs and exercising mechanic art [Hutcheson 1749, p. 273]

Few authors made this connection explicitly—those who did were treated less charitably than Hutcheson. Consequently, we are left with a tradition of reading about the compassion of Smith, Ricardo, and even Malthus. Compared with others of their day, no doubt they were. We have only to refer to the brutal language of "The Well Wisher to Mankind" to see the standards against which the classical political economists were measured.

To show that classical political economy was not altogether benign does not prove a personal failure on the part of its practitioners. Rather, it illustrates the manner in which our social conscience is molded by the economic formation in which we find ourselves. To pursue this matter further is important, especially insofar as it reveals forces in capitalist society that might otherwise escape our attention.

According to classical political economy, all social conditions and all social institutions were to be judged merely according to their effect on the production of wealth. One can almost hear the jingling of coins in reading the words of Jeremy Bentham, that vigorous advocate of freedom of commerce, as he dreamed of the profits that would accrue from the use of the inmates of his proposed prison, the fabled Panopticon. The attraction of unfree labor was obvious to all. He wrote:

> What hold can another manufacturer have upon his workmen, equal to what my manufacturer would have upon his? What other master is there that can reduce his workmen, if idle, to a situation next to starving, without suffering them to go elsewhere? What other master is there whose men can never get drunk unless he chooses that they should do so? And who, so far from being able to raise their wages by combination, are obliged to take whatever pittance he thinks it most his interest to allow? [cited in Ignatieff 1978, p. 110; see also Foucault 1979]

Perhaps the only adequate commentary on this literature came from the acid pen of Jonathan Swift, whose modest proposal to consume the flesh of children was patterned after the typical economic proposals of the time (see Wittkowsky 1943; Swift 1729).[3] As the struggle to create a proletariat intensified, the ruling class took special care to separate the household economy from its means of production. Workers lost their capacity to be self-reliant. Foreign visitors were struck by the final result of this arrangement, noting that "not one of all the many thousand English factory workers has a square yard of land on which to grow food if he is out of work and draws no wage" (Escher 1814, p. 35).

The separation of workers from the land was justified in terms of progress. McCulloch denounced the security associated with the ownership of small plots of land as being:

> uniformly associated with poverty, frequently degenerating into destitution; it gives use to the most revolting of all combinations, that of penury, pride, and laziness. . . . The happiness of peasant proprietors seems very much akin to that of the oyster—they are ignorant and satisfied.[4] [cited by Coats 1971, pp. 159–60]

Workers generally understood the strategic importance of these measures to foster primitive accumulation. Thomas Spence, a courageous working-class

---

[3] Wittkowsky finds numerous stylistic parallels to support his contention that Swift's "modest proposal" had been chiefly modeled after Petty's work (Swift 1729; see also Wittkowsky 1943). Allusions to Petty are also made by Gulliver's description of the "odd kind of arithmetick . . . in reckoning the numbers of our people by a computation drawn from the several sects among us in religion and politicks" (Swift 1726, p. 131).

[4] A stunning commentary on the classical analysis of *satisficing*!

advocate, proclaimed, for example, that "[It] is childish . . . to expect. . . to see anything else than the utmost screwing and grinding of the poor, till you quite overturn the present system of landed property" (cited in Thompson 1963, p. 805).

The system, however, was not overturned. It just became stronger. The workers were forced to surrender their traditional periods of leisure (see Hill 1967 and Reid 1976, pp. 76–101). The working day was lengthened (Hammond and Hammond 1919, pp. 5–7). The working class, in the person of Thomas Spence, cried out:[5]

> Instead of working only six days a week we are obliged to work at the rate of eight or nine and yet can hardly subsist . . . and still the cry is work—work—ye are idle. . . . We, God help us, have fallen under the hardest set of masters that have ever existed. [cited in Kemp-Ashraf 1966, p. 277; see also Tawney 1926, esp. p. 223]

This statement was eloquent enough to earn its author a sentence of three years' imprisonment after its publication in 1803. Here we see that whenever the working class and its friends effectively protested against capitalism, silent compulsion gave way to compulsory silence.

Progressive historians have managed to rescue some part of the people's life from obscurity. My project in the remaining portion of this chapter is more modest. I merely intend to show how their struggles were reflected in the works of classical political economy.

Sir William Petty and Richard Cantillon

Classical political economy was a period of adolescent brilliance. Perhaps none of its practitioners was so brilliant or so adolescent as the irrepressible William Petty, whom Marx credited with being "the father of English political economy" (Marx 1970, p. 52n, and 1977, p. 384).

Petty was a polymath. Before winning his spurs as a political economist, he had achieved both fame and notoriety as a doctor. He had also served as a professor of music and had dabbled in the design of ships. After his appointment as the chief medical officer to Cromwell's forces in Ireland, he won the contract to survey the newly defeated land. Speed was of the utmost necessity, since measurement was required before the spoils could be divided

---

[5] Spence's biographer asserts that Owenism and the subsequent heritage of British socialism follows a direct line of descent from Spence's critique of capitalism (Rudkin 1966, pp. 191ff). Indeed, journalists of the day agreed (see Halevy 1961, p. 44fn). Knox's contrary evaluation of Spence as a "radical crank" (Knox 1977, p. 73) finds an adequate response in Kemp-Ashraf (1966).

among the conquerors. Petty's work was quick enough, but in the process, he picked up a great deal of land for himself in direct violation of the terms of his initial agreement.

Although his ensuring legal intrigues sapped most of his energy, he still managed to set political economy on the course it was to follow for the next three centuries. Petty's experiences put him in touch with some of the most dynamic forces of his era. His early life as a cabin boy, and perhaps his military duties in Ireland, suggested England's future as a sea power to him. Whereas most observers were reluctant to move against the peasant society too quickly because of its ability to produce inexpensive foot soldiers (see Marx 1977, pp. 880–81n; Smith 1937, p. 655; and Weulersse 1910; 1: 246), Petty called for an acceleration of primitive accumulation. England's future lay with a strong navy so far as Petty was concerned. England's geographical position gave naval power considerably more importance than was the case in other nations. Consequently, England could afford to sacrifice some of her peasantry in the course of forming a new society in which defense would rest primarily upon the navy (see Moore 1966, p. 30). Sailors were, for Petty, simultaneously soldiers, artisans, and merchants (Petty 1690; 1: 259). He used the following calculation to demonstrate the advantage of his implicitly proposed social division of labor: "The Husbandman of *England* earns but about 4s. *per* Week, but the Seamen have as good as 12s. in Wages, Victuals (and as it were housing) with other accommodations, so as a Seaman is in effect three Husbandmen" (Petty 1690: i, p. 259).

The navy Petty envisioned only made sense if the people could be led to produce sufficient commodities for export. Petty found confirmation of his proposal in the experience of Holland, which relied on the international economy for much of its food (ibid., p. 266; see also Appleby 1976, Chapter 4). The importance of creating a new social division of labor in England was so integral to Petty's mission that he even attempted to design the ships that would best support it (see Strauss 1954). Although his naval designs were not successful, his social program was. The navy, nonetheless, became the eventual foundation of the British imperial system (Frank 1978).

Petty's scientific activities led him to extreme technological optimism. In his enthusiasm, he predicted that the day would come "when even hogs and more indocile beasts shall be taught to labour; when all vile materials shall be turned to noble use" (cited in Strauss 1954, p. 137). In general, however, his views were based on his keen powers of perception. Like others of his day, he caught a glimpse of the power of capital accumulation in the rapid reconstruction of the wealth of London after the Great Fire of 1666 (Petty 1690, p. 243; see also Appleby 1976, p. 502). He also recognized that the prospects for the future could be advanced through changes in the system of social organization. Not only did he perceive that a more rational organization of society could increase the quantity of labor; he also seems to have been the first writer to describe the improved efficiency resulting from the division of labor within the workshop (Petty 1960; 1: 260, and 1685; 2: 473; see also George 1964, pp. 173–75).[6] Moreover, he took notice of the changing social division of labor: "The Trade of food was branched into Tillage of Corn and grazing of Cattle, that of clothes into Weaver, Tinker, and Taylor, Shewmaker and Tanner and that of Housing in Smith, Mason and Carpenter" (Petty 1927; 1: 212). Petty, as was common in his age, wanted to set everybody to work: thieves, robbers, beggars, "fustian and unworthy Preachers in Divinity in the country schools, . . . Pettifoggers in the Law, . . . Quacksalvers in Physick, and . . . Grammaticasters in the country schools" (cited in Strauss 1966, p. 137).[7] To this end, he insisted that food be kept sufficiently scarce; surplus grain was to be put into granaries rather than allowing it to be "abused by the vile and brutish part of mankind to the prejudice of the commonwealth" (Petty 1690; 1: 275).

The value of high food prices was commonly advocated at the time (see Furniss 1965 and Wermel 1939, pp. 1–14, 17, and 24), although not always in language as vigorous as Petty's. In his wonderful audacity, he called upon the government to hasten the development of a proletariat by removing a million Irish to England, leaving the remaining population to manage Ireland as a cattle ranch, as a "Kind of Factory" (Petty 1687: ii, p. 560; see also 1927, pp. 58–61).[8]

Petty lived in an age where people did not accept wage labor as a matter of course. Perhaps because the household economy was too solidly entrenched, he did not raise the question of the incentives that might make people forego producing for their own needs. Choice was not an issue.

---

[6] His example of the manufacture of watches was one of the few areas in which England was a technical innovator rather than an imitator (George 1953). The strategic importance of this new method of organizing production may well be connected with his naval experience. Dutch shipbuilding had achieved a remarkably refined division of labor within the industry (Kindleberger 1976). The combination of Petty's interests in the architecture of ships and in the special division of labor also lends support to Engels's speculation that the division of labor originates in the military (see Marx and Engels 1975, pp. 90–91).

In addition, unlike the other practitioners of classical political economy for whom the division of labor was a matter of theory, Petty profited from it handsomely in his capacity as the organizer of the great survey of Ireland. Petty taught hundreds of untrained workers the rudiments of the separate parts of the profession of surveying in order that the spoils of conquest could be divided among the English as soon as possible (Strauss 1966).

[7] This passage is one that seems to have inspired Swift.

[8] Swift also parodied this passage (see Swift 1731, p. 175).

Instead, the government was assigned the responsibility for the creation of a new social division of labor. Petty appropriated the language of bullionism to lend theoretical support to his advocacy of a new social division of labor. He calculated:

> the *Wealth* of every Nation, consisting chiefly, in the share which they have in the Foreign Trade with the whole *Commercial World*, rather than in the Domestick Trade, of ordinary *Meat, Drink,* and *Cloaths*, &c. which bring in little *Gold, Silver, Jewels,* and other *Universal Wealth*. [Petty 1690; 1: 295]

Petty's universal wealth was merely a sign of power, derived from the development of the economic forces of the nation. Thus he estimated that England was substantially more powerful than her great rival, France (ibid.). This wealth was closely associated with the rise of a new social division of labor. This connection is expressed even more clearly in a similar passage which directly follows his estimates about the superior productivity of seamen (pp. 259–60).

Petty demonstrated a lifelong interest in stimulating the government to take actions that would reduce the vitality of household production. Specifically, he recognized the strategic importance of transferring workers out of agriculture (Petty 1690: i, pp. 256, 267). In his chapter of *Verbum Sapienti* entitled "How to Employ the People, and the End Thereof" he explained that an efficiently run society must set people "upon producing Food and Necessaries for the whole People of the Land, by few hands" (Petty 1691: i, pp. 118–120).

The age of Petty had witnessed only the beginnings of the creation of a proletariat. Much more needed to be done to organize society. Consequently, we find many more explicit discussions of the relationship between the restriction of opportunities for domestic production and the willingness to accept wage labor. For example, one author of 1767 exclaimed, "Nor can I conceive a greater curse upon a body of people, than to be thrown upon a spot of land, where the productions for subsistence and food were, in great measure, spontaneous, and the climate required or admitted little care for raiment or covering" (Forster 1767, p. 10 cited by Marx 1977, p. 649n; see also Steuart 1966; 1: 45–46).

Richard Cantillon, the second major figure of classical political economy, was a shadowy presence. Much of what we know of his life comes from court records. Where Petty was frequently hauled into court for his land speculation, Cantillon was deeply involved in litigations concerning his dealings in credit. He lent people money to buy shares in John Law's scheme. As security, he required that the shares be left in his custody. Anticipating a fall in their values, he sold them. Those to whom he lent the money were not satisfied that Cantillon stood ready to buy new shares. Instead, they charged that he had betrayed their trust (see Fage 1952 and Hayse 1971).

Unlike most of the writers encountered in the study of primitive accumulation, Cantillon's importance lies mostly in the realm of theory. True, he complained about the excessive number of holidays enjoyed by the people in the countryside (Cantillon 1755, p. 95), but so did almost every other political economist at the time. Cantillon also wrote "Individuals are supported not only by the produce of the Land which is cultivated for the benefit of the Owners but also at the Expense of these Same Owners from whose property they derive all that they have" (p. 43).

Although numerous writers took up this theme in arguing for policies that promoted primitive accumulation, the real importance of this citation is its suggestion of the notion that the land generates a surplus (see Walsh and Gram 1980, p. 19). Even more fundamentally, Cantillon went far beyond William Petty's call for reorganization of the economy. According to Cantillon, a system of prices could give the same final result as a system of direct command over labor (Cantillon 1755, pp. 63ff; Walsh and Gram 1980, p. 298). Thus he recognized for the first time that market relations could be an effective means of control. In this sense, his contribution to the political economy of primitive accumulation is incalculable.

The Physiocrats

Eventually, Petty's vision came to be more or less realized. England "presented a unique and amazing spectacle to the enquiring foreigner; it had no peasants" (Hobsbawm and Rude 1968, p. 3; see also Deane and Coale 1967, pp. 3, 256). What was the meaning of English experience? Forster, cited above, seemed to interpret it in terms of natural history. In the same vein, Hume blamed the poverty of France, Italy, and Spain on its benign climate and rich soil (Hume 1752, p. 16); however, in France, the physiocrats understood that social conditions could not be explained by an act of God. They had to be created. The physiocrats looked upon England as the most successful example of a well-functioning society. Accordingly, they sought to emulate the British system. Nonetheless, they modified the English model of the social division of labor by calling for the initial concentration of wage labor in agricultural pursuits. Textile production, for example, the mainstay of the industrial revolution in England, was initially looked upon with suspicion as an unwelcome competitor for agricultural labor (Weulersse 1959, p. 28n.).

The physiocratic movement differed from British political economy in one other important respect. Although all agreed that the French peasants were lazy (Weulersse [1910] i, p. 321),[9] the physiocrats did not adopt an ostensibly hostile attitude toward them. Unlike the British, whose tone was contentious at best when discussing the common people, the French often expressed concern about the countryfolk. Such differences came down to matters of style. Where the British violently opposed hunting by the common people, the French expressed concern that people had to content themselves with coarse food such as chestnuts (Weulersse 1910; i, p. 488), now an expensive gourmet item. The Parliament of Toulouse lamented the fate of women who spun at night after spading or even plowing during the day (ibid.; 2: 687). With a more free form of commerce, such women were promised lighter workloads. Enclosures were even recommended as a method for expanding the demand for labor (Weulersse 1959, p. 149).

More typically, the expected beneficiaries of the now social division of labor were landholders. Thus the physiocratic identification of the surplus and rent reflected a more general opinion in French society. At the time, the French bourgeoisie was incapable of imagining any other source of wealth and power than landed property (Nallet and Servolin 1978). For example, the legal framework they constructed gives no indication of an awareness of the potential expansion of capital (ibid.).

As might be expected, the physiocrats themselves were to be counted among those who would profit from the changes they proposed. Quesnay took a special interest in the earnings he derived from his lands (see Ware 1931). According to his economic table, which was a schematic analysis of the new social division of labor, the expected rate of return on agricultural investment was between 250 and 300 percent (Weulersse 1910; 1: 354).

Even the physiocrats understood that small-scale, labor-intensive agriculture could produce substantially higher yields (Weulersse 1910: ii, p. 317). Recall the success of M. Ponce and the Parisian market gardeners discussed in Chapter I (see also Kropotkin 1906, p. 20; 1899, pp. 62ff; and Ponce 1870, pp. 32–49).

True, these market gardeners devoted a prodigious amount of labor to their work. Mirabeau claimed that the majority of the Paris gardeners slept with a pail of water near their bed to quench the thirst of their plants when they gave off sounds that indicated the need for moisture during the night (Weulersse 1910: ii, p. 317); however, even if their working day had been halved, their output would still have remained substantial.

The techniques of market gardening have much to offer, even under trans-

---

[9] Was there ever a nation in which the rich found the poor to be sufficiently industrious? The universal howl of "indolence" could be heard as far away as nineteenth century Japan (see Smith 1966, p. 120).

formed social relations. Along these lines, Bukharin and Preobrazhensky predicted an important future for the technology of market gardening, based on the experience of the first two years of the Soviet Republic (Bukharin and Preobrazhensky 1922, pp. 303–4).

What, then, was the advantage of the new technology of large-scale farming? The answer from England, where the French first learned about the new husbandry, seemed clear:

> The proprietor of the land, cultivating his farm under the old system, was obliged, we will suppose, to keep ten horses, ten labourers to plough, sow and reap, ten women to card and spin. Under the present system of providing a series of different crops in succession, we may assume that five horses and five labourers are sufficient to carry on the work of the same farm, and that the use of machinery in carding, spinning, and weaving, may enable two women the same quantity of wrought goods, which formerly required the labour of ten.[10] [Edwards 1827, p. 417]

In short, the new technology seemed to save labor. On closer examination, this savings becomes more ambiguous. To begin with, much of the improved economy of labor was not due to the production of more output with a lesser quantity of labor. Instead, it was a result of the intensification of labor. For example, with Adam Smith, traditional agriculturalists are pictured as "slothful and lazy" (Smith 1937, p. 8). However, he observed that "improvements in husbandry . . . leave the husbandman as little leisure as the artificer" (p. 659; see also Smith 1978, p. 340). Marx, too, made the same point (Marx 1977, p. 908), directing his reader's attention to the work of Sir James Steuart (1767: i, chap. 16).

The intensification of labor associated with the new husbandry was rarely discussed elsewhere. Steuart, as we shall see, was a unique figure in political economy. Marx also did not always agree with the opinions of the majority of the classical political economists. In *The Wealth of Nations*, Smith raised the issue only when discussing the difficulty of fitting military training into the

---

10 The author of this citation, according to Hilton (1977), was Edward Edwards, the purported author of the books by Piercy Ravenstone, generally considered to be two of the most noteworthy representatives of "Ricardian Socialism," at least so far as Dorfman is concerned (Dorfman 1966a). In the article cited above, the author does not argue so much against profit as for rent. This divergence supports Sraffa's contention that the author of the Piercy Ravenstone works was Richard Puller (see the editorial note in Ricardo 1951–73; 11: 64).

schedule of the agriculturalist. In his *Lectures on Jurisprudence*, it set off the grandest display of obfuscation known to political economy (see Chapter 5 below).

Labor was not merely speeded up in the new system (see Smith 1937, p. 659); it was also redirected to meet the needs of capital. Under the old system, labor was not required for agricultural tasks for long periods of time. Consequently, "the occupier of any tenant must have maintained in his own house, or at least within the limits of his own farm, a number of hands, sufficient, not only to perform the work of tillage, but to manufacture all the articles of clothery required by himself, his family, and his working people" (Edwards 1827, p. 416).

Thus although the new agricultural technology was accompanied in the long run by a far-reaching expansion of the productive powers of labor, a major attraction at the time appeared to be the reduction in the expense of maintaining labor over the extensive periods previously devoted to household production. Consequently, workers who had previously divided their hours between the production of grain and the production of their other domestic needs were required to more or less specialize in grain. As a result, the net product would increase, since fewer workers would be required on the farm to perform those tasks specifically directed to the production of grains (Weulersse 1910; 2: 314–15).

Thus Mirabeau, the "Friend of the People," justified capitalist farming by virtue of its ability to force people to cease from living at the expense of the proprietor (Weulersse 1910; 2: p. 350; see also Cantillon 1775, p. 47). Under the physiocratic program, as Abeille recommended in his *Principles sur le liberte du commerce de grains*, the worker was to be considered as a commodity like all other commodities (Abeille 1768, p. 95, cited in Weulersse 1910; 2: 686).

To give this program theoretical support, the physiocrats excluded grain consumed by cultivators (and presumably also all other goods they produced for their own needs) from the national wealth (see Maitland 1804, pp. 125–27).

The physiocratic contention that the success of agriculture should be judged by the net product did not go uncontested. Others such as Forbonnais countered that the support of people was an end in itself (Weulersse 1910: ii, pp. 314–15). In effect, the physiocrats regarded agriculture as a commodity-producing enterprise directed toward the creation of surplus value; their critics analyzed agriculture from the point of view of the production of use values. Thus the much vaunted success of the capitalist agriculture recommended by the physiocrats was not merely the product of technical improvements.

In conclusion, with the physiocrats, as with Sir William Petty, we get some idea of the connection between the creation of a new social division of labor and the rise of capitalism, a connection that is generally expressed in terms of hostility toward the self-sufficient household.

chapter 3

Sir James Steuart's Secret History of Primitive Accumulation

A river may as easily ascend to its source, as a people voluntarily adopt a more operose agriculture than that already established.

Steuart, *An Inquiry into the Principles of Political Economy*, vol. 1: pp. 177–78

Steuart's Scotland

The conflict between the traditional economy of the household and capitalist development is most clearly reflected in the work of Sir James Steuart, the first systemizer of economic theory. Marx paid handsome tribute to Steuart, crediting him with a "sense of the *historical* differences in modes of production, a gift belonging to no other classical political economist except Richard Jones" (Marx 1963–71, pt. 3, p. 399). Elsewhere, Marx expanded on Steuart's importance:

> His service to the theory of capital is that he shows how the process of separation takes place between the conditions of production, as the property of a definite class, and labour-power. He gives a great deal of attention to this *genesis* of capital—without as yet seeing it directly as the genesis of capital, although he sees it as a condition for large-scale industry. He examines the process particularly in agriculture: and

he rightly considers that manufacturing industry proper only came into being through this process of separation in agriculture. In Adam Smith's writings this process of separation is assumed to be already completed. [Ibid., pt. 3, p. 43]

Steuart's work is especially interesting since it has been largely ignored by modern historians of political economy, a breed noted for its excellence in perusing the most obscure documents.[1] This neglect is astonishing considering that Steuart was the author of the first complete English treatise on political economy. Moreover, besides *The Wealth of Nations*, no others were published until Ricardo's *Principles*.

In fact, Steuart was the most important economist of his day. So why the thundering silence with respect to Steuart? The answer seems to lie with his blunt honesty about the nature of capitalist development, especially with respect to the destruction of the self-sufficient household. The connection between the creation of a widespread wage-labor relationship and the social division of labor was essential to Steuart, who had the opportunity to witness the unfolding of capitalist development from the vantage point of the Scottish countryside, where the household economy maintained an exceptional degree of self-sufficiency (see Marx 1977, p. 472, 616n; see also Smith 1937, p. 17; and Anderson 1777, pp. 12–15).

Eighteenth-century Scotland was a land of stark contrasts. In some ways, it could be compared to ancient Athens when it was being transformed from a tribal to a civil society. Like Athens, Scotland was a center of intellectual ferment. Like Athens, it was to fall victim to the superior military might of a neighbor.

The tribal aspect of Scotland was strongest in the Highlands. Daniel Defoe remarked, "Our geographers seem to be almost as much at a loss in their description of this north part of Scotland as the Romans were to conquer it" (Defoe 1724–26, p. 663). Samuel Johnson recalled his tour of the Highlands: "I got an acquisition of more ideas by it than anything that I remember. I saw quite a different system of life" (Boswell 1799, p. 199).

The common people of the Highlands lived relatively independent of the market. Defoe noted, "Their employment is chiefly hunting . . ." (Defoe 1724–26, p. 664). Despite the unfavorable environment, the people of the rugged Scottish Highlands could furnish themselves with provisions with remarkable ease, as we can see in the reports of Daniel Defoe, an enthusiastic

---

1 With the exception of Sen (1957) and Chamley (1965), the social content of Steuart's work has been scrupulously avoided. For a convenient bibliography of such literature, see Akhtar (1979).

prophet of early capitalism: "[H]owever mountainous and wild the country appeared, the people were extremely well furnished with provisions (Defoe 1724–1726, pp. 666–67). Defoe specifically mentioned the availability of venison and salmon.

Before the union with England, the Highlands were ruled by the clan chiefs, who received goods in kind as well as military service from their people. The self-sufficiency of the Highlands largely extended to the clan chiefs as well. Adam Smith observed: "In a country where there is no foreign commerce, nor any of the finer manufactures, a man of ten thousand a year cannot well employ his revenue in any other way than in maintaining, perhaps, a thousand families, who are all necessarily at his command" (Smith 1937, p. 389; see also 1978, pp. 202, 248).

During the eighteenth century, this tightly knit military society began to crumble. Some lairds started to shift their reference point from the clan to Lowland and English aristocracy. A hunger for money set in (see Smith 1978, p. 262; see also Johnson 1774, pp. 85, 94). Smith's reference to an effete nobility purchasing a diamond buckle for an amount that could maintain a thousand men (Smith 1937, p. 389; Carter 1980, p. 384) was symptomatic of the changes that were occurring: "It was a tradition that in the days of the Scots Parliament . . . , when the sessions closed, the Cannongate jail was crowded with peers, whom their creditors could seize the moment their period of immunity ceased" (Graham 1937, p. 29).

After the Union with Britain in 1707, the lairds saw a market rise in the value of cattle, their chief produce, which could more easily find their way into the lucrative English market (Smith 1937, p. 149, 220–22); however, rents were fixed by custom at a nominal sum or a lamb or a sheep (Smith 1937, p. 386). The Battle of Culloden had a twofold effect on this situation. First, it reduced the need for the military services of the clan members; second, it offered a pretext for the conversion of the traditional feudal system of land tenure. Instead, the lairds became landlords and their land a source of rent (Anderson 1777, pp. 12–14). In the process, a large number of their people were thrown off the land in the name of agricultural improvements.

The forced migrations subsequent to the first Jacobite rebellion, as well as the Battle of Culloden, resulted in concentrations of people available for employment. Concerning these matters, Thomas Pennant rhapsodized:

> Let a veil be flung over a few excesses consequential to a day of so much benefit to united kingdoms. . . . The Halcyon days are near at hand: oppression will beget depopulation, and depopulation will give

us dear-bought tranquility.[2] [Pennant 1772, p. 145; and 1774; 3: 145]

No wonder the classical political economists could lay claim to the virtue of humanitarianism! The most important industry was the labor-intensive business of gathering kelp (Gray 1951; Carter 1980, p. 372; Smith 1937, p. 145; and Matsukawa 1965), work that employed as many as 50,000 people (see Ross 1953, p. 230). This primitive industry provided the alkali needed for the dynamic textile industry. Without kelp, scarce timber would have been burnt for potash. Thus the furthering kelp industry was rather strategically placed during the early years of the industrial revolution (see Thomas 1980, p. 7). All of the elements of a capitalist development seemed to be in place. Unfortunately, manufacturing did not take a firm hold in Scotland. The fine Scottish woolen industry, as well as most other manufactures, was swamped by English competition (Campbell 1953, p. 12). Scottish prosperity did not extend much beyond Glasgow, which benefited from the extension of the Navigation Acts to Scotland (ibid., p. 12; Devine 1976).

Intellectual Roots

Steuart was well suited to be the theoretician of Scottish development. His native Lanarkshire, although not far from Edinburgh or Glasgow, was surrounded by "the wildest country" that Defoe saw during his tour of Scotland (Defoe 1724–26, p. 617). Steuart's father led an erratic career compromised by involvements in Scottish conspiratorial politics; nonetheless, eventually he was appointed Solicitor-General of Scotland. Steuart's grandfather was Lord Provost of Edinburgh. Steuart was not only connected with traditional Scottish society; he also had ties with recent capitalistic developments. His mother, "for the sake of finding employment to her mind, had taken coal work" (Kippis 1842, p. 282).

Although Steuart was not as dependent on the printed word as Adam Smith, he did make some use of his predecessors. His work bears a strong resemblance to Mirabeau's *Friend of the People* (1756). Skinner believes that Steuart benefited from Mirabeau's work (Skinner 1966, p. xxxvii), whereas Chamley suggests the flow of ideas may well have gone in the other direction (Chamley 1965, pp. 76–81).

A third possibility does present itself. The books of both Steuart and Mirabeau bear a striking similarity to the work of Richard Cantillon. Mira-

---

[2] Compare with Samuel Johnson, author of another important travel report: "to hinder insurrection, by driving away the people, and to govern peaceably, by having no subjects, in an expedient that argues no profundity of politicks" (Johnson 1774, p. 97).

beau claimed to have been in possession of Cantillon's work for sixteen years. He had planned to publish it as his own, but he did not. Then, in 1755, just after Steuart arrived in Paris, Mirabeau finally published it (Higgs 1931).

Steuart's work was connected with Cantillon in a more roundabout fashion. He twice cited the English version published as the work of Phillip Cantillon (Steuart 1767; 2: 22, 67). In his first book, *Principles,* completed by 1759, the parallels with Cantillon were more pronounced. Yet there, Cantillon was not cited.

The handwritten version of this book was dedicated in 1759 to Lady Mary Wortley Montagu (1689–1732), whom Steuart had met in Venice during the previous year (Chalmers 1805, p. 372). This brilliant English woman of letters was often immersed in scandal that was not always literary in nature (see Halsband 1956, pp. 268–79). The very same Lady Mary Wortley Montagu had become, a quarter century earlier, the close friend of Mary Anne Mahoney, the wife of Richard Cantillon (see Wortley 1966–1967; 2: 25, 29). She wrote to her sister that Cantillon's wife "eclipses most of our London beauties" (ibid., p. 25). In 1741, she seems to have been referring to Cantillon as "One of the prettiest men I ever saw in any country," in writing of an affair between Cantillon and the wife of the British consul in Naples, where she was staying (ibid., p. 213). Almost two decades later, while taking a deep interest in the work of Steuart, she probably would have called Cantillon's book to the attention of her protegé in the case that he himself had not already been familiar with the theories of that most important earlier peripatetic economist.

Books were not as important to Steuart as what he saw for himself. His perception of the world around him was colored by a distinct antagonism toward the self-reliant household.[3] Long before he had begun the formal study of political economy, he expressed concern about "the laziness of the people," such as the peasants he saw in Spain (letter to Sir Thomas Calderwood, 5 March 1737, printed in Chamley 1965, p. 127). He did not even seem to think the self-sufficient peasant worthy of even working unimproved

---

[3] In this respect, Steuart displayed one of his numerous affinities with the physiocrats (see Weulersse 1910; 2: 697). One can see numerous similarities between Steuart and Harrington (on Harrington, see Hill 1964 and Macpherson 1962). Harrington opposed small holders, called for high rents to stimulate labor, attempted to calculate an appropriate balance among classes in which the nobility were to oversee agriculture and bear arms (see Macpherson 1962, pp. 187 and 178–79). Another influence of probable importance was Wallace's *A Dissertation on the Numbers of Mankind,* published in 1753, the year after Hume, in his *Political Discourses,* challenged him to publish it (see Hume 1752b, p. 108, and Hume to Montesquieu, June 1753, cited in Rotwein 1955, p. 184).

land. He asked his readers, "[H]ow can extended tracts of bare land be improved, but by subdividing them into small lots of about ten, fifteen or twenty acres, and letting them to those *who make their livelihood (by doing) . . . things for hire"* (Steuart 1769, p. 328; emphasis added). He considered it to be "evident" that these lands would be so finely subdivided that it "is in no way sufficient to enable the possessors to maintain themselves, and pay their rents out of the product. The land will contribute towards maintaining themselves and their family; their industry must support their family and pay the rent" (ibid.). No doubt he would have approved of the vigorous measures taken by the descendant of his wife's cousin, the Duchess of Sutherland, from whose land about 15,000 inhabitants were evicted between 1814 and 1820. In Marx's words:

> All their villages were destroyed and burnt, all their fields turned to pasturage. British soldiers enforced this mass of evictions, and came to blows with the inhabitants. One old woman was burnt to death in the flames of her hut she refused to leave.[4] It was in this manner that this fine lady appropriated 794,000 acres of land which belonged to the clan since time immemorial. . . . By 1825, the 15,000 Gaels had been replaced by 131,000 sheep. [Marx 1977, pp. 891–92; see also Smout 1969, pp. 353–54; and Ross 1973, pp. 182–93]

In fact, Steuart himself associated the march of progress with the replacement of cropland by pasture (see Steuart 1767; 2: 56–57).[5] Steuart's program owed not a little to Hume, who called for the employment of *"superfluous hands"* as soldiers to extend the power of the state (Hume 1752, pp. 289–90). In Hume's words:

> Where manufactures and mechanic arts are not cultivated, the bulk of the people must apply themselves to agriculture; and if their skill

---

4 This particular method of eviction has been used recently on tenants in India (see Perelman 1977, p. 149). Lest our sympathies for the disposed divert our attention too far from Steuart, we should take note that Sismondi reported that a few years later, the unfortunate proprietor of the estate was extremely anxious about the precarious state of her fortunes (see Sismondi 1827, p. 52; see also Ross 1953, p. 242). For other reasons, the kindly Nassau W. Senior wrote of this event as "one of the most beneficient clearings since the memory of man" (Senior 1868, p. 282; also cited in Marx 1977, p. 892).

5 Marx enlisted Steuart in condemning the clearings in his *New York Tribune* article by means of a rare misquotation. Marx cited Steuart to the effect that "a plot of land in the highlands of Scotland feeds ten times more people than a farm of the same extent in the richest provinces" (Marx 1853a, p. 491). Steuart had actually written "value," where Marx cited the word "extent" (Steuart 1767: i, p. 137).

and industry increase, there must arise a great superfluity from their labour beyond what suffices to maintain them. They have no temptation, therefore, to increase their skill and industry; since they cannot exchange that superfluity for any commodities, which may serve either to their pleasure or vanity. A habit of indolence naturally prevails.

Everything in the world is purchased by labour. . . . When a nation abounds in manufactures and mechanic arts, the . . . superfluity, which arises from . . . labour is lost; but is exchanged with manufactures for those commodities, which men's luxury now makes them covet. [ibid., p. 293]

Taking his cue from his countryman Hume, and consistent with Turgot and the physiocrats, Steuart joined in the call for the elimination of the "free hands" who resided on the land.[6] For Steuart, they represented a substantial "burden on the husbandman" (Steuart 1767; 1: 40, 43; see also Hume 1752, p. 293; Turgot 1766, paragraphs 4 and 8; Weulersse 1910; i: 350; and Quesnay 1758, p. vi). Elsewhere these same people were categorized as nothing more than "superfluous mouths (Steuart 1767; 1: 58, 198). Steuart's proposals for economic development were ostensibly presented in terms of their potential efficiency; however, we do not have to search long before we learn that that his underlying concern was a more general attack on the household economy. Enclosures and clearings such as the Sutherland affair may well have been conducive to progress in the long run, but their immediate effect was more dubious. Recall that the increase in pasturage was followed by an expansion in deer parks.

Steuart's brutal terminology suggests the uniqueness of his position in political economy. In his youth, he was compromised by his involvement in Jacobite conspiracies. Consequently, he was forced to spend fourteen years in exile on the Continent. Steuart seemed to believe that his distance from his homeland gave him an advantage in comprehending it theoretically. In his dedication of his handwritten manuscript in 1759 to Lady Mary, he wrote, "The best method I have found to maintain a just balance . . . has been, in discussing general points, to keep my eye off the country I inhabit at the time, and to compare the absent with the absent" (cited in Chamley 1965, p. 137). By availing himself of this method, even before his return to the British Isles, he was able to anticipate the exceptional nature of what was occurring in his native Scotland.

Steuart himself stood with one foot firmly implanted in the old way of life

---

6 This interpretation of rural development was recently made fashionable by W. A. Lewis (1954).

(see Marx 1974, pp. 83–84) and the other tentatively pawing at the new modes of existence. As a result, he differed from Adam Smith by pointing to the nobility as the appropriate source of class leadership for the future. Unlike Smith, who mocked pretensions of the nobility and lauded prudence (Smith 1759; bk. 6, chap. 1), Steuart complained that the middle class only held the nobility in contempt during peacetime. At times of military crisis, those same characteristics that impede the nobility's success in the humdrum world of bourgeois calculation become admirable qualities (Steuart 1767; 1: 83).

Steuart went much further. In contrast to classical political economy, in general, Steuart's work was openly undemocratic.[7] He considered the poor to be incapable of self-government (Steuart 1767; 1: 98). In fact, he traced the "principle cause of decay in modern states [To] . . . liberty" (ibid.: p. 93). For Steuart, "the most perfect plan of political economy" was to be found in the Spartan republic of Lycurgus (ibid.: p. 332; see also Hume 1752, pp. 290–91). At one point, he even seemed to have been comparing himself with Lycurgus, "a profound politician, who had travelled over the world with a previous intention to explore the mysteries of the science of government" (ibid.: p. 334).

Steuart admitted the futility of his hope of recreating a Spartan republic based on slave labor supporting a commercial society of frugal warriors. Capitalism, so it seemed, was the next best alternative.

Such words may shock to modern ears, but they were more or less common when Steuart was writing. The admiration of Lycurgus owed much to Rousseau, who popularized Sparta's collectivism and antipathy to trade (see Therborn 1980, pp. 119–24). Scottish writers generally portrayed Sparta favorably. For example, Adam Smith's "never to be forgotten Dr. Hutcheson" (Smith to Dr. Archibald Davidson, 16 November 1787 printed, in Mossner and Ross 1977, p. 309), in his chapter "Of the Nature of Civil Laws and their Execution," also commended Lycurgus to modern legislators (Hutcheson 1755; 2: 310). What made Steuart's use of Sparta unique was not his approval of totalitarian methods, but his straightforward recognition that these methods could be used to further capitalist development. Steuart accepted that the future lay in capitalism. He clearly recognized the advantages of moving with the times. The nobility could not support themselves by trading, since they lacked the requisite funds (Steuart 1767; 1, p. 84). To become mere shopkeepers was unthinkable. The proper course for them was

---

[7] Yet capitalism was credited with unleashing the dread forces of democracy (ibid.; 2: 23). In this sense, his project threatened to come apart at the seams even though he never gave any indication that democratic rights would extend to the working class.

to support themselves as prosperous capitalist farmers. Steuart's suggestion that the gentry engage in capitalist farming represented a call to break with the tradition of maintaining customary rents. Steuart himself noted that "[r]aising . . . rents was thought to be robbing the present possessor" (Steuart 1769, p. 286). Nonetheless, he came out squarely in favor of the new husbandry by virtue of its ability to raise rents (Steuart 1769, pp. 287ff and Steuart 1767; 1: 280ff). In this sense, the new husbandry may be said to have been most successful. Benjamin Franklin noted in 1773, "It seems that some of the Scottish Chiefs, who delight no longer to live upon their Estates . . . chuse rather a Life of Luxury . . . , have lately raised their Rents most grievously to support the Expense" (Franklin 1959–; 20: 523). During the third quarter of the nineteenth century, for example, Highland rents quadrupled (see Johnson 1775, p. 38). Unfortunately, this process reflected a future of poverty rather than prosperity. Steuart rejoiced at the thought of an augmentation in rents. Higher rents were justifiable because "the surplus of the farmers . . . goes for the subsistence of others." Moreover, "the surplus I show to be the same thing with the value of rents" (Steuart 1767; 1: 204; see also 1: 55). Steuart's position about rents is reminiscent of the physiocrats, but with a significant difference. In spite of the relatively extensive nature of the new husbandry that they proposed, the physiocrats could suggest that the commercialization of farming would increase the supply of food on account of the large tracts of unused land in France. Steuart made no such claim. In fact, since he identified the increase of the surplus with the extension of pasture (ibid., 1: pp. 55ff), he admitted that the mass of food produced would fall with the changes he recommended (Steuart 1767; 1: 282; see also Malthus 1976, pp. 106–7). The advantage of pastures was that they require a minimum of labor, thereby leaving almost all the proceeds of the land to its owner.

What of the people who had previously lived and worked on the land? Their mode of existence was appropriate only for "rude and uncivilized societies" (Steuart 1767; 1: 111). So long as they had been free to live off the spontaneous fruits of the earth, they could content themselves with a few wants and much idleness (ibid., 1: 48, 62). Thus Steuart called for the "separation between parent earth and her laborious children" in order that they no longer be "suckle[d] in idleness" (ibid., 1: 65, 77; see also Marx 1977, p. 649). Otherwise, "who will increase his labour, voluntarily, in order to feed people who do not work for himself?" (Steuart 1767; 2: 174). Benjamin Franklin cited an issue of the *Edinburgh Courant* in 1773, which claimed that 1500 people had emigrated from Steuart's Sutherlandshire in a space of two two years (Franklin 1959– ; 20: 523). As Thomas Pennant observed, "the great men begin at the wrong end, with squeezing the bag, before they have helped the poor tenant to fill it, by the introduction of manufactures" (1771, p. 180; see also Boswell 1799; 5: 221).

Steuart had no doubts about transforming traditional agriculture. The lives of rural workers had to be turned to purposes not of their own choosing. According to him, "Any person who could calculate his labours in agriculture purely for subsistence, would find abundance of idle hours. But the question is, whether in good economy such a person would not be better employed in providing *nourishment* for others, than in providing for other wants" (ibid.; 1: 110; see also Weulersse 1910; 1: 687). Steuart even went so far as to state that insofar as a person exercised the art of agriculture, "*as a direct means of subsisting . . .*, the state would lose nothing though [he] . . . and his land were both swallowed up by an earthquake" (Steuart 1767; 1: 116; see also 4: 314).

Steuart and the Organizing of Economic Development

Steuart's concern with purging the land of free hands, together with his antagonism toward subsistence farming, was clearly connected with the rise of commodity production:

> Now the frequent sale of articles of the first necessity makes a distribution of inhabitants into *labourers,* and what we have called "free hands." The first are those who produce the necessaries of life; the last are those who buy them. [Steuart 1767; 2: 80]

Here we come to the heart of Steuart's work. Steuart found himself in a land in which labor had not yet been fully subjugated to the needs of capital. Steuart himself appears to have been adept at the new husbandry (Steuart 1805, p. 377; Campbell 1953, pp. 25–26). In the words of one contemporary report on his agricultural practices, "No person who is acquainted with Sir James Stewart [sic], but must admire his genius and zeal to promote agriculture" (Wight 1778–84; 3: 544–46). However, his agricultural success necessitated a victory over the rights of his tenants.

Steuart's agricultural experience was well suited to equip him to become the theorist par excellence of primitive accumulation. Yet Steuart went much further. He seemed to recognize that merely throwing the people off the land would not necessarily lay the path for a smooth transition to capitalist social relations. Three important barriers stood in the way.

In the first place, Steuart stressed that one cannot overlook the tempo at which changes are introduced.[8] What may be disastrous when suddenly

---

[8] The followers of W. A. Lewis failed to take this factor into account while they dismantled traditional agricultural systems around the world.

introduced might well be beneficial if it could be accomplished more slowly (Steuart 1767; 1: 160–61, 284 and chap. 19). For this reason he called for the gradual conversion of corn fields into pasture (ibid.; 1: 181). The second difficulty was more substantial. Steuart knew full well that the Scottish gentry were able to throw masses of people off the land, but eviction alone was not sufficient to ensure the transition to wage labor. Time and time again, Steuart repeated that the crux of his investigation was to discover how people came to submit voluntarily to authority (ibid., 1: 8, 29, 237). In a capitalist society, this submission implied the acceptance of the wage relationship.

The third difficulty was closely related to the second. This particular barrier has been more recently discussed by Rosenstein-Rodan (1943),[9] who wondered about the possibility of creating a shoe factory in an economy in which households were largely self-sufficient (See also Hume 1752, p. 293). Workers might be willing to exchange some of their time for shoes, but also they have other needs. Since the factory would presumably be the first institution to be found in the economy, the workers there could not exchange their wages to obtain the goods which they are accustomed to consuming. Consequently, the shoe factory presumes the existence of other entities that manufacture consumer goods for sale.[10] How, then, would the first factory come into existence?

We already know something about Adam Smith's basic answer. We shall analyze it later in more detail. According to Smith, the first institutions were not large factories, but the works of small artisans who gradually increased the scale of their operations. Unfortunately, this response does not shed any light on the origins of wage labor. Unlike Smith, Steuart did not trust the market to bring about economic development. Thus his analysis of the rise in industry brought market and nonmarket forces into play. Steuart called upon the state to guarantee an appropriate social division of labor:

> I conclude, that the best way of binding a free society together is by multiplying reciprocal obligations and creating a general dependence between its members. This cannot be better affected, than by appropriating a certain number of the inhabitants, for the production of food

---

[9] Nurske later credited this program to the "big push" to the Smithian tradition (Nurske 1953), but as shall see in Chapter 5, it is the very antithesis of Smith's proposal. For Steuart, however, politics, rather than the market, was the fundamental determinant of economic progress.

[10] This phenomenon was doubly important in eighteenth-century England, where the absence of coin of small denomination led to the practice of paying workers with a share of their product, which they had to market on their own.

required by all, and by distributing the remainder into proper classes for supplying every other want. [Steuart 1767; 1: 110]

For Steuart, these reciprocal obligations were not understandable merely in terms of Smith's "bartering and trucking spirit" (Smith 1976, p. 27n). They were the creation of the statesman to manipulate the people:

> [N]othing is impossible to an able statesman. When a people can be engaged to murder their wives and children, and to burn themselves, rather than submit to a foreign enemy; when they can be brought to give their most precious effects, their ornaments of gold and silver, for the support of a common cause; . . . I think I may say, that by properly conducting and managing the spirit of a people, nothing is impossible to be accomplished. [Steuart 1767; 1: 15]

If people could be moved so far to support pre-capitalist ends, why should the capitalist statesman be less able to direct society? Consequently, the creation of a social division of labor should not raise serious difficulties for capable leaders.

Steuart frequently returned to the theme of the need to create an appropriate social division of labor in order to ensure a proper structuring of reciprocal wants (see Steuart 1767; 1: 3, 20, 33, 46, 86, 211, and 316; and 2: 158). His position was diametrically opposed to that of Adam Smith, who counted on market forces alone to create the appropriate structure. Steuart expected the statesman "to lay down his plan of political economy, and chalk out a distribution of its inhabitants" (ibid. 2: 175). Elsewhere he was more specific, calling upon the statesman to "regulate the distribution of . . . classes of his people" (ibid., 2; 17). He stressed the importance of this objective (ibid., 1: 46). He explicitly stated that the "object of our enquiry hitherto has been to discover the method of engaging a free people to concur in the advancement of one and the other, as a means of making their society live in ease, by reciprocally contributing to the relief of each others' wants" (ibid., 2; 157).

Steuart called upon his statesman to act "with an impartial hand" (ibid., 2: 183).[11] For Steuart, the statesman had an obligation to restrict profits from rising above a certain standard (ibid., 2: 185). He sounded more emphatic, however, when he warned that "when a statesman looks coolly on, with his arms across, or takes it into his head, that it is not his business to interpose, the prices of the dextrous workman will rise" (ibid., 1: 314). Steuart was not

---

[11] Could the use of the term "impartial" have referred to the famous spectator of Adam Smith's Theory of Moral Sentiments (e.g., Smith 1759, p. 26)? We will return to the relationship of Smith and Steuart later.

blind to the underlying social relations of his program. He understood that
the same object of mutual dependence could be obtained by slavery. However, he considered slavery to be a more "violent method (for) making men
laborous in raising food" (ibid., 1: 51). In the past, "*men were . . . forced to labour
because they were slaves to others; men are now forced to labour because they are slaves to
their own wants*" (ibid., 1: 52).[12]

> One reviewer took Steuart to take on this point: In plain English,
> that by one way or another, men are made slaves by statesmen, in
> order that the useful may feed the useless. This is, indeed, the present
> state of what is called liberty in England. But, in fact, they are not made
> slaves to their passions and desires, for that is common to all men. It
> is the hard hand of necessity at present, like that of the taskmasters
> in preceding times, which compels them to work. The hired husband-
> man has, indeed, one passion that engages him to become a slave, and
> to labour; it is the goading dread of starving that enslaves him, and
> urges him to toil without desire. [Anon. 1767b, p. 127]

This review should not be read as a refutation of Steuart, but as a clarifica-
tion. Whether we refer to hunger and poverty as "wants" is irrelevant.
Steuart's attention was turned to an overriding question: How were these
wants to be structured so that they would effectively enslave people?

The traditional Highlanders also had wants, but they were not yet "slaves"
to their wants in the sense that Steuart used the term. The solution envisioned by Steuart required that the nobility become capitalist farmers thereby, separating large numbers of such people from their means of subsistence.

Steuart's conception of primitive accumulation did not require that continual force be applied directly against the Highlanders. The market, properly arranged, would accomplish much of what was necessary. In a letter of
14 October 1777, he described the process in words that could have come
from Adam Smith:

> The allurement of gain will soon engage everyone to pursue that
> branch of industry which succeeds best in his hands. By these means
> many will follow manufactures and abandon agriculture; others will
> prosecute their manufactures in the country, and avail themselves at
> the same time of portions of land, proper for gardens, grass for cows,

---

12 "The whole magic of well-ordered society is that each man works for others,
while believing that he is working for himself" (Mirabeau's *Philosophie Rurale* cited in
Meek 1963, p. 70). Mirabeau was acquainted with Steuart. In many respects, however,
their work differed (see Chamley 1965, pp. 73ff).

and even for producing certain kinds of fruit necessary for their own maintenance. [cited in Chamley 1965, p. 87]

Higher rents would also serve to drive those remaining on the land to intensify agricultural production. As a result of such "silent compulsion" farmers would no longer produce as many goods as use values. They would specialize in the production of commodities for the market.

According to Steuart, once workers have ceased the production of a diverse set of use values, a regime of "good economy" would be expected to commence. Leisure would be restricted (Steuart 1767; 1: 35; see also Pollard 1978, p. 144) and labor would become more intense (ibid., 1: 139; and 2: 176). Thus although wage earners, unlike slaves, are formally free, Steuart understood that workers would be subject to an increasingly strict discipline. The labor of children would be expected to be mobilized especially effectively as capitalist social relations began to gel. Their time would no longer be dissipated on such chores as the herding of a few geese. Along with women, they would be set to work spinning (ibid., 1: 136–38). Eventually, the working class was expected to develop that most wonderful of all qualities, "a taste for labour" (ibid., 1: 200 , 202)—all as a result of a well-designed market.

Steuart recognized the complexity of the underlying dynamic of primitive accumulation. Much caution was required: "A young horse is to be caressed when a saddle is put upon his back" (ibid., 1: 175). Steuart even expressed some humanistic concerns, observing that eventually "Those who become servants for the sake of food, will soon become slaves" (ibid., 1: 28). He opposed "excessive misery among the poor" (ibid., 1: 277). His standards of humanism, however, were not high: he supported enslavement without slavery.

Steuart believed that a proper wage could be calculated from the expense accounts of hospitals and workhouses that were hardly the seats of opulence (Steuart 1767; 1: 415). He also called for the systematic collection of poor children into workhouses (Steuart 1767; 1: 98, 378–79),[13] a policy that would seem to be incompatible with high wages. One can only guess at the expected fate of the poor without the protective measures advocated by Steuart. Once capitalist relations would take hold, Steuart expected that the typical farm would come to be regulated by a precise economy:[14] "cattle consume the exact quantity of grain and forage necessary; what remains is money; a superfluous egg is money; a superfluous day of cart, of a horse, a superfluous

---

13 Leading perhaps to a deeper meaning of the term "infant industries."
14 Tribe wrongly ascribes to Steuart a precommercial understanding of economics (Tribe 1978, pp. 88, 94).

hour of a farmer is all money to the farmer" (ibid., 1: 72). In an apparent anticipation of the modern economic theory of labor (Schultz 1968), Steuart recognized that with development, "Time becomes more precious" (Steuart 1767; 1: 230; see also pp. 303ff), although he gave no indication that the working people would ever benefit from this increasing value.

Steuart and the Dialectics of Household Production

Steuart's seemingly casual observation about time was linked to a rich theory of the role of self-provisioning in the course of development. Steuart was the only classical economist to clearly express the dialectical nature of the household economy. On the one hand, the masses' access to their traditional means of subsistence had to be restricted in order to ensure their "voluntary subordination" (ibid., 1: 29, 8, 62). On the other hand, a high degree of self-provisioning meant that the wage rate could be held very low (ibid., 1: 197, 304). For example, Steuart estimated the wage rate of a day laborer according to the cost of grain required for subsistence. Since the worker was assumed to have a vegetable garden and a potato patch, in addition to a cow, the meager earnings of his wife's spinning were assumed to be sufficient to meet all other expenses (Steuart 1769, pp. 291–92). Recall also Steuart's observation that two days' wages were required to nourish a spinner for a single day (ibid., 1: 304; see also Smith 1937, p. 117). The proper degree of reliance on such gardens is, of course, difficult to ascertain. The more people who are able to feed themselves, the lower will be the price of grain (Steuart 1767; 2: 89–99). When food is cheap, even those people without access to any substantial degree of self-sufficiency will not feel as much compulsion to labor.[15] Thus Steuart's hostility to the household economy was conditional since he recognized its value as a prop to early capitalist accumulation. In the stage of emergent capitalist development, a cottage industry supported by a high degree of self-provisioning was the preferred course to take. The sort of putting-out system that Steuart recommended, developing in tandem with the strong household economy, could allow business to begin with a minimum of investment in plant and equipment. In Steuart's words, "[p]eople . . . must glean before they can expect to reap" (ibid., 1: 397).

Over time, the variable capital per worker would increase with the subsi-

---

[15] This tension continued between cheap food and a tractable labor force. For example, the agent of the Duke of Sutherland, in attempting to get textile entrepreneurs to invest in factories on his employer's property, spoke honestly of the tenants: "[T]hey have all some land—labour remarkably cheap" (cited in Ross 1973, p. 228). Yet, profit-seeking business people did not stake their money on Scottish Highland labor.

dence of the household sector, but the increasing mass of labor as well as its heightened productivity allow capitalists to pay a larger wage bill. In addition, as more commodities come on the market, the problem that Rosenstein-Rodan described recedes.

Eventually, Steuart's program was designed to so modify the condition of labor so that it would be "powerless as an independent force, that is to say, [it would be unable to exist] *outside* of this capitalist relationship" (Marx 1963–71, pt. 1, p. 391). More and more people would have no choice but to accept wage labor. Steuart, however, did not sense the full potential of capital. Like the physiocrats, he still saw the world from the standpoint of the profit it would yield to capitalist farmers. Thus he developed his plan to throw small farmers off the land after they had improved barren holdings (Steuart 1767; 1: 112–13; see also 1769, p. 328). Nonetheless, Steuart was still able to see further and clearer than all his contemporaries.

Steuart's Contribution and Legacy

With Steuart, we find a very sophisticated application of the classical theory of primitive accumulation. For half a century, we find nothing else of the kind. Steuart was not one to base his work on the airy fiction of a social contract (Steuart 1767; 1: 320). Instead, he sought out the real forces that impelled people to produce surplus value for others. In this respect, he was far more honest than all the rest of the classical political economists combined. Whereas most of his contemporaries described historical evolution in terms of the romance of natural law, Steuart was willing to investigate the forces that caused "men . . . to submit to labour" (Steuart 1767; 1: 237). From the first, he understood the uniqueness of his efforts. He observed:

> No problems of political economy seem more obscure than those which influence the multiplication of the human species, and which *determine the distribution and employment* of them, so as best to advance the prosperity of each particular society.[16] . . . I have nowhere found these matters treated to my wish, nor have I ever been able to satisfy myself concerning them". [Steuart 1767; 1: 89; emphasis added]

Steuart's modern editor, a scholar with wide-ranging knowledge of both Steuart and his milieu, departs from his usual detached attitude with respect to Steuart to insert the comment: "Statements of this kind are all that Steuart

---

[16] Postlethwayt also touched on this point in arguing that "prosperity of a trading nation to consist in the multiplying of the number of new trades; that is to say, in the multiplying of the different species of mechanics, artificers and manufactures" (Postlethwayt 1751; 1: 118).

had to offer on the division of labour" (Steuart 1966; 1: 89n). Indeed! Such remarks merely confirm the usual practice of relegating Steuart to the status of an obscure mercantilist.[17] Accordingly, we would expect to have little to learn from what he saw or said concerning the development of capital. We are thus encouraged to turn from Steuart to the likes of Adam Smith, whose analysis is considered to represent a more scientific viewpoint.

Steuart's contemporary readers understood that he was an important figure. One unsympathetic reviewer was nonetheless forced to credit him as a "penetrating genius" (Anon. 1767, p. 125), and another still less sympathetic one termed his work "a code for future statesmen and ministers" (Anon. 1767a, p. 32). In fact, Steuart's advice was solicited by the East India Company, which later gave him a diamond ring as a token of gratitude for his efforts (see Chalmers 1805, p. 381).

Yet public acclaim eluded Steuart. Indeed, he seemed to realize that he was flying in the face of the prevailing fashion in political economy. He asked his readers, "Is it not of the greatest importance to examine with *candour*, the operations by which all of Europe has been engaged in *a system of policy so generally declaimed against, and so contrary to that which we hear daily recommended as the best*" (ibid., 1: xix; emphasis added).

Steuart recognized that he could have eliminated some of the resistance to his book by adopting a style that would "prevent certain expressions here and there interpreted, from making the slightest impression upon a reader of delicate sentiments":

> [N]othing would have been so easy as to soften many passages,
> where the politician appears to have snatched the pen out of the hand
> of the private citizen; but as I write for such only who can follow a
> close reasoning, and attend to the general scope of the whole inquiry,
> I have, purposely, made no correction; but continued painting, in the
> strongest colours. [Ibid., 1: xvii]

Steuart grossly misjudged the reaction of his readers. Despite the reviewers' obvious respect for Steuart's insights, they wanted to reject his conclusions. The anonymous reviewer in *The Scots Magazine* admitted as much. Following the line of reasoning we associate with Smith, he wrote: "It is the common interest which is properly subject to laws; while the management of the particular interest of each individual, not interfering with that of the public,

---

[17] One exception is Dockes (1969), who sees von Thunen as a mere derivative of Steuart. Since von Thunen is credited with anticipating much marginal analysis, conventional economic theory might well afford Steuart some of the honors usually poured on Smith for his occasional modernisms.

ought to be left to itself" (Anon. 1767c, p. 199). Yet Steuart offered a very different tale from that presented by exponents of classical liberalism. One reviewer charged that in Steuart's work, "[w]e behold the dismal prospect of *millions* enslaved for the gratification of the few" (ibid.). Yet the reviewer could not easily dismiss him:

> The observations he has made, and the intelligence he has acquired, during his residence in several parts of Europe have furnished him with the most authentic facts for the foundation of his reasoning; and a capacious philosophical genius which has been employed in producing a composition which cannot fail to be admired by all who are able to comprehend it. But whether this admiration may not, in some sort, resemble that which we bestow on a well-constructed instrument of war, calculated either to defend or to destroy, according to the hands that it falls into [is an open question].

The public did not seem to appreciate Steuart's interpretation of the role of government in stimulating economic development. The same reviewer who described Steuart's work as a "code for future statesmen" feigned surprise in this regard: "We have no idea of a statesman having any connection with the affair, and we believe that the superiority which England has at present over all the world in point of commerce is owning to her excluding statesmen from the executive part of commercial concerns" (Anon. 1767a, p. 412).[18]

The Reverend Joseph Townsend, the Well Wisher of Mankind, may have been favorably referring to Steuart when he wrote that "the best politicians in Europe" agreed with his own condemnation of the poor laws (Townsend 1786, p. 430). Townsend wrote that that particular "nobleman, who stands foremost among the literati in the North of Britain, has more freely and more fully delivered his opinion" (ibid., p. 430). Indeed, the sixth section, which discussed the role of a wise legislator and the need to "confirm the natural bonds of society," sounds more than a bit like Steuart (ibid. pp. 406ff).

Occasionally, published works would refer to Steuart's views on money

---

18 For Smith, the statesman was a "crafty and insidious animal" (Smith 1937, p. 435). In the paragraph following the metaphor of the invisible hand, Smith argued:

> [T]he statesman, who should attempt to direct private people in what manner they ought to employ their capitals, would not only load himself with a most unnecessary attention, but assume an authority which could safely be trusted, not only to no single person, but to no council or senate whatever, and which would nowhere be so dangerous as in the hands of a man who had folly and presumption enough to fancy himself fit to exercise it. [ibid., p. 423]

or other matters, but generally he was received in silence. The public had to wait until almost a quarter-century after Steuart's death for a strongly positive note from a British author. In a rather obscure work, Daniel Wakefield judged Smith to be an "inferior copy" of Steuart (Wakefield 1804, p. 3). Wakefield charged:

> Few writers have been under equal obligations to another, as Doctor Adam Smith to Sir James Steuart, and but few have been so entirely destitute of candour and gratitude, as in no place to acknowledge the debt, or to pay a tribute to the fame of their instructor. The style of *The Wealth of Nations* renders the work popular, though . . . obscurity frequently supplies the place of profundity. [ibid.; see also Marx 1859, pp. 167–68]

Wakefield was the first of a series of writers to comment on the practice of plagiarizing "that great MASTER of political science, to whose invaluable work, succeeding writers have had recourse, as to the grand storehouse of knowledge" (ibid., p. 3). Two years later, a reviewer of Steuart's collected works mentioned Steuart's writings concerning "the influence of political economy on civil government." He noted: "To this topic, also, Dr. Smith has only incidentally averted; and here, likewise, in the few observations he makes on it, we find him tread closely in the footsteps of his precursor" (Anon. 1806, p. 115).

One of the most remarkable echoes of Steuart is found in Arthur Young's *Travels in France*. In assessing the importance of Young, the longtime secretary of the Board of Agriculture, keep in mind that almost none of the major figures of classical political economy except Steuart had much agricultural experience. The one exception to this generalization was Richard Jones, an avid gardener, whom Harriet Martineau addressed as "My dear King of Roses" (cited in James 1979, p. 283), the same Richard Jones whose knowledge of growing plants supplied him with the insight to demolish classical rent theory.

Although Young is rarely counted among the important classical economists, all of his contemporaries seemed ready to grant him credit as a major authority on agricultural affairs. His response to Steuart represents a test of the practical value of Steuart's work by an individual who had little sympathy for matters of pure theory. Young described Steuart as "a genius of superior cast" (Young 1794, p. 366). Like Steuart, Young judged the success of an agricultural system by its contribution to the deepening of the social division of labor (ibid., p. 365). After a long discussion of the subject, Young concluded: The size of farms is most beneficial, in general, which secures the greatest produce *in the market*; or, in other words, converted into money (ibid.,

p. 312), although he later qualified this conclusion with the remark "In the preceding observation, I have had rented farms only in view" (ibid., p. 315). Nonetheless, Young was no great friend of self-provisioning. In a long passage that reflected the ideas of Steuart, although the latter's name was misspelled, Young wrote:

It is a remarkable circumstance in the agriculture, or rather in the domestic economy of France, that the culture of hemp or flax, for home uses pervades every part of the kingdom. It is a curious question how far this is beneficial or not to the general interests of the national prosperity. On the one hand, in favour of this system it may be urged, that the national prosperity being nothing more than the united prosperity of single families, if any such article of economy be advantageous to individuals, it must be so to the nation at large; that it cannot fail of being beneficial to a poor man's family to have the women and children industriously employed on clothing the whole rather than forced to buy such articles at an expense of money which they may not be able to procure. By means of industry, thus exerted, a poor family is rendered as independent as its situation admits. All of them are likewise warmer, and more comfortably clothed, as far as linen is concerned, than if it were bought; for whatever demands money will be consumed with much more caution than if the result merely of labour. . . . A modern society flourishes by the mutual exchange of the products of land for the manufactures of towns; a natural connection of one with another, and it may be remarked, that in proportion as the exchange is rapid from a great consumption, in such proportion will a people generally flourish. If every family in the country have a patch of flax or hemp for its own supply of all the manufactures founded on these materials, this beneficial intercourse of the country with the town, is so far cut off, and no circulation takes place. If the practice be good in flax, it is good in wool; and every family should have a sufficient number of sheep, to cloth [sic] themselves woolens; and if every little village have its little tanner, the same supposition may be extended to leather. A patch of vines furnishes the beverage of the family; and thus, by simple domestic industry, all wants are supplied; and a poor family, as it would be improperly called, would have no occasion to resort to the market for any thing *to buy*. But with nothing *to sell*; . . . [A] minute division of the soil into small properties always attacks the existence of towns, that is to say, of what Sir James Steuart calls the *free hands* of a society. A countryman living on his own little property with his family industriously employed in manufacturing for all their own wants, without exchange, connection, or dependence on any one, offers, indeed, a spectacle of rural comfort, but a species absolutely inconsistent with the prosperity of a modern society. [Young 1794, p. 427]

In what sense was this spectacle of rural comfort inconsistent with the prosperity of modern society? Young estimated that French agriculture was able to deliver food to market at a very low cost:

> Living is reckoned cheap here. . . . As I conceive the English to have made far greater advances in the useful arts, and in manufactures, than the French have done, England ought to be the cheaper country. What we meet with in France, is a cheap *mode of living*, which is quite another consideration. [ibid., p. 27]

According to his detailed calculations, "The consumption of bread, and the price of labour [were] about 76 percent cheaper in France than in England" (ibid., pp. 339–40), just as Steuart had predicted would be the case under such circumstances. The problem lay elsewhere. Primitive accumulation was a prerequisite of the development of the social relations of capitalist production. Again, Young clearly revealed the logic of the early marketplace:

> [T]he most industrious and hard labouring of our poor peasants, are not those who keep their little gardens in the best order and cultivation; but such, on the contrary as make inferior earnings, that mark something of debility. . . . No labour is so wretchedly performed, and so dear, as that of hired hands accustomed to labour for themselves; there is a disgust, and a listlessness, that cannot escape an intelligent observer; and nothing but real distress will drive such little proprietors to work at all for others; so that I have seen, in the operosely cultivated parts of France, labour comparatively dear, and ill performed, amidst swarms of half wild people. . . . Can anything be apparently so absurd, as a strong hearty man walking some miles, and losing a day's work which ought to be worth 15 or 20s. in order to sell a dozen of eggs, or a chicken, the value of which would not equal the labour of conveying it, *were the people usefully employed?* This ought to convince us, that these small occupations are a real loss of labour [ibid., p. 322].

Just what did Young mean by a real loss of labour? Certainly, he did not mean that peasants who worked on their account were lazy. Young himself had written, "Give a man the secure possession of a bleak rock, and he will turn it into a garden" (ibid, p. 45). With a revealing turn of a phrase, Young recalled, "I saw nothing respectable on small properties, except a most unremitting industry" (ibid., p. 316). Thus unremitting work was not respectable unless it was performed for wages. What of the time dissipated in carting insignificant quantities of produce to market? On several occasions, Young sneered at peasants who dissipated their energy in trifling transactions (see ibid., pp. 81 and 306).

Yet Young knew enough peasant life to realize that market day was not strictly an economic affair. It was a time for socializing by people who were often cut off from society. The peasant whom he met carrying two chickens to a market twenty-four miles away may not have been behaving economically, but we have no reason to believe that he was acting irrationally (ibid., p. 306). All in all, Steuart could not have asked for a more devoted disciple than Young.

Just like Young, Jean-Baptiste Say misspelled Steuart's name when citing him as an authority (Say 1880, p. 206), but Say's reference merely lumps Smith and Steuart together "in thinking, that the labour of the slave is dearer and less productive than that of the freeman" (ibid.). When dealing with more important questions, he left any debt to Steuart unacknowledged. I refer specifically to a chapter in his *Cours Complet* entitled "The Influence of Social Life on the Production of Riches" (Say 1843, pp. 253–58). There Say scrupulously avoided any mention of any conflict in creating a social division of labor. In the place of primitive accumulation, Say wrote of "a concert of wills" (ibid., p. 233).

Once the matter of primitive accumulation was put aside, Say could then address the relationship between the division of labor and the social division of labor:

> I will not repeat here, Sirs, what I have said about the division of labor. . . . You have to recall that this prodigious growth of human power is principally due to the possibility of concluding exchanges. . . . The progress of industry establishes bonds, relations among men, by means of which they are at the same time each independent on his side, and yet obliged to manage himself reciprocally. [ibid., p. 234, 237]

Steuart's name, however, was not mentioned in this discussion. The next flash of recognition came from none other than Dugald Stewart, Adam Smith's eulogist, who told his students:

> With respect to NATIONAL WEALTH, I have all along recommended, and must beg leave again to recommend, Mr. Smith's *Inquiry*, as the book with which the student may, with the most advantage, *begin* his researches on the subject; not only on account of the comprehensive outline it exhibits of its various parts, but as it is the *Code* which is now almost universally appealed to, over all Europe, as the highest authority which can be quoted in support of any political

argument. The work of Sir James Steuart, too, besides some ingenious speculations of his own, contains a great mass of accurate details. [Stewart 1855; 2: 458]

An anonymous reviewer, in praising Smith's virtues with respect to his great mercantilist rival, emphasized Steuart's emphasis on detail (Anon. 1806, pp. 231–32), but this apparently disparaging remark bears some similarity to Marx's complementary evaluation of Steuart.

Steuart never learned how far his influence carried. In the last year of his life, frustrated by the lack of public recognition of his work, he wrote of his deceased dog, "were I to write his life, it would be a work as voluminous as my *Political Oeconomy* and perhaps as little relished by the public" (cited in Skinner 1966, p. iv).

The reference to dead dogs brings up a curious coincidence. Marx, writing of Steuart's eclipse, said: "Steuart remained even more of 'a dead dog' than Spinoza appeared to be Moses Mendelson in Lessing's time" (Marx 1859, p. 167). On another occasion, Marx applied the very same metaphor to Hegel (see Marx to Kugelmann, 27 June 1870, in Marx and Engels 1975, p. 225). Over the years, Hegel's reputation fared much better than Steuart's. To some extent, however, Steuart may have been responsible for the reception both of them received. Steuart's frank treatment of the process of capital accumulation proved to be an embarrassment. Thus Steuart suffered obscurity. Yet his honesty allowed him to produce a very insightful theoretical system.

The temptation to claim such original research as one's own was more than some people could resist. Malthus, for example, praised Steuart in private correspondence with Ricardo (see Ricardo 1951–73; 6: 33–35), yet we search his published work in vain looking for a reference to Steuart. Other writers (see Young 1792, p. 318; Steuart 1767; 4: 315 and Stewart 1855; 1: 150–51), including even Adam Smith, fell to publishing Steuart's ideas as their own. In his youth, Hegel also drew upon the unacknowledged Steuart, all the while praising Smith (see Chamley 1965, pp. 142–47). In the words of Adam Smith's pupil and lifelong friend, the Earl of Buchan:[19]

> As for the great work, the *Political Oeconomy*, it is needless to praise it, for the public will do ample justice to it, when it has thrown from its literary meal the high-seasoned cookeries of the plagiarists, who have obtruded Sir James's facts, principles, and reasoning, on the

---

[19] We might value the Earl's words more highly if they were not lifted verbatim from those published earlier by Archibald Hamilton (see Chamley 1965, p. 26).

world, without acknowledging from whence they were derived. [cited in Chamley 1965, p. 26]

Thus Steuart, the greatest classical theorist of primitive accumulation, found himself the victim of a primitive accumulation of a literary sort. We are all the poorer for the lack of attention given to this seminal mind.

chapter 4

The Classics as Cossacks: Classical Political Economy Versus the Working Class

The head of the new school, Mr. Ricardo has, they say, declared himself that there are no more than twenty-five people in England that had understood his book. Perhaps he had cultivated obscurity, so that those who understood him . . . had become a sect of adepts with a new language.

Sismondi, *Nouveaux principes d'economie politique*, p. 324

The Scotland of Steuart and Owen

Robert Owen was a successful cotton spinner. Like others of his trade, he discovered that the creation of a capitalist society in Scotland, or elsewhere, was no easy task. "The Highlander," it was said, "never sits at ease at a loom; it is like putting a deer in a plough" (Pollard 1965, p. 261). Robert Owen maintained that the "regularly trained Scotch peasant disdained the idea of working early and late, day after day, within cotton mills" (Owen 1857, p. 58). Children could be bound to the factory by indentures of apprenticeship for at least seven years and usually until they were twenty-one (Mantoux 1927, p. 410). "Lots of fifty, eighty or a hundred children were supplied [by the Poor Law authorities] and sent like cattle where they remained imprisoned for many years" (ibid., p. 411).

Sidney Pollard points out that "[i]n Scotland, significantly, factories were referred to as 'public works,' showing the mental association with work-houses, and migration to factory districts was likened to transportation" (Pollard 1965, p. 194; see also Kuczynski 1967, p. 70). The feeling against factories ran so strong that Richard Oastler's father sold his business rather than employ the "machine [which] symbolized the encroachment of the factory *system*" (Thompson 1963, p. 548), machines that he regarded as "a means of oppression on the part of the rich and of corresponding degradation and misery to the poor" (cited in Thompson 1963, p. 549).

Given the widespread revulsion created by factory work, employers had to go to great lengths to snatch labor from the depths of the urban centers. They also had to be quick to take advantage of fortuitous events; for example, David Dale, a famous Scottish cotton lord, upon hearing of 200 emigrants shipwrecked on a nearby coast, rushed off to recruit them (Pollard 1965, p. 261). Such occasional opportunities, however, were obviously insufficient.

Dale's famous son-in-law, Robert Owen, recognized that "[t]wo modes then only remained of obtaining these labourers, the one to procure children from the various public charities of the country, and the other to induce families to settle around the works" (Owen 1813, p. 26). As a result, Dale, like other cotton magnates, eventually found it expedient to create entire villages in order to maintain a labor force (Robertson 1971, pp. 150–51; Pollard 1965, pp. 231–42; Collier 1930). Dale's village, located in Lanark County, home of Sir James Steuart, passed into the hands of Owen, who established a nursery school for young children and night schools for older ones. He developed a support fund to take care of the injured, sick, and aged. Workers were also served by a savings bank and stores that undersold private dealers (on this latter point, see Ricardo 1951–73; 5: 218).

Owen's establishment won the admiration of people around the world.[1] His workers seemed to enjoy a better life than the urban proletariat, even though he paid them below the going rate. More important, his factory earned a healthy, but not unusual profit (Robertson 1971, pp. 147–48). Although Owen's community had many progressive features, it suffered from the paternalism inherent in such operations.[2] The workers themselves complained:

---

[1] One exception was Malthus, who entered into his diary, in 1810: "About fifteen hundred people are employed at the cotton mill, and great debauchery prevails among them" (Malthus 1966, p. 233); however, his next sentence describes the thirteen-hour, six-day-per-week schedule. No details about the debauchery are supplied.

[2] One need only follow its course of development in the evolution of company towns from Francis Cabot Lowell's attempt to re-create what he saw at New Lanark (Dillard 1967, pp. 328–29; Marx 1967; 2: 516), including the emphasis on discipline (see Ware 1924, pp. 78–79) through the town that bears George Pullman's name, which was

> We view it a grievance of considerable magnitude to be compelled by Mr. Owen to adopt what measures so ever he may be pleased to suggest to us on matters that entirely belong to us. Such a course of procedure is most repugnant to our minds as men, and degrading to our characters. [cited in Robertson 1971, p. 150]

To his credit, Owen understood this shortcoming of his work and attempted to create alternative communities with more self-governance, although the *Black Dwarf* still denounced his planned community as a "nursery for men" (cited in Hollis 1973, p. 31).

Owen's involvement with the cotton industry educated him in many respects. He came to recognize that labor was being driven from the country-side much more rapidly than it could be absorbed in the factories. In this regard, Owen seems also to have been influenced by Spence, whose call for land reform was cited earlier (Rudkin 1966, pp. 191ff); however, with Owen, the Spencian demands for collective ownership of the land were softened. Rather, he had hoped that the wealthy, including the royal family, would help him in establishing villages that could set labor back to work on the land. Like Steuart and Spence, Owen recognized that the social division of labor in food production was a vital element in the determination of the level of real wages. In a letter dated 25 July 1817, and published in the London newspapers five days later, Owen declared, "Value must be restored to manual labour, and this cannot be done except by employment on the land" (cited in Owen 1857, p. 74).

Owen's idea was by no means novel. Owen himself discovered that much of his analysis, as well as much of his solution, had already been proposed by John Bellers in the late seventeenth century. Bellers, considered by Marx to be "a veritable phenomenon in the history of political economy" (Marx 1977, p. 619), proposed that capitalists invest in colleges of industry that could educate the poor, teach them industry, and shelter them from earthly cares. Although he observed that "the labour of the poor . . . [is] the mine of the rich" (Bellers 1696, p. 164), Bellers argued that a decent life for the poor was compatible with a wholesome rate of profit for the rich.

---

designed to "attract and retain a superior type of workingman, who would in turn be elevated and refined" by the physical setting (cited in Harvey 1976, p. 283) to the grotesque system engineered by Ford, with a "staff of over thirty investigators [who] visited workers' homes gathering information and giving advice on intimate details of the family budget, diet, living arrangements, recreation, social outlook and morality" (Flink, 1975, p. 89; see also Sward 1972, pp. 228–29, and Harvey 1976, p. 277).

And why was profit necessary? Bellers answered naively, "Because the rich have no other way of living but by the labour of others" (Bellers 1696, p. 177). This naive philanthropist hoped to benefit all humanity by virtue of an improved social division of labor in which the cooperation of concentrations of labor would result in a tremendous expansion of productivity. In Bellers's words: "[A]s one man cannot and ten must strain to lift a ton weight, yet one hundred men can do it only by the strength of each of them" (Bellers 1696, p. 176).

Owens designed a plan for villages based on labor-intensive agriculture. He stressed the social, rather than the technical advantages of his own plan calling upon the wealthy, and even the government, to invest with him in a program to correct the imbalances in the social division of labor. Some members of the royal family were duly impressed.

Although most of the attempts to put Owen's ideas into practice met with failure, the Ralahine community in County Clare, Ireland was, in fact, quite successful, even on purely monetary grounds, until its owner gambled away his fortune (Garnett 1971, pp. 47–52; see also Bray 1841; 2: 580–585).

A Brief Digression on Land Reform

Owen's ideas were echoed by later calls for land reform. In Britain and the United States, workers were in the forefront of the struggle for land reform, even though they not might never get the opportunity to work the land themselves (Thompson 1963, pp. 231, 295; Foner 1975, pp. 44–45).[3] The Chartists, for example, even bought up land during the 1840s to lease back to their members (see Engels 1845a; Tsuzuki 1971, pp. 18–19). According to Feargus O'Connor:

> The first use the land would be to them was to ease the labour market of its surplus; the second was to create a certainty of work for the people; and the third was to create a natural rate of wages in the artificial market; for so long as there was a surplus to fall back on, or a warehouse from which to procure labour, so long would work be uncertain and wages low. [*Northern Star*, 7 June 1845, cited in Prothero 1969, p. 99]

O'Connor had intended that workers could be drawn off into agriculture in such a way that "the number working at each trade [could be adjusted] to

---

[3] This activity does not prove the existence of a permanent solidarity of interests between urban and rural workers. The AFL-CIO, for example, has resisted the training of rural workers that would enable them to compete for jobs in the urban labor market (see United State House of Representatives 1961, p. 99).

the amount of produce required from each as to ensure a healthy settlement of demand and supply" (O'Connor 1845). Unfortunately, O'Connor's perspective was limited. He denounced "communism" as "a fascinating theory [that] opens a wide field for indulgence of the wildest of visionaries" (O'Connor 1848, p. 55). He wanted "to make idleness a crime" (ibid., p. 56). More important, O'Connor looked backward to a system of petty commodity production. Not surprisingly, the left wing of the Chartist movement, as well as Marx and Engels, could not support his project, just as they could not endorse Kriege's land reform activities in the United States (see Draper 1978, pp. 411 and 420–425).[4]

Yet the Chartist plan might have worked to raise the wages of labor in the short run. The case of Mr. R. F. Powell, hired by wealthy philanthropists as superintendent of the Philadelphia Vacant Lots Cultivation Association, illustrates this point.[5] (Dudden 1971, p. 36). As a follower of Henry George, Mr. Powell was keenly aware of the extent of vacant land held for speculative purposes in his city, which he estimated to have amounted to one-quarter of the urban area (see Kelley 1906, p. 306). Mr. Powell helped to set almost 1,000 families to work raising gardens on these lots. For the especially needy, Mr. Powell would hire them as gardeners at only twelve-and-a-half cents per hour, although the organization would not have suffered a loss even if the wages had been raised to forty cents per hour. Why were wages set at the lower level? The board of directors of the association, composed of wealthy businessmen, would not allow a higher wage. Powell informed Florence Kelley, the translator of the American edition of Engels's *Conditions of the Working Class*: "It would make no end of trouble. . . . If these people were to find that they could earn as much as that they would either leave the factories or demand as much pay there" (Kelley 1906, p. 306). In any event, the Chartists' plan failed and the capitalist system continued; so did its intended "screwing and grinding" (Spence, cited in Thompson 1963, p. 805).

David Ricardo

Owen's schemes stirred up a great deal of controversy. Classical political economy was drawn into the fray. The importance of this controversy is what it reveals about the attitude of classical political economy with respect to the social division of labor and self-provisioning. Ricardo, for one, became

---

4 However, a program to give peasants land was progressive in the context of less advanced economic conditions, such as were found in Germany (see Marx and Engels 1846a, pp. 351–55).

5 I owe this reference to T. J. Bassett, Department of Geography, University of California, Berkeley.

a reluctant participant in this wrangling. No one should have expected Ricardo to offer much support to Owen's plan. Although most modern commentators cite Ricardo's words of sympathy for the poor, they fail to note that this sympathy was rather abstract. In his very first speech to Parliament, he warned his fellow members against being overly tender to the children of the poor, lest such actions encourage the poor to breed more offspring (Ricardo 1951–73; 5: 1). He was not at all critical of the attempts of employers "to keep down the recompense to the labourer to the lowest rate" (Ricardo 1951–73; 9: 54).

Attending a meeting of the Owenites along with Robert Torrens, he found himself appointed to a committee to study the idea. Ricardo was skeptical that the scheme could be administered in the socialistic form envisioned by Owen. He wrote to his friend, Trower:

> Can any reasonable person believe with Owen, that a society, such as he projects, will flourish and produce more than has ever yet been produced by an equal number of men, if they are to be stimulated to their private interest? Is not the experience of ages against him? [Ricardo 1951–73; 8: 46]

The objections Ricardo raised in Parliament were not limited to such philosophical speculations on human nature. There he charged Owen with the grave error of building "a theory inconsistent with the principles of political economy, and in his [Ricardo's] opinion . . . calculated to produce infinite mischief to the community" (Ricardo 1951–73; 5: 30). While both Ricardo and Owen argued that the then existing social division was brought about by matters of individual self-interest, Owen interpreted the result to be detrimental to the well-being of labor.

By contrast, Ricardo reasoned on a very different basis, assuming that if labor-intensive technologies were beneficial to society, then they would turn out to be more profitable. Consequently, he told Parliament, "as soon as the farmer knew that it was in his interest to pursue a different system, he would adopt it as a matter of course" (Ricardo 1951–73; 6: 31n).

Given this position, Ricardo could accept Owen's diagnosis: "For what did the country want at the present moment? A demand for labour. If the facts stated of spade husbandry were true, it was a beneficial course, as affording that demand" (Ricardo 1951–73; 5: 31).

Owen's prescription, however, was totally unacceptable. Ricardo was only willing to go so far as to ascertain if spade husbandry would be more profitable. The market could take care of the rest.

Ricardo on Machinery

Ricardo, however, was forthright enough to express a growing skepticism about the market. In his *Notes on Malthus*, he explicitly recognized that an alternative agricultural technology might very well improve the position of the working class even though it might not be more profitable to individual farmers:

> It might be possible to do almost all the work performed by men with horses, would the substitution of horses in such case, even if attended with a greater produce, be advantageous to the working classes, would it not on the contrary very materially diminish the demand for labour? All I mean to say is that it *might* happen with a cheaper mode of cultivation the demand for labour *might* diminish, and with a dearer it might decrease. [Ricardo 1951-73; 2: 239]

Two qualifications cast additional light on Ricardo's position. First, he recognized in an earlier note that "diminished [net] production is compatible with an increased consumption, *by human beings*" (Ricardo 1951-73; 2: 238). In other words, although the farmer's monetary costs might be higher with more manual labor, the amount of grain available for human consumption (i.e., measuring the profits of the farmer in terms of grain plus the grain consumed by the workers) might also be higher. If, however, the labor replaced by horses might be productively employed elsewhere, then presumably Ricardo would have considered the measure of "consumption by human beings" to be irrelevant. The very fact that he even stopped to reflect upon this concept indicates that he sensed something amiss in the marketplace.

Second, Ricardo wrote and then deleted the thought: "This is perhaps the only case in which the substitution of labour for fixed capital, if horses can be so called, is not attended with advantage to the capitalist yet is nevertheless beneficial to the working class" (Ricardo 1951-73; 2: 239n). Senior suggested the identical idea: "I do not believe that there exists upon record a single instance in which the whole annual produce has been diminished by the use of *inanimate* machinery" (Senior 1831, pp. 39-40; emphasis in original); however, Senior was concerned about the excessive use of horses (Senior 1868; 2: 43).

His observation that food was diverted from human use to horses seems to have been common at the time. A horse was estimated to typically require about three pecks of oats and a gallon of beans daily in addition to its hay (Ashton 1972, p. 55). A writer in 1799 spoke of the horse as "the most dangerous moth in the whole web of agricultural economy" (cited in ibid., p. 55). To make such a statement did not necessarily mean an acceptance of Ricardo's later idea that machinery in general could operate to the detriment of labor, although Samuel Hollander attempts to make such a case (Hollander 1971; see also Maital and Haswell 1977). Senior, for example, never accepted the later Ricardian position on machinery.

Horses could be regarded as a special case for one of two reasons. On the one hand, both the input, grain, and the output, food, were more or less identical. Consequently, the typical descriptions of the indirect beneficial effects of the actions of supply and demand were not convincing. On the other hand, the substitution of horses for people, associated in part with the enclosure movement, reflected a change in the mode of production, whereas the adoption of machinery in general took place within the capitalist mode of production. Thus on some level the case of horse husbandry may have been assumed to be unique, even though most political economists held that, in spite of the suffering engendered by the initiation of market relations, the development of the market would make life better in the long run.

Whether or not horses were a special case, to his credit, Ricardo's reflections on the matter publicly gave confirmation, albeit indirectly, to Owen's more pessimistic perspective. In his famous chapter "On Machinery" in the *Principles*, Ricardo indicated the conditions by which labor could be harmed by the introduction of labor-saving techniques (Ricardo 1951–73; 1, chap. 31).[6] He even went so far as to speculate that "if machinery could do all the work that labour now does, there would be no demand for labour" (Ricardo 1951–73; 8: 399–400). Under this assumption, "Nobody would be entitled to consume who was not a capitalist, and who could not buy or rent a machine" (ibid.). Such discussion, however, was presented in the form of an abstract principle absolutely unrelated to any particular point of policy. According to Ricardo's interpretation, machinery could harm only labor under the very special conditions of capital scarcity (see Berg 1980, pp. 65–75). Thus he claimed to be "not aware that I have ever published anything respecting machinery which it is necessary for me to retract" (Ricardo 1951–73; 1: 386). However, he added what seemed to be an admission that he had not treated Owen altogether fairly: "yet I have in other ways given my support to doctrines which I now think erroneous" (ibid.). How far he intended these words to be taken is not clear in the context.

The Corn Laws in England

At that time, Parliament was in fact actively enforcing a policy that was discouraging labor-intensive agriculture; namely, the infamous Corn Laws.

---

6 The examples found in that chapter are industrial. Ricardo, however, suggests that agriculture in his day might well be more capital-intensive than manufacturing (Ricardo 1951–73; 5: 77–78).

According to the conventional wisdom, the Corn Laws would be expected to increase the demand for agricultural labor. Indeed, Hilton suggests that even if higher bread prices had restricted the demand for industrial labor, prior to the 1820s, this diminution would have been more than offset by the greater amount of labor employed in agriculture (Hilton 1977, p. 120). Not only was recourse to foreign production impeded by the Corn Laws, but the labor demands per bushel were higher on marginal lands. Some explicitly used this line of reasoning to support the Corn Laws at the time (ibid., 1977, p. 125). The *Northern Star* repeated this argument as late as 1840 (see Hollis 1973, pp. 280–81). Ricardo, in effect, also relied upon higher labor costs on marginal soil in constructing his theory of comparative advantage (Ricardo 1951–73; 1, chap. 7), although he treated the total demand for labor as fixed.

The defenders of the Corn Laws regarded England as preeminently agricultural. They spoke as if a greater demand for agricultural labor were tantamount to a larger aggregate demand. The empirical support for this position is not entirely clear because the marginal lands were brought into production mostly with heavy investments. The extent of these sunk costs, in fact, was what made the pressure for the Corn Laws so intense.

These investments served two purposes. To some extent, they substituted for the natural conditions of the raw and unimproved land. For example, a substantial portion of the investments were designed to provide better drainage for the land. The second purpose was to substitute for labor.

Strictly speaking, this separation of investments cannot be made precisely. Labor can also substitute for land. For example, extra labor might be an alternative to the installation of drainage tiles. The reason for making the distinction between the two effects of agricultural investment is to suggest that not all the money spent for agricultural improvements was directed toward compensating for the lack of natural productivity; some went to save labor on tasks that were then being performed on less-capitalized farms located on more fertile lands. Although such investment may have appeared economical under wartime conditions, it need not have been after demobilization.

Those improved farms located on previously idle land were in the forefront of agricultural improvement. They would not necessarily use less labor than the typical less-capitalized wheat farm. Consequently, these farms actually may not have used less labor than the typical less-capitalized wheat farm. Thus we might guess that the effect of the Corn Laws in increasing the demand for the growing of grain might be less than would be expected from the proportional increase of domestic production.

The Corn Laws had a negative effect on agricultural employment in one respect. Wheat uses relatively little labor compared to most crops. Conse-

about substantial cost reductions for those with adequate access to capital (see Nelson and Cochrane 1976). Indeed, Anderson and some of the supporters of the earlier Corn Laws justified the legislation in similar terms (see Anderson 1777a and Hollander 1979, Appendix C), as did the British government in 1815 (Hilton 1977, p. 112). Taking all these effects together, we could interpret the Corn Laws as a measure primarily designed to help the larger farmers who marketed the majority of their produce at the expense of small ones. Consequently, the number of small farms fell as their places were taken by still smaller operations that were used to supplement nonfarm wages (see Wordie 1974).

Since the shift to grain production might well mean a fall in agricultural employment, the overall effect of the Corn Laws on the supply of labor could have been substantial. Not surprising, this process was felt most severely by agricultural labor. John Barton, whose study is sometimes credited with prompting Ricardo's changed stand on machinery, showed the appalling poverty of agricultural labor during the early nineteenth century (Barton 1817 and 1833).[10] The effect of a glut of agricultural labor would spill over into industrial labor markets, although the impact would not have been particularly strong for those specific skills that were in high demand. To the extent that real wages fell, the Corn Laws also served to help establish labor discipline.

To make matters worse, the shift from manufacturing to agriculture, which one should expect to occur as a result of the Corn Laws, might have tended to make capital more scarce in industry. Ricardo himself told Parliament on 9 May 1822 that he doubted that agriculture was less capital-intensive than industry (see Gordon 1976, pp. 139–40). Assuming that Ricardo was correct, artificial stimulation of grain production might increase the ratio of profits to wages, even if we disregard the undermining of small-scale, labor-intensive farming. After a good number of the small farmers had been converted into industrial workers, and industrial workers had come to accept the norms of factory work, a lower cost of food would result in a higher rate of surplus value. At that point, the Corn Laws could be conveniently abolished.

My understanding of the Corn Laws parallels a related thesis proposed by Nallet and Servolin, who have interpreted the persistence of relatively small-

---

[10] Barton associated poverty with a falling price of corn. A higher price was taken to be an indication of a higher demand for agricultural labor. This result is consistent with my reasoning. I am suggesting that without the Corn Laws, the falling demand for some types of agricultural labor would be more than compensated for by other, less seasonal farm labor demands.

scale agriculture as an essential part of capitalist development (Nallet and Servolin 1978). Although the farmer's Janus-like appearance—half-farmer, half-worker—frequently is seen as inconsistent with capitalist development, in fact, this arrangement is very efficient in providing cheap food and raw materials. The government allows this system of petty producers to feel a constant level of stress to spur them on. At the same time, the government provides a certain degree of protection to this seemingly archaic system of production, knowing full well that agriculture organized on a more strictly capitalist basis would prove to be substantially more costly. Nallet and Servolin argue their case on the basis of the French experience, but my own research of the United States system seems to bear them out (Perelman 1981).

The Corn Laws were not discussed in terms of their impact on the small farmer.[11] Certainly some small farmers would have found the higher cost of their subsistence a burden. Given the level of economic sophistication found in the better works of English political economy, we can only ascribe the almost universal absence of comment on this effect of the Corn Laws to an insensitivity to the conditions of the small producer.

The majority of political economists of the day are generally treated as firm opponents of the Corn Laws. Accordingly, they would seem to be blameless in the question of responsibility for the hardships created by the laws. In reality, however, Ricardo was far less doctrinaire in this matter than he was in his opposition to Owen (see Hollander 1979, chap. 2). Rather than calling for their immediate abolition, he recommended that the Corn Laws be gradually eliminated over a decade (Ricardo 1951–73; 4: 243–44 and 263–64).[12] The eventual elimination of the Corn Laws would have been slight consolation for those small producers without the means to wait until cheaper food became available.

This analysis of the Corn Laws runs counter to the common discussion of this legislation, which is generally depicted as the consequence of a struggle between business and landed interests. Certainly, more was involved than a simple question of large- versus small-scale farming; nonetheless, we still need to address the relationship between Ricardo and the state of the largely self-sufficient household or petty-commodity producer. Ricardian political economy was a continuation of those policies that "favored those agriculturalists who had access to capital without the need to mortgage estates" (Gordon 1976, p. 231; see also Johnson 1909, pp. 122–23). Ricardo's alliance with

---

[11] Marx did briefly note a connection between the Corn Laws and the scale of farming (see Marx 1845, p. 289).

[12] Ricardo was not unique in this respect. None of the major figures of classical political economy called for outright repeal (see Grampp 1960, Chapter 2).

this class of farmers went deeper than the Corn Laws. According to Gordon, Ricardo's deflationist policies generally favored "the interest of the rentier . . . which included the wealthier land owning aristocrats but took little cognizance of the needs of the entrepreneur" (ibid., p. 153) and, one should add, the small-scale farmer.

RICARDO ON IRELAND

> Poor *Ireland* maketh many rich.
> Jonathan Swift, *The Drapers Letters*, p. 132

Ricardo's hostility to small-scale agriculture was especially evident in his private correspondence. In response to his friend Trower's suggestion that "no permanent or substantial good [in Ireland] can be done until all *small farms* and small tenancies are got rid of" (Ricardo 1951–73; 9: 145), Ricardo agreed with the goal of eliminating small-scale agriculture in Ireland (Ricardo 1951–73; 9: 153); however, he believed small farms were an effect rather than a cause of conditions in Ireland. Nonetheless, Ricardo was far from being a staunch advocate of cheap food. In words almost indistinguishable from those of Malthus, he wrote to Francis Place:

> The evil of which the Irish ought to complain is the small value of food of the people compared with the value of other objects of their consumption, and the small desire they have of possessing other objects. Cheap food is not an evil, but a good, *if it be not accompanied by an insensibility to the comforts and decencies of life.* [Ricardo 1951–73; 9: 56; emphasis added]

Ricardo's fear of cheap food in Ireland was so great that he suggested:

> The evil they (the Irish) experience proceeds from the indolence and vice of the people, not from their inability to procure necessaries. By reducing their population, you reduce food in perhaps a larger proportion, and rather aggravate rather than remove their misery. [Ricardo 1951–73; 7: 48]

In the first edition of his *Principles*, he repeated the idea that the population of Ireland might be insufficiently large to encourage the people to work enough:

> The facility with which the wants of the Irish are supplied permits that people to pass a greater part of their time in indolence; if the population were diminished, this evil would increase, because wages would rise, and therefore the labourer would be enabled in exchange

for a still less portion of his labour, to obtain all that his moderate
wants require. [Ricardo 1951–73; 1: 100; see also 7: 334]

This section is worth examining in more detail. The relevant portion began:

> In those countries where there is abundance of fertile land, but
> where from ignorance, indolence, and barbarism of the inhabitants,
> they are exposed to all the evils of want and famine, and where it has
> been said that the population presses against the means of subsistence,
> a very different remedy should be applied from that which is necessary
> in longly settled countries, where from the diminishing rate of the
> supply of raw produce, all the evils of a crowded population are ex-
> perienced. [Ricardo 1951–73; 1: 99]

The first edition read: "In the one case, misery proceeds from the inactivity
of the people. To be made happier, they need only to be stimulated to
exertion." This passage reads much like something from the mercantilist
literature, or even Joseph Townsend. After this section came under the
critical scrutiny of George Ensor, Ricardo changed its tone, but not its meaning.

> To be made happier, they require only to be better governed and
> instructed, as the augmentation of capital, beyond the augmentation
> of people would be the inevitable result. [Ibid]

Ricardo's comments in the first edition continued:

> In some countries of Europe, and many of Asia, as well as in the
> islands in the South Seas, the people are miserable, either from a
> vicious government or from habits of indolence, which make them
> prefer present ease and inactivity, though without security against
> want. . . . By diminishing their population, no relief would be afforded,
> for productions would diminish in as great, or even in a greater propor-
> tion. The remedy for the evils under which Poland and Ireland suffer,
> which are similar to those experienced in the South Seas, is to stimulate
> exertion, to create new wants, and to implant new tastes. . . . The
> facility with which the wants of the Irish are supplied, permits that
> people to pass a great part of their time in idleness: if the population
> were diminished, this evil would increase, because wages would rise,
> and therefore the labourer would be enabled in exchange for a still less
> portion of his labour, to obtain all that his moderate wants require.
> Give to the Irish labourer a taste for the comforts and enjoyments
> which habit has made essential to the English labourer, and he would
> be content to devote a further portion of his time to industry, that he

might be enabled to obtain them. Not only would all the food now produced be obtained, but a vast additional value in those other commodities, to the production of which the now unemployed labour of the country might be directed. [Ibid., p. 100]

Ensor roundly attacked Ricardo for these words. He pointed out that the English labourer "is no object of admiration." Then he asked: "How are these tastes to be excited in Irish labourers? Is it supposed that they are not like other human creatures? but that they make choice of privations?" (Ensor 1818, p. 106 cited in ibid., p. 100n).

In discussing the Irish problem with its attendant poverty, Ricardo fell silent about the great wealth flowing from Ireland. Instead, like so many of his contemporaries, he viewed that troubled isle as England's "most formidable" agricultural rival (Ricardo 1951–73; 8: 369). Indeed, more than 7 percent of the wheat consumed in England in 1844 came from Ireland (Pollard 1978). The Irish agricultural potential was seen as virtually unlimited at that time (Hilton 1977, pp. 4, 11, 23, and 278).

The extraction of Irish foodstuffs as a counterbalance to the claims of Irish rent recipients was thought to be unconnected with Irish poverty. The fault, according to political economy, lay with the wretched peasantry itself. The people had to learn to desire more luxuries, which were to be purchased by means of the proceeds of wage labor (see Black 1960). Even worse, Senior told his students of 1847–1848: "Races which like the Celts, have neither docility nor intelligence must be governed by fear" (Senior 1926: i, p. 233).

In Ireland, classical political economy confronted a people not yet subdued by capital. The results were frustrating. Consider Adam Smith's letter to Lord Carlisle on Ireland:

> [Ireland] is ill provided with [coal and] wood; two articles essentially necessary to the progress of Great Manufactures. It wants order, police, and a regular administration of justice both to protect and restrain the inferior ranks of people, articles more essential to the progress of Industry than both coal and wood put together. [cited in Mossner and Ross 1977, p. 243]

Simple market solutions were not sufficient. Thus the Irish civilization was written off as barbarians, while barbaric measures were condoned in the name of civilization. Although Ricardo was far less extreme in his attitude toward Ireland than Senior, his call for population growth there shows how casually laissez faire ideology was cast aside when it ran up against barriers.

Ricardo changed his discussion of Ireland in later editions of his *Principles*. Instead, he inserted his oft-cited idea: "The friends of humanity cannot but wish that in all countries the labouring classes should have a taste for comforts and enjoyments" (Ricardo 1951–73; 1: 100). This version, which is often used as evidence of Ricardo's humanitarianism, was actually a cover for his objection that the wages of Irish workers should not be allowed to rise. Notice also that Ricardo's first-edition version contained all the essential elements of the classical theory of primitive accumulation.

Under conditions such as Ricardo saw in Ireland, workers chose leisure rather than wage labor. They did not want to exchange many hours of wage labor for a few hours' worth of consumer goods. Thus measures to eliminate indolence were of the utmost necessity, although Ricardo only specifically mentioned increasing a taste for luxury. If the workers could be harnessed to wage labor, "a vast additional value in . . . other commodities would be produced." Presumably only a portion of these would do to satisfy the newfound tastes of the Irish workers.

Ricardo understood who was to benefit from the more intensive work that he advocated. In a private letter to Malthus, he admitted that the workers might even be behaving rationally in preferring leisure to increased consumption:

> Happiness is the object to be desired, and we cannot be quite sure that provided he is equally well fed, a man might not be happier in the enjoyment of the luxury of idleness, than in the enjoyment of a neat cottage, and good clothes. And after all we do not know if these would fall to his share. *His labour might only increase the enjoyments of his employer.* [Ricardo 1951–73; 7: 184; emphasis added]

In his unpublished *Notes on Malthus*, Ricardo repeatedly dismissed Malthus's concern about the ease with which food can be obtained (see Ricardo 1951–73; 2: 334–35, 339–41, and 286–87; notes 223, 226, and 237); but there he made his case only on the formal grounds that the examples Malthus used were inapplicable to England, that has "a dense population, abounding in capital, skill, commerce, and manufacturing industry, and with tastes for every enjoyment that nature, art or science will procure"; however, Malthus did not have England in mind, but Ireland (see ibid., p. 344).

The identification of self-provisioning as the primary cause of the poverty of Ireland continued to be espoused by Ricardo's disciple, John Ramsay McCulloch. He informed a parliamentary committee on Ireland:

> I consider the combination of manufacturing and agricultural pursuits to be a proof of the barbarism of every country in which it exists. . . . I consider that the more labour is subdivided, the greater will be the quantity of produce obtained by each individual labourer. When you combine in the same family, the trades of manufacture and

farmer, neither the one nor the other can be well carried out. [McCulloch 1825a, p. 812]

McCulloch praised the Scottish restrictions on subletting (see Ross 1953, p. 245), which "has made the tenants more respectable by making farms, or tending to make them large; it has prevented all but people possessed of considerable capital, from taking farms in Scotland." McCulloch even alleged:

> [I]t has been extremely advantageous to the labouring class. By preventing the splitting of farms once joined together, it has tended to occasion cultivation by means of large farms, and . . . so that there has not been that facility of obtaining slips of land and the means of support which there had been in Ireland. [Ibid., p. 833]

McCulloch's parliamentary questioner pressed him on this point: "Do you think that the condition of the labouring class is better, in consequence of their not being able to obtain land?" McCulloch responded, "Certainly, that is my clear opinion." Although Ricardo was not as explicit as McCulloch, we might expect that he was just as concerned about the situation of the mass of Irish people. After all, Ricardo sat in Parliament as their representative. However, he had merely purchased his seat; not once did he set foot in his constituency of Portlington.

Nonetheless, Ricardo, the political economist, had a clear understanding of the nature of the Irish economy, which was substantially different from that of England. Ireland was distinguished by the vigor with which people resisted capital. By contrast, England appeared to have reached the point at which it could rely on "silent compulsion," which becomes effective only after the "advance of capitalist production develops a working class which by education, tradition and habit looks upon the requirements of that mode of production as self-evident natural laws" (Marx 1977, pp. 899–900).

Thomas Robert Malthus

Compared to Malthus Ricardo appeared to be sympathetic to the household economy. According to Malthus, to allow people the means to produce for their own needs was to generate a widespread pattern of indolence among the masses (Malthus 1820, pp. 381–82). Where food could be produced with little effort, he observed:

> We ought always to find a small portion of the population engaged in agriculture, and a large proportion administering to the other wants of society. . . . But in examining the state of unimproved countries what do we really see?—almost invariably, a much larger portion of

the whole people employed on the land than in those countries where the increase of population has occasioned the necessity of resorting to poor soils; and less time instead of more devoted to the production of conveniences and luxuries. [Malthus 1820, pp. 334, 380]

Like Ricardo, Malthus wished that the Irish would develop a greater preference for commodities such as "ribands, lace and velvets" relative to leisure (ibid., p. 314; see also Berkeley 1740, p. 423, and Hume 1752, for earlier variants on this theme, see Appleby 1976, pp. 505ff),[13] but this recommendation was not realistic.[14] Malthus complained that in a country such as Ireland, "where the necessary food is obtained with so little labour, it is perhaps impossible that the time not devoted to the production of food should create a proportionate quantity of wealth, without a decided taste for conveniences and wealth among the lower classes of society" (Malthus 1836, p. 348).

Malthus's attitude smacked of opportunism. The earliest edition of his *Essay* was meant to forestall any plans to ameliorate the workers' standard of living. Their lot, he believed, was hopeless in the long run. In 1798, when he wrote his *Essay on Population*, he explicitly stated that "The consumable commodities of silk, laces, trinkets are . . . the revenue only of the rich, and not of society in general" (Malthus 1798, p. 112).

The workers' only hope was a temporary increase in their consumptions of necessities. According to the *Essay*, the availability of food ultimately would result in population growth that would soon eat up the increase in necessities. The later revisions were intended to address other problems. Malthus was no longer arguing for the futility of charity for the victims of primitive accumulation; instead, he was developing the position that the poor share in prosperity of capitalism if they worked hard. By the third edition of the *Essay*, he was arguing, "The condition of the labouring . . . cannot be essentially improved by giving them a greater command over the means of subsistence" (cited in Gilbert 1980). In the fifth edition, he went even further, asserting that "the comforts of the lower classes do not depend solely upon food, nor even upon strict necessaries" (ibid.).

Malthus recognized that untrammeled growth could severely worsen the lot of the poor (see Gilbert 1980). Supply and demand were inadequate

---

[13] As Sismondi emphasized, however, luxuries become attractive only when they are bought with the labor of others (Sismondi, p. 106; see also p. 127 and Edmonds 1833, chap. 7).

[14] In the colonies, missionaries assisted capital by instructing the people in a proper devotion to commodities as well as to God (see Magabane 1979, p. 60). More recently, that responsibility has fallen on the shoulders of development advisers (see Moser 1966, p. 34).

guides for economic action. At some point workers would likely challenge the system. The government had to ensure a proper balance of agriculture and industry lest employment fall too low. To keep workers from challenging the system, Malthus counseled political economy to hold out the promise of a future of ribbons, lace, and trinkets.

In many respects, Malthus anticipated the sort of problems the Atlantic economies faced during the 1930s. His position won him the endearment of John Maynard Keynes, but it was totally inappropriate for Ireland, which he offered as a proper field for the application of his theory. To suggest that the Irish workers should concern themselves with luxuries when they were lacking the basic necessities was downright ridiculous.

Malthus did chide the Irish for having too few wants. In addition, he charged that they were also guilty of the further offense of "supplying [their wants] principally at home" (Malthus 1836, p. 349). He even went so far as to claim, echoing Steuart, that the basic problem in Ireland was production "with a view to support rather than sale" (Malthus to Ricardo, 17 August 1817 in Ricardo 1951–73; 7: 175). Malthus offered further insight into his attitude toward the Irish small-holders during a parliamentary examination by a member of the 1826–27 Committee on Emigration who asked him if it were not true that "if a thousand [Irish] labourers . . . were to die, the wealth of the country would not be diminished by their decrease?" Malthus answered affirmatively (cited in Inglis 1971, p. 233).

Since the working class seemed disinclined to exchange an excessive amount of labor time in return for commodities of relatively little value, Malthus was willing to allow for extraeconomic pressures on the poor. Although he did not elaborate on how he wished to accomplish his objective, he opposed the use of the potato in Ireland on the grounds that it allowed the poor to survive with less effort (Malthus 1820, pp. 344–45).

Malthus even expressed serious misgivings about the work of Count Rumford, whose soups could feed the poor for slightly more than one-quarter penny per day (Rumford 1795, p. 187). Rumford, whose scientific stature was considerably more solid than his political reputation, alleged that water was the major source of nutrients (ibid., p. 172). Although Malthus admitted that Rumford's soups might be "excellent inventions for the public institution," he hoped that they "should not be adopted as the general food of the common people" (Malthus 1826; 2: 232). Malthus's ostensible concern was that cheap food resulted in low wages, but it did not take him more than a page to get from Rumford's soups to the dreaded indolence that threatened to plague capital.

Malthus was also skeptical of Owen's plan. He asked Arthur Young: Pray can you tell me in what *small* work I can obtain the best information respecting spade husbandry which has been lately talked of. I should also like to know what you think of it, and whether you are not of the opinion, that independently of the object of employing Parish Poor, our wastes are not likely to be cultivated by saving labour on the land, rather than increasing it. The great obstacle to the cultivation of Wastes is surely that the produce does not pay the expense of procuring it; and that this difficulty it appears to me is only to be overcome by skill and prices—not mere labour. [letter of 21 November 1819, cited in James 1979, p. 325]

Malthus tended to prefer a smaller scale of agriculture on the grounds that more people would be elevated to the status of property owners (see e.g., Malthus 1976, p. 115; see also 1820, pp. 385–89). He appreciated the modest prosperity of the Scandinavian small-holders (Malthus 1966, p. 145), but he opposed holdings as small as were found in France (Malthus 1836, p. 378). He insisted that "all the great results in political economy, respecting wealth, depend upon *proportions* (ibid., p. 376). The proper dimensions of a farm were to be determined by the aggregate quantity of luxuries that the owners would demand.

Malthus proved himself to be an irreconcilable foe of all sorts of measures that might improve the ability of the poor to maintain themselves, including even the very means that could help them follow Malthus's own advice— birth control. He warned, "Prudential habits among the labouring classes of a country mainly depending upon manufactures and commerce might ruin it" (Malthus 1820, p. 221) "although the greatest resource of the labouring classes for their own happiness must be in those prudential habits" (ibid., p. 291, and Malthus 1836, p. 261).[15] This curious manner of analyzing class conflict is worth some future study. Only the purist J. B. Say seemed to notice the anomaly between this position and the famous principle of population (Say 1821, p. 30). In addition, Malthus was a stout advocate of the Corn Laws. Over and above his support for the Corn Laws, he opposed providing families with plots of land for cows or gardens; he even favored the tearing down of rural cottages (Cowherd 1977, pp. 7, 32, 50, and 162).

Malthus went much further than Ricardo on the subject of self-provisioning because of one major difference between their interpretation of English society. Each took a different mode of production for his frame of reference. Malthus was not convinced that enough workers had accepted wage labor.

---

[15] Say also opposed Malthus by means of the classical model of the household described in Chapter I. According to Say, since a celibate worker needs less to maintain a household, wages would be certain to fall (Say 1880, p. 333).

By contrast, Ricardo felt that England had already reached the point where household economy was no longer a serious problem for capital. The time had almost arrived to increase the relative surplus value through the importation of inexpensive grain. To obtain this end, Ricardo would resort to ideological argumentation that was contrary to the historical experience of capital; however, in Ireland, the question was not purely ideological. Irish household production was still an extremely strong force and capitalism proper still had to be fostered. Consequently, Ricardo stood alongside Malthus when the discussion turned to Ireland.

Robert Torrens

Malthus and Ricardo were not alone in wanting to fashion a suitable social division of labor. Colonel Robert Torrens felt that unemployment would more properly be managed through emigration, and he considered Owen's project in particular to be a serious threat to capitalist society. He denounced Owen's plan as "nothing more than a Spencian project in disguise" (Torrens 1817, cited in Robbins 1958, p. 149). This heresy had to be eliminated root and branch. Torrens complained, "Inasmuch as his plans extend to make villages consume within themselves whatever they produce, the division of labor, whether territorial or mechanical, will be superseded" (Torrens 1817, pp. 453–77). If Owen's scheme were put into effect, Torrens predicted that "the whole net revenue would be required to supply the merely animal wants of the people: that art, literature, and science, would be abandoned; a more than Gothic ignorance prevailed" (Torrens 1817, pp. 515–16). Even though Ricardo was a personal friend of Owen (Owen 1857), he approved of Torrens's position (Ricardo 1951–73; 8: 159).[16]

Torrens's close associate Edward Gibbon Wakefield went even further. If Owen's ideas were put into practice, "All the people would be . . . precisely like another" (Wakefield 1835; 1: 38).[17] Wakefield ridiculed Owen's vision of a voluntaristic division of labor in which one is found "now digging, then

---

[16] Thweat (1974) argues that McCulloch had a hand in this article; however, O'Brien and Darnell (1978) have made a powerful case for dismissing that contention.

[17] Wakefield's verdict that "a monotonous people are necessarily dull and ignorant" (Wakefield 1835; 1: 38) and Torrens's prediction of a "more than Gothic ignorance" find support in Marx's comment that a collection of self-sufficient households make up a society "much as potatoes in a sack form a sack of potatoes" (Marx 1852; 1: 478). Although Marx finds merit in Smith's charge that factory routine can dull the intelligence (see Marx 1977, p. 483), he considered that ultimately the scientific improvements in technology would call for a more sophisticated labor force (Marx 1974, p. 705).

trading, then mending a shoe" (Wakefield 1835; 1: 42).[18]

Political economy recoiled from Owen's plan for different reasons. Owen began with the intent of raising the demand for labor. Steuart had also earlier understood the social mechanics of spade husbandry. He fretted that to increase the number employed in self-sufficient farming would reduce the number available for the production of the surplus (Steuart 1767; 1: 175). Profits would thereby suffer. Such honesty was nowhere to be found in later classical political economy.

Torrens was a partial exception. Because he was Irish, Irish poverty was a preoccupation with him (Robbins 1958, p. 145). In addition, he was an officer in the marines, promoted to the rank of colonel as a reward for his gallantry in the defense of Anholt, an island in the Kattegat (Robbins 1958, p. 3). This background colored his economics.

Although the market could be counted upon to take care of certain matters, Torrens called upon the government to play an activist role in some crucial respects. Just as Steuart wanted farmers to rid the land of "superfluous mouths," Torrens wanted the nation to deposit its excess labor in the colonies. He also favored restrictions on the export of machinery.

In addition, Torrens was the most realistic theorist of imperialism among those who are usually recognized as major classical political economists. In his first work, *The Economists Refuted*, he wrote of the territorial division of labor (Torrens 1808, pp. 14–15, cited in Robbins 1958, p. 20). He emphasized that England's proper role was to trade finished products for the raw materials of the less developed countries. He informed his constituents:

> It is not to France—it is the countries comprising the Russian empire, to the two continents of America, to our colonial possessions, to India, and to China, that we must look for new and extending markets. The measure which should be adopted, in order to open these vast regions to our commerce, must, however, be the subjects of future communications. [Torrens 1833, p. 56]

Torrens warned that colonies would most likely suffer from their relationship with imperial England, at least in the short run. He wrote, "unless timely and energetic measures of precaution be adopted, Ireland, in advancing towards wealth and prosperity, must necessarily pass through a period of the most aggravated and intolerable distress" (Torrens 1828, pp. 39–42, cited in Robbins 1958, p. 151). Such realism was not often found in the annals of classical political economy. William Petty, knowing only an early sort of

---

[18] Compare Wakefield's comments with the vision expressed by the early Marx in a similar metaphor (see Marx and Engels 1846), pp. 35–36).

imperialism, never rose beyond the rank of cabin boy in the ship of state, whereas Robert Torrens spoke like a true colonel in the royal marines.

Nassau Senior and Primitive Accumulation in Ireland

The 1840s brought ample confirmation of Torrens's prediction of "aggravated and intolerable distress." Scrope and Mill both called for land reform as a means of invigorating the Irish economy, but they were in a distinct minority. For most, the catastrophe of the Irish potato famine was further evidence to carry on with the process of primitive accumulation. Only fully developed capitalism could save the Irish.

No one addressed this thesis more eloquently than Nassau William Senior, although he actually denied that the Irish were as poor as had been claimed. He deduced that since the Irish population had been growing, he had grounds to doubt "that the great majority of the inhabitants of Ireland are in the state of destitution which is popularly ascribed to them" (Senior 1832, p. 6).

In his *Conversations and Essays Relating to Ireland,* Senior collected information just as if he were organizing one of the many government reports he had prepared. Most informants were given the opportunity to read over Senior's transcriptions of their conversations. Just enough personal detail was retained to give an appearance of spontaneity to his carefully crafted work.

We have already met with Senior's opinion of the Irish race. Thus "ribands, lace and velvets" could do little to change the ways of the Irish people. An unnamed Englishman told him: "They are less industrious than the English, less cleanly, less decent, and less comfortable, but they do not feel the want of comfort, or decency, or cleanliness" (cited in Senior 1868; 1: 163).

Senior placed great hope in education. In his opinion, "the political economy of the poor" appeals to the uneducated because "though it is in the power of human institutions to make everyone poor, they cannot make everybody rich; . . . they can diffuse misery, but not happiness" (Senior 1871; 1: 150). In this same spirit, he longed to convince the Irish to abandon their antagonism to market relations. He visited schools, observed the classes, and even questioned the children about their knowledge of political economy:

> I repeated the question which I have proposed in other schools [see ibid.: ii, p. 125]—"What would be the consequence of every man's being able to do four times as much as he can now?"
>
> "To make all the working people," they said, "poor for there would be no demand for their work."
>
> "Would not," I said, "the things which they consumed be much more abundant?"

"Perhaps so," they said, "but they would have no money to buy them."

"Why so?"

"Because only rich people have enough now, and would employ one one-fourth of them."

This must be the obvious opinion, for I have always met with it.

The poor seem to be unaware of the indefinite variety and extent of men's wants. [Ibid., 2: 137]

Senior hoped that the Irish would reject their political economy of class conflict once Irish society as a whole changed. As evidence, he noted that the Irish became excellent workmen once they reached the United States (Senior 1928; 2: 348).

Senior and his friends were acutely aware of the dimensions of their project of remaking Irish society. Although the poor people in the countryside did not actually own the land that they worked, the reorganization of Ireland amounted to something very much akin to primitive accumulation. A revealing conversation between Senior and a Dr. G. is worth citing in detail in this respect. Dr. G. began by explaining the beneficial impact of the recent famine:

Before the famine, the tenant had no creditor except his landlord. He sold only to pay his rent, and he bought nothing; he depended on his potatoes, his pig, and (when he was prosperous) his cow. . . .

Though he had an abundance of leisure, he seldom sought to work for wages. Indeed, he worked little even for himself, as the state of his fences and his copious crops of weeks showed. . . . He no longer depends for everything on his land; he feels—what he never knew before—that a man may starve with his land, and may live without it. [Senior 1868; 2: 274]

Then Dr. G. offered a very concise description of the program of the classical theory of primitive accumulation:

"I believe," continued Dr. G., "that the struggle now going on in Ireland between cottiers and farmers, between agriculture on a large scale, takes place in almost every country that has been feudal, and is therefore in the hands of large proprietors—at a certain stage of its improvement.

When there is little capital, and therefore few manufactures, the bulk of the population are tillers of the ground. There are few cattle or sheep. Meat is little used. The best soils only are cultivated, and, by profuse labour, a large *gross* produce, though a small *surplus* produce, of grain is produced. "Much food," says Solomon, "is in the tillage of the poor: but there is that which is destroyed by want of judgement." As wealth increases, and with it the demand for cattle and sheep, landlords find it profitable to substitute pasture for arable, and large farms for small ones. There is more surplus produce, more rent, and less trouble.

The first result of every such change is, at the same time, to turn the small farmer and cottier into an agricultural labourer, and also much to diminish the demand for labour. The existing occupants of the land suffer in every way. They lose the freedom and the apparent security of their former state. They must obey a master, keep his hours, give up the frequent holiday of the wake and the fair, and work for wages which a sudden supply of labourers must render low. . . .

No friend to Ireland can wish the war to be prolonged—still less, that it should end by the victory of the tenants; for that would re-plunge Ireland into barbarism, worse than that of the last century. The sooner it is over—the sooner Ireland becomes a grazing country, with the comparatively thin population which a grazing country requires—the better for all classes. [Ibid., pp. 264–66]

In 1832, before the famine, Senior had addressed the question of Irish agriculture. He recognized that the Irish worker produced a surplus: "for every bushel that the Irish labourer consumes, he enables more than a bushel to be gathered" (Senior 1832, p. 48)—yet this inveterate advocate of the market saw greater profits resulting from a shift to wage labor. He recommended the "extension of farm, and the consequent conversion of cottiers into hired labourers . . . which may be assisted by Government, if money is advanced . . . to facilitate by emigration the consolidation of farms" (ibid., 1832, p. 20). This call for public funds to be spent to encourage larger farms is found in a work largely intended to warn the government of the dangers created by expending money to provide work for the impoverished Irish. Senior's response to Dr. G. was more circumspect. He restricted himself to restating the doctor's case in positive terms consistent both with the tenets of classical political economy as well as words of his informant:

The suffering of England . . . gradually and slowly wore away, as the surplus agricultural population was absorbed by the spread of manufactures, and the increase of towns.

The absorption of the surplus population of the Highlands of Scotland . . . was assisted by a large emigration, and in the case of Sutherlandshire—one of the largest and *most beneficial* clearing on record.

But in Ireland, there are scarcely any manufactures, except at Belfast.

The trades-unions have destroyed them, or prevented their existence everywhere. [Ibid., p. 266; emphasis added]

Senior's prescription for the ills of Ireland was fairly simple. He called for legislation to "enable the establishment of manufactures, by freeing the manufacturing population from the tyranny of the trades-unions" (ibid., p. 266). With these words the enormities of English policy took on the mantle of liberty: Crush unions in the name of freedom. Political economy, even in Ireland, maintained the posture of laissez faire.

Senior was far more sympathetic to Irish small producers when he was taking responsibility for his own views. In his *Edinburgh Review* article of 1844, republished in his *Journal*, he wrote:

> The Material evils are the want of Capital, and the want of small Proprietors. A people, indeed, ill-provided with capital cannot enjoy much division of labour. Its labour, therefore, cannot be productive, its manufactures must be few and rude; the bulk of its members must be agricultural. . . . A middle class is the creature of capital. But though without a middle class, and without the diffusion of moral and intellectual cultivation which a middle class produces, such a population, if it consists of proprietors, may be happy. . . .
>
> On the other hand, in a country possessing abundant capital, the absence of small proprietors of land, though attended by considerable political inconvenience and danger—inconvenience and danger, perhaps, outweighing its economical advantages—is not inconsistent with general comfort and prosperity; and perhaps is a condition necessary to the greatest productiveness of labour, and to the greatest accumulation of wealth. [Ibid., 2: 22ff]

Thus a study of Senior not only shows how classical political economists analyzed primitive accumulation; it also demonstrates the manner in which they attempted to avoid responsibility for what it wrote.

chapter 5

The Revisionist History of Professor Adam Smith

They were standing on a plank which had been laid across a tanning pit; the doctor, who was talking warmly on his favorite subject, the division of labor, forgetting the precarious ground on which he stood, plunged headlong into the nauseous pool. He was dragged out, stripped, and carried with blankets and conveyed home on a sedan chair.

Biographical sketch of Adam Smith,
The London Times, 6 August 1790

Adam Smith and James Steuart

The meaning of Adam Smith's *Wealth of Nations* can best be seen against the backdrop of the work of Sir James Steuart. The stylistic difference between these two writers is apparent at the outset. Smith's prose was a joy to read, whereas Steuart's was heavy and dense. Smith wrote of a familiar world. He began, "The annual labour of every nation is the fund which originally supplies it with all the necessaries and conveniences of life" (Smith 1937, p. lvii). Steuart's first words were "It is with great diffidence . . ." (Steuart 1767, vol. 1). He then went on to defend his project and apologize for his style. The defense carried little weight with the public, since the apology made the book no less easy to read. This difference was, no doubt, related to the nature of Steuart's book. As Schumpeter noted:

Steuart's work did not ride, like Smith's, on the wave of a single and

simple policy that was rapidly conquering public opinion. [O]ne cannot fail to be struck by the number of points that indicate more
originality and deeper thought than does the *Wealth of Nations*. . . . In
the theories of population, prices, money and taxation Steuart went
much below the smooth surface on which A. Smith happily sailed his
course. [Schumpeter 1954, p. 176]

Steuart was said to have been a persuasive speaker; indeed, Smith himself
acknowledged that he understood his rival's system better from their conversations than from reading Steuart's book (Rae 1895, p. 62; Chalmers 1805,
p. 378). By contrast, Smith's conversation was punctuated by frequent lapses
of memory, whereas his book displayed an elegance of style. In Steuart, we
see the grim face of primitive accumulation. By contrast, Smith appears to
be one of the most humanistic figures of classical political economy. Certainly, with the possible exception of John Stuart Mill, he was ostensibly more
considerate of the interests of labor than any other political economist.

Although Smith was rather coy about his intentions, *Wealth of Nations* was
a direct challenge to Steuart's authority. After the first rewriting of the
history of capital, he would use the resulting ideology to refute the sort of
administrative measures Steuart recommended. Both of these projects were
fused together in the *Wealth of Nations*. Smith never once mentioned the name
of Steuart in his book, although his heated denunciations of the mercantile
school were probably aimed, at least in part, at Steuart. For example, in his
advertisement to the fourth edition, Smith attacked all previous works on the
Bank of Amsterdam as "unintelligible" (Smith 1976, p. 9). His modern editors point out that Steuart's perceptive work on that subject could hardly be
liable to that charge (Smith 1976, p. 9n). They mention numerous other
instances where notice of Steuart's work would have been appropriate. Marx
judged Smith's omission of Steuart harshly in this regard:

Adam Smith records the results of Steuart's researchers as dead facts.
The Scottish proverb ["Mony mickles mark a muckle"] that if one has
gained a little it's often easy to gain much, but the difficulty is to gain
a little, has been applied by *Adam Smith* to intellectual wealth as well,
and with meticulous care he accordingly keeps the sources secret to
which he is indebted for the little and turns it into much. [Marx 1859,
pp. 167–68]

Smith's silence concerning Steuart could not be charged to ignorance. After
all, he attended the same Burgh School of Kircaldy, where Sir James had
earlier appropriately acted the king in a production of *Henry the Fourth* (Rae
1895, p. 5). By the time Smith wrote *Wealth of Nations*, Steuart was the most
eminent political economist of Scotland. Although Smith may not have

personally known Steuart until the latter's long period of exile had ended, in later years Smith and Steuart belonged to several of the same clubs (see Bell 1960).

In a private letter dated 3 September, 1772, he wrote to William Pultney: "I have the same opinion of Sir James Steuart's book that you have. Without mentioning it, I flatter myself that any fallacious principle in it will meet a clear and distinct confutation in mine" (Mossner and Ross 1977, pp. 163–64; Rae 1895, pp. 253–54).

This letter is doubly interesting since it also concerned Smith's attempt to win an appointment to an East India Company committee that was to travel to India to investigate administrative malpractices. Fortunately for Smith's reputation as a stalwart opponent of entrenched monopolies, although he was selected, the mission was never completed (Ambirijan 1977, pp. 2–3). Smith may well have been aware that the East India Company had already commissioned Steuart to analyze the state of the coinage in Bengal (see Steuart 1772). Smith's reference to the views he shared with Pultney on the "disorders of the coin of Bengal" (ibid., p. 164) suggest that the letter may have been intended to deprecate Steuart both as author and consultant.

The basic thesis of Smith's attempted refutation of Steuart was appealing: The interest of individuals might clash, but society as a whole, as well as the classes of which it is composed, have a common interest. Primitive accumulation, a term which Smith inadvertently helped to coin, was an unnecessary, if not nonexistent, element in economic development.

Among Smith's contemporaries, almost everyone believed that Scottish development would have to be administered. For example, Smith's patron, Lord Kames, was a leading member of the Board of Trustees for Fisheries Manufactures and Improvements in Scotland, set up to rescue the "Highlands from its archaic backwardness" (Rendall 1978, p. 11). Smith and Bentham appear to have been virtually alone in their opposition to a scheme of Steuart to create a fishing village along the Scottish coast (Viner 1965, pp. 92–93; Mossner and Ross 1977, p. 327; Rae 1895, p. 409; see also Steuart 1767; 2: 194).[1] At least, the industrious Jacob Viner could find no other indication of dissent (Viner 1965, p. 92). With Smith, that part of history concerning the means by which the reign of capital was reinforced by the state falls from view. The litany about the lethargic nature of labor comes to an end.[2] Instead, we are treated to a theory of the essential harmony between labor and capital. Therein lies the nature of his revision.

---

[1] Wallace was a forerunner of the proponents of this scheme (Wallace 1809, p. 159).
[2] With the significant exception of the worker who could afford to divide his time between farming and weaving (Smith 1937, p. 8).

Not surprisingly, *Wealth of Nations* was an enormous commercial success in England. Booksellers decorated their display windows with busts of the author (Viner 1965, pp. 39–40). Even Smith's first book, *The Theory of Moral Sentiments*, won the lavish praise of Edmund Burke, who wrote that "a dry abstract of the system would convey no juster idea of it, then the skeleton of a departed beauty would of her form and allure when she was alive" (Burke 1759, p. 488). Steuart's book suffered a far different fate. One month before his death, he wrote to a correspondent that his "opinions . . . have little weight, they have long been printed, little read and less considered" (cited in Skinner 1966, p. lv).

In spite of the enthusiastic reception Smith enjoyed, his success as an economic theorist was more limited. During the eighteenth-century parliamentary debates, "the number of citations of Smith's is minute compared with . . . other writers," such as John Locke, Sir William Petty, David Hume, Gregory King, Charles Davenant, Sir Josiah Child, Dean Josiah Tucker, and Arthur Young (Willis 1979, p. 510).

Here we must make a distinction between Smith's contributions to economic theory and his influence on economic administration. Smith was an important influence on tax policy, although his authority as a political economist was not generally recognized in Parliament until the early nineteenth century. As one student of Smith's parliamentary prestige wrote: "Even twenty-five years after the publication of the *Wealth of Nations*, the Houses of Parliament were largely indifferent to its tenets, suspicious of its truth, and uncertain of its applicability" (ibid., p. 544).

As we shall see, by 1830, political economy had openly embraced Wakefield's theories, which directly contradicted those of Smith (see Chapter 7 below). Indeed, except for a brief period when Smith's ideas flourished, political economy, reaching back from the theoretical prehistory of the mercantilist epoch to the triumph of the Wakefield school, was a continuous affirmation of the need for government action to sustain the interests of capital.

Smith's Project

Smith's theory of primitive accumulation has heretofore passed unnoticed. The reason is not hard to fathom. Adam Smith was a highly abstract writer who used his charming prose to disarm his readers. In fact, Smith, who is supposed to reveal so much about the nature of economic activity, had remarkably little to say about the most significant contemporary developments in English economic society.[3] This silence is most apparent in his discussion of the production of commodities. For example, we hear of pin factories instead of textile mills. Kindleberger (1976) attempts to explain this aspect of the *Wealth of Nations* by writing off the author as an "unworldly" professor. Indeed, Smith himself deprecated the story of pin manufacture as a "frivolous example" (Smith 1978, p. 343). Along the same lines, the usually perceptive Coats explains this lack of material on commodity production by labeling Smith as an "economist . . . the domestic period" (Coats 1962, p. 47).[4] Such terminology does nothing to resolve the paradox of Smith as a scientific economist. Nor should his omissions and oversights be accounted for by his lack of foresight, as Koebner (1959) argues. What could the Smith of Kindleberger, Coats, or Koebner teach us about the wealth of nations?

No, Adam Smith was far from the unworldly professors his commentators made him out to be. He won the close friendship of the wealthy merchants of Glasgow (Stewart 1811, p. 300). In fact, he owed his initial appointment as a professor, in part, to his close connections with the wealthy merchants of Glasgow (Scott 1934). Later in life, he became the intimate of some of the most powerful members of British society (Hartwell 1978, pp. 130–35). Nor should we be led to believe that these relationships were purely social. Even the Prime Minister of England is said to have declared himself to be a Smith's disciple (Rae 1895, p. 404).[5] Such people sought out his advice, and often with good reason.[6]

That the *Wealth of Nations* was apparently initially begun in response to a request from Townshend for material on "French finance, its administrative method, taxation and public borrowing" may be indicative of the value which was placed on such advice (Fay 1956, p. 151; see also Mossner and Ross 1977, pp. 328n, 378n, and Campbell and Ross 1981, p. 88; but see Viner 1965, p. 86). His appointment as a Commissioner of Customs may well have been a reward for this work (see Campbell and Ross 1981, p. 88). His experience as a commissioner later left its mark in the revised third edition of *Wealth of Nations* of 1784 (see Campbell and Mossner 1977, pp. 263–64, 266, and Mossner and Ross 1981, p. 88). Smith also drew upon his business friends,

---

3 Smith made some passing reference to modern industry (see Smith 1937, p. 263).

4 Seligman made an almost identical claim (Seligman 1910, p. xi).

5 Nonetheless, this illustrious disciple wished to set pauper children to work in workhouses to be known as "colleges of industry" (Pollard 1965, p. 192).

6 Stewart commended Smith's works as, with few exceptions, of greater practical utility "to businessmen and politicians than that of the physiocrats" (Stewart 1877, p. 306), although some later commentators believe that Smith's recommendations on colonial taxation were responsible for the import duties that sparked the American Revolution (Fay 1956, p. 116; Smith 1977, letter 302; and Winch 1978, chap. 7).

such as Alexander Cochrane, in preparing the original edition of his book (see Scott 1937, p. 81).

Why, then, would Adam Smith, now reputed to be the premier political economist of his time, be so frequently interpreted as one who was out of touch with his own age? In answering this question, a comparison with Steuart is once again instructive. Steuart was widely praised for his detailed information, but his basic message was swept aside. His grim advocacy of primitive accumulation was far too blunt. Smith's cheerful optimism, by contrast, was just what polite society wanted to read: Curb the government; unleash the forces of the market; and all will be well.

This vision presented by Smith could be achieved only by substantially violating the truth. Joan Thirsk's comments in this respect are worth citing in detail:

> He [Smith] was not concerned with the personal lives led by individuals and could achieve the superb clarity of his exposition by detaching his theory from any sensitive consideration of the human beings whose labors created the wealth of the nation. Yet at every turn their lives obtruded themselves, insisting on inserting question marks at the end of his confident expositions. For example, he had to explain inequalities in the wages of labour. [Thirsk 1978, p. 152]

The defect Thirsk points to is not the absence of fact or detail in general, but rather their omission when dealing with the delicate question of conflict between classes.

The contradictory nature of *Wealth of Nations,* which is at once full of detail and devoid of much of the most important phenomena of the time, is understandable when we recognize that this work consists of two different projects. On the one hand, Smith developed a handbook of practical administration of the sort that Townshend requested (see Mossner and Ross 1977, p. 328n). Here we find an abundance of factual material. On the other hand, Smith was the architect of a cleverly written revision of political economy and history in which the harsh reality of capitalist development was recast in as favorable a light as possible. In this project, Smith relied mostly on what his student Dugald Stewart termed "conjectural history" (Stewart 1855, p. 36; Stewart 1811, p. 450),[7] an approach that Stewart defended by claiming that "in want of direct evidence, we are under a necessity of supplying the place of fact by conjecture" (ibid., p. 449). The facts that

---

[7] William Robertson described the early period of Scottish history as "The region of pure fable and conjecture and ought to be totally neglected or abandoned to the industry and credulity of antiquaries" (Robertson 1781, p. 6).

Smith lacked were those needed to support his revision of political economy; for his theory of administration, he had a mass of information on which to rely. Smith's two works are not physically separated, but we can roughly isolate them. The book of practical administration should be read by starting at the end of *Wealth of Nations,* then working backward. The ideological work begins on page one and continues forward as it blends in with the book on political administration.

The intended lesson of the ideological work is that economic progress should be explained in terms of the voluntary actions of mutually consenting producers and consumers in the marketplace. In some respects, this message was a step forward.

Smith attempted to ground his work in a materialistic theory of society that could "explain the origin and something of the progress of government . . . not as some writers imagine from any consent or agreement, but from the natural progress which men make in society" (Smith 1978, p. 207; see also Meek 1977b). Smith himself considered his application of this theory to the economy to be original. Indeed, by 1749 he had already written:

> Little else is requisite to carry a State to the highest degree of opulence from the lowest barbarism, but peace, easy taxes and a tolerable administration of justice; all the rest being brought about by the natural course of things. All governments which thwart this natural course, which force things into another channel, or which endeavour to arrest the progress of society at a particular point are unnatural and to support themselves are obliged to be oppressive and tyrannical. [cited in Stewart 1811, p. 322]

He further obscured conflict between the rich and the poor by means of his psychological analysis of wealth. Consider how he dismissed the problem of poverty in *Theory of Moral Sentiments.* He speculated, "Avarice overrates the difference between poverty and riches" (Smith 1759, p. 149). He supposed that "the greater part of them [the misfortunes which people had suffered] have arisen from [people] not knowing when they were well, when it was proper for them to sit still and to be contented" (ibid., p. 150).

Smith counseled his readers to lead a life without luxury, even of the most modest sort:

> How many people ruin themselves by laying out money on trinkets of frivolous utility? . . .
> Power and riches appear then to be, what they are, enormous and operose machines contrived to produce a few trifling conveniences to the body, consisting of springs most nice and delicate, which must be kept in order with the most anxious attention and which in spite

of all our care are every moment to burst into pieces, and to crush in their ruins their unfortunate possessor. They are immense fabrics, which it requires the labour of a life to raise, which threaten every moment to overwhelm the person that dwells in them, and which while they stand, though they may save him from some of the smaller inconveniences, can protect him from none of the severer inclemencies, can protect him from summer shower not the winter storm, but leave him always as much, and sometimes more exposed than before, to anxiety, to fear and to sorrow, to diseases, to danger, and to death. [Ibid., pp. 180–83]

Yet, Smith seemed to approve of what he later referred to as the "natural effort of every individual to better his own condition" (Smith 1937, p. 508; see also pp. 324–25). Although he argued in *Wealth of Nations* that "this principle is so powerful . . . that it is alone, and without any assistance capable of carrying on the society of wealth and prosperity" (ibid.), he claimed not to value accumulation on account of its contribution to prosperity.

People were deceived in working toward material success. In *Theory of Moral Sentiments*, Smith wrote a chapter entitled "Of the Origin of Ambition, and of the Distinction of the Ranks," beginning with the notion that "we pursue riches and avoid poverty" only to avoid the humiliation of poverty, even though "[t]he wages of the meanest labourer [can] supply the necessities of nature" (Smith 1759, p. 50). According to Smith, the "meanest labourer" spends a "great part [of his wages] . . . upon conveniences, which may be regarded as superfluities, and that, upon extraordinary occasions, he can give something even to vanity and distinction" (ibid.). Yet the vain desire for ostentation served a noble purpose:

> And it is well that nature imposes upon us in this manner. It is this deception which rouses and keeps in continual motion the industry of mankind. It is this which first prompted them to cultivate the ground, to build houses, to found cities and commonwealths, and to invent and improve all the sciences and arts which enable and embellish human life; which have entirely changed the whole face of the globe, have turned rude forests into agreeable and fertile plains. [Smith 1759, p. 183

That the concluding words of the citation were identical to his translation of a passage from Rousseau's "Discours sur l'origine de l'inegalite" published in Smith's "Letter to the Editors of the *Edinburgh Review*" hints at the ideological nature of Smith's approach (see Smith 1755–1756, p. 250). There, he was disputing Rousseau's contention that the acquisition of private property caused inequality. In the *Theory of Moral Sentiments,* in the very same paragraph in which Smith repeated his words about changing rude forests, he wrote:

> They [the rich] are led by an invisible hand to make nearly the same distribution of the necessaries of life, which would have been made, had the earth been divided into equal portions among its inhabitants. [Ibid., p. 184]

Smith's discussion of the game laws offers an additional instance of his blurring of class conflict. Recall that he minimized the importance of game laws as a means of primitive accumulation. According to him:

> There can be no reason in equity for this. . . . The reason they give is that this prohibition is made to prevent the lower sort of people from spending their time on such unprofitable employment; but the real reason is the delight they take in hunting and the great inclination they have to screw all they can out of their hands [Smith 1978, p. 24]

In this citation, the conflict between labor and capital is hidden behind two layers of assertions. To begin with, the gentry are ostensibly concerned with an intense exploitation of the people. Smith is undoubtedly correct here, but his silence conveys the additional sense that capital is disinterested in matters of primitive accumulation. Then Smith went on to assert that the gentry's claim to an interest in economic success was spurious, arguing that their real concern was noneconomic. The gentry were merely interested in their love of hunting and of dominating their fellow human beings. Here, as in the rest of his work, the most pervasive of all human faults is held to be folly. Rational thought (read "capitalism") would seem capable of excluding exploitation and misery from the world. Smith's avuncular posture makes for charming reading, but it is hardly satisfactory either as history or political economy.

To understand Smith's purpose, a perusal of his early essay on the history of astronomy is rewarding (Smith 1790). He asserted that the mind becomes uncomfortable in the face of contradictory phenomena. Science began as an attempt to discover the underlying harmonies in order to "sooth[e] the imagination" (ibid., p. 46). Smith's science seems to have a similar origin.

For Smith, feudalism was a system of conflict and discord, whereas capitalism was a system of harmony. According to Smith: "[T]he nobility are the greatest opposers and oppressors of liberty that we can imagine. They hurt the liberty of the people even more than an absolute monarch" (1978, p. 264).

Even worse than the powers exercised by the nobility was the effect on the people being dependent on the lords:

> Nothing tends so much to corrupt and enervate and debase the mind

as dependency, and nothing gives such noble and generous notions of probity as freedom and independency. Commerce is one great preventive of this custom. The manufactures give the poorer sort better wages than any master can afford. [Ibid., 1978, p. 333]

Although this last comment refers to the state of servants, Smith's discussion of the same notion in *Wealth of Nations* extended to all the common "inhabitants of the country, who had before lived almost in a continual state of war with their neighbours, and of servile dependency upon their superiors" (Smith 1937, p. 385). Smith went so far as to assert here that the elimination of dependency was "by far the most important of all [the] effects" of commerce (ibid.), but he neglected to add that the work cited here was largely written while he was supported by the funds of a rich and powerful nobleman. Are any psychohistorians listening?

Smith's emphasis on the harmony of the marketplace was conceivable only after capital no longer had to rely as extensively on external compulsion to create wage labor.[8] With the establishment of an epoch in which "the silent compulsion of economic relations" was in effect (Marx 1977, p. 899), Smith could interpret both labor and capital as willing partners in a mutually rewarding transaction.

Certainly, Smith is as welcome to such illusions as were others of his day; however, we have the obligation to scrutinize his falsification of historical relation between labor and capital. Considering that he was engaged in producing a history of wage labor, we have a right to demand an answer from him to the question later explicitly posed by von Thunen: "How has the worker been able to pass from being the master of capital—as its creator—to being its slave?" (Dempsey 1960, p. 335; see also Marx 1977, fn. p. 772). In other words, Smith had to account for the forces that would induce self-sufficient households to exchange labor power for wages.

Smith might have taken the position that people who were impoverished

---

[8] On a political level, Smith's project was anticipated by Hobbes (see Macpherson 1962, p. 89); however, many decades passed after the publication of *Leviathan* before many people came to believe that labor could be employed without some means of coercion (see Wiles 1968 for some exceptions). Thus Coats dates 1760 as the point at which people first began to mention the possibility that the system could rely on high wages rather than external compulsion (Coats 1958, p. 35; and see Hobsbawm 1974). However, skilled English workmen were prohibited from emigrating until as late as 1815 (Marx 1977, p. 719). This restriction was considered to be a matter of prime importance to employers of skilled labor. Wedgewood even wished to authorize the postmaster to open letters of "suspected persons" (cited in McKendrick 1961, p. 47). So pervasive was this selective reliance on market forces that no one saw anything unusual in proposals such as Wedgewood's.

under precapitalist formations chose marginally higher earnings from wage labor. As we shall see later, Lenin did, but Smith did not. He obstinately attempted to prove that capitalism would naturally evolve within a community of independent households.

Unlike Steuart, who advocated extra economic measures to create "a free and perfect society which is a *general tacit contract, from which reciprocal and proportional services result universally between all those who compose it*" (Steuart 1767; 1: 109), Smith was obliged to indicate how a social division of labor would naturally evolve from market relations. As Bagehot charged, "Political Economy does not recognize that there is a vital distinction between the main mode in which capital grows in England now, and the mode in which countries grew at first (Bagehot 1880, p. 419). Smith used two different approaches to evade this challenge. First, he relied on abstract analysis of the division of labor. Second, he proposed the colonies of North America as an example of the harmonious relations between labor and capital (see Skinner 1976, p. 78).

Evidence from America

> The differences of circumstance between this and the old countries of Europe, furnish differences of fact whereon to reason, in questions of political economy, and will consequently produce sometimes a difference of result.
>
> 　　　　　　　　　　Thomas Jefferson, letter to J. B. Say, 1 February 1804

What did Smith claim to have seen in North America? He told his readers that in the Colonies of North America, where "[t]he plenty and cheapness of good land are such powerful causes of prosperity, . . . the very worst government is scarce capable of checking the efficiency of their operation" (Smith 1937, p. 537; see also 523, 538–539 and 592). Since land was relatively easy to obtain in the Colonies, Smith could explain how capital could develop in the absence of a thorough program of primitive accumulation. On a less abstract level, since the wages of labor were relatively higher in the Colonies, Smith wished to use the colonial evidence to demonstrate that economic development was compatible with high wages.

Smith's discussion of the labor markets in North America began at a crucial point in his analysis of wage labor. His theory of price led him to state, "These ordinary or average rates may be called the natural rates of wages . . . at the time and place in which they commonly prevail" (ibid., pp. 55–56). The use of the term "natural" in this context would usually convey the acceptance of the status quo. In Smith's case it did not.[9]

Smith was concerned about the distributive equity of the existing British wage system. More than any other classical political economist, Smith came out squarely for a comfortable standard of living for the worker:

> Is this improvement in the circumstances of the lower ranks of society to be regarded as an advantage or as an inconveniency to society? The answer seems at first sight abundantly plain. . . . But what improves the circumstances of the greater part can never be regarded as an inconveniency to the whole. No society can surely be flourishing and happy, of which the far greater part of the members are poor and miserable. It is but equity, besides, that they who feed, cloath and lodge the whole body of the people, should have such a share of the produce of their own labour as to be themselves tolerably well fed, cloathed and lodged. [Ibid., pp. 78–79]

Yes, Smith recognized that realities of the labor market would work to the disadvantage of wage earners:

> It is not . . . difficult to foresee which of the two parties must . . . have the advantage in the dispute [over wages], and force the other into a compliance with their terms. The masters, being fewer in number, can combine much more easily; and the law, besides, authorizes or at least does not prohibit their combinations, while it prohibits those of the workmen. [Smith 1937, p. 66]

He concluded a page-long discussion of the advantages enjoyed by employers of labor with the comment: "The workmen, accordingly, very seldom derive any advantage from the violence of those tumultuous combinations, which, partly from the interposition of the civil magistrate, partly from the superior steadiness of the masters, partly from necessity . . . generally end in nothing but the punishment of ruin of the ring-leaders" (ibid., p. 67). But what could workers expect from the free play of supply and demand?

---

[9] The prevailing use of the term "natural" implied a rather broad vision of society. According to Smith's friend, Hume:

> The word *natural* is commonly taken in so many senses and is of so loose a signification that it commonly seems vain to dispute whether justice be natural or not. If self-love, if benevolence be natural to man; if reason and forethought also be natural, then may not the same epithet be applied to justice, order, fidelity, property, society? . . . Natural may be opposed to what is *unusual, miraculous,* or *artificial.* [Hume 1751, pp. 275–76]

In the next paragraphs, Smith suggested that the lower bound to wages was set by the minimum level of subsistence (ibid., pp. 67–68). Although Smith elsewhere indicated that the wages of the English workmen were above this lowest possible rate (Smith 1974, p. 74), he did not interject that opinion at this point. Nor did he recall his earlier discussion of the "superfluities" of "the meanest labourer." Instead, he shifted his readers' attention to dependence of labor on "the funds which are destined for the payment of wages" (Smith 1937, p. 69).

What can we make of this welter of conflicting assertions? Were the capitalists supposed to be the benefactors of labor who add to the wages fund or the enemies of labor who use the organized power of the state to oppress the working class? Or was Smith merely groping for an answer to that question? Considering the relative strengths of the previous paragraphs, one gets the distinct feeling that the obvious answer did not sit well with his ideology.

His attempted escape from this dilemma was found in the Colonies. Thus Smith attempted to use the Colonies as evidence that a high level of wages was conducive to a thriving economy. Smith would seem to favor what Bentham later called "practical equality—the sort of equality . . . which has place in the Anglo-American United States: meaning always those in which slave holding has no place" (Bentham 1954, p. 442-43n).

According to him, the essential feature of America was:

> Every colonist gets more land than he can possibly cultivate. He has no rent and scarcely any taxes to pay. No landlord shares with him in his produce, and the share of the sovereign is commonly but a trifle. [Smith 1937, p. 532]

The conditions of the Colonies appeared to be ideal. Under these circumstances, Smith believed that profits were "commonly very great." Only one difficulty stood in the way: "[T]his great profit cannot be made without employing the labour of other people in clearing and cultivating the land" (ibid., p. 533). In light of the scarce supply of labor, the employer "does not, therefore, dispute about wages, but is willing to employ labour at any price" (ibid.).[10] Moreover, "the interest of the two superior orders obliges them to treat the inferior one with more generosity and humanity" (ibid., p. 532).

The "generosity and humanity" of the employers might seem to support Smith's contention about the harmony of classes; however, readers of his recently discovered *Lectures on Jurisprudence* can also learn that "the slaves in the

---

[10] The wages of skilled labor, however, were approximately equal in both Britain and North America (see Habbakuk 1967; Cole 1968, p. 64).

American colonies on the continent are treated with great humanity, and used in a very gentle manner" (Smith 1978, p. 183). Only where slave owners' wealth had progressed to the level of the lords of the sugar islands would slavery degenerate to a barbaric relation (ibid., pp. 183-87). Following this line of reasoning, we could just as well assert the essential harmony between slave and master.

  Although Smith alleged that in the Colonies, high wages and high profits were compatible (ibid., pp. 392-93), the colonial employers did not appreciate this environment of "generosity and humanity." Indeed, high wages were a constant lament in that part of the world (see, for example, Dorfman 1966; 1: pp. 44-47, 63-64, 117, and 214; Bogart 1927, pp. 67, 82).

  Not only was wage labor expensive, it was rather impermanent. Even in England, "in years of plenty, servants frequently leave their masters, and trust their subsistence to what they can make by their own industry" (Smith 1937, p. 83). In the North American colonies, the situation was more serious.

  The more wages capital paid out to its workers, the sooner they accumulated enough money to become independent farmers. Consequently, labor was relatively expensive to hire. Gabriel Thomas wrote from Pennsylvania in 1698:

> The chief reason why Wages of Servants of all sorts is much higher here than there, arises from the great Fertility and Produce of the Place; besides if these large stipends were refused them, they would quickly set up for themselves, for they can have Provision very cheap, and Land for a very small matter, or next to nothing in comparison of the Purchase of Land in England. [Thomas 1698, cited in Bidwell and Falconer 1941, p. 33]

By the nineteenth century, two or three years of farm labor were said to be sufficient to save enough to acquire the land and equipment with which to begin farming (see Williams 1809 and Ogg 1904 cited in Bidwell and Falconer 1941, pp. 118, 163).[11] In Smith's day, even less time may well have been required. In other words, we come up against the substitution of household labor for wage labor, the very opposite of the movement that initially Smith set out to explain. Smith, in fact, noted the ease with which workers could gain access to the land (Smith 1937, pp. 92, 575). At one point he even admitted that the conditions in North America were incompatible with wage labor:

---

[11] Danhoff's figures suggest that more time might have been required (Danhoff 1941).

In our North American colonies, where uncultivated land is still to be had for easy terms, no manufactures for distant sale have yet been established in any of their towns. When an artificer has acquired a little more stock than is necessary for carrying on his own business in supplying the neighbouring country, he does not in North America, attempt to establish it with manufacture for distant sale, but employs it in the purchase and improvement of uncultivated land. From artificer he becomes planter, and neither the large wages nor the easy subsistence which that country affords to artificers, can bribe him to work for other people than for himself. [Ibid., p. 359]

Smith's Theory of Economic Development

What conclusions did Smith draw from the fact that workers would not remain long in the employment of others? He speculated that the Colonies would adopt a position in the world market as a supplier of raw materials:

Agriculture is the proper business of all new colonies; a business which the cheapness of land renders more advantageous than any other. . . . In new colonies, agriculture either draws hands from other employments, or keeps them from going to any other employments. There are few hands to spare for the necessary, and none for the ornamental manufactures. The greater part of the manufactures of both kinds, they find it cheaper to purchase of other countries' than to make it themselves. [Smith 1937, p. 575]

Smith approved of this sort of arrangement:

If the society has not acquired sufficient capital to cultivate all its lands, and to manufacture in the completest manner the whole of its rude produce, there is even a considerable advantage that the rude produce should be exported by a foreign capital, in order that the whole stock of the society may be employed in more useful purposes. [Smith 1937, pp. 359-60]

He reasoned that "land is still so cheap, and consequently, labour so dear among them, that they can import from the mother country, almost all the more refined and more advanced manufactures cheaper than they could make them for themselves" (Smith 1937, p. 549). Smith believed the colonists to be fortunate in this respect. He noted that their "wealth is founded altogether in agriculture" (Smith 1937, p. 392; see also p. 347); consequently, their growth was more rapid than that of Europe. Moreover, he taught that agriculture was "of all the arts the most beneficial to society" (Smith 1763, p. 224).

At times, one could almost believe that the colonists were getting the better of the British, who were left to shoulder the burden of the carrying trade (ibid., pp. 347-48). As a result, the Americans were free to specialize in agricultural production. Consequently, the economy prospered, since the "capital employed in agriculture . . . not only puts into motion a greater quantity of productive labour than any equal capital employed in manufactures, but in proportion to the quantity of productive labour it employs" (ibid., p. 345).

Smith's optimistic prognosis for the Colonies flew in the face of his own theory of the division of labor. The first sentence of *Wealth of Nations* read: "The greatest improvement in the productive powers of labour . . . seem to be the effects of the division of labour" (Smith 1937, p. 3). Three pages later we are told, "The nature of agriculture . . . does not admit of so many subdivisions . . . as manufactures" (ibid., p. 6).

Yet Smith held that because of the heavy reliance on agriculture, the Colonies were enjoying an extremely rapid increase in prosperity (ibid., pp. 347, 392-93). He insisted that agriculture "adds much greater value to the annual produce of the land and labour of the country, to the real wealth and revenue of its inhabitants" (ibid.). Thus he concluded, "Of all the ways in which a capital can be employed, it is by far the most advantageous to the society" (ibid.).

This analysis comes in the same chapter in which he wrote:

> Were the Americans, either by combination or by any other sort of violence, to stop the importation of European manufactures, and by thus giving a monopoly to such of their own countrymen, . . . divert any considerable part of their capital into this employment, they would retard instead of accelerating the further increase in the value of their annual produce. [Smith 1937, p. 347]

Given the advantages of agriculture, we might expect Smith to have supported protection for agriculture in England. He did not. He predicted that "[e]ven the free importation of foreign corn could very little affect the interest of the farmer of Great Britain" (ibid., p. 428).

Piecing together Smith's remarks suggests a pattern consistent with the thesis that he favored a system in which the Colonies were to produce raw materials for the mother country to work up into finished products. Would specialization in agriculture actually lead to prosperity in the Colonies? Some years later de Tocqueville noted:

> Agriculture is perhaps, of all the useful arts, the one which improves most slowly in democratic nations. . . . To cultivate the ground prom-

ises an almost certain reward . . . but a slow one.[12] In that way you only grow rich by little and with toil. Agriculture only suits the wealthy, who already have a great superfluity, or the poor, who only want to live. . . . [T]he great fortunes . . . are almost always of commercial origin. [de Tocqueville 1846, pp. 551-53]

Smith, too, understood that agriculture was not the quickest path to personal affluence:

> We see every day the most splendid fortunes that have been acquired in the course by trade and manufactures, frequently from a very small capital, sometimes with no capital. A single instance of such a fortune acquired by agriculture in the same time, and from such a capital, has not, perhaps occurred in Europe during the course of the present century. [Smith 1937, p. 355]

He explained the disadvantages of agricultural investments in Europe in terms of the prevailing policies there (ibid., p. 355). No such disadvantage need exist in the Colonies. In fact, just before a discussion about the role of the Colonies in the international division of labor, Smith went to some lengths to discuss the "beauty," "tranquility," and "charm" of a rural lifestyle (ibid., p. 358). After noting that "man . . . seems . . . to retain a predilection for this primitive employment," Smith's next paragraph abruptly begins with the idea that a social division of labor that includes industry is required for an efficient agriculture (ibid., p. 358). One might be led to believe that the humanitarian British were about to sacrifice their idyllic existence so that the fortunate colonists might be allowed to live in harmony with nature.

Smith's theory did have other flaws so far as the colonists were concerned. So long as the Colonies adhered to Smith's recommendations, their military capacity would be limited, since the financing of warfare through the export of raw materials is always inconvenient (Smith 1937, pp. 412-13 and 1978, pp. 196-97). Thus the Colonies would remain a de facto appendage to England. Under this arrangement, England would prosper, since "a small quantity of manufactured produce purchases a great quantity or rude produce . . . while . . . a country without trade and manufactures is generally obliged to purchase, at the expense of a great part of its rude produce, a very small part of the manufactured produce of other countries" (Smith 1937, p. 642). Smith linked this very same idea with the benefits which foreign markets

---

[12] The same phenomenon struck observers of nineteenth-century Japan (see Smith 1966, p. 66).

bring for the development of economies of scale in manufacturing (Smith 1937, pp. 644-45).

The weakness of Smith's theory of development is apparent to many of us. It should have been obvious to Smith himself. He should have benefited from his observations of Scotland, which remained a supplier of raw materials even in the absence of mercantile prohibitions of native industry such as those which crippled Ireland. More than fifty years after Defoe first criticized Scotland's position as a mere supplier of raw materials (Defoe 1724-26, pp. 634-37), Anderson found it necessary to repeat the same idea (Anderson 1777, pp. 395-97). Each produced an almost identical list of imports. Other than some textiles, Scotland was said to export no manufactured goods to England. Much of its imports were manufactured. Anderson complained that the situation in Scotland was, if anything, a more extreme dependence than that found in the United States. "[A]n equal number of the inhabitants of North America, who hardly take any other articles from England but cloathing and hardwares, cannot consume more English manufactures than an equal number of the Scots do" (ibid., p. 397).

Smith, however, did not see dependence in the Scottish economy. Instead, he focused on its backwardness, which made people less dependent on purchased commodities, such as the farmer who doubled as "butcher, baker and brewer." Nonetheless, such independence and self-sufficiency are a common characteristic of peripheral lands. Smith recognized no structural reason for the backwardness he saw in Scotland. Improved roads would seem to be sufficient to modernize an area (Smith 1937, pp. 17-18).

No, Smith the theorist of economic administration was not nearly the doctrinaire free trader that he is generally thought to be. He warned that "freedom of trade should be restored only by slow gradations" (Smith 1759, p. 438; see also Smith 1937, p. 435-38). In Britain, Smith was in favor of using various devices to encourage industry. Although he recognized that some duties were justified to counterbalance taxes levied on domestic producers (Smith 1937, pp. 431-32), Smith favored duty-free importation of raw materials as an encouragement to industry. In the next paragraph, he criticized the low duty on linen yarn on the grounds that the work of spinners made up four-fifths of the labor used in the production of sail-cloth (ibid., p. 608). He did not make the case, as he might have, that spinning might have helped such people carry on their agricultural pursuits. Instead, he relied on a mercantilistic allusion to the creation of employment. Similar reasoning led to his recommendation of duties on the export of wool (ibid., p. 653).

In financial matters, Smith also called for the prohibition of the issue of small denominations of bank notes (Smith 1937, pp. 307, 313). Recall that Smith earned a strong rebuke from Bentham (1787 and 1790) for his acceptance of laws to prohibit usury (Smith 1937, p. 339).

Smith's prescription for administration was so much at odds with his ideology that he claimed, "The great object of political economy of any country is to increase the riches and power of that country" (ibid., p. 352). The postulate is found in the very same chapter of *Wealth of Nations* where Smith recommended agricultural pursuits to the colonists.

In summary, Smith took a pragmatic approach to laissez faire policies. In spite of his philosophical ruminations about the psychology of wealth and accumulation, Smith was an advocate of economic *Realpolitik*.[13] With respect to his work on international trade and development, Smith's interest lay as much with the nations of wealth as the wealth of nations. We might well credit Adam Smith, the teacher of economic administrators, with being the first theorist of neoimperialism.[14]

The American Reception of Smithian Economics

All seemed to know Sir James Steuart. Adam Smith's *An Inquiry into the Nature and Causes of the Wealth of Nations* would often be cited along with Steuart, but always within the framework of that variant of mercantilism to which the author adhered.

> Joseph Dorfman, *The Economic Mind in American Civilization, 1606–1865*, vol. 1, p. 242

Steuart's work was never very popular in England, a nation where capital had risen to ascendancy. The household economy was becoming not so much a competitor of capital, but rather a useful complement. By contrast, his book was popular where capital had not matured. The Irish, French, and German editions fared rather well (Sen 1957, p. 13). Steuart's work was also popular in the Colonies.

Let us now review the reception of Smithian theory in North America, a part of the earth where independent farmers made up the majority of the nonslave workers. After all, Smith himself had time and time again held out the market-oriented economy of the northern Colonies as an example for the still partially mercantile English economy to follow. We might reason that, since Smith's theory was meant to explain conditions in these colonies, it would be embraced by the people who resided there; however, the support for this line of reasoning is scanty.

---

13 T. Perronet Thompson, before departing to Africa as a colonial governor, wrote to his fiancee, Miss Barker, "I am beginning my course of study for the time being of Adam Smith on the *Wealth of Nations*, as fitting a subject I guess for the Sierra Leone as can be devised" (Thompson 1808, p. 33).

14 Dean Tucker could also lay claim to this distinction (see Schuyler 1931, pp. 35–36).

Indeed, much of Smith's perspective had been anticipated by his illustrious namesake, Captain John Smith, a century and a half before the appearance of *Wealth of Nations*. The earlier Smith wrote of New England:

> And here are no hard landlords to racke vs with their many disputations to Ivstice. . . . [H]ere every man may be master and owner of his owne labour; or the greatest part in a small time. If hee have nothing but his hands he may set vp trade; and by industrie quickly grow rich. [Smith 1616, pp. 195-96]

The reality of the Colonies was not as simple as Captain Smith suggested. For example, Governor Pownall of Virginia provided Smith with an insightful critique of *Wealth of Nations* (Pownall 1766). Pownall understood that the object of economics was to analyze *"those laws of motion*[15] . . . which are the source of, and give direction to, the labour of man in the individual; which form that reciprocation of wants and intercommunion of mutual supply that becomes *the creating cause of community"* (Pownall 1766, p. 337). The parallel with Steuart is striking, although Pownall gave no indication of familiarity with his work. As was mentioned already, Pownall rejected Smith's reliance on speculative anthropology.

Pownall also recognized the relationship between the social division of labor and the *"division of objects,"* i.e., property (ibid., p. 343). Finally, he emphasized the advantages of using administrative means to speed up the creation of markets and the accumulation of capital (ibid., p. 371). Pownall, however, was an administrator. Consequently, he might have been instinctively more attuned to the doctrines of Steuart than those of Smith.

What was the attitude of those who supported the revolution against the mercantile interests of England? Should not they be likely disciples of Adam Smith? Jefferson praised *Wealth of Nations* as "the best book extant" (Jefferson 1950-; 8: 111), although by 1817 he felt that Say's presentation was superior (Jefferson 1817). Madison recommended to Jefferson that Congress purchase the works of both Steuart and Smith (Madison 1962-; 6: 86). In John Adams's opinion, "the pith and marrow of science were contained in . . . the great works of Sir James Stuart *[sic]*, and of Adam Smith" (Adams 1819, pp. 384-85).

This weak testimony to the influence of Smith, cited above, must be taken with a grain of salt. After all, Adams was not a very accomplished student of political economy. In the same letter in which he recommended the works

---

[15] Compare with Marx (1977, p. 92); however, the use of this expression was probably widespread. For example, Fourier also claimed to have revealed the "laws of social motion" (see Ainikin 1975, p. 353).

of Steuart and Smith, he confessed himself unable to understand the physiocratic school. Jefferson predicted that Ricardo's "muddy reasoning . . . could not stand the test of time" (cited in Spengler 1968, p. 7). William Appleman Williams judges Madison to have been greatly affected by Sir James Steuart (Williams 1966, p. 145). Madison himself lamented "the present anarchy of our commerce" (Madison 1962-; 8: 502). To remedy the situation, he relied upon the authority of Steuart's "anti-quantity theory of money" as a means of improving the organization of economic activity (Dorfman 1966; 1: 221).

Eventually, Smith's ideas did win wide circulation, especially as a result of the 1821 translation of Say's *Treatise*, which was the first consciously composed textbook in economic theory (see Spiegel 1960, p. 65; see also James 1965).[16] List, for example, in a speech at the dinner given in his honor by the Pennsylvania Society for the Promotion of Manufacturers in 1827, expressed regret that he found Say's book "in the hands of every pupil" (cited in O'Connor 1944, p. 34). One would thus expect Smith to have exercised a wide influence in the United States, but the schools and colleges were run by the churches. Their economic teaching was notoriously out of touch with the real business world (see O'Connor 1944).

Symbolically perhaps, Steuart was reprinted in the Colonies by 1771; the first American edition of *Wealth of Nations* did not appear until 1789 (see ibid., p. 22). Of all the founding fathers, Hamilton was most inclined to political economy. Scholars have noted parallelism between the work of Hamilton and the *Wealth of Nations* (Gourne 1894; Mitchell 1962; 2: 144, 146, and 149; and the editorial notes in Hamilton 1961; 10: 1-240). Indeed, William Grampp even suggests that a reading of *Wealth of Nations* was sufficient to wean Hamilton of his mercantilist notions (Grampp 1965, pp. 134–36). Nutter goes so far as to credit Smith with bringing Benjamin Franklin into the liberal fold (Nutter 1976). A more accurate verdict on the perceived merits of Smith came from Fisher Ames, who remarked in 1789: "The principles of the [*Wealth of Nations*] are excellent, but the application of them to America requires caution" (Ames 1854 1: 49, cited in Nutter 1976, p. 16).

Hamilton's ideas were close to those of Steuart. He approved of Steuart's popular monetary theories because they would "cement more closely the union of states" (Hamilton 1961-; 7 70).[17] The same metaphor can be found

---

16 "We are, however, not yet in possession of an established textbook on the science of political economy, . . . a work which . . . results are so complete and well arranged as to afford each other mutual support, and that may everywhere, and at all times, be studied with advantage" (Say 1880, p. xlx).

17 Debt and the army were also praised as cement for the union (Hamilton 1961-; 2: 635, 402; see also 3: 429).

in Steuart, where statesmen are called upon to "cement" their society (Steuart 1767; 2: 191).

Steuart's influence is readily apparent in Hamilton's *Report on the Establishment of a Mint*, which drew heavily on the work of his master (Hamilton 1961-; 10: 462). Although Steuart was not explicitly acknowledged, an early draft did refer to him as "an English writer of reputation who appears to have investigated the point with great accuracy and care and who accompanies his calculations with their data which are confirmed by other authority" (ibid., p. 482). The actual role of Smith in the development of Hamilton's thought is suggested by one source, who noted that Hamilton had actually prepared a critique of *Wealth of Nations* during his term in the Continental Congress (ibid., p. i, and Hamilton 1879, 2: 514). In his most systematic study of the limits of the market, Hamilton lashed out at those "who maintain that trade will regulate itself" (Hamilton 1961-; 3: 76; see also ibid., 15: p. 467). He continued:

> Such persons assume that there is no need of a common directing power. This is one of those wildly speculative paradoxes, which have grown into credit among us, contrary to the practice and sense of the most enlightened nations (ibid.).

Hamilton's most noteworthy contribution to economic theory proper was his *Report on the Subject of Manufacturers* (Hamilton 1961-; 10: 1-340). In spite of the frequent appropriations of observations from Smith, the intent of the document was decidedly unsmithian (ibid., p. 7; see also Cooke 1967, p. 81). Hamilton wrote of the division of labor, but his division of labor was Steuart's, not Smith's. He began with the assertion:

> It has just been observed, that there is scarcely anything of greater moment in the economy of a nation, than the proper division of labour. The separation of occupations causes each to be carried to a much greater perfection, than it could possibly acquire, if they were blended. [Hamilton 1791, p. 249]

To create an appropriate social division of labor, Hamilton called for the "separation of the occupation of the cultivator, from that of the Artificer" (Hamilton 1961; 10: 251) by "diverting a part of its population from Tillage to Manufactures . . . leaving the farmer free to pursue exclusively the cultivation of his land and enabling him to procure with its products the manufactured supplies requisite either to his wants or to his enjoyments" (Hamilton 1961; 10: 216, 261-62). He rejected "the proposition, that Industry, if left to itself will naturally find its way to the most useful and profitable employment: whence it is inferred that manufacturers without the aid of government will grow up as soon and as fast, as the natural state of things and the interest of the community may require" (ibid., p. 266). Steuart could not have said it better.

The Conjectural History of the Social Division of Labor

> For why should he that is at libertie make himself bond?
> Sith then we are free borne,
> Let us all servile base subjection scorne.
> Spenser, "*Complaints. Mother Hubbard's Tale*, p. 130

Adam Smith was wrong to look for practical confirmation of his theories in the North American colonies. As we shall see later, he would have done better to have investigated the impoverished countryside of lands like Russia. Instead, Smith, the ideologist, attempted to produce a theoretical proof of his proposition that capitalism had no need of governmental action to promote the creation of a more refined social division of labor. He pictured the division of labor as unfolding naturally within the bosom of the country-side.

Smith's theory of the evolution of the division of labor served an important purpose in his work. His teacher, Frances Hutcheson, took every possible opportunity to oppose the works of Bernard Mandeville. In one of Smith's earliest works, he took both Mandeville and J.-J. Rousseau to task for "suppos[ing] that there is in man no powerful instinct which necessarily determines him to seek society for its own sake.

Smith returned to his theory of the harmonious evolution of human society in his later works. He traced the social division of labor back into the dark recesses of prehistory. Indeed, a social division of labor may be seen in pre-agricultural societies. Harmonious cooperation can even be found among the flora and fauna (Engels 1954, pp. 402-405; see also Wynne Edwards 1962); however, to analyze the social division of labor as a natural history is to sacrifice all hopes of understanding the mechanism which governs its evolution in human society.

At first, Smith fell somewhere between the world of natural science and the world of political economy. He wrote:

> The compleat division of labour . . . is posterior to the invention of agriculture . . . . The smith, . . . the carpenter, the weaver and the tailor soon find it in their interest not to trouble themselves with cultivating the land.[18] [Smith 1978, p. 584]

---

[18] This assertion contradicts his analysis of the relationship between stock and the social division of labor made earlier.

Later he added that "without the assistance of some artificers, indeed, the cultivation of the land cannot be carried on but with great inconvenience and continual interruption" (Smith 1937, p. 358). These artificers eventually settled down into towns or villages that evolved a relatively well-developed division of labor.[19]

Smith's observation about the "invention of agriculture" does not refer to the technological innovations that modern anthropologists describe by those words; the "invention of agriculture" and the "compleat division of labour" would seem to be synonymous. Both expressions seem to mean nothing more than a pattern of specialization whereby some people farm and others work as carpenters, weavers, and tailors. The posteriority of one to another would seem to be either wrong or ridiculous.

Both of Smith's statements about the social division of labor suggest that its evolution was determined by the extent of scientific knowledge. In reality, a relatively primitive social division could persist even though a society might be in possession of the understanding required for a more complex arrangement. For example, Smith noted that in "the Highlands of Scotland, every farmer must be a butcher, baker and brewer for his own family" (Smith 1937, p. 17; see also Marx 1977, p. 616n, citing Dugald Stewart), although the technologies of "the smith, the carpenter and the tailor" had been available for millenia. Much the same was true of the Colonies in which Smith placed his hopes (see Bidwell and Falconer 1941, pp. 126-31, 162-63; see also Peffer 1891, cited in Luxemburg 1968, pp. 396-98). In fact, the farmers' self-reliance was at the heart of Smithian development theory, according to which nations with limited capital are said to specialize profitably in agriculture (see, for example, Smith 1937, p. 345).

Worse still, Smith's utterances about the social division of labor point us away from what should have actually been his concern. As a scientific economist, Smith was obligated to delve into peculiar features of the society in question. By implying that (1) the contemporary social division of labor was the result of mutually advantageous adjustments and (2) that this process is a continuation of social behavior that stretches back into prehistoric time, Smith presented the misleading inference that the creation of the social division of labor was a natural process, devoid of conflict. We are left with

---

[19] Towns, in contrast, were founded as artificial units that were granted special privileges (see Merrington 1976, pp. 180-82). Later, however, capital shifted much of its activity to places such as Leeds, Birmingham, Manchester, where it could be less encumbered by traditional labor regulations of workers to pass through apprenticeships (Ashton 1972, pp. 15-16 and 94). In the northern colonies of North America, however, towns did seem to develop much in the way that Smith envisioned them to evolve (see Bidwell 1916, pp. 256-62).

his fable about hunters and artificers of bows and arrows specializing according to their particular skills.

Clearer thinkers such as Marx and Wakefield were in agreement that the origins of the differentiation among employments should more properly be sought in slavery rather than purely technical explanations (Marx 1977, p. 335). One can even find such a suggestion in Smith's own work (see Smith 1978, p. 196). True, market forces could eventually lead to a more elaborate social division of labor. A decline in self-sufficiency could create a home market for mass-consumption goods; however, such a home market begins from a very small base and could not reach a substantial size overnight.

The mercantile school, in particular, did not care to wait for the maturation of a home market. The mercantilists wanted a more immediate response.[20] They preferred to tap the riches of world markets as soon as possible. To this end, they were willing to launch an immediate attack on the self-sufficient household as a first step in stimulating the production of commodities for export (Marx 1967; 3: 785). Thus for Steuart, trade first begins with government support of luxury exports. Gradually, inland commerce takes on more importance (Steuart 1767; 1: 347-49).

Smith, by contrast, saw the acceleration of domestic exchanges as a consequence of the expansion of internal markets. He associated this tendency with "natural" progress as opposed to the contrived commerce that Steuart interpreted as the motor force (Smith 1937, p. 360). As a result, Smith preferred to wait for the household economy to atrophy as the market withdrew economic energies away from the traditional activities of the household. Smith left this analysis vague because he presumed the institution of wage labor to be in existence prior to the initiation of the process of development. Consequently, he never faced the issue of the change in the mode of production as the self-sufficient household gave way to wage labor. The difference between the Smithian and the mercantile path was substantial:

> [T]he characteristic feature of the interested merchants and manufacturers of that period, which is in keeping with the stage of capitalist development represented by them, is that the transformation of feudal

---

[20] Luxemburg, discussing the course of the transformation of colonial expansion noted:

> If capital were here to rely on the process of slow internal disintegration, the process might take centuries. To wait patiently until the most important means of production could be alienated by trading . . . [would be] tantamount to renouncing the production forces of these territories altogether. [Luxemburg 1968, p. 370]

agricultural societies into industrial ones and the corresponding industrial struggle of nations on the world-market depends on an accelerated development of capital, which is not to be arrived at along the so-called natural path, but rather by means of coercive measures. *It makes a tremendous difference whether national capital is gradually and slowly transformed into industrial capital, or whether this development is accelerated by means of a tax which they impose through protective duties mainly upon landowners, middle and small peasants, and handicraftsmen, by way of accelerated expropriation of the independent direct producers, and through the violently accelerated accumulation and concentration of capital, in short by means of accelerated establishment of conditions of capitalist production. It simultaneously makes an enormous difference in the capitalist and industrial exploitation of the natural national productive power.* [Marx 1967; 3: 785; emphasis added]

Smith commended his own policies because he argued that they would lead to rapid development. He weakened his own case because of his insistence of the role of "stock" in promoting the social division of labor. Even though he could argue that the market would lead to a vigorous pace of capital accumulation, stock would be largely confined to agriculture.

Recall that Smith had taught that "[t]he nature of agriculture . . . does not admit of so many subdivisions of labour, nor of so complete a separation of one business from another, as manufactures" (Smith 1937, p. 6). Consequently, the effect of the accumulation process would be limited; yet Smith insisted that capitalism was perfectly capable of developing out of the local initiative and enterprise of the countryside. He believed that such a process would proceed rapidly even in the absence of government intervention. Of course, Smith never went so far as to imply that capitalism could develop independently of towns. He merely argued that the interests of town and country were parallel: "The inhabitants of the town and the country are mutually the servants of one another" (ibid., pp. 358-59; see also pp. 128, 384-86, and 649-50). (One might expect Smith to have added a similar observation concerning the international center and periphery.) In spite of its failures and inconsistencies, Smithian ideology eventually won widespread acclaim. Before Adam Smith's *Wealth of Nations*, Arthur Young reflected the prevailing attitude when he characterized "trade and manufactures of . . . sickly and difficult growth; if you do not give them active encouragement they presently die" (Young 1774, p. 298, cited in Deane 1957, p. 88; see also Young 1794, p. 436). By the turn of the century, most of the writers on political economy had fallen in line with Smithian dogma (see Deane 1957, p. 88).

The Practical Rejection of Smith's Theory

Even though they proclaimed their adherence to their master's theory, Adam Smith's professed disciples went to elaborate lengths to support the manipulation of the institutions of society so as to foster the growth of markets and the elimination of remnants of the preexisting mode of production (see Samuels 1966, pp. 22-23; see also Samuels 1973 and Thompson 1963, p. 82). Perhaps nowhere do we see this contradictory role more clearly than in the elaborate projects of Jeremy Bentham. We just have to think back to his panopticon (see Foucault 1979, pt. 3).

The practical men of affairs in the Colonies were not willing to stake their future on the market. They relied instead upon controls. For example, the Massachussets Bay Company had earlier attempted to enforce wage ceilings (Bailyn 1955, p. 32) and restricted access to the land. The English Board of Trade and Plantation noted in 1732 that "the height of wages and the high price of labour in general rendered it impracticable for people there to manufacture their linen at less than twenty percent more than the rate in England" (cited in Bogart 1927, p. 61).

More important, capital understood that great profits were to be made as a result of unfree labor. Great American fortunes were made on the triangular trade that hinged on the sale of slaves. After the slaves reached their final destination, they continued to provide a market for American goods. In 1766, Pennsylvania was able to import 500,000 pounds worth of British goods while exporting only 40,000 back to Britain. Benjamin Franklin told Parliament that the balance was made good through exports to the West Indies (Franklin 1959-; 13: 133). Even where profits were based on the employment of labor in the Colonies, the workers were mostly in a state of bondage, either as slaves or as indentured servants (Herrick 1926 and Abbot Smith 1927, chap. 2). Moreover, much of the profits earned in the northern states were derived from the surplus originating on the plantations (North 1966, esp. pp. 6, 68, 105).

Some authors have suggested that this so-called "cotton-thesis" is too strong (see Rattner et al. 1979, pp. 223-26). Others have concentrated their attacks on particular links in the mechanism whereby slavery imparted growth to areas outside the South. For example, an attempt has been made to explain away the prosperity that northern and western farmers owed to southern food deficits, since much of the produce arriving in the South was destined for New Orleans and other large cities (see Lee and Passell 1979, pp. 146-51). This effort fails on several counts. First, such cities were also part of the cotton system. Second, one might also take into consideration the food sent to northern workers who manufactured goods for the South.

Northern capitalists profited from a host of other activities such as sales, financial services and shipping. Almost all the wealthy families of the Northeast owed their fortunes to such lines of business (see Pessen 1973, chap. 4). Finally, the farmers were but a single connection in a complex set of linkages. Even if slavery had not been the major source of growth, we are all familiar with the manner in which a relatively small acceleration in the growth rate can lead to a major transformation of society.

Cliffe Leslie has offered us an ironic commentary on the dependence of slavery on the demands of "free enterprise." Although he intended a very different lesson, his ambiguous words can be read as a summary of my position:

> It is said, indeed, that we owed to slavery the produce which sup-plies the principal manufacture of Britain. But the whole of this production was in truth credited to free industry. . . . The possibility of the profitable growth of so much cotton was caused by the com-merce and invention of liberty. [Leslie 1888, p. 17]

In conclusion, Smith's idea that the Colonies provided a proof of the success of "free labor" was subject to numerous objections, but Smith did not bother to acknowledge them. He was too zealous in promoting his ideology.

In one part of the world, Smithian ideology actually resulted in major changes in social relations. The West Indies were the last bastion of British colonial slavery. The actual implementation of an antislavery policy had disastrous consequences for the possessing classes. Although slavery was officially abolished in 1834, blacks were kept in a state of virtual slavery for four additional years.[21] After that period elapsed, sugar production plum-meted. Annual production in the period 1839-46 was 36 percent below what it had been during the period 1824-33 (Temperly 1977).

Smith himself had recognized that great profits were being made in the slave plantations. He commented, "[I]t is commonly said, that a sugar planter expects that the rum and the molasses should defray the whole expense of his cultivation, and that his sugar should be clear profit" (Smith 1937, p. 157).

In his opinion, such gains neither reflected the efficiency of slavery nor the exploitation of slaves. According to Smith, they were the result of a combi-nation of price supports and temporary shortages in European markets (Smith 1937, pp. 156-59, 366). Indeed, slavery was described as "the dearest

---

[21] McCulloch charged the British with hypocrisy on this count. Why abolish sugar slavery when British industry continued to depend on cotton slavery (McCulloch 1845, p. 341)?

of any" system of production relations (Smith 1937, p. 365; see also p. 80, and Millar 1806, pp. 261-82). The irony goes further. At the very time, Smith was asserting that slavery was uneconomical, Scottish salters and miners were still being held in a state of virtual slavery, even to the point of having to wear collars engraved with their master's name (Mantoux 1961, p. 74, Millar 1806, pp. 289-92, and Duckham 1969).[22] Recall, in this regard, that Steuart's mother was the proprietor of a coal mine. Thus, his advocacy of slavery might not have been as abstract as it might seem (Miller 1806, pp. 289-92, and Duckham 1969).

In keeping with his practice of maintaining almost absolute silence on the subject of rural poverty in Scotland (Viner 1965, p. 101), in *Wealth of Nations* Smith never once mentioned the existence of slavery in Scotland. He did cite Montesquieu's comparison of the Hungarian mines worked by wage labor with the inefficient Turkish mines worked by slaves (Smith 1937, p. 648). He also compared the wages of colliers in Scotland and England without commenting upon the status of the Scottish miners (Smith 1937, p. 104). Without taking note of their unfree status, Smith estimated that these workers earned approximately four times as much as farmhands (ibid., p. 104 and Smith 1976, p. 121n). He also estimated that the Scottish slave earned more than a British worker in comparable occupations (Smith 1937, p. 104), although this estimate is both debatable on factual grounds (Viner 1965, p. 115) and open to the complex objections that make most comparisons of this kind questionable (see Thompson 1963, chap. 6).

Smith argued that Scottish slaves escaped to seek employment from British mines in spite of a lower wage. Thus the institution of wage labor for these Scottish workers would benefit all parties. This vestige of earlier times served no economic function according to Smith. It was the result of the "love of domination and authority over others, which I am afraid is naturall to mankind" (Smith 1978, p. 192). However, in 1765, only a few years after Smith's lectures, British masters endeavored to turn the British system of "a yearly bond into a slavery as gross as that which was . . . in Scotland" (Hammond and Hammond 1919, pp. 12-13).

Smith's reluctance to address the question of the status of the Scottish miners was surprising. The subject was a matter of considerable public interest. In 1774, while Smith was busily at work on *Wealth of Nations*, the Lord Advocate of Scotland, Sir Alexander Gilmore, prepared a bill at the instigation of the Earl of Abercorn and other coal masters (Arnot 1955, p. 8). The

---

[22] Ashton noted that iron founders in South Wales were also tied to their employers for their lifetime (Ashton 1948, p. 112).

primary reason for its introduction was given in its preamble: "[T]here are not a sufficient number of colliers, coal-bearers, and salters, in Scotland, for working the quantity of coal and salt necessarily wanted" (cited in ibid., p. 8). As a secondary consideration, it intended to "remove the reproach of allowing such a state of servitude to exist in a free country" (ibid.).

Twenty-five years later, however, the law had proven itself highly ineffective in freeing the slaves. The old system of bondage had lost much of its potency. Pitmen enlisted in the navy or restricted their work to three or four days per week (ibid., p. 10). Not until 1799 did the Scottish slaves officially receive their full freedom. The immediate consequences of emancipation were not exactly what Smith had predicted. After 1799 wages steadily rose until the beginnings of the Napoleonic Wars. Once the shock of demobilization occurred, coming on top of a strong influx of Irish immigrants, the wage level sank back to from 45 to 70 percent of its peak (Smout 1969, pp. 434-35).

Slavery and wage labor are not the linear phenomena that Smith supposed them to be. When labor is scarce and the price it can command for its services is high, capital has good reason to prefer slavery (Domar 1970). The same logic explains the second serfdom in Eastern Europe, which was characterized by the reinstitution of old feudal obligations following the period of labor scarcity after the Thirty Years' War (Dobb 1963, p. 57).

Smith ignored such considerations. Instead, he blithely asserted that slavery was not economical. Yet he inferred by his own remarks on the United States that southern slavery also may have been profitable in spite of his theory about the costly nature of slave labor. He observed, "[T]he late resolution of the Quakers in Pennsylvania to set at liberty all their Negro slaves, may satisfy us that their number cannot have been very great" (Smith 1937, p. 366). Smith had a clear grasp of the logic of commodities. He added, "Had they made any considerable part of their property, such a resolution could have never been agreed to" (ibid., p. 366).

Slaves were an inconsequential part of the labor force in Pennsylvania only because typical small-holders did not possess enough cash to purchase a slave for life; instead, they had to content themselves with indentured servants the labor of which could be obtained with a much lower initial outlay (see Kalm 1770-71; 1: 388; Anon. 1775, pp. 121-22; see also Tulley 1973 and Main 1965, p. 33). In fact, "apart from the Puritan migration to the northeastern colonies, something between a half and two-thirds of all white emigrants to the Colonies were convicts,[23] indentured servants or redemptions" (Rich

---

[23] *"Place us on an equal footing with New South Wales, by giving us a share of the benefits which must, more or less, accrue from . . . convict labour"* (Anon. 1824, cited in Wakefield 1829, p. 127).

1967, p. 342). Thus only two years after the publication of *Wealth of Nations*, a suggestion to free the indentured servants of Pennsylvania elicited stern response from the legislature, which insisted that "all apprentices and servants are the property of their masters and mistresses, and every mode of depriving such masters and mistresses of their Property is a Violation of the Rights of Mankind" (cited in Hughes 1976, p. 111). Only a fool could have expected property owners in the South, where slaves made up a substantial proportion of the wealth (Wright 1978, p. 35), to have willingly shown more humanity. Planters in Georgia, the only southern state to be founded on the concept of "free labor," pleaded a hopeless inability to recruit enough labor. They insisted that "it is clear as light itself, that Negroes are as essentially necessary to the cultivation of Georgia, as axes, hoes or any other utensil of agriculture" (cited in Taylor 1972). After the Civil War, slave labor became unavailable for all (see Ransom and Sutch 1977, pp. 44-46). In part, because of a preference for leisure and, in part, because black families profited from devoting much of their female labor to subsistence production (Wright 1977, p. 62), cotton production fell precipitously. This experience again demonstrated how narrow Smith's doctrine of wage labor was.

We might also have expected some discussion of slavery with respect to the tobacco trade. Smith mentioned tobacco upon occasion, but he never hinted that the prosperity of his friends, the Glasgow merchants, depended upon their monopoly of the trade (see Smith 1937, p. 353, and Smout 1969). The tobacco merchants became the chief partners of the first Glasgow banks, established in 1750. Between 1754 and 1764 tobacco imports doubled to 11,500 tons per annum (Soltow 1959). Although Smith observed that the trade of Glasgow was said to have doubled in the fifteen years following the founding of the banks, he did so only to indicate the beneficial effect of such financial institutions (Smith 1937, p. 281).[24] The fact that this trade was based on slave labor was not broached. After 1776, when the merchants lost their access to tobacco, the town fell on hard times (Kindleberger 1976, p. 12), but Smith did not inform his readers of this situation in later editions of his book.

In summary, Smith failed dismally in his attempt to use the conditions of labor in the Colonies to demonstrate how the social division of labor would naturally evolve. Not only was he stymied by stubborn contradictions such as the fable of slavery, but he relied on incorrect assertions, which could have

---

[24] The leading authority on the subject of Scottish banks was most likely Steuart, whose modern editor noted an "interesting" absence of reference to him at this point in *Wealth of Nations* (Skinner 1966, p. xlii; see also Steuart 1966, bk. IV, pt. 2).

been avoided if he had just taken the trouble to verify them (see Skinner 1976, pp. 71-73).

THE ORIGINS OF WAGE LABOR: SMITH'S THEORETICAL EXERCISE

Smith made one other attempt to rationalize the institution of wage labor. Although he admitted to his Glasgow students of 1762-63 that "[t]he labour and time of the poor is in civilized countries sacrificed to the maintaining of the rich in ease and luxury," he apologized for this situation with the modest claim that the most disadvantaged members of society enjoy a far greater degree of "plenty and opulence" than they would in a "savage state" (Smith 1978, pp. 340, 338). In fact, he asserted that "an ordinary day labourer . . . has more of the conveniences and luxuries than an Indian [presumably Native American] prince at the head of 1,000 naked savages" (Smith 1978, p. 339).[25] Considering that the Scottish slaves were alleged to have enjoyed a higher income than comparable wage laborers, Smith might have just as well used this last argument to justify slavery. Instead, he tried to explain the voluntary origins of wage labor based on his theoretical analysis of the division of labor. In this endeavor, Smith was not very successful either. Although he is reputed to have made a great contribution to the theory of the division of labor, Marx charged that he did less "to bring out the capitalist character of the division of labor" than earlier writers such as Petty and the anonymous author of *Advantages of the East-India Trade* (Marx 1977, p. 486n; see also Cannan 1929, pp. 96-100, and Rodbertus 1899, pp. 78-79).[26]

In effect, Smith theorized that the social division of labor could be understood in terms of the individual division of labor within the workshop; thus the "separation of different trades and employments from one another seems to have taken place in consequences" of the advantages of the division of labor in the workshop (Smith 1937, p. 5). This analogy formed the founda-

---

[25] Smith here went further than Locke, who had merely asserted that the English worker "feeds, lodges and is clad" better (Locke 1698, pp. 314-15). Native Americans did not seem to share Smith's assessment. For example, Ojibways who visited London in the 1840s are reported to have told the English who attempted to engage them in conversation:

> [We are] willing to talk with you if it can do any good for the hundreds and thousands of poor and hungry children we see in your streets every day. . . . We see hundreds of little children with their naked feet in the snow, and we pity them, for we know they are hungry. . . . [W]e have no such poor children among us. [cited in Tobias 1967, p. 86]

[26] On the authorship of this tract, see Barber (1975, p. 57n).

tion of Smith's basic argument: Since within the workshop a more refined division of labor is economical, surely people would choose to arrange their employments in a manner that would create a more progressive social division of labor.

In spite of the importance of this aspect of Smith's work, only Wakefield, among all the later commentators, seems to have divined Smith's intentions. He noted, Smith "appears to be composing, not a theory, but a history of national wealth" (Wakefield 1835; 1: v). Wakefield correctly chided Smith for confounding this aspect of the division of labor with the social division of labor (ibid., p. 30). He even insinuated that Smith was "not thoroughly acquainted with . . . this subject" (ibid., p. 21).

Smith Versus Small-Scale Producers

No matter how hard he tried, Smith was unable to come to grips with the transition from the self-sufficient household to the capitalist mode of production. He could come as close as barter or even simple commodity production, but the leap to wage labor was beyond him. Exchanges, in and of themselves, could not explain such a fundamental modification of the economic system (Marx 1967; 3: 325-27). To make matters worse, poor but independent small farmers and petty producers frustrated Smith's theory. They were not the "bustling, spirited, active folks, who can't brook oppression and are constantly endeavoring to advance themselves [and who] . . . naturally join in with the democraticall part of the constitution and favour the principle of . . . the Whig interest" (Smith 1978, p. 320; see also Smith 1959, pt. 1, sec. III, chap. 3). True, many rural people worked very hard. Smith himself had recognized as much: "Those improvements in husbandry . . . which the progress of arts and manufactures necessarily introduces, leave the husbandman with as little leisure as the artificer" (Smith 1937, p. 659). Here Smith was addressing a practical problem. Since the demands on their time were so great, country folk could not form a militia. Thus the state must spend more money for national defense.

Smith knew that continual activity was not the chosen way of life for all concerned. Although some peasants were rapidly advancing themselves, many resisted the new ways. His disgust with those who clung to the old burst out in his description of the country weaver:

> A country weaver, who cultivates a small farm, must lose a good deal of time in passing from his loom to the field, and from the field to his loom. When the two trades can be carried on in same workhouse, the loss of time is no doubt much less. It is even in this case, however, very considerable. A man commonly saunters a little in turning his hand from one sort of employment to another. When he first begins the new

work he is seldom very keen and hearty; his mind, as they say, does not go to it, and for some time, he rather trifles than applies to good purpose. The habit of sauntering and of indolent careless application, which is naturall, or rather necessarily acquired by every country workman who is obliged to change his work and tools every half hour, and to apply his hands in twenty different ways almost every day of his life; renders him almost always slothful and lazy, and incapable of any vigorous application even on the most pressing occasions. [Smith 1967, pp. 8-9; see also Smith 1978, pp. 345-46, 491]

Such antagonism reveals another side of the apparently benign Smith. Joan Thirsk, a keen student of English rural life, described this passage as a "grotesque caricature" (Thirsk 1978, p. 151). John Stuart Mill took issue with Smith: "This is surely an exaggerated description of the inefficiency of country labour. Few workmen change their tools oftener than a gardener; is he incapable of vigorous application?" (Mill 1848; 2: 126).

Why was Smith so hostile to the small producer? He assumed that the "natural effort of every individual to better his own condition" (Smith 1759, p. 508) was foreign to the indolent and sauntering country weaver. Such people would not seem to respond quickly enough to develop a rapidly deepening social division of labor. Yet that is just how Smith imagined that the social division of labor would "naturally" evolve:

[When industry is not] introduced . . . by the violent operation of the stocks of particular merchants or undertakers, who established them in imitation of some foreign manufactures . . . , manufactures for distant sale . . . grow up of their own accord, by the gradual refinement of those coarser manufactures . . . in this manner have grown up naturally, as it were of their own accord . . . . Such manufactures are the offspring of agriculture. [Smith 1937, pp. 381-82]

Smith had the good sense to recognize that the actual unfolding of the social division of labor was bound up with the rise of capital. He perceived that capital was just as essential to the evolution of wage labor, but he could not grasp how these phenomena were systematically connected. He speculated, "in that rude state of society in which there is no division of labor, in which exchanges are seldom made, and in which every man provides enough for himself, it is not necessary that any stock should be accumulated" (ibid., 259; see also Marx 1967; 2: 140n). Of course, this assertion is utter nonsense. Are we to believe that people plowed with their fingernails and cut wood with their teeth?[27] Smith's expression "stock" must be translated to mean *"capital."* With no real explanation, a new principle suddenly becomes dominant: Capital appears and demands a profit on its stock. Piercy Ravenstone must have had a this sort of logic in mind when he wrote:

> [T]he word capital is sufficient to account for every thing. If nations grow populous, it is the effect of capital. If they direct their industry to the cultivation of their fields, it is capital lends them lands. . . . If they build cities, and encourage manufactures, it is still the effect of capital. . . . Whence came the capital that creates all these prodigies? Adam left none to his children . . . Capital like all the productions of man, has had a beginning; but how that which is the result of accumulation could act before accumulation took place, could be its cause is a problem. [Ravenstone 1824, p. 38-39]

According to Smith, "As soon as a stock has accumulated in the hands of *particular* persons, some of them will *naturally* employ it in setting to work *industrious* people" (Smith 1937, p. 48; emphasis added). Why do the industrious people need these particular persons to set them to work? Smith's answer was that "the greater part of the workmen stand in need of a master to advance them the materials of their work, and their wages and maintenance" (ibid., p. 65).[28]

Smith gave further indication of the degree of his befuddlement in his chapter on money. Here he began with a historical treatment of money as a unit of account (bk. 1, chap. IV). He seemed unable to move beyond that point; after a long series of anecdotes about ancient money, he ventured to promise to examine the rules that determine exchangeable value. Suddenly, he shifted to a paragraph on the difference between use values and exchange values (ibid., pp. 28-29). What follows, however, is a disappointing introduction to his superficial treatment of value as the sum of the component parts of wages, profits, and rent. Never once did he mention how he was able to justify his jump from the armor of Diomede to the wages of labor (ibid., p. 23).

Smith was unable to comprehend the move from the "rude state" to one in which people who were once able to live without "stock" now find themselves "stand[ing] in need of those particular persons," the capitalists

---

[27] "Imagine a number of intelligent and industrious men, paced in a fertile country . . . utterly destitute of capital. With what difficulty could they eke out a miserable subsistence, possessing no tools except what they could fashion with their hands, and teeth, and nails" (Longfield 1834, p. 190).

[28] Many of these workers owned their own tools (see Ashton 1972, p. 217).

who are able to claim a reward for their "stock." On the one hand, he asserted that "the accumulation of stock must, in the nature of things, be previous to the division of labour" (ibid., p. 260). On the other, he alleged that the "compleat division of labour . . . is posterior *[sic]* to the invention even of agriculture" (fragment reprinted in Meek 1977a, p. 52).

We have already noted that Smith's confusion seems to have put Marx on the track of his theory of the so-called primitive accumulation. This confusion can be seen more clearly by turning our attention to the nature of Adam Smith's anthropological speculations.

Adam Smith's Curious Anthropologies

Two separate principles are at work in Smith's version of social evolution. First, precapitalist societies such as the Hottentots developed a social division of labor because of the economies associated with specialization (Meek 1977a, p. 52). Thus Smith, the anthropologist, discovered a historical motivation for the social division of labor, which is not "the effect of any human policy" but is rather "the necessary consequence of a natural disposition . . . to truck, barter and exchange" (cited in Meek 1977a, p. 38, and Smith 1976, p. 27n). This sort of anthropology was not, by any means, novel. John Wheeler, in his *Treatise on Commerce* (1601), had observed, "[T]here was nothing in the world so ordinarie, and naturall unto men, as to contract, truck, merchandize, and traffike one with another" (cited in Appleby 1978, p. 94). Smith's merit was to have pushed this principle further than anyone else.

In reality, Smith did not believe in his own anthropology. Trucking and bartering were the predilections of the emergent middle class. The gentry were not so inclined. As early as 1618, Francis Bacon had advised that prosperity requires that a nation not be overburdened by clergy or nobility, "for they bring nothing to stock" (cited in ibid 1978, p. 115). Defoe, too, had charged that "the gentry have no genius to trade; 'tis a mechanism which they scorn; . . . they would not turn their hands toward business" (Defoe 1724–26, p. 596). Steuart also felt trading to be beneath the gentry (Steuart 1767, p. 84).

Because of this aloofness from the market, Smith launched an attack on the gentry. The creation of a shirt was held to be productive if it were eventually purchased, unproductive if it came from the hands of a servant (Smith 1937, p. 315).[29] Why? Because the gentry were pictured as refusing to engage their savings in capitalistic ventures. By disconnecting his critique

---

[29] Of course, households that produced their own goods were also guilty of not engaging in productive labor.

of the gentry from his anthropology, Smith managed to hide the class nature of his analysis of human society, thereby lending an illusion of universality of this principle.

Smith discovered another more explicitly class-based principle to explain the social division of labor. This second principle depends upon the existence of "stock" or, to be more precise, capital.

According to the first approach, the progressive social division of labor is understood exclusively in terms of the anthropological principle of the natural disposition of man. Any attempts to affect the division of labor through political action must be prohibited as "evident violations of natural interest of every society that things such as this kind [i.e., the creation of a new social division of labor] should never be forced or obstructed" (ibid.). Thus drawbacks were also criticized as destructive of "the natural division and distribution of labor in the society" (ibid., p. 466).

In spite of these theoretical offerings, Smith was still able to tell his students that the exclusive privileges of corporations were able "to bring about . . . the separation of trades sooner than the progress of society would naturally effect" (Smith 1978, p. 88). This last point may be interpreted as an aside noted down by a diligent student. Certainly nothing of the sort is found in *Wealth of Nations,* for it would have conceded much ground to the theory of Steuart.[30]

In general, the distinction between the two principles relates to the division of the economic process by occupations and by classes. Each principle has its own underlying anthropology. Each has its own intended use.

The division of the social labor process into occupations was a useful tactic to explain the harmony of the marketplace through the example of the mutually beneficial nature of barter among independent workers. This approach is limited. As Bagehot observed:

> [T]he main part of modern commerce is carried on in a very different manner; it begins and ends at a different point. The fundamental point is the same: the determining producer—the person on whose violation it depends whether the object should be produced or not—goes on so long as he is satisfied. . . . But the determining producer is now not a laborer but a capitalist. [Bagehot 1880, p. 361]

Capitalist social relations can no longer be explained by a "natural disposi-

---

30 However, he does concede that a "particular manufacture . . . may sometimes be acquired sooner" by virtue of encouragement (Smith 1937, p. 425); but such actions are alleged to slow down the process of accumulation, thereby hindering the "natural evolution" of the social division of labor.

tion . . . to truck barter or exchange." As Governor Pownall of Virginia explained to Smith, "[B]efore a man can have the propensity to barter, he must have acquired something somewhat" (Pownall 1776, p. 338). Smith understood this objection, for he posited a substantially different anthropology for capitalist society made up of separate classes in which the poor are possessed by "passions which prompt [them] to invade property, passions much more steady in their operation, and much more universal in their influence" (Smith 1937, p. 670). Consequently, government is necessary to protect the property of the rich (see Smith 1937, p. 670ff). For example, in discussing the poverty of Ireland, Smith observed:

> It is ill provided with [coal and)] wood; two articles essentially necessary to the progress of Great Manufactures. It wants order, police, and a regular administration of justice both to protect and restrain the inferior ranks of people, articles more essential to the progress of Industry than both coal and wood put together. [letter to Lord Carlisle, 8 November 1799, cited in Mossner and Ross 1977, p. 243]

The limits of Smith's anthropology of harmony were evident when he observed that although "the relief and consolation of human misery depend upon our compassion for [the poor] the peace and order of society is of more importance than even the relief of the miserable" (Smith 1759, p. 226; see also Part II, Section 1). Smith even went so far as to teach his students:

> Laws and government may be considered in . . . every case as a combination of the rich to oppress the poor, and preserve to themselves the inequality of the goods which would otherwise be soon destroyed by the attacks of the poor, who if not hindered by the government would soon reduce the others to an equality with themselves by open violence. [Smith 1978, p. 208; see also p. 404]

A few weeks later, he emphasized the necessity of inequality as a stimulant to commerce (ibid., p. 262).

Two points are of interest here. First, the market is not mentioned as a means of eliminating poverty. Second, stringent measures are required to keep people (meaning the lower classes) in line. On the whole, Smith's class-based theory was more consistent than his theory of occupational cooperation. Moreover, the former was presented as a system of administration to be implemented in practice, whereas the occupational-based theory is found in the ideological sections.

The contrast between an occupational-based or a class-based analysis of society, although not made wholly explicit by Smith, remains a great achievement nonetheless. Thus, for example, we learn that the socially desirable self-interest of the butcher, brewer, and baker leads to beneficial results (Smith 1937, p. 14), whereas the interest of capital in general "has not the same connexion with the general interest of society" (ibid., p. 250). Smith could superficially resolve the contradiction between the class-based and occupational-based interests by invoking the market. Accordingly, we read in *Theory of Moral Sentiments* that "the rich . . . are led by an invisible hand to make nearly the same distribution of the necessaries of life which would have been made had the earth been divided into equal portions among all its inhabitants" (Smith 1769, pp. 184-85; see also 1937, pp. 594-95), but he later explained the same point by the "narrow capacity of the human stomach" (ibid., p. 164). In other respects, marked differences separate classes.

Smith's invisible hand does not resolve the confusion between his two anthropologies. To make this line of reasoning coherent, he should not have addressed the subject in terms of the " distribution of the necessaries of life," but rather with regard to the distribution of the means of production. After all, he himself had strongly emphasized the importance of "stock." Even if he had been justified in ignoring the distribution of the means of production, he very well understood that consumption goods, in general, were not shared equally among all people. He had observed that in spite of the invisible hand, "for one very rich man, there must be at least five hundred poor, and the affluence of the few supposes the indigence of the many" (ibid., p. 670; see also Meek 1977c, p. 11).

This case reveals a great deal about Smith's method of analysis. He recognized the conflict between his class-based explanation of the evolution of the social division of labor and his alternative explanation framed in terms of market forces. Yet when dealing with class antagonisms, the issues were muddied.

For example, Smith often appears to take the side of labor versus capital. Baumol (1976) collected a number of extracts to "prove" the existence of this aspect of Smith. All but one of these citations were written, not for the support of labor, but to attack corporate business, which then meant firms that enjoyed exclusive privileges or to denounce anti-competitive behavior typical of entrenched business interests. The only exception in Baumol's collection is a paragraph that concerns business' tendency to criticize high wages while remaining silent about high profits (Smith 1937, p. 98).

Baumol, however, neglected to mention an almost identical passage pointed out by Cannan in the edition that Baumol cited as evidence for his argument. The context of this other citation indicates that Smith again had corporate business in mind (ibid., p. 566). Moreover, when Smith relied on his market-based explanation, he was less than honest. To return to the "invisible hand" passage, the casual reader might be left with the impression that Smith was suggesting that the market would be conducive to equality.

When we read the later citation, we understand that Smith had said no more than Steuart, who had earlier written, "The most delicate liver in Paris will not put more of the earth's productions into his belly than another: he may pick and choose, but he will always find that what he leaves will go to feed another" (Steuart 1767; 1: 193). In fact, we might well expect to find the same sort of equality to which the invisible hand leads in Steuart's dream for resurrection of the Spartan slave-republic.

Recapitulation

Steuart's ideas are shocking to a modern reader. Smith's appear benign. Yet this appearance of benevolence is dangerous since it deadens our critical facilities. The occasional references to the conflict between labor and capital throw us further off guard. Although we can read in Smith that the interests of labor and capital are "by no means the same" (Smith 1937, p. 66), we are within only a couple of pages of the story of labor in North America. A touch of realism makes us more credulous by the time we reach the tale of the harmonious conditions of labor and capital in North America. Nothing could be more subtle.

In spite of Smith's obvious talents, *Wealth of Nations* can be counted as less than a total success. All too often Smith became entangled in his own ideology. A lesser mind could have put together a flat yet consistent story. Smith could not, perhaps because he recognized the underlying reality he was trying to deny. He also failed as a result of the contrary nature of his two objectives. On the one hand, he attempted to put together an ideology of class harmony; on the other hand, his theory of political and economic administration required an explicit analysis of class conflict.

Generally, his ideological perspective conflicted with his administrative principles. The one case where his two approaches to economics coincided was in his analysis of the colonies of North America.[31] Both ideology and good government led him to call for a regime of laissez faire; however, this accord was achieved only by ignoring reality while proposing numerous violations of this theory (see Viner 1927, p. 229). Certainly Jacob Viner was correct in noting that Smith "displayed a fine tolerance for a generous measure of inconsistency" (Viner 1927, p. 230).

I might also add that Smith's own life was not altogether free of contradictions. Did he sense the irony of the patron saint of free trade collecting a pension from a nobleman or a salary as a commissioner of customs? Did he feel a tinge of hypocrisy when he sought the appointment to the committee

---

[31] For a conventional view of Smith's analysis of the Colonies, see Stevens (1975).

of the East India Company? To see these inconsistencies in Smith's life does not prove that he was attempting to deceive his readers. As Peter Berger, a student of such mentality, has observed: "deliberate deception requires a degree of psychological self-control that few people are capable of. . . . It is much easier to deceive oneself" (Berger 1963, p. 109).

The *Wealth of Nations* is not merely a product of self-deception. It is a great book. Its greatness rests, in part, on Smith's treatment of his own contradictions, "which he does not solve, but which he reveals by contradicting himself" (Marx 1963-71, pt. 2, p. 151). At times, his work becomes so absurd that we are signaled that we have come upon a matter of importance.

A case in point is Smith's attempt to explain capitalist production by a natural history of commodities. We are told that stock is not important because of the social relations of capitalist production. Its importance derives from the nature of commodities. He informed his students: "The number of hands employed is business depends on the stored stock in the kingdom. . . . Many goods produce nothing for a while. The grower, the spinner, the dresser of flax, have no immediate profit" (Smith 1978, p. 365).

Although such goods may have been in existence before capitalism, we can wonder how they were produced without stock; yet according to Smith, only the increase in capital was capable of bringing about an increase in production (Smith 1937, p. 326).

Is Smith's insistence on the crucial nature of stock an isolated lapse? Smith's friend Turgot,[32] whom nobody has to my knowledge accused of being an unworldly professor, used an almost identical line of reasoning in his *Reflections on the Formation and Distribution of Wealth*. In the first two sections, Turgot indicated how diversity of land can lead to barter but not wage labor. The institution of wage labor arises out of a natural history of commodities quite similar to Smith's. Wheat must pass from grain to flour and then to bread; cattle raised, their hides tanned and then made into shoes. "If the same man who cultivates on his own land these different articles, and who raises them to supply his wants was obliged to perform all the intermediate operations himself, it is certain he would succeed very badly" (Turgot 1966, p. 5). Consequently "[e]veryone profits" from a more refined social division of labor (Turgot 1966, p. 6); however, in the next paragraph, Turgot began by introducing us to a new individual, the "mere workman, who depends only on his hands and his industry . . . [who] has nothing but such part of his labour as he is able to dispose to others" (ibid., p. 7). He neglected to explain exactly how the transition from an equal ownership of land with which he

---

[32] The parallelisms may not have been coincidental (see Viner 1965, pp. 128–38), although Groenwegen makes the case that they may have been (Groenwegen 1969).

began his exposition to a situation in which some are reduced to the status of "mere workmen" is in the interest of these people. Such is the nature of political economy! Yet Smith went further than even Turgot. In fact, he attributed so much importance to stock that we are told "stock cultivates the land; stock employs labour" (Smith 1937, p. 800). In his absurd anthropology, Smith even lumped together "labouring cattle" and "productive labourers" (ibid., p. 344).[33]

What would press a thinker of the stature of Smith to resort to such ridiculous reasoning? Wakefield noted in his commentary on Smith's chapter "On the Profits of Stock":

> Treating labour as a commodity, and capital, the produce of labour, as another, then, if the value of these two commodities were regulated by equal quantities of labour, a given quantity of capital would, under all circumstances, exchange for that quantity of capital which had been produced by the same amount of labour; antecedent labour, as capital has been termed, would always exchange for the same amount of present labour. [Wakefield 1835; 2: 230-31n]

In other words, Smith was on the verge of coming to grips, perhaps unconsciously, with the concept of surplus value. He plucked out his offending eye in a primitive ritual whereby the category of stock was deified. The *Wealth of Nations* emerged as an epic poem of a strange world where "things are in the saddle and ride mankind" (Emerson 1940). No wonder Wordsworth wrote of him as "[t]he worst critic, David Hume excepted, that Scotland, a soil to which that sort of weed seems natural, has produced" (Wordsworth 1802, p. 418).

Adam Smith's Discovery of the Division of Labor

> It is chiefly in the description of Adam Smith's intellectual progress and in the analysis of influences which went to make the *Wealth of Nations* that there may be room for something further.
>
> J. M. Keynes, "Adam Smith as Student and Professor," p. 330

The section of Adam Smith's *Lectures on Jurisprudence* dealing with the subject of police gives us, perhaps, the most remarkable insight into the origins of his theory of the division of labor. Smith began by commenting that the state had the obligation to maintain the cheapness of commodities (Smith 1978, p. 333). He then went on to note that, in spite of the rarity of some materials,

---

[33] "Thus the Grass my Horse has bit; the Turfs my Servant has cut; and the Ore I have digg'd . . . become my *Property*" (Locke 1698, p. 307).

advance in production could make things much more affordable (ibid., p. 337). Such progress requires the enforcement of the law, which is necessary to the preservation of "that useful inequality in the fortunes of mankind" (ibid., p. 338). This unexceptional discussion seems to have somehow aroused Smith's curiosity about the equity of the law.

Are the poor merely victims of the law? Recall that Smith observed that laws were required to protect the rich from the poor. This idea sat poorly with Smith, the ideologue. Consequently, he took a page from John Locke, who had noted the English worker "feeds, lodges and is clad" better than the Native American (Locke 1698, para. 41). Smith may well have come by this thought by way of Mandeville, who wrote (Mandeville 1723, p. 26): "the very poor Liv'd better than the Rich before."

Smith then turned to another thought of Mandeville: The production of a fine crimson or scarlet cloth requires a multiplicity of trades working together in its manufacture (Mandeville 1723, pp. 356-57). The democratic Smith used the example of a blue coat of a worker, but the thought was unchanged.

Next Smith returned to his idea of the relative affluence and comfort of his contemporaries. How could the poor of his day live better than the rich Indian prince? He mused:

> But that the poor day labourer or indigent farmer should be more at ease, notwithstanding all oppression and tyranny, should be more at his own ease than the savage, does not appear so probable. Amongst the savages there are no landlords nor userers, no tax gatherers, so that every one has the full fruits of his own labours, and should therefore enjoy the greatest abundance; but the case is otherwise. [Smith 1978, pp. 339-341]

So here is the key: The poor laborer has more commodities but less leisure than the savage. Smith ended his lecture without explaining why the laborer would choose to substitute commodities for leisure. Indeed, Smith did not even say that the transformation was voluntary. In his earlier works, he had addressed the role of class in the evolution of leisure. He noted, "In civilized nations, the inferior ranks of people have very little leisure, and the superior ranks have many other amusements" (Smith 1790a, p. 187; see also 1790, p. 50).

The next day Smith expanded upon his remarks from the previous lecture:

> The labour and time of the poor is in civilized countries sacrificed to the maintaining of the rich in ease and luxury. The landlord is maintained in idleness and luxury by the labour of his tenants. The

moneyed man is supported by his exactions from the industrious merchant and the needy who are obliged to support him in ease by a return
for the use of his money. But every savage has the full enjoyment of
the fruits of his own labours; there are no landlords, no userers, no tax
gatherers. . . . [T]he poor labourer . . . has all the inconveniences of the
soil and season to struggle with, is continually exposed to the inclem-
ency of the weather and the most severe labour at the same time. Thus
he who as it were supports the whole frame of society and furnishes
the means of the convenience and ease of all the rest is himself possessed of a very small share and is buried in obscurity. He bears on his
shoulders the whole of mankind, and unable to sustain the weight of
it is thrust down into the lowest parts of the earth from whence he
supports the rest. In what manner then shall we account for the great
share he and the lowest persons have of the conveniences of life? [ibid,
pp. 340-41]

This last sentence is curious. In the previous lecture, Smith had asserted that
the poor laborer was better fed, clothed, and housed than the savage. In this
session, just as students were hearing about the same laborer's "small share,"
Smith suddenly asked them to account for the "great share he [has]
. . . in the conveniences of life." What follows is just as remarkable. His next
words were, "The division of labour amongst different hands can alone
account for this" (ibid., p. 341). No wonder Schumpeter could complain of
the lack of attention given to the *use* of the division of labor by Smith.
Schumpeter emphasized, "[N]obody, either before or after A. Smith ever
thought of putting such a burden upon division of labor" (Schumpeter 1954,
p. 187). Perhaps his blue coat reminded him of Mandeville, who had earlier
written of the division of labor (see Mandeville 1723, p. 284). In any case,
we hear nothing more about the effect of the increased working day. Instead,
Smith turned the attention of his audience to a "frivolous" example, the pin
factory.

Indeed, Smith seems to have stumbled onto the classical theory of primitive accumulation. Rather than work within this framework, he fled from it
into his theory of the division of labor. However, the division of labor was
completely irrelevant to the question at hand, namely the condition of the
poor laborer.

In the concluding few lectures, we find a compressed version of *Wealth of
Nations* (see Stewart 1811, p. 275). In short, Smith seems to have developed
his great work as an attempt to avoid the logic of the classical theory of
primitive accumulation.

The Eclipse of Adam Smith

Smith's revision of history was proved to be an unworkable basis of economic administration, but as ideology it served a useful role. For example, Francis Horner, famous member of the Bullion Committee and editor of the *Edinburgh Review*, was requested to prepare a set of notes for a new editor of *Wealth of Nations*. He explained his refusal in a letter to Thomas Thomson, written on 15 August 1803:

> I should be reluctant to expose S's errors before his work had operated its full effect. We owe much at present to the superstitious worship of S's name; and we must not impair that feeling, till the victory is more complete. . . . [U]ntil we can give a correct and precise theory of the origin of wealth, his popular and plausible and loose hypothesis is as good for the vulgar as any others. [cited in Horner 1843; 1: 229]

In spite of the caution of people like Horner, ideological conflict broke out. The actual behavior of the contending classes eventually decided this ideological conflict. A string of repressive legislation, including the Combination Acts of 1799 and 1800, repeal of the justices' power to fix wages in 1813, the Apprenticeship clauses in 1814, as well as the Poor Law Amendment Act of 1834, are irrefutable testimony of the use of the state to further the interests of capital (see Pollard 1978, p. 151). The only exception was the repeal of the Combination Act in 1824, which was intended to reduce economic protests (see Hollis 1973, pp. 102-15, and Marx 1847, p. 170) and prove the correctness of the Wages Fund Theory to the working class (see Wallas 1919 and Halevy, pp. 204-8). By 1830, Senior was ready to reestablish these restrictions on labor in an apparent admission of the failure of this unique experiment (see Levy 1970, pp. 71-73).

After the 1830s, political economy came to embrace the ideas of Steuart, which reappeared in the works of Wakefield, to whom we will turn in a subsequent chapter. Indeed, the modern literature of economics has recorded neither the battle between Smith and Steuart, nor Smith's subsequent defeat. We hear little mention of Steuart except that he was a trifle more modern than the run-of-the-mill mercantilist.

The obliteration of Steuart's contribution was marked in a recent publication entitled *The Market and the State: Essays in Honour of Adam Smith* (Wilson and Skinner 1976). This title suggests a detailed analysis of Smith's response to the question of state intervention. Indeed, some of the contributions do bear titles that relate to this subject matter, but a review of the body of the articles proves disappointing. One contributor was irreverent enough to venture the opinion that "industrialization required government action" (Lewis 1976,

p. 139),[34] but that particular article had nothing to do with the Smithian theme of the title. Thus, in a book, one of whose co-editors produced an earlier edition of Steuart's *Inquiry*, not one mention of Steuart can be found.

---

[34] This verdict is shared by Kroos and Gilbert (1972, p. 162) and Kuznets (1965, p. 108). It was almost universally accepted up until the time of Smith (see Deane 1957, p. 89).

chapter 6

Benjamin Franklin and the Smithian Ideology of Slavery and Wage Labor

That few in public affairs act from a mere view of the good of their country, whatever they may pretend; and tho' their actings being real good to their country, yet men primarily considered their own and their country's interest was united and did not act from a principle of benevolence.

"Observations on my *Reading History in The Library*," in
The Papers of Benjamin Franklin, vol. 1, pp. 192-93

Adam Smith was not alone in his interest in the Colonies. During the time in which the *Wealth of Nations* was being written, North American colonial affairs were very much in the minds of the English. Between 1720 and 1784, about 10 percent of all books, pamphlets, maps and prints published in London concerned these colonies (Bonwich 1977, p. 35 citing Adams 1971). Similarly, from 1774 to 1779, about 20 percent of all books and pamphlets published in England were related to the colonies of North America (ibid.; see also Adams 1969). Of all the sources of information on colonial affairs, the most famous was Benjamin Franklin, whose opinions on this subject were said to be "a degree of credit little short of proofs of holy writ" (Knox 1769, p. 111 cited in Benians 1926, p. 252).

We are all familiar with the genial Franklin, a man of great wit and inventiveness. In real life, Benjamin Franklin was a much more complex character than the hagiographies of Americana would have us believe. No political economist, with the possible exception of Petty, was either as mercurial or as engaging as Franklin. Consequently, some biographical material will be useful in gaining a perspective on his prolific writings on political economy. Franklin made his debut as a political economist in 1729, while still in his early twenties, with a splendid "application" of William Petty's *Treatise of Taxes and Contributions* (1662) (Franklin 1959-; 14: 76-86). Franklin himself seems to have been originally drawn to the subject by William Rawle's pamphlet on paper money, which Franklin printed in 1725 (see Fetter 1943, p. 472n). Thereafter, he expressed so many contradictory opinions that one Franklin scholar compared him to a chameleon (Eiselen 1928, p. 29).

The relative weights of his various works are difficult to assess because his pen was frequently used to further his own interest rather than the truth. For example, shortly after his first pamphlet appeared, Franklin was rewarded with a contract for printing the paper money, which he so ably advocated in that work (Franklin 1964, p. 124). Later, pamphlets written to argue against smuggling and for the maintenance of low wage rates appear to have been designed to win him a more lucrative position with the British government (see Conner 1965, p. 37, and Franklin 1959-; 15: 14-16, 159-64; and 16: 162).

Franklin was not above plagiarism. Whole paragraphs of his pamphlet on paper money appear to be lifted directly from Petty (see Wetzel 1895). This practice was not limited to his works on economics. For example, Davis alleged that many of Franklin's most famous words were borrowed by him without proper attribution (see Davis 1803; 2: 25-36).

The difficulties of evaluating Franklin's activities are so pervasive that even his commitment to the colonial cause has been brought into question. According to Dennys DeBerdt, colonial agent for Massachusetts, Franklin "stood entirely neuter [with regard to the Revolution] till he saw which way the cause would be carried, and then he broke out fiercely on the side of America" (cited in Currey 1965, p. 148). A more hostile interpreter charged that Franklin's opportunism led him to work as a double agent for the British during the Revolutionary War (Currey 1972). Whether or not we accept such a damning verdict, Franklin was an undeniable master of saying whatever would accrue to his own advantage (see Currey 1965).

Although Schumpeter is undoubtedly correct in his judgment that Franklin's work offers "little to commend for purely analytic features" (Schumpeter 1954, p. 192), he had great influence. He was able to convince William Petty's great grandson, Lord Shelburne, the powerful president of the British Board of Trade and later Prime Minister, that he was "one of the [three] best authorities for anything related to America" (Franklin 1959-; 14: 325; see also the editor's cautionary note).

The strongest claim for Franklin's influence on political economy can be traced to Franklin himself. A Mrs. Logan, widow of a friend wrote:

> Dr. Franklin once told my husband that the celebrated Adam Smith, when writing his *Wealth of Nations,* was in the habit of bringing chapter after chapter, as he composed it, to himself, Dr. Price and other literati of that day, with whom he was intimate; patiently hearing their observations, and profiting by their discussions and criticisms. . . . Nay, that he has sometimes reversed his positions and rewritten whole chapters, after hearing what they had to remark on the subject before them . [cited in Carey 1928, p. 126]

As Lewis Carey pointed out, Franklin as well as Richard Price were indeed in London during the period 1773-75, when Smith was there working on his book (Carey 1928, p. 115; see also Viner 1965, pp. 42-45). Franklin and Smith met for the first time in Edinburgh in 1759 (ibid.). Both men, as well as Price, were members of the Royal Society of London (Carey 1928, p. 118). Finally, both were both very close to Strahan, the publisher of *Theory of Moral Sentiments* and a member of the firm that first published *Wealth of Nations* (Fay 1956, Chapter 9).

Although Smith had begun his book long before the period in question, Carey noted that Franklin would have good reason to be unaware of the extent of its period of gestation (Carey 1928, p. 119); however, the subjects upon which Smith was working during 1773-75 included the chapter "Of Colonies," written in October 1773, and the passages on American wages in the chapter "Of the Wages of Labour" (Carey 1928, p. 120).

In fact, Franklin's influence, of course, may have begun earlier than 1773. Franklin and Smith first met in 1759. By the early 1760s, Smith had begun an early draft of the *Wealth of Nations.* In the draft, we find the assertion that Pennsylvania and some of the New England colonies were wealthier than Virginia (Scott 1965, p. 363). Also, Native Americans are used as an example of a society with an underdeveloped social division of labor. Unless these thoughts occurred only after meeting Franklin, we might expect that Smith would have been eager to take advantage of the eminent visitor's expertise. We do get a hint, however, that in spite of the cordial correspondence between Franklin, on the one hand, and Lord Kames and Hume, on the other, that something may have gone amiss during this visit. In Reminiscing about the natural tendency to avoid disputation, Franklin listed as exceptions: "Lawyers, University Men, and Men of all sorts that have been bred at Edinborough" (Franklin 1964, p. 60).

We have no direct evidence of Smith's esteem for Franklin; however, the opinion of his closest friend, Hume, may be indicative. In 1762, a few years after first meeting Franklin, Hume praised him: "America has sent us many good things: gold, silver, sugar, tobacco, indigo, etc.; but you are the first philosopher, and indeed the first great man of letters for whom we are beholden to her" (Franklin 1959-; 10: 81-82). By 1774, Hume's attitude had changed. He asked Smith:

> Pray what strange account are these we hear of Franklin's conduct? I am very slow in believing that he has been guilty in the extreme degree that is pretended, tho' I have always known him to be a very factious man, and Faction next to Fanatacism is of all the passions the most destructive of morality. [cited in Rae 1895, p. 267]

The incident to which Hume refers is the theft of the letters of the governor and lieutenant-governor of Massachusetts in which Franklin was implicated. Consequently, he was required to appear for examination before the Privy Council on 29 January 1774 by Solicitor-General Wedderburn, a former student under Smith and a friend of Hume (Carey 1928, p. 117). Franklin's action in this affair may have cut short Smith's association with him, but probably not before he had the opportunity to supply Smith with much information on the impact of plentiful lands and high wages characteristic of the northern colonies of America (see Carey 1928, pp. 123-25).

This material is extremely important in *Wealth of Nations* because it is the only concrete example Smith offered in his attempt to prove that labor could prosper without seemingly damaging the interests of capital. Consequently, it played an essential role in the creation of the Smithian ideology of the noncoercive nature of wage labor. Accordingly, we should be careful in evaluating Franklin's contribution.

The proof of Franklin's influence is not conclusive. His name does not appear in *Wealth of Nations*, but neither does that of Steuart, whom Smith was challenging, nor that of Turgot, whose work was embarrassingly similar to Smith's own (see Viner 1965, pp. 128-38). Smith did repeat statements similar to those made in Franklin's essays suggesting that the population of North America doubled in twenty or twenty-five years (Smith 1937, pp. 70, 393).[1] The most likely written source for such estimates would be Franklin's essays

---

[1] Smith's editor, Cannan, overlooked Franklin as the source of this statement. Instead, he suggested that this estimate may have come from Richard Price (Smith 1937, pp. 70, 393). Later editors as well as Carey dismissed Price on the basis of a letter written by Smith: "Price's speculations cannot fail to sink into the neglect that they always deserved. I have always considered him a *factious* citizen, a most superficial Philosopher and by no means an able calculator" (Carey 1928, p. 126, and Smith 1976, p. 88n; emphasis added).

Here Price is judged to be guilty of the same sin as Franklin; Smith's use of the

Observations Concerning the Increase of Mankind (1751) (Franklin 1959-; 4: 227-34) and *The Interest of Great Britain Considered* (1760) (Franklin 1959-; 9: 47-100), both of which Smith possessed. In fact, Smith's analysis of the prosperity of North American colonies commences with this discussion of population growth. Thus, both pamphlets are particularly relevant because of their possible role in shaping Smith's opinions concerning the relations between labor and capital in the economic development of North America. The first work, *Observations*, was a remarkable piece of argumentation. McCulloch saw it as an "excellent specimen of the penetrating sagacity and compressed and clear style" of Franklin (McCulloch 1845, p. 253). Malthus hailed it as a forerunner of his own work (Malthus 1826, pp. 1, 5), but it was not what we might consider Malthusian, even expressing a wish for an increase in the numbers of the "Body of White People on the Face of the Earth" (Franklin 1959-; 4: 234). This work was written in response to the British Act of 1750, which prohibited the erection of additional slitting and rolling mills, plating forges, and steel furnaces in the American colonies (Franklin 1959-; 4: 225-26). Franklin did not question the right of the English to frame such legislation. Instead, he argued that it was not in the best interest of the mother country because of the political conditions of the Colonies .

At the time, some people had already noted the strategic importance of a strong British settlement, considering the struggle between France and England for control of the Continent (Franklin 1959-; 4: 224). Yet to argue for the potential vitality of the colonial economy on such political grounds would play to the worst fears of those who wished to nip their potential

---

concept of Factiousness was highly subjective. As he wrote to Lord Shelburne, "For tho' a little faction now and then gives spirit to the nation, the continuance of it obstructs all public business and puts it out of the power of [the] best Minister to do much good" (Mossner and Ross 1977, p. 28).

Since the verdict on Price is dated twelve years after the appearance of *Wealth of Nations*, the ever controversial Price could have fallen from grace long after 1773. The tone of a letter addressed to Price by Franklin in 1780 suggested that the two may have suffered a common ostracism stemming from their methods of supporting the cause of the colonists: "Your Writings, after all the Abuse you and they have met with, begin to make serious Impressions on those who at first rejected the Counsels you gave; and they will acquire new Weight every day and be in high Esteem when the Cavils against them are dead and forgotten" (Franklin 1905-07; 8: 6). In any case, Price would have most likely received his information on the subject of the Colonies from his American associate. Cannan suggested a second possible source of Smith's information; namely Dr. John Mitchell's *The Present State of Great Britain and North America with Regard to Agriculture, Population, Trade, and Manufactures* (1767) (Smith 1937, p. 70n). An equally likely candidate would have been *American Husbandry*, believed by some to have also been written by Dr. Mitchell (Anon. 1775; see also Anon. 1776 and Carrier 1918, pp. 48, 52-53, and 123).

competitors in the bud. Franklin deftly sought to resolve the contradiction by proving that the economic future of the Colonies would be complementary to that of Britain. The economy of North America would grow, but its growth would be agricultural.

Franklin's pamphlet was a masterful brief on behalf of colonial industry. He attempted to demonstrate that industrial development would be forestalled because of the handicaps imposed on the use of both slave and wage labor in the Colonies. First, the "Labour of Slaves can never be so cheap here as the Labour of working men is in Britain" (Franklin 1959-; 4: 229). Second, "Land being thus plenty in America, and so cheap as that a labouring Man, that understands Husbandry, can in a short Time save Money enough to purchase a Piece of new Land sufficient for a Plantation, whereon he may subsist a Family," manufacturing based on wage labor would be uncompetitive in the foreseeable future (Franklin 1959: iv, p. 228). The Colonies would have to remain agrarian until the time would arrive when the crush of population became too great to allow the common workman to become an independent farmer. The English thus had no reason to fear competition from the Colonies.

Franklin's conclusion was generally accepted by the leaders of the United States. For example, Jefferson wrote:

> [I]t is impossible that manufactures should succeed in America from the high price of labour. This is occasioned by the great demand of labour for agriculture. A manufacturer from Europe will turn to labour of other kinds if he finds more can be got by it, and he finds some emploiments [sic] so profitable that he can lay up enough money to buy fifty acres of land to the culture of which he is irresistibly tempted by the independence in which it places him. [letter to Thomas Digges, 19 June 1788, in Jefferson 1950-: 13, p. 260]

John Adams concurred:

> Among men of reflection the sentiment is generally . . . that no power in Europe has anything to fear from America. The principal interest of America for many centuries to come will be landed, and her chief occupation agriculture. Manufactures and commerce will be but secondary objects and subservient to the other. America will be the country to produce the raw materials for manufactures; but Europe will be the country of manufactures, and the commerce of America will never increase but in a certain proportion to the growth of agriculture, until its whole territory of land is filled up with inhabitants, which will not be in hundreds of years. [Adams 1780, p. 255]

A few years later, Madison predicted that the extent and fertility of the Western soil would for a long time give to agriculture a preference over manufactures (Madison 1787, pp. 98-99).

Franklin's argument was internally consistent concerning the threat of colonial competition. The English were said to have nothing to lose and everything to gain from the granting of more freedom to the colonial economy. One might question why colonists should be concerned by laws that compel them to do what they would have done in the absence of any such legislation, but to raise such a question would be to apply a standard that was foreign to such pamphlet literature. Franklin's intent was merely to dispel English fears about the colonial economy.[2]

Although Franklin's pamphlet was an admittedly unscientific work, it does reflect greater consistency concerning alternative modes of production than the great *Wealth of Nations*, which it seems to have influenced. Whereas Smith argued that slaves were more costly to use than wage labor without reference to any particular historical situation, Franklin made the far more modest claim that slave labor could not be so cheap as wage labor in Britain. In the colonial economy, however, slaves were understood to be advantageous. In Franklin's words:

> Why then will Americans purchase Slaves? Because Slaves may be kept as long as a Man pleases, or has Occasion for their Labour; while hired Men are continually leaving their Master (often in the midst of his Business), and setting up for themselves. [Franklin 1959-; 4: 230]

The same ideas recur in *The Interest of Britain Considered* written in 1760. The issue at hand was whether the English should claim Canada or Guadeloupe in consequence of the French surrender at Montreal in 1759. The debate over this question was heated. Pitt queried "some are for keeping Canada; some Guadeloupe; who will tell me which I shall be hanged for not keeping?"

---

[2] Franklin seemed to have maintained an interest in making the English complacent about the strength of the colonial economy for some time. For example, after the colonial governors were requested to supply Britain with a summary of their industrial strength in 1766, Franklin advised his son, whom he had arranged to be appointed governor of New Jersey, "You have only to report a glass-house for coarse window glass and bottles, and some domestic manufactures of linen and woolen for family use that do not clothe half the inhabitants, all the finer goods coming from England and the like" (Franklin 1959: xv, p. 77). His son complied almost to the letter.

Of course, industry had not taken hold to any great extent by that time in any case. Only North Carolina boasted of its 50 saw mills on a single river (ibid.), but that industry was hardly a threat to Britain. Governor Moore of New York replied with a long description of the difficulty of retaining the employment of workmen who took up farming as soon as possible (see Rabbeno 1895, p. 73).

Alvord 1917; 1: 19) Franklin's contribution was again an exceedingly clever brief prepared on behalf of the American interests. Guadeloupe was a slave island with little demand for English wares, since the majority of its inhabitants were slaves. Canada would serve the English purposes much better. To make this case, Franklin stressed the complementary, rather than the competitive, characteristics of the colonial mainland. Here we have another instance of Franklin adopting whatever measures were required to win a point. To make his argument appear more convincing, he posed as an English writer:

> [Until the colonies become more populous] this nation must necessarily supply them with the manufactures they consume, because the new settlers will be employ'd in agriculture, and the new settlements will so continually draw off the spare hands from the old, that our present colonies will not . . . find themselves in a considerable degree, much less for those who are settling behind them. [Franklin 1959-; 10: 78]

Why would the Colonies fail to develop their own industry? According to Franklin:

> [N]o man acquainted with political and commercial history can doubt [that] Manufactures are founded in poverty. It is the multitude of poor without land in a country, and who must work for others at low wages or starve, that enables undertakers to carry on a manufacture, and afford it cheap enough to prevent the importation of the same kind from abroad, and to bear the expense of its exportation. But no man who can have a piece of land of his own, sufficient by his labour to subsist his family in plenty, is poor enough to be a manufacturer and work for a master. Hence while there is land enough in America for our people, there can never be manufactures to any amount of value. [Franklin 1959-; 9: 73]

This image of the future is hardly what Adam Smith had envisioned. Thus Smith's use of Franklin was very selective.

Benjamin Franklin and Adam Smith

Despite of probable correctness of Franklin's claim of influence on Smith, broad divergences occur between the two authors. Franklin had merely argued that the English had no need to legislate against the development of colonial manufactures; Smith implied that the English had no need of any colonial relationship whatsoever. Such ties placed an unnecessary burden on England since the Colonies would necessarily remain within the British orbit with or without the formalities of colonial bonds. In this respect, Smith stood shoulder to shoulder with Dean Tucker (1776: pp. 30-31), although Smith's analysis was far more subtle. Franklin's call for colonial independence was not necessarily intended to create the same result.

More important, Smith, the ideologist, sought evidence for the harmonious coexistence of the factors of production in North America. He contended that the Colonies offered proof that capital could flourish in the face of high wages. Franklin, in contrast, described conflict between labor and capital, as expressed by the desire of workers to become independent farmers.

How are we to understand this difference? To argue that Smith was unaware of Franklin's position would be untenable. We saw that Smith knew Franklin personally and was in possession of some of his writings. On one occasion, he even criticized one of Franklin's scientific works that was bound together with the very pamphlets which we have been discussing (Carey 1928, p. 122). Moreover, Smith would have had difficulty in misunderstanding Franklin's meaning in these pamphlets. Although the wily American frequently contradicted himself, these particular pamphlets were perfectly clear.

Smith's own contradiction of Franklin's description might be explained by the Scotsman's confusions, such as those to which we referred earlier when analyzing his treatment of the noncoercive origins of wage labor. The same symptoms of befuddlement pervade his discussion of the Colonies. For example, we have already alluded to the section in which Smith recognized the necessity of wage labor as a prerequisite for earning great profits in colonial agriculture (Smith 1937, p. 533). The high wages that the proprietors were forced to pay were understood to be consistent with rapid capitalist development because they encouraged "population and improvement" (ibid.). However, with so much land unoccupied by the colonists, the effects of higher population were expected to take a very long time. At least, such was the message of Franklin's pamphlets. Even the most optimistic observers of the North American Colonies understood that wage labor would be restricted to those few industries in which employers could afford to pay high wages due to the special advantages of abundant resources or labor-saving technology (see Hamilton 1961-; 10: 272 for one of the most favorable views of American circumstances; see also Raymond 1823, p. 242, and McCulloch 1825, p. 136). Smith himself concurred. He saw the Colonies as advancing only within the sphere of dependency—at least for the foreseeable future.

Smith's ideological analysis also required him to explain why workers would willingly engage in wage labor. One side of his formula of "population and improvement" suggested that wage labor would take hold as a result of Malthusian pressures, which would eliminate the very phenomenon he set out to explain. The other he seemed to rule out in his analysis of the future of the Colonies as producers of raw materials. However, instead of trying to reconcile his contradictory assertions, Smith irrelevantly interjected his opinion that "the progress of many of the ancient Greek colonies toward wealth and greatness, seems accordingly to have been very rapid" (Smith 1937, p. 533).

Wakefield was quick to respond to that dodge: "In no Greek colony did anyone ever sell his labour; or anyone pay wages, high or low. [The work was] performed exclusively by slaves" (Wakefield 1834, p. 236; see also Wakefield 1829, p. 154). Smith's allusion to slavery seems to reflect a subconscious recognition of the force required to ensure that workers allow employers to extract surplus value. Smith, the ideologue, never gave full expression to this semirepressed insight. Had he done so, *Wealth of Nations* might well have conformed to Benjamin Franklin's interpretation of colonial development.

Unlike Smith, Franklin did express racist sentiments in *Observations*, but in later life he appeared to be unalterably opposed to the institution of slavery (see Carey 1928, chap. 4, and Mellon 1969, pt. 1).[3] In a later edition of that work, he had the good sense to alter the phrase "almost every Slave being *by Nature* a Thief" to "almost every Slave being from the nature of slavery a Thief" (Franklin 1959-; 4: 239n). Franklin's "Conversation on Slavery," published in the *London Public Advertiser* in 1770, seems to have played a significant role in preparing for the emancipation of the Scottish bondsmen who lived in a state of virtual slavery (Franklin 1959-; 4: 227-34; see also Viner 1965, pp. 113-14). Addressing himself to a hypothetical Scotsman, he wrote, "Sir, as to your observation, that if we had a real love of liberty, we should not suffer such a thing as slavery among us, I am a little surprised to hear this from you . . . in whose own country, Scotland, slavery still subsists" (cited in Viner 1965, p. 114). Although Franklin had a low opinion of slavery, before 1770 he gave few indications that North American producers could bridge the gap between household manufactures and industry based on wage labor. In 1769 when Franklin communicated his approval of the Resolutions of Non-Importation, he gave little suggestion of an industrial future:[4]

For their Earth and their Sea, the true Sources of Wealth and Plenty, will go on producing; and if they receive the annual Increase, and do

---

[3] Although his position was politic in Quaker Pennsylvania, he continued to hold it long after he could expect much gain from local political conditions. His opposition to slavery may be the only example of a strongly held ethical position in his life.

[4] The physiocratic doctrine that Franklin espoused at this period sat well with his intense involvement in land speculation (Currey 1965, p. 89).

waste it as heretofore on Gegaws of this Country (i.e., England), but employ their spare time in manufacturing Necessaries for themselves, they must soon be out of debt, they must soon be easy and comfortable in their circumstances, and even wealthy. [Franklin 1959; 16: 209; see also Coxe 1794, pp. 442-43]

A few months earlier, Franklin suggested to Lord Kames, Smith's patron (Rae 1895, p. 31), that the true value of manufactures was to concentrate value so that "Provisions may be more easily carried to a foreign market" (Franklin 1959-; 16: 109). Elsewhere, he made use of a biblical allusion (John 6:12) to recommend manufactures on account of their ability to *"gather up fragments* (of time) *that nothing may be lost"* (Franklin 1959-; 15: 52; repeated in 21: 173).

Franklin's Theory of Accumulation

The citations above indicate that Franklin believed manufacturing would remain a part-time adjunct to the independent farm. In his marginal notes to "The Constitutional Means for Putting an End to the Disputes between Great Britain and American Colonies," Franklin remarked, "There is no Necessity for their leaving their Plantations; they can manufacture in their Families at spare Times" (Franklin 1959-; 16: 295; see also Coxe 1794, p. 442).[5] Franklin also observed that families who practice this sort of economy were the healthiest in the nation (ibid., 20: 442-45). Unless these jottings were meant to prepare Franklin for a public encounter, we might expect that they represented his true beliefs.

Yet this state of affairs was transitional. Franklin said as much in the two pamphlets under discussion. Manufacturing would eventually take root, but only after the country became more populated. At that time, he had predicted that the appropriate conditions would be in the distant future. A few decades later, in 1786, he indicated in a promotional tract that North America had already reached that point. Reading the pamphlet in question, we can easily see how Franklin's attitude might well have appealed to the author of *Wealth of Nations*:[6]

---

5 In effect, he anticipated that the Colonies would follow a development path similar to that of Japan and Taiwan to which we alluded earlier (see Chapter 1).

6 "Where do the inhabitants live most on an equality, and most at their ease? Is it not in those inland parts where agriculture gives health and plenty, and trade is scarcely known? Where, on the contrary, are the inhabitants most selfishly luxurious loose and vicious; and at the same time most unhappy? Is it not along the sea-coasts, and in the great towns, where trade flourishes and merchants abound?" (Price 1783, see also de Crevecoeur 1782, pp. 40, 58, and 89).

Whoever has travelled thro' the various parts of Europe, and observed how small is the Proportion of People in Affluence or easy Circumstances there, compared with these in Poverty and Misery; the few rich and haughty Landlords, the multitude of poor, abject, and rack'd Tenants, and the half-paid and half-starv'd ragged Labourers; and view here the happy Mediocrity,[7] that so generally prevails throughout these States, where the Cultivator works for himself, and supports his Family in decent Plenty, will . . . be convinc'd that no Nation that is known to us enjoys a greater share of human Felicity. [Franklin 1905-07; 10: 120]

Yet Franklin observed other tendencies that suggest very different forces were at work:

[N]ever was the Farmer better paid for the Part he can spare Commerce. . . . The Lands he possesses are also continually rising in value with the Increase of Population; and, on the whole, he is enabled to give such good Wages . . . that . . . in no Part are the labouring Poor so well fed and well cloth'd, and well paid as in the United States of America. [Franklin 1905-07; 10: 118]

Indeed, the very period in which Smith was completing his *Wealth of Nations* seems to be the point at which wealth in the northern Colonies was beginning to become more concentrated (Williamson and Lindert 1977). The course of development charted by Steuart seemed to be coming to pass in North America.

Farms were becoming more commercialized. In southeastern Pennsylvania, the region Franklin knew best, the typical farm of 1790 was marketing about 40 percent of its produce (Lemon 1967, p. 69). Economic relations were becoming monetized. Franklin noted, "These Workmen all demand and obtain much higher Wages than any other Part of the World would afford them, and are paid in ready money" (Franklin 1905-07; 10: 118). Moreover, industry that began as an adjunct to agriculture began to take on a life of its own, although many workers, even in urban environments, continued to grow much of their own food (see Smuts 1959, pp. 11-13, and Ware 1924, pp. 39, 74).[8]

---

[7] "Each man owns the house he lives in and the land with which he cultivates, and everyone appears to be in a happy state of mediocrity" (Weld 1800, p. 170).

[8] Urban food production was important elsewhere in the world. London was largely self-sufficient with respect to milk until the 1870s (see Atkins 1977). It also had extensive backyard agriculture, chicken coops, sheep folds, and pig sties above and below ground (see Dyos and Wolff 1973, p. 898). Not all these activities were made consistent with the public's health.

True, Adam Smith could have interpreted such development as a vindication of his doctrine of "population and improvement" (Smith 1937, p. 533). In part, his claim might have some slight validity; however, the prosperity of these urban centers owed much to the surplus produced by slaves.

As the social division of labor became more elaborate, the opportunities for self-employment became less common. Franklin saw this evolution well before Smith had published his *Wealth of Nations*. These transitional conditions explain how Franklin, in 1769, in the paragraph following his comments on part-time domestic manufacturing in the aforementioned margin notes on *The Constitutional Means . . .* observed: "But some Manufacturers may be more advantageous to some Persons than the Cultivation of the Land" (Franklin 1959–; 16: 295). Franklin explained the meaning of his note in an earlier discussion with Gottfried Achenwall, professor of jurisprudence at the University of Göttingen. According to Achenwall's account, Franklin stated: "There is land enough for the rich and poor, and the former prefer the larger profits from waste to the small return from the land" (Achenwall 1767, p. 354).

Franklin left another marginal comment on *The Constitutional Means* that also alludes to the declining welfare of the independent farmer: "No Farmer of America, in fact, makes 5 percent on his Money. His Profit is only being paid for by his own Labour and that of his Children" (Franklin 1959; 16: 294).

Thus, with rising land values and relatively low returns to subsistence farming, we are but a short distance from the institution of wage labor. To say as much does not indicate that Franklin saw America as replicating English conditions. Indeed, he took pride in the uniqueness of the colonial experience. In marginal comments on another anonymous pamphlet, *The True Constitutional Meaning*, Franklin offered some more private thoughts on class relations in England:

> And ought the Rich in Britain, who have such numbers of Poor by engrossing all the small Divisions of Land; and who keep the Labourers and working People Poor by limiting their wages; ought these Gentry to complain of the Burthen of maintaining the Poor that have work'd for them at unreasonably low rates all their Lives? [Franklin 1959–; 16: 290]

What Franklin saw in Ireland was even more distressing. In response to an English gentleman who wondered why North America did not rival Ireland in the export of beef, butter, and linen, Franklin snapped back that "the Reason might be, *Our People eat Beef and Butter every Day, and wear Shirts themselves*" (Franklin 1959–; 19: 22).

Franklin and Smith Once Again

Franklin may well have shared his disdain for the Irish system with liberal friends such as Smith and Hume. This hypothesis is all the more likely since Franklin's hopes for success in speculating on Ohio Valley lands were checked, in part, because powerful Irish interests, in the tradition of Child,[9] feared economic losses resulting from the migration of their tenants to the American West (Franklin 1959–; 13: 414; Currey 1965, p. 221; Alvord 1917, p. 121). By contrast, the Scottish gentry welcomed the exodus of their "free hands," who had only recently lost their traditional rights to the use of the land (see Johnson 1774, p. 97), at least until the rate of emigration reached a point that threatened to lower rents (see Franklin 1959–; 20: 522–28).

The greater tolerance for emigration in Scotland may be explained, in part, by the less labor-intensive cropping system used there. Another major difference between the two cases may well have been the disposition of firearms (see Pettengill 1981). As Defoe noted, "[T]he Highlanders not only have all of them fire-arms, but they are all excellent marksmen" (Defoe 1724–26, p. 667).

Although a certain degree of poverty was required to establish wage labor, the relatively egalitarian society of the northern Colonies provided a welcome comparison with England. Smith, no doubt, shared such an appreciation of colonial conditions. In other words, the American wage rate was coming closer to the ideal of a "normal" or "natural" rate or wages under which capital could prosper without driving labor into utter destitution (see Thompson 1977).

These desired conditions were coming to be met. Although the prerevolutionary farmers in the North may have been relatively prosperous (see Sachs 1953), between 1700 and 1736, the number of landless whites had already risen from 5 percent to 12 percent (Mayer and Fay 1977, p. 44). The average size of landholdings per adult male had declined from approximately 150 acres in the early seventeenth century to 43 acres in 1786 (ibid.).

In presenting the advantages of the state of "happy mediocrity" in which workers could earn relatively high wages while capital profited, both Smith and Franklin could paint a picture of relative harmony between labor and capital. True, it was not as idyllic as Smith's ideological project required, but it was still attractive.

Unfortunately, both neglected to inform their readers of the coercive relations that made colonial development so rapid. Franklin found slavery in

---

[9] Josiah Child, in his *New Discourse on Trade*, argued against plantations by writing "that lands (tho' excellent) without hands proportional, will not enrich any kingdom" (see Child 1751, p. 134). Thus, labor should be kept in the mother country.

Scotland; Smith in history or in far-off Turkey. Neither addressed the role of the temporary servitude of indentured labor, let alone the harsher lot that fell to the blacks, who suffered a lifetime of slavery.

Smith's silence on the subject of slavery is especially troubling since he obtained much of his information about the Colonies from the Glasgow tobacco merchants and planters who had returned from the Colonies (Fay 1956, pp. 264–66). Even if Smith disregarded southern conditions, he still should have understood the importance of the plantation for the rest of the economy. Although slavery did not exist to a great extent in the Northeast, great profits of that region were derived from slave trade. In addition, when manufacturing did mature there, it found its markets in the regions in which slavery flourished. Even in Franklin's adopted home of Pennsylvania, it was "white servitude" that planted in its "fertile soil . . . the seeds of a great industrial future" (Herrick 1926, p. 76). Was Franklin or Smith so naive as to believe that slavery and indentured servitude were irrelevant to the development of the American colonies?

Even if we turn our attention away from the more directly coercive relationships of indentured servitude or slavery pure and simple, problems still remain. How could we be sure that the emergent labor force would willingly forego leisure, even with the promise of a relatively high rate of wages? Poor Richard said, "a fat kitchen, a lean will" (Franklin 1959: i, p. 315). Franklin himself confronted this question with a curious anthropology. In his pamphlet in which he wrote of the conditions which suggested a strengthening of the wage relationship in America, he asserted that "there seems to be in every nation a greater proportion of Industry and Frugality, which tend to enrich, than Idleness and Prodigality, which occasion Poverty; so that upon the whole there is continued accumulation" (Franklin 1905–07; 10: 121). This notion would appeal to Smith, of whom it has been said that he believed "there was a Scotchman inside every man" (Bagehot 1889; 5: 343).

Franklin, however, did not always express such confidence in the industry of the populace. In a valuable letter written to Peter Collison, he observed that when British workers came to the Colonies, where "Labour is much better paid than in England, their Industry seems to diminish in equal proportion" (Franklin 1959–; 4: 479). Noting that the same did not hold true of the German immigrants, Franklin supposed that the variation must be traced to "Institution" (ibid.). The institution to which he referred was the Poor Laws, which lent support to the unfortunate.

In the Native Americans, Franklin saw proof of the "proneness of human Nature to a life of ease, of freedom from care and labour." Although they understood the advantages that "Arts, Sciences, and compact Society procure . . . they have never shown any Inclination to change their manner of life" (ibid.). Not only the Native Americans educated in white society, but even whites taken prisoner by the Indians, inevitably drifted back to the primitive society in preference to the civilized one (ibid.).[10]

Franklin generally expressed a fondness for the values of the Native American (see, for example, ibid., 15: 148–57), which contrasted with his impatience with any white who would not labor diligently. The happiness of the Native Americans was explained on account of their few natural wants, which were easily supplied; whereas, the civilized community had "infinite Artificial wants, no less craving than those of Nature, and much more difficult to satisfy" (ibid., 4: 482). Franklin applauded the simplicity of other pre-capitalist cultures. After being informed by members of Captain Cook's crew about the behavior of the inhabitants of New Zealand, Franklin termed them "brave and sensible" (ibid., 18: 210). What especially struck Franklin's imagination was their refusal to accept the presents of the visitors. He exclaimed, "Behold a Nation of Philosophers! Such as him [meaning Socrates] we celebrate as he went thro' a Fair, *How many things there are in the World that I don't want*" (ibid.). Nonetheless, he later took an active part in a proposed project to carry the benefits of civilization to New Zealand (Franklin 1959–; 20: 522–28).

The same Franklin, in the very letter in which he heaped lavish praise upon the Native Americans for their simple ways, called for the erection of workhouses, where the indigent would be "obliged to work at the pleasure of others for a bare subsistence and that too under confinement" (ibid., 15: 148–57). Given this perspective, not just poverty, but grinding poverty would be required to ensure the accumulation of capital. In spite of all the pious sentiments about the naturalness of a liberal wage rate, the hard liners would seem to be correct after all, at least so far as Franklin was concerned.

Franklin defies easy interpretation. Despite his advocacy of Spartan simplicity, Franklin saw advantages in the finer things in life (McCoy 1980, p. 75). In his letter of 26 July 1784, Franklin asked Benjamin Vaughan: "May not Luxury, therefore, produce more than it consumes, if without such a Spur People would be as they are naturally enough inclined to be, lazy and indolent" (Franklin 1905–07; 9: 244). He then told a story to illustrate his point:

> The skipper of a shallop employed between Cape May and Philadelphia, had done us some small service for which he refused to be paid. My wife understanding that he had a daughter, sent her a present

---

[10] On this score, Madison fretted that American society as a whole might fall back into the "savage state" of the indigenous people (see Branson 1979, p. 241; see also de Crevecoeur 1782, p. 52, and Morgan 1975, pp. 65–66).

of a new-fashioned cap. Three years after, this skipper being at my house with an old farmer of Cape May, his passenger, he mentioned the cap, and how much his daughter had been pleased with it. "But," said he, "it proved a dear cap to our congregation." "How so?" "When my daughter appeared with it at meeting, it was so much admired, that all the girls resolved to get such caps from Philadelphia; and my wife and I computed that the whole could not have cost less than a hundred pounds." "True," said the farmer, "but you do not tell all the story. I think the cap was nevertheless an advantage to us; for it was the first thing that put our girls upon knitting worsted mittens for sale at Philadelphia, that they might have wherewithal to buy caps and ribbons there; and you know that that industry has continued, and is likely to continue and increase to a much greater value, and answer better purposes." [ibid., pp. 243–44]

I am struck by the fact that Franklin seems to have promoted trade for the Colonies, when he had much to gain from the favor of the British, although he promoted self-sufficiency for the newly emerging republic. Moreover, his writings about the noble savage served his own self-interest. Who in English society could match his knowledge (real or imagined) about primitive life? Finally, Franklin attributed the same values to the savages which he associated with yoeman farmers of North America. In a letter to Joshua Babcock, he wrote:

Had I never been in the American colonies, but was to form my judgement of Civil Society by what I have lately seen [in the British Isles], I should never advise a Nation of Savages to admit of Civilization. . . . [T]he Effect of this kind of Civil Society seems only to be, the depressing Multitudes below the Savage State that a few may be rais'd above it. [Franklin 1959–; 19: 6–7]

Franklin seems to have been so pleased with this anthropological flourish that he repeated it in another letter written on the same day (ibid., pp. 16–24).

Was Franklin's anthropology conveyed to Smith? Reading *Wealth of Nations*, we find too much of a love of anecdotes from ancient and classical sources to believe that Smith would not have questioned a visitor with first-hand information about the rude state of society.

This subject was a matter of great importance for Europeans (see Whitney 1924, p. 370). In the words of John Locke, "In the beginning all the world was America" (Locke 1698, p. 319; see also Hobbes 1651, chap. 13, and Meek 1976, pp. 66–67, 136–45, and Meek 1977b, p. 30). In the words of William Robertson, in his *History of America*:

Much discovery of the New World . . . presented nations to our view, in stages of their progress, much less advanced than those wherein they have been observed in our continent. In America, man had to subsist under the rudest norm in which we can conceive him to subsist. We behold communities just beginning to unite, and may examine the sentiments and actions of human beings in the infancy of social life. [Robertson 1777, pp. 50–54 cited in Rendall 1978, pp. 190–91]

Even de Tocqueville saw Tacitus's Germans in the Native Americans (de Tocqueville 1848, pp. 328; see also p. 32). Whitney pointed out that Smith owned at least thirty books of travel and collections of voyages to exotic regions (Whitney 1924, p. 370).

Smith himself saw Native Americans as living in a society that approximated the "rude state" (Smith 1937, p. 653). Besides the numerous examples from the lives of the Native Americans in his *Lectures on Jurisprudence*, Smith speculated that the ancient Scots must have been like that people (Smith 1978, p. 239). We should expect that Smith would have been very interested in what Franklin would have had to say concerning the indigenous people of the New World. Whether the implications of such stories as Franklin had to offer concerning these people would register was another matter.

The final irony of the history of Franklin and Smith is that Franklin not only participated in the Smithian project of using the experience of the New World as an object lesson in the virtues of laissez faire, but he also instructed the New World in the lessons to be derived from European development. Here we find Franklin is far more in tune with Steuart than with Smith:[11]

Every Manufacturer encouraged in our Country, makes part of Market for Provisions within ourselves, and saves so much Money to the Country as must otherwise be exported to pay for the manufactures he supplies. Here in England it is well known and understood that

---

[11] In one of his promotional tracts, Franklin did take a position much like that advocated by Smith. He stated that when the state does subsidize individual industries, "it has rarely succeeded, so as to establish a Manufacture, which the Country was not so ripe for as to encourage private Persons to set it up. Labor being generally too dear there and Hands difficult to be kept together, every one desiring to be a Master, and the Cheapness of Lands inclining many to leave trades for Agriculture" (Franklin 1905–07; 8: 609–10). In the same essay, however, he recommends America on account of the convenience of going about without being shocked by having to see an atheist. Unless the good doctor Franklin absented himself from America in order to protect the pious sensibilities of the immigrants, one might sense some hypocrisy here.

when ever a Manufacture is established which employes a number of Hands, it raises the Value of Lands in the neighbouring Country all around it; partly by the greater Demand near at hand for the Produce of the Land; and partly from the Plenty of Money drawn by the Manufactures to that Part of the Country. It seems therefore, in the Interest of all our Farmers and owners of Lands, to encourage our young Manufacturers. [Franklin 1959–; 18: 82]

All in all, Franklin's ideas about economic development were much closer to those of Steuart than to those of Smith. Like Steuart, Franklin saw industry as beginning as an adjunct to agriculture evolving with a more intensive use of time, although Steuart was more favorably inclined toward manufactures than was Franklin. Patricia James recently speculated that Steuart's claim for the wholesomeness of cities was, in fact, a direct response to Franklin (see James 1979, p. 106). Franklin, however, understood as well as Steuart that increasing population could push labor into accepting full-time employment in manufacturing. Otherwise, Franklin's work was decidedly inferior to Steuart's.

Despite Franklin's similarities with Steuart, neoclassical economists enjoy interpreting Franklin as a Smithian. Grampp (1979) and Nutter (1976) both stress Smith's influence on Franklin. Indeed, Franklin's contribution to Whateley's pamphlet, "Principles of Trade," indicates a militant free-trading spirit (Franklin 1959–; 21: 169–77). However, we must again be on guard against taking Franklin at face value. In the first place, industry was more firmly rooted by 1774, when the work was written, than was the case when Franklin wrote his "Observations and the Interest of Great Britain Considered." More important, the doctrine of free trade lent support to the colonial cause. Although this pamphlet was published pseudonymously, people soon learned who wrote such works.

Thus Franklin's evolution was influenced less by Smith than by the conditions of the society in which he lived. His infatuation with a system of happy mediocrity was appropriate to the early stage of the accumulation process. It was comparable to Steuart's analysis of domestic industry. Later, as a satisfactory labor supply seemed to be put in place, Franklin supported a more conventional theory in which markets, utility, and luxury have more prominence. Even in this late period, Franklin's work bore a marked similarity to Steuart's. In fact, Smith's eulogist, Dugald Stewart, cited Franklin's story of the woolen cap in describing Steuart's analysis of economic development. Stewart introduced the citation with the comment that Franklin's "trifling anecdote . . . places the whole of this natural process in a stronger light than I can possibly do by any general observations" (Stewart 1855; 2: 154).

The case for Smith's influence on Franklin is slim, to say the least. We have no evidence that Franklin ever seriously studied *Wealth of Nations*. Its message, however, was in the air. In contrast, we know Franklin did study Steuart. He made several pages of notes on Chapter XI of Book II of Steuart's *Principles* (printed in Carey 1928, pp. 144–46).[12] The choice of this chapter is significant, since it contains Steuart's most coherent analysis of the transition to capitalist social relations from a system of self-sufficiency.

Smith gave no indication that he recognized this aspect of Franklin's work. His selective appropriation of Franklin's analysis of North American development lends further support to the thesis of Smith's falsification of the political economy of the wage relationship, a relationship which appears clearly in the writings of Franklin and Steuart.

---

[12] Unfortunately, the otherwise thorough editors of Franklin's works omitted these notes. One of the editors has assured me that they will be printed in a subsequent volume.

chapter 7

The Counterattack

The discovery of America . . . by opening a new and inexhaustible market to all the commodities of Europe . . . gave occasion to new divisions of labour and improvements of art, which, in the narrow circle of the ancient commerce, could never have taken place for want of a market to take off the greater part of their produce. The productive powers of labour were improved, and its produce increased in all the different countries of Europe, and together with it the real revenue and wealth of the inhabitants. The commodities of Europe were almost all new to America, and many of those of America were new to Europe. A new set of exchanges, therefore, began to take place which had never been thought of before, and which should naturally have proved as advantageous to the new, as it certainly did to the old continent. The savage injustice of the Europeans rendered an event, which ought to have been beneficial to all, ruinous and destructive to several of those unfortunate countries.

> Adam Smith, *An Inquiry into the Nature and Causes of the Wealth of Nations*, p. 416

Robert Gourlay

Robert Gourlay was not a political economist. He does not even seem to have read much political economy, yet he seems to have provoked others to read Smith in a new light. Gourlay was experienced in agriculture. He recalled:

> When a young man, having time and money at command, I travelled over England for fifteen months together as an agriculturist, and dur-

ing that time became acquainted with the late secretary to the Board of Agriculture. One day, in conversation with him, we hit upon a subject to which each of us had devoted peculiar attention. My father, and indeed my grandfather, had been in the habit of letting out small portions of land on a kind of perpetual lease, called in Scotland a *feu*, to labouring people, whereon each man might build a dwelling house, and enjoy the convenience of a garden. I had marked the wonderful influence which the possession of such a little property had upon the characters of the people. . . .

I had noticed with what serene delight a labourer, especially of the sedentary class, would occupy himself in his garden at hours not devoted to his trade, and I had calculated what an addition, as well to individual as to national wealth and happiness, such economical arrangements, generally adopted, might produce. [Gourlay 1822, pp. 83–84]

Arthur Young wanted to amend general enclosure law so that "a portion of land sufficient to keep a cow should be secured to each man in lieu of his ancient right of pasturage" (ibid., p. 84). Young asked Gourlay to go to the "counties of Rutland and Lincoln, where the practice prevailed of letting the poor have land and cows" (ibid., p. 84). Gourlay recognized the powerful impact of primitive accumulation. He protested:

Year after year, at this place and that, the poor, seeing themselves unjustly deprived of advantages which they had inherited from time immemorial, grumbled, rioted, and were put down. The process of stealing gradually on, the strength of the mass was subdued piece meal; and, finally, a change was effected, in the condition of English labourers, through a variety and succession of causes, but little reflected on or noticed by political economists. [Ibid., p. 86]

Gourlay was far from radical in his vision. He claimed to have "an absolute abhorrence of the spade husbandry, as proposed by the benevolent Mr. Owen" (ibid., p. 156). He wanted the distribution of land to be tied to the interests of employers. He reminded his readers:

[T]he half acre of land is condescended upon as being such a quantity as any poor man could make the most of at his spare hours, and from which he could raise sufficient food for a cow, along with his liberty of pasturage on the common:; but there are reasons which would make it politic and right to diminish both the extent of the common and the garden plot. A quarter of an acre is the proper size for a garden, and 25 instead of 50 acres of common would be quite sufficient.

A rood of land, under good garden culture, will yield a great abundance of every kind of vegetable for a family, besides a little for a cow and pig. . . . It is not the intention to make labourers professional gardeners or farmers! It is intended to confine them to bare convenience. The bad effects of giving too much land to labourers was discovered more than thirty years ago, in the lowlands of Scotland. . . . The bad effects of the little potatoe farms in Ireland are well known; and nothing but dirt and misery is witnessed among the *Crofters* of the Highlands of Scotland. A tidy garden, with the right of turning out a cow in a small well-improved and very well-fenced field, would produce efforts of a very different kind indeed. [Ibid., p. 154–55]

Gourlay "despaired of seeing anything effectual accomplished by the Board of Agriculture (ibid., p. 86). Consequently, he said "[I]mpressions as to the necessity of changing somehow the system of the poor laws became more and more riveted in my mind" (ibid.). The poor laws, he charged were "the greatest evil which overshadows the fate of England" (ibid., p. 83). How did he come upon this revelation? He said that he was struck by the marked difference between the conditions of agricultural laborers in England and Scotland:

In the one [Scotland], labourers were independent and improving their condition, even in the face of growing taxation: in the other they were verging to extreme poverty and degradation, while all was flourishing around them. In Scotland it was more generally the custom to accommodate farm labourers with cows than in England, but this was far from constituting the difference. [Ibid., p. 87]

Gourlay laid the blame on the poor laws. He did not join in the familiar lamentation that the poor rates were too high. Instead, he pointed out that the poor laws were meant to serve the interest of farmers:

[F]armers had chiefly in view to hold down . . . wages of single men. . . . Thus, while the statute laws have been framed to prevent manufacturing labourers from combining to raise their pay, a most powerful combination . . . was at work to keep down husbandry labour below its proper level; and thus it was that I could hire an English ploughman for 12 pounds per annum, while I could not hire a Scotch ploughman of the same appearance at less than 18 pounds. [Ibid., p. 109]

By the time Gourlay was ready to publish his work, Scottish wages had fallen from 12 to 9 pounds, while English plowmen continued to earn the same wage as before (ibid., p. 104). The superior wages earned in England were not a cause for rejoicing. In such times, wages should fall so that both worker and employer could share in the losses that hard times bring.

Gourlay had a plan to rid England of its poor laws. It should unburden itself of its poor by having them emigrate to Canada. Thus taxes in Britain could be lower. Only one difficulty remained if the Canadian economy were to enjoy the benefit of the new supply of labor. Canada was cursed with an excess of cheap land. According to Gourlay:

> It should never be forgotten that wild land is the chief bane of this country, and no fair means should be left unemployed to lessen it. . . . Land in America is the very lubber-fiend which checks its own improvement. Could nine-tenths of it be sunk into the sea, and after-wards emerge by tenths, gradually, as it became absolutely necessary for the wants of mankind, there would be infinite gain in every way. The people of the States are wasting their strength by spreading too rapidly over their wide domain. [ibid., pp. 414, 385].

He complained that the average Ontario farmer owned 237 acres, of which only 38 were cultivated (ibid., p. 415). Land should not be granted freely; nor should it be held tax-free.

I confess that I have made Gourlay's argument considerably more coherent than he did. His writing style was as bizarre as his personal life. For example, when Brougham neglected to respond to one of his letters, Gourlay horse-whipped him (Mills 1915, p. 136). His ability to antagonize powerful people frequently led to incarceration. The economic theorizing was part of a more urgent agenda of personal rehabilitation. In the middle of the book he bursts out, "I have exhibited my case . . .: produced documents: stated what course I was pursuing, and was about to pursue for redress" (ibid., p. 317). It is full of bile and invective, with matters pertaining to his economic program randomly scattered about. Although his economic reasoning may seem rather common-place, its influence turned out to be profound. Now let us see how Gourlay's ideas worked their way through the world of political economy.

Edward Gibbon Wakefield

One of the handful of people who paid some tribute to Gourlay was Edward Wakefield, Sr., land agent to David Ricardo and brother of the first author to have credited Steuart with superiority over Smith. Regarding an early work of Gourlay's, he wrote: "From my personal knowledge of that gentleman, I am inclined to pay very great attention to his opinion, for few have seen so much of England in a practical way as this intelligent North Briton" (Wakefield 1812, cited in Gourlay 1822, p. 89). Some years later, Wakefield's son, Edward Gibbon Wakefield, seems to have drawn some inspiration from Gourlay.

The younger Wakefield never gave much public acknowledgment to what Mills had called his "obvious debt to Gourlay" (Mills 1915, p. 139). His endorsement of Gourlay's book was lukewarm. In an article for the *Spectator* he wrote:

> The author . . . has mixed up with much valuable statistical informa-
> tion an account of his own pre-eminent misfortunes and a picture of
> his own mental sufferings, so distressing, or so annoying, to the reader,
> that it becomes difficult to extract from his book those parts which are
> merely useful. [Wakefield 1831a cited in Mills 1915, p. 136]

Aside from citing Gourlay in his pamphlet, "A Statement of the Principles and Objects of a Proposed National Society for the Cure and Prevention of Pauperism," which he published in 1830 (see Mills 1915, p. 136), and printing a few extracts from Gourlay in the Appendix to *England and America* (1834, pp. 351–56), Wakefield refrained from mentioning Gourlay. According to Gourlay, Wakefield readily acknowledged his debt in private when they met in Canada in 1838. Gourlay claimed[cited in Mills 1915, p. 139]:

> He introduced himself—Mr. Wakefield (the same who had been
> announced in the newspapers as accompanying Lord Durham, to in-
> struct as to the settling the wild lands of Canada). He told me that he
> was the writer of letters which appeared in the London *Spectator* ["Let-
> ters by P."] some 7 years ago, regarding me. I called to mind the letters:
> they were highly complimentary, and intended to draw towards me
> the notice of the Grey Ministry. Never before having known to whom
> I was thus obliged I thanked Mr. Wakefield. . . . He then went on to
> say that he was also the author of a pamphlet on Colonization ["A
> Statement . . ." cited above], which was sent to me, soon after, under
> the frank of Lord Howick. . . . Mr. Wakefield said he had taken his
> ideas on colonization from my book. I replied that it gave a very
> imperfect view of my projects: . . .
>
> Mr. Wakefield added, "Nevertheless, Government has established a
> colony on your principles in Australia".

The importance of Wakefield's work cannot be overestimated. As Lionel Robbins has written, "The arrival [of Wakefield] on the scene may be com-pared to the descent of some gorgeous tropical bird among the sober denizens of a respectable farmyard" (Robbins 1958, p. 154). To translate this metaphor into more understandable terms, we might say Smithian ideology was trium-phant in England until it met the challenge of Edward Gibbon Wakefield.

Wakefield was a most unlikely person to have effected such a revolution in economic thought. His mother despaired of her son's ever putting his bright mind to good use, but while confined in Newgate prison for the abduction of a wealthy schoolgirl, Wakefield came into contact with many candidates for transportation to Australia. As might be expected, travel books were very popular in Newgate (see Tobias 1967, p. 66). Wakefield wrote, "[W]hilst in Newgate, I had occasion to read with care every book concerning New South Wales and Van Dieman's Land, as well as a long series of newspapers published in these colonies" (Wakefield 1931, p. 266). On the basis of such books, newspapers, and probably information gleaned from other prisoners, Wakefield wrote a book that purported to be the product of an English colonist in Australia.

Surprisingly, Wakefield was able to reconstruct the social relations of labor and capital in a very realistic fashion (Wakefield 1829). He scoffed at the notion that the social division of labor was the product of voluntary consent. Its creation required authority, hierarchy, and, generally, slavery (Wakefield 1935; 1: 46–47). In his words, "Slavery appears to have been the step by which nations have emerged from poverty and moved toward wealth and civilization" (Wakefield 1841; 4: 333, cited in Robbins 1958, p. 160; see also Engels 1894, p. 217).

Wakefield was not as hesitant to embrace slavery as was Steuart. In his pretended letter from Australia, after bemoaning the scarcity of labor, he cried out:

> How often, in my presumption, had I cursed the memory of Las Casas, for bribing the first planters of Hispaniola to spare the inhabitants of that island, by suggesting that they might obtain slaves from Africa! How scornfully, in my ignorance of cause and effect, had I abused the Democrats of North America for cherishing the horrors of slavery! In moments of weakness, how I had sighed, and even shed tears of compassion and anger, at the damnable cruelties which I saw inflicted upon Blacks at the Cape of Good Hope! And yet, in spite of my reason and every better feeling of my nature, I brought myself to find excuses for the Spaniards, Americans, and Dutch; aye, even to think that a few thousand Negroes would be a great acquisition to New South Wales! So they would; and they would conduce to the wealth, and—deny it who will—even to the *civilization* of these colonial landowners. [Wakefield 1829, p. 112]

Wakefield insisted that the importance of slavery had not disappeared, even in his day. He predicted that if slavery were abolished in the United States, the great cities of the North "would sink into insignificance" (Wakefield

1836; 11: 2, cited by Winch 1965, p. 97n). By extension, England itself was dependent on slavery. A disciple of Wakefield, Herman Merivale, an Oxford professor, whose lectures on the subject of colonizations and colonies delivered between 1839 and 1841 won him an appointment as Under-Secretary for India, explained to his fellow countrymen whose sensibilities were too delicate to accept the morality of slavery:

> What raised Liverpool and Manchester from provincial towns to great cities? What maintains now their ever active industry and their rapid accumulation of wealth? The exchange of their produce with that raised by American slaves and their present opulence is as really owing to the toil and suffering of the Negro as if his hands had excavated their docks and fabricated their steam engines.
>
> [Everyone connected with the commerce between Britain and the United States] . . . is in his very own way an upholder of slavery: And I do not see how any consumer who drinks coffee or wears cotton can escape from the same sweeping charge.[1] [Merivale 1841, p. 295; see also McCulloch 1845, p. 341]

Merivale instructed his Oxford students:

> In the old civilized countries, the worker, although free, is by a law of nature dependent upon the capitalist. [In the colonies] it is of the highest importance to find some artificial substitute for the slave and convict labour, by which our colonies have been hitherto rendered productive. [Merivale 1841, pp. 235–314, cited by Marx 1977, p. 937; Merivale 1841, p. 262]

Wakefield and his school recognized that the key to maintaining this dependence was the high price of land; for where land is to be had cheaply, workers "cease to be labourers for hire; they . . . become independent landowners (Wakefield 1834, p. 203, and 1849, p. 347). Much of the power of Wakefield's system stems from his recognition that this simple observation of his contradicted the sacred laws of political economy:

> At length the true light broke upon me. The *scarcity of labourers* was an insuperable bar to any mode of cultivation that requires the employment of many hands! I profess my self to be little versed in the laws of political economy; but the fact was self evident. [Wakefield 1829, p. 108]

---

[1] The first citation appears to be an accurate paraphrase rather than a direct quotation.

According to Wakefield's interpretation of the North American colonies, "[T]he doctrine of Adam Smith concerning the effect of cheap land and dear labour, in producing national wealth has been refuted by the safest of all arguments—an ample experiment" (ibid, p. 156). An experiment, I should add, of Smith's own choosing. In contrast in Australia, "During forty years we have combined the fire and water of political economy—dear land and cheap labor" (ibid., p. 127).

Wakefield expressed pride in the novelty of his ideas, although, in reality, his ideas were anything but novel (see Marx 1977, p. 932). In Locke we find vague hints of Wakefield's idea (Locke 1698, p. 316). Hobbes displays striking similarities (see Hobbes 1651, chap. 30, p. 387).

The problem of labor leaving for more accessible lands in the colonies was a fairly common theme in British mercantile literature after 1600 (see Appleby 1978, p. 135). Remember that Franklin's plans to colonize the Ohio Valley came to naught because, in part, the president of the Board of Trade, Lord Hillsborough, was afraid that further immigration from Ireland would reduce the profitability of his extensive Irish holdings (Franklin 1959–; 13: 414; Currey 1965, p. 221; Alvord 1917; 2: 121; and Plath 1939, p. 231).

Franklin had understood these forces earlier; his *Observations* was published in 1755. The following year, the Marquis de Mirabeau published his views on the importance of land scarcity in *L'Ami des hommes*. Mirabeau's brother was a governor of Guadeloupe despite his objection to slavery (Davis 1966, p. 428). Whether or not Mirabeau received the idea from his brother or from Franklin is a matter of conjecture. Such ideas were in the air.

The Revolutionary War did not end British concern about the lure of cheap land in the United States (Herrick 1926, pp. 156–59). As late as 1814, skilled mechanics employed in the British machine-making industry were prohibited from emigrating on pain of severe punishment (see Marx 1977, p. 719–21). In 1816, some Britons were still calling upon their government to stop migration to the United States, although the rationale was to stifle development in the New World (Anon. 1816, p. 62).

The settlers in the Colonies also knew the importance of restricting access to the land. For example, landholdings of the poor in the Massachusetts Bay Colony were limited, partly for the purpose of preventing what Governor Winthrop termed the "neglect of the trades" (Goodrich and Davison 1935, p. 168). In seventeenth-century Virginia, the same object was achieved by the extensive claims staked by earlier settlers (see Morgan 1975, pp. 218–23); however, such restrictions were not always as effectively enforced by the time Wakefield was writing. As Daniel Webster noted, in New England, where settlers were "nearly on a general level in respect to property . . . their situation demanded a parcelling out of the land" (Webster 1920, pp. 43–44; see also Fite and Reese 1965, pp. 30–33; Harris 1953; and a similar assertion by Sir Robert Peel cited in Tuttle 1967, p. 221). The resulting situation in New England was so unfavorable to would-be employers of wage labor that parents had to take measures to restrict the marriages of their sons lest the farmstead lose its only labor supply (see Fobre 1980, pp. 6–7).

Employers resented the effects of cheap land. According to an eighteenth-century French ambassador, a group of influential Americans wished that Spain would close the Mississippi River to stop people from being able to live relatively unattached to commercial society (see Morgan 1976, p. 111). Later, politicians attempted to maintain a restrictive land policy, especially in the West (see Zahler 1941).

Politicians such as ex-president John Quincy Adams and Senator Foote of Connecticut were especially vocal in calling for restrictions on the availability of public lands (see Schlesinger 1945, p. 347). This debate was a major policy issue in the United States. Readers of political economy could learn of it from Thomas Cooper, who denounced "the cunning and selfish management of the manufactures . . . [that] discourages the low price of western lands, that the door of emigration may be closed on their slavish operatives" (Cooper 1833, p. 107, cited in O'Conner 1943, p. 220).

Nonetheless, western land remained cheap by international standards. The relative accessibility to land in Britain and the Colonies is reflected by the following comparison: in 1830 a British farm worker could purchase about one-tenth acre of land with his annual wage; an Illinois farm worker could afford 800 times that area (Gates 1960, p. 276; see also Shireff 1835, p. 466).

Wakefield argued that capital could not remain viable in such an environment. It would have to resort to coercion. History seems to bear him out in this regard. According to Wakefield's interpretation of history, "cheapness of land [was] . . . the cause of slavery" (Wakefield 1834, p. 152; see also Domar 1970).

As proof of this proposition, Wakefield offered the example of Virginia. According to one estimate: "[O]ne man may prepare and husband so much grounde . . . with less than foure and twenty hours, as will yield him his victuall for a twelve month" on 25 square yards of ground (Heriod 1588; 1: 343). This account may have been probably exaggerated. The author of a similar description of Virginia also reported grapes so plentiful that a single vine could fill a London cart, potatoes as thick as a child's thigh, a frogs leg large enough to feed six Frenchmen (see Marx 1964, pp. 75–80). Although one could take issue with the particulars, land was still plentiful in the Colonies. A more reliable source, George Bancroft, wrote:

> Labour was valuable; land was cheap; competence promptly followed industry. There was no need of a scramble; abundance gushed

from the earth for all. . . . It was "the best poor man's country" in the world. [Bancroft 1854; 1: 234]

It was not, however, the best rich man's country. The resulting struggle between the poorer farmers and the wealthy plantation owners that 1676 was "the greatest social conflict of pre-revolutionary North America" (Brenner 1977, p. 89). According to Wakefield, only slavery "saved" Virginia (Wakefield 1834, pp. 201–23; see also Morgan 1975).

Wakefield did no more than to bring a well-established practice into the discourse of economic theory. He dared to speak openly of such matters only because his program promised huge dividends at home and abroad.

Writing at a time, however, when labor was temporarily in surplus, Wakefield had no particular reason to express concerns about induced labor shortages in England. For example, Senior believed that the reduced poor rates would more than pay for the cost of removing workers from England (Senior 1831, p. xvi). Also, Senior felt that emigration promised to reduce the pressure for social revolution (see Levy 1970, p. 70). Of course, much of the emigration to Australia was not voluntary. Convicts were routinely sent to Australia. Many of these people were guilty of the heinous crime of poaching (see Wakefield 1829, p. 105).

The removal of the poachers eliminated those from England who were most likely to resist the demands of capital. An additional benefit from emigration would be the substitution of seasonal workers from Ireland for the more expensive permanent employees, who were to be removed to the colonies (Cowherd 1977, p. 158, Pollard 1978, p. 112). Yet for the Australian employers, labor was still too scarce.

Wakefield's remedy for this situation was merely to make land artificially scarce by putting a sufficient price on it, thereby removing the worker's opportunity to become self-sufficient farmers. This program, which he dubbed "systematic colonization," was clearly designed to limit access to the land. He recommended these measures on account of their encouragement of "natural slavery . . . that natural subordination in which the greater part of mankind always has been and probably always will be" (cited by Semmel 1970, p. 111). In effect, Wakefield argued that market relations would be incompatible with wage labor when access to the land was too easy. Capital would have to resort to coercion.

Wakefield was convinced that slavery, whether "natural" or enforced, had the advantage of allowing a more advanced division of labor (Wakefield 1835; 1: 46). Thus it could also lead to an expansion of social productivity. Like Steuart, Wakefield preferred natural slavery to its more direct variant.

Wakefield even called upon English workers to join with him in a program to restrict access to land in the Colonies. He argued, "In order to raise wages immediately, the field for employment of English capital and labour must be enlarged" (Wakefield 1834, p. 130). Consequently, workers were advised that their self-interest required that capital be granted satisfactory conditions in the Colonies; yet the more English labor was drawn to the Colonies to avail itself of the cheap resources, the better the condition of the remaining workers should be.[2]

Wakefield did not mention that labor would be better off if the workers had freer access to the colonial lands.[3] Instead, he played down the artificial glutting of colonial labor markets by invoking Bellers' principle: that concentration of workers can make enough of an addition to the total product to allow for increased benefits to both labor and capital (Wakefield 1835, pp. 51ff). Consequently, the combination of expensive land and wage labor would allow a great influx of labor to be absorbed. Systematic colonization promised higher profits as well as a better standard of living than the free market could offer.

In spite of his supposed concern for the working class, the essential message of Wakefield was that where workers found alternatives to wage labor, capital would even resort to slavery. Thus Smith's optimistic evaluation of wage labor had to be amended. According to the calculations of the Wakefield school, "slave labour is dearer than free *wherever abundance of free labour can be procured*" (Merivale 1841, p. 256). In short, capital would submit itself to the rules of the marketplace only after labour had been made to submit itself to capital.

Wakefield's Reception by Political Economy

By suggesting that wage labor developed out of slavery, or, even worse, that the prosperity of England continued to be dependent, even in part, on slavery, the Wakefield school undermined any humane pretensions of political economy. Yet Wakefield's ideas won him the support of virtually every major economist of his day (Winch 1975, pp. 128–35, Semmel 1970) with the sole exception of McCulloch.[4] Moreover, Wakefield became the major influence in the settlement of New Zealand, the land to which Franklin had earlier proposed introducing the benefits of capitalist civilizaton.

After reading *England and America* (1834), Scrope wrote to the author, "I cannot remember reading any work with greater interest, or more thoroughly

---

2 Disregarding numerous other contradictory impacts.

3 The rights of indigenous people did not merit a trifle of concern.

4 In the United States, Wakefield's interpretation of North American history, as it has been passed down from Achille Loria through Frederick Jackson Turner, has been thoroughly assimilated in academic thought (Benson 1950).

going along with any author in his views, opinions, and sentiments" (cited in Mills 1915, pp. 87–88).

Nassau Senior, an outspoken foe of the working class, announced:

> It is a remarkable instance of the slowness with which political knowledge advances that though colonization has been vigorously carried on for about 3,000 years . . . the mode of affecting it in the manner most beneficial to the mother country and to the colony was discovered only twenty-five years ago. The discoverer was Edward Gibbon Wakefield. [Senior 1928, pp. 351–52]

In spite of such fulsome praise, Wakefield is generally passed over in silence. Even Schumpeter's encyclopedic *History of Economic Analysis*, which brings together a discussion of the most obscure texts, fails to give Wakefield a single mention (Schumpeter 1954).

We might expect to find a clear exposition of Wakefield's theories in the work of his avowed disciple, John Stuart Mill; however, Mill felt compelled to dress up his master's ideas to make them more presentable. Accordingly, he introduced Wakefield to generations of students with a curious fable. Mill asked his readers to "suppose that a company of artificers provided with tools, and with food sufficient to maintain them for a year, arrive and establish themselves in the midst of" a population of self-sufficient households (Mill 1848; 2: 119).[5] Consequently, he noted, "The economical position of the landed population is now materially altered.[6] They have an opportunity given them of acquiring comforts and luxuries" (ibid.).

Just in case his readers missed his point, Mill, the colonial administrator, shifted ground to recommend that "the best chance for an early development of the productive resources of India consists in the rapid growth of its exports of agricultural produce (cotton, indigo, sugar, coffee, etc.) to the markets of Europe" (Mill 1848; 2: p. 121).

Mill's effort is remarkable. In the first place, he attempted to take the sting out of Wakefield's program by allowing a Smithian extension of the division of labor. But where did he look? To India! India had never been used to translate Smith's ideology into practice; the administrators had always been congenial to the mercantilist conception of development. Finally, in Mill's fable, it would seem that wealth flowed from Britain, the home of the "company of artificers," to India. Repatriation of profits was not mentioned.

---

[5] Compare with a similar fable in Steuart (1767; 1: 254–62).

[6] See Marx (1967; 3: 327, 331–32), where he argues that the mode of production cannot be transformed merely by the actions of merchant capital.

Stripped of its fantasies, however, Mill smacks of Wakefield pure and simple:

> [T]he influence exercised on production by the separation of employments is more fundamental than, from the mode in which the subject is usually treated, a reader might be induced to suppose. . . . The truth is much beyond this. Without some separation of employment, very few things would be produced at all. [Mill 1848; 2: 118]

Wakefield and Primitive Accumulation

Marx reserved his last chapter of Volume I of *Capital* for Wakefield. He was not so much concerned with Wakefield's discovery of colonization. Those ideas were found more than a half century earlier in Mirabeau, as we mentioned before (Marx 1977, p. 932), as well as by Franklin and other Americans. Rather, for Marx, the importance of Wakefield was that "he discovered, not something new *about* the colonies but *in* the *colonies*, the truth about capitalist relations in the mother country" (Marx 1977, p. 932). Most economists have ignored Marx's characterization of Wakefield's work. The major exception is Lionel Robbins, who reluctantly accepted Wakefield's importance (Robbins 1958, p. 154n):

> This judgement is a complete reversal of a view which I expressed some thirty years ago when, in the course of controversy about some Marxian theorems, I reproached my opponent, Mr. Maurice Dobb, with paying too much attention to Wakefield's propositions.

Professor Robbins, while recognizing Wakefield, was still not willing to accept the lesson Marx drew from his work. Robbins chides Marx for misrepresenting Wakefield in the final line of *Capital*, Volume I:

> [T]he capitalist mode of production and . . . capitalist private property have for their fundamental condition the annihilation of that private property which rests on the labour of the individual himself; in other words, expropriation of the worker. [Marx 1974, p. 940]

Robbins cites Wakefield's *Letter to the South Australian Commissioners* to prove his case against Marx:

> Let it be clearly understood, that the object in putting a price on public land is not to prevent labourers for hire from ever becoming landowners. On the contrary, every one wishes that all the labourers taken out should be able to obtain land and servants of their own, after, and by means of, a few years of labour for hire. . . . In my own calculations . . . I have supposed that three years would be long enough

for the capitalist and short enough for the labourer. [Robbins 1958, p. 163]

Wakefield's key assumption was the requirement that the stream of immigrants be sufficiently large that the expanding population of employers could continue to have a satisfactory supply of labor. Such a condition would be rather unlikely. Consider the case of the United States. Many observers estimated that frontier labor could save enough to become independent within the three-year period recommended by Wakefield, but he regarded the result with displeasure. He described the frontiersman as "grossly ignorant, dirty, unsocial, delighting in rum and tobacco, attached to nothing but his rifle, adventurous, restless, more than half-savage (Wakefield 1834, p. 196). Thus one must take his supposed support for easy access to the land with a grain of salt.

While an adequate labor force might have been theoretically maintained in the United States when people could obtain land within three years, in England, obviously, too few immigrants were arriving to supply enough wage labor to satisfy employers. Labor had to be shaken loose from the countryside. In this sense, Wakefield demonstrates the need for the sort of primitive accumulation that actually occurred in England.

If Robbins wished to find fault with Marx's words, he could have pointed to the fact that capital can actually benefit from the workings of household production, as Sir James Steuart had clearly demonstrated. Wakefield himself, however, had comparatively little direct comment on the English economy proper. He emphasized that Smith was correct to teach that "as capitals increase in any country, the profits that can be made by employing them necessarily diminish" (Smith 1937, p. 336; see also p. 128). Wakefield allowed for two means of improving the situation of capital: "Colonization and the importation of Food" (Wakefield 1835; 1: 254). Cheap imported food obviously implies that the same monetary wage would exchange for a greater use value. Wage labor could consequently become slightly less abhorrent compared to the alternative of domestic labor.

Colonization is another matter. Here Wakefield, in anticipation of Lenin, recognized that the export of capital can improve the rate of profit, providing the proper climate for colonization exists—namely, lack of access to cheap land. Beyond this point, Wakefield was very evasive about what he found within the English economy. In his commentary to the *Wealth of Nations* we read: "When a body of men raise more food than they want, and employ that surplus food as capital, paying it in wages to other labourers, those other labourers act in concert or combination with those capitalists" (Wakefield 1835; 1: 29).

We have no need to go further. In the first place, Wakefield carefully obfuscates the cleavage between those who employ labor and those who labor. Once he has gone this far, he can simply slide into the technical advantages of the division of labor. Such a contrived performance teaches us more about Wakefield than about political economy.

Wakefield seems to have recognized that an honest exposition of the workings of the domestic economy would have made his theories too embarrassing for political economy to embrace. In describing his manner of presentation, he explained, "By dwelling altogether on the former question [of the distribution of shares], we make bad blood between the two classes; . . . by examining the latter question [of the total product], we may prove that masters and servants have one and the same interest" (Wakefield 1834, p. 83).

When Wakefield did come close to the truth, he presented it as nonsense, perhaps to make it more palatable. For example, after asking himself, "Why does *any man ever* produce of anything more than he himself can consume," he satisfied himself with the Smithian fantasy: "Solely because he expects that some other man will take from him that portion of his labours which he does not want, giving him in exchange something which he wants" (Wakefield 1834, p. 242; emphasis added).

Where Wakefield did attempt to justify the relationship between labor and capital, he became even more ridiculous. He repeated a variant of Locke's naive fable about the social compact (Locke 1698, p. 320). Accordingly, we are told, "Mankind has adopted a simple contrivance for promoting the division of labour: they have divided themselves into owners of capital and owners of labour" (Wakefield 1834, p. 26). Wakefield even went so far as to propose that these two groups complimented each other's psychological needs: The capitalists are happy to save because they can expect to have workers to employ, and the workers are happy to spend because they can expect to find employment (ibid., p. 26).[7] At one point, immediately after picturing the English farm worker as "a miserable wretch," Wakefield suggested that "the agricultural class seems to have come to an understanding with the other classes, to separate its employment from the manufacturer and dealer" (ibid., p. 29).

To his credit, Wakefield signaled us when he was serious. Consequently, we can easily separate the wheat from the chaff. Moreover, Wakefield's importance did not depend upon his analytical gifts, but rather on his ability, generally, to keep from getting confused by the ideology around him, including his own. Perhaps Wakefield owed this advantage to his thorough

---

[7] Compare with Rousseau (cited in Marx 1977, p. 909).

grounding in Irish affairs.[8] He was easily able to recognize that where small, self-contained households predominated, leisure would take precedence over production. Thus he maintained that "the labor of an Irish coal-heaver or pavior in London, whose labour, when he was without the means of exchanging, did just suffice to maintain his family, produced enough for the maintenance of perhaps a half-dozen families" (Wakefield 1835; 1: 77). We do not have to accept that the standard of living of the coal-heaver was so elevated even when compared to the impoverished Irish peasant, *except in terms of money income.*

The crucial point here is the intensification of labor as a consequence of capital. According to Wakefield, the lesser performance of the Irish peasant is attributable to what he cites McCulloch as calling "the apathy and languor that exist in a rude state of society" (ibid., p. 76). Even Smith criticized "the habit of sauntering and indolent and careless application [that] . . . renders [the peasant] almost always lazy and slothful" (Smith 1937, p. 8).

We need not belabor the point: Wakefield did not see the opportunities for exchange naturally evolving out of the higgling and haggling of the marketplace. Like Steuart, Wakefield attributed the unenthusiastic labors of the Irish peasant to the lack of opportunities for exchange (Wakefield 1835; 1: p. 77). And, like Steuart, he attempted to encourage non-market forces to create the appropriate opportunities.

What concerned Wakefield most was the power of the employer to exchange wages for labor power. Given the alternative of producing for themselves, the peasant household displayed a marked aversion toward wage labor. The household members valued their *opportunity not to exchange* many hours of labor for the equivalent of the value of fewer hours. Moreover, even when wage labor offered pecuniary advantages, workers still frequently chose the independence of a less regimented life (Pollard 1965, pp. 166, 173). Wakefield seemed to have much more to say on the subject, but he remained judiciously silent:

[I]t must be confessed, that the power of exchanging has not been

---

8 Wakefield, although not Irish, was closely associated in his works with his father, author of *Ireland, Statistical and Political,* which was considered to be the best work of that period on the subject of Ireland. Pitt supposedly consulted him on Irish affairs (Lee 1879, p. 449). Torrens also was Irish. Werner Stark commented on the importance of the Irish perspective in later British economic thought: "The apostles of historicism in England . . . were Irishmen. This is certainly no mere chance" (Stark, p. 49n).

However, we must not let an overemphasis on his Irish interests lull us into forgetting his exposure to the working classes at Newgate prison.

thoroughly analyzed by any writer on the subject. Of what element is that complex power composed, and by what circumstances it is apt to be increased or diminished; these are questions which would occupy much space in political economy. [Wakefield 1835; 1: 32]

Moreover, Wakefield recognized that this question of the social division of labor represented a theoretical challenge to political economy:

One cannot use capital merely by wishing to use it, nor can a single workman practice "division of labour," but the capital and the "division of labour" arise from some anterior improvement. [Wakefield 1834, p. 25]

Wakefield's insight into the political economy of wage labor might seem to be self-evident as to be judged unworthy of consideration as theoretical analysis. Yet, the same matter has often been perplexing to first-rate economists. For example, Ricardo, toward the end of his chapter on machinery, theorized that because of cheap food in America "there is not nearly such great temptation to employ machinery" (Ricardo 1951–73; 1: 395). If workers in both locations earned the same real wage, Ricardo might have found himself on solid ground.

More recently, Peter Temin, who excels at the application of economic tools to historical material, argued that extensive supplies of land should not have made industry in the United States require more intensive mechanization than in England (Temin 1971; see also David 1975, pp. 19–91).[9] In reality, by restricting the growth of the industrial reserve army, the homestead was a great threat to profits. Had all workers been wage earners, the equations used to develop the argument might have been more sensible; however, even on the eve of the Civil War, a mere 28 percent of the northern labor force was estimated to have worked for wages (de Canio and Mokyr 1977). Wakefield, who was far more realistic in this matter, realized that only 10 percent of the labor force in the northern states earned wages (Wakefield 1834, p. 30).

Those economists who do correctly apprehend the conditions of employers in the early United States cannot resist obscuring the matter in a haze of

---

[9] Temin qualified his position by noting that industry in the United States would be more capital-intensive if interest rates were higher than in England. The high proportion of farmers, traditionally debtors, did serve to push interest rates up. Although he based his conclusion on different premises, List proposed as a general rule that interest will always be higher in agricultural societies (List 1841, p. 332). For a useful rectification of other aspects of Temin's work, see Clarke and Summers 1980, pp. 129–39.

neoclassical jargon. Fleisig, for example, does not interpret the situation in terms of labor's opportunity to secure employment outside of the wage nexus; rather he pictures potential employers being denied outlets for their supply of entrepreneurial expertise (1966).

Wakefield, in this sense, represents a high point in the study of wage labor. Political economy did not rouse itself to follow it up until the appearance of *Capital*, exactly 100 years after the publication of Steuart's *Inquiry*. Unfortunately, it fell back into a comfortable slumber shortly thereafter.

John Rae and the Moral Value of Primitive Accumulation

Another frontal attack on Adam Smith's theories came from the remarkable John Rae, namesake of both Smith's famous biographer and the no-less renowned Arctic explorer. Such fame eluded this John Rae. Although Rae was a doctor of medicine who made significant contributions in the fields of geology and linguistics, as well as a political economist and magistrate in Hawaii, he is little remembered today. He was even less recognized in his own lifetime. True, John Stuart Mill quoted from him extensively (Mill 1848); Irving Fisher was also generous toward Rae, even dedicating his *Theory to Interest* to the memory of Rae and Boehm-Bawerk (see James 1965, p. 182). Acknowledgment from other quarters was almost nonexistent.

John Rae's assault on Smithian economics was even more significant than that of Wakefield, who never had any real pretensions as an economic theorist. By contrast, Rae was a sophisticated theorist. In addition, he knew about economic development first-hand by virtue of his long experience living on the Canadian frontier, where he could study the meaning of primitive accumulation.

Rae does not seem to have owed anything to Wakefield, but he may have been indebted to Gourlay. Rae's personal life bore some similarity to that of Gourlay. Each wrote the bulk of his work in Canada. Each seemed to embark on long journeys after the onset of some personal troubles (see Goodwin 1961, p. 7, and James 1965, pp. 14–15). Rae's proposal for dealing with the land set aside to finance the Canadian clergy had much in common with Gourlay's recommendations (see James 1965, p. 28).

Rae's appraisal of Gourlay's work was very similar to that of Wakefield. In 1840, after Rae's only major work on political economy had appeared, Rae published a prospectus of another book that he intended to complete. In comparing his prospective book with earlier works, Rae wrote:

> It is believed that no work approaching in plan to the present, has been published by anyone personally acquainted with the country, with the exception of Dr. Dunlop's *Backwoodsman*, and Gourlay, Bouchette and Rolph's volumes.... With regard to the other books it may

be remarked that Mr. Gourlay's book was published under very unfavorable circumstances that the talent which portions of it evidently display, lies buried under a heterogeneous mass of uninteresting matter. [cited in James 1965, p. 71]

Rae is a very difficult figure to approach. In some ways, his work is strikingly modern. He anticipated Boehm-Bawerk's capital theory as well as Thorsten Veblen's notion of conspicuous consumption. On two different occasions, he even described consumption as "conspicuous" (see Rae 1834, pp. 287, 310). In another respect, he was almost a medieval thinker, since his economics was ostensibly derived from an explicit theory of morality.

How might a writer as important as Rae get caught up in disputes over morality (see James 1965, pp. 134–35)? In 1820, the North West Company was merged with the Hudson Bay Company. Consequently, Montreal lost its dominant role in the fur trade. This new arrangement opened the way for the merchant families of Montreal to increase their strength and influence in the economic life of the region. The merchants were mostly of Rae's faith; the majority of the masses were Catholic French Canadians. Dissimilar language, religion, and social customs among classes are familiar ingredients of violent turmoil. Canada was no exception. By 1837, armed conflict had broken out.

Rae was a Scotch Presbyterian, who "was intimately associated with the Montreal merchants and their friends and in due course was to become one of their philosophers and publicists" (James 1965, p. 134). His sister ran a boarding school that catered to the well-to-do merchant families. Her husband and brother-in-law were both successful merchants (ibid., p. 134).

Rae became active in the movement that called for subsidies for the Protestant church. According to Rae, the church had a legitimate claim on the one-seventh of Upper Canada, which was set aside "for the support and maintenance of a Protestant clergy" (31 Geo., c. 31, sec. 36). The Church of England held the position that the Presbyterian church was not intended to be included in the phrase cited above. Rae's involvement in this controversy seems to have helped shape his economic theories, as we shall see.

Apparently, Rae's moral sensibilities put him in conflict with the theories of Adam Smith while he was still young. In 1819, the Scottish public favored the reduction on duties levied on alcohol. Rae recalled:

Almost everyone thought that great good would result from such a change of system and laughed at the fears which few entertained of its bad effects on the general morals of people. The authority of Adam Smith was cited as decisive of the question, and the measure was carried through amid a general acclaim of approbation. I own that I was among the doubters.... Time has now shown that I was not far wrong. [Cited in James 1965, p. 13]

One would not expect a person with this mindset to contribute much to our understanding of the market, but Rae did. Rather than merely rail against the market as an amoral institution, he analyzed economic activity as a subset of morality. To understand his method, recall Gourlay's concern about the Canadian farmers' excess land. In the same vein, Rae challenged his readers to ask a farmer:

[W]hy, instead of stone fences around his fields, which decay, or hedges which require constant trimming and dress, he does not put iron railings, he will answer, "it does not pay." Ask the house builder, why this is not cut stone, instead of brick, that oak instead of pine, this again iron, instead of oak or that copper instead of iron, and consequently the whole fabric doubly durable.

He will also reply, "it will not pay." In all these cases, and a thousand others that ought to be put, the answer is abundantly sufficient as regards the individual, but is no answer at all as regards the society.[10] [Rae 1834; 2: 206; see also Anon. 1775, p. 54]

Rae's comments were aimed as much at those farmers who recently came from the British Isles as native-born Canadian farmers. Even though a farmer may initially look with disdain on the farming methods of the New World, the logic of profit maximization will force the adoption of the techniques that Rae decried: "His neighbors will tell him, indeed, from the first, that if he expects the same profit as they have, he must have less dead stock on his hands, and he must give more activity to his capital; but he is slow of believing them" (Rae 1834; 2: 207).

Elementary economics predict such a result. The New World was short of capital. Thus farmers as well as other businesses would be wise to ration capital very sparingly. Many other observers noticed the same phenomena as Rae (see, for example, Morgan 1975, p. 141; Boserup 1965, p. 63; Grigg 1977, pp. 63, 70, and Kalm 1770–71). We can also point to John Ramsay McCulloch, who noted that British farmers who visited Flanders resolved to farm as carefully as the Flemish, but "a few years' experience... throws them back by a kind of necessity into their former habits; a falling off which they

---

[10] A few years earlier, Thomas Cooper used a similar image of a stone fence to illustrate the advantages of improvements in agriculture relative to industry on account of the less durable nature of investments in manufacturing.

attribute to indolence or the incapacity of those whom they employ" (McCulloch 1824, p. 123n).

I cannot resist comparing the performance of McCulloch and Rae at this point. McCulloch came within a hair's breadth of stumbling onto Rae's brilliant insights. Instead, he attributed the failure of Flemish-style agriculture in England to the availability of land at a low rent. Thus he did not push his observation beyond the agricultural sector. In contrast, Rae used the same idea to develop theories of both capital and the social division of labor.

Rae's theory of the social division of labor evolved out of his concept of what he called "dead stock." In a society made up of identical self-sufficient households, each one would have a complete outfit of the means of production. If some were to specialize in a particular trade, then society could economize on the total capital requirements (see Rae 1834, chap. 8). In Rae's words:

> The exercise of the arts of the weaver, the blacksmith, the carpenter, the farmer, implies the existence of a great variety of tools with which they may be carried on. But, as a man can do only one thing at once, if any man had all the tools which these several occupations require, at least three fourths of them would constantly lie idle and useless. [Rae 1834, p. 164]

This idea was not entirely new. We can find it in Turgot (1766), but nobody else seems to have given it much thought. With Rae, the division of labor is a passive factor in economic development. This interpretation of the division of labor put him in direct conflict with Adam Smith, who intended to show the division of labor as the principal motor of economic development. Rae stressed invention:

> Among a people chiefly agricultural, in the early stages of human society, some persons, more ingenious than the rest, make discoveries and improve the natural products in a variety of modes, whence gradually arise the division of labour, the difference of professions, and a new distribution of wealth among mankind. [Rae 1825, p. 196]

Rae was not giving the credit to those who displayed business acumen. He considered science to be the driving force in economic development. He boldly challenged Smith's interpretation of the division of labor:

> In the *Wealth of Nations*, the division of labor is considered the great generator of invention and improvement, and so of the accumulation of capital. In the view I have given it is represented chiefly as proceeding from the antecedent progress of invention. [Rae 1834, p. 353]

Rae's seemingly casual remarks about the techniques used by Canadian farmers also implied a sophisticated analysis of capital. Consider two alternative methods of constructing a fence. A farmer could use either wood or stone. The wooden fence would be cheaper, but less durable. A profit-maximizing farmer would have to weigh the relative costs. Imagine that the stone fence were produced in two stages. First a wooden fence would be created. Then some additional work were done to give the fence the durability of stone. Profit maximization would require that the extra expense of purchasing the durability be weighed against the cost of tying up the extra capital required to produce that durability. Where the rate of interest would be high, investors would be reluctant to tie up much of their investment in durability. The discounted cost of future maintenance or replacement would be relatively low.

Rae seems to have been the first political economist to have given this idea any thought. Had he gone no farther, he would have earned himself a place of honor. In fact, he did not stop his analysis at this point. He noted that, other things being equal:

> Every individual endeavors to exhaust, as speedily as he can, the capacity of the instruments which he possesses. By rapidly exhausting the capacity of any instrument, the returns yielded by it are not lessened, but quickened. [Ibid., p. 164]

In order to be able to compare technologies with widely differing characteristics, Rae made some simplifying assumptions. To begin with, he supposed that each piece of equipment lasted for a specific time. Next, he expressed their capacity in terms of how much labor would be required to do an equivalent amount of work. Finally, he proposed to measure how much time would have to elapse before an implement yields a quantity of work double that required to build in the first place. Finally, he implicitly assumed that those technologies that produce an effect equal to twice the original effort expended in their production in the shortest period of time will be the least durable. In other words, the least durable method of production will have the highest rate of return. Nonetheless, as was the case with his example of the iron fence, those techniques that yield the highest rate of return are the least efficient.

I am using the term "efficient" in a special sense here. I mean that such investments require the most labor over the long run. For instance, the iron fence might require ten times more labor to install. The wood fence might require one-tenth as much labor to maintain it in a constant state of repair. The average annual amount of labor devoted to fencing will equal the initial expenditure plus the sum of annual inputs of labor. Over a long period, the iron fence will need a lower annual average labor input, even though it would have cost more labor initially.

In effect, Rae had come close to Boehm-Bawerk's theory of capital by identifying more efficient techniques with a lengthening of the lapse of time before investments repay themselves. True, iron fences would not imply inefficiency to most modern economists. High interest rates in Rae's Canada reflected a shortage of capital. Restricting investment to those techniques that yielded a high rate of return indicates a sensible rationing of scarce capital resources.

Rae seems to agree. Recall that he presumed that all individuals attempt to exhaust their capital as rapidly as possible. He even used this logic to expand upon his theory of the social division of labor:

> It is not perhaps likely, that this was the manner in which that division of occupations with which we are now familiar was originally produced, but it must evidently have been produced in this way . . . that even now it is thus brought to pass in the progress of settlements in North America. In such situations, every man is at first probably obliged to be his own carpenter, glazier, tanner, cobbler, and perhaps to a certain extent his own blacksmith. As the settlement fills up, and the population becomes sufficiently dense, he gives us this multifarious industry, and takes to some particular branch. [Ibid., p. 165]

In reality, Rae could not accept the logic of modern economics. He reasoned that capital was not scarce because of the natural conditions in which Canadian settlers found themselves, but because of a moral and ethical failure on the part of the people. Primitive people do not use more simple tools as a rational adaptation to economic conditions. According to Rae, they use such technologies because they have too little regard for the future. In Rae's words, such people have an insufficient "effective desire of accumulation" (ibid., chapt. 8). At times, this moral defect was explained in environmental terms. For example, Rae supposed:

> The life of the hunter seems unfavorable to the perfect development of the accumulative principle [and] necessarily improvident. . . . [T]he future presents nothing, which can be with certainty either foreseen, or governed. . . . [E]very member of such a community thinks of nothing but whether the supply of game will be plentiful, or scanty. [Ibid., p. 131]

Thus the resulting "naturally low degree of strength of the accumulative principle among nations of hunters, prevents them . . . from forming instruments of sufficiently slow return" (ibid., p. 147). Accordingly, Rae assumed: "Circumstances have given to every community a peculiar character; the moral and intellectual powers of every people have received different degrees of development" (ibid., p. 162).

Rae did not explain how a community might advance to a higher level. Instead, he attributed progress to race. He argued that those who saw parallels between European civilizations and the aboriginal peoples of America were mistaken. The Europeans were not hunters. Rae admitted that "it is our business to inquire how he [the hunter] could be induced to adopt [the ways of the pastoralist]" (ibid., p. 148).

This line of reasoning led him to contradict his other theory—that science was the cause of development. New technologies would be put into use only if people had a sufficiently advanced effective desire of accumulation. He noted:

> [T]he possession of flocks and herds, implies a considerable degree of care and foresight both in protecting, and making provision for them, and in avoiding to consume too great a number of them. It also implies the existence of private property to a large amount, and, consequently, of strength in the ties binding families together. [Ibid., p. 143]

Yet Rae offered no reason, other than race, to indicate why the Europeans had come to practice animal husbandry (ibid., p. 144). He also saw race as the cause of the poverty of the Chinese, a people whom he described as "abandoned to gross sensuality, to drunkenness, and degrading licentiousness" (ibid., p. 151). Bad as the Chinese were, their "effective desire of accumulation [was] . . . greater than that of other Asiatics" (ibid., p. 151). Based on their racial defects, he deduced:

> We should, therefore, a priori, suppose that the instruments formed by them must be of orders of quicker return, and embracing a less compass of materials, than those constructed by European nations; but of slower return . . . than those to which the strength of the accumulative principle carries the other nations of Asia. [Ibid., p. 151]

As proof, he cited testimony of travelers who described the simple instruments used by the Chinese (ibid., p. 152). True, the intricate system of terraces and water works were evidence of long and hard work, but they owed their existence to public officials rather than to individual choice (ibid., p. 284). Not having the benefit of the recent work of Joseph Needham, Rae accepted the prevailing European view that Chinese science was inferior to that of Europe (ibid., p. 156; see also Needham 1969). Thus he concluded: "[I]t will I think be admitted as a fact, that Europeans in general far exceed

Asiatics both in vigor of intellect, and in strength of moral feeling" (ibid., p. 155).

Late in life, Rae went so far as to claim that the "succession of race to race seems to have been one of the main causes of the progress of mankind" (Rae 1862, p. 370).

Race was not the only determinant of the effective desire of accumulation. Like many other classical political economists, Rae attributed the same values to lower classes and to supposedly inferior races. Thus the lower classes were criticized for a failure to give sufficient attention to the future. Their improvidence keeps them in a state of poverty (Rae 1834, p. 200). Rae saw the small quantity of household utensils in the working-class homes as proof that such people had an inadequate desire of accumulation (ibid., p. 202). They squandered their funds on alcohol and tea instead of better pots and pans, which could have allowed them to reduce the amount of food that they waste (ibid., pp. 202–4).[11]

Rae's ideas about capital and the social division of labor combined to form a moralistic theory of primitive accumulation. If people could be induced to have a higher effective desire of accumulation, the prevailing rate of return would be lower. With a lower rate of return, the class composition of society would be transformed. Rae wrote:

> Where, as in Hindostan, the loom is merely a few sticks, it would save one individual very little to employ another to weave for him. It is accordingly, in countries where the population is most dense, the facility of communication greatest, and instruments wrought up to the more slowly returning orders, that employments are most divided. [Rae 1934, p. 166]

According to Rae's conception of the world, the society of North America was most primitive:

> [I]n most communities where the population is scattered and the internal communications are bad, many trades are practiced in the farmers' houses and by their own families. In this way it is that, in very many of the recently settled parts of North America, every operation that the wool undergoes, from the taking off of the fleece to the cutting and making up the cloth, is performed in the farmer's house and by his own family. A similar state of things caused a similar practice to

---

11 Those who are inclined to psychologizing might ponder on Rae's criticism of the lower classes. Rae's own consumption of alcohol may have played a part in his dismissal as a teacher (see James 1965, p. 95). Rae often identified an effective desire of accumulation with a desire for offspring, yet Rae seems to have had no children.

prevail in England a century ago, and, at present, keeps up many of those manufactures which are properly termed domestic, in many other parts of Europe. In Canada it is not uncommon for the farmer to have, not only the whole processes that wool undergoes til it comes to be worn, carried on by members of his own family, but also to get a great variety of other things made by them, which he could not procure otherwise by sending to an inconvenient distance. . . .

[T]he vegetables that supply his table, the animals he slaughters for it, the cider that refreshes his meals, the very sugar that sweetens his tea, and all that variety of fruits, that would attract the most fastidious appetite, are the produce of his own fields, and orchards, and woods. [ibid., pp. 57, 230]

Consequently, "There is not, in truth, a prouder man than the Canadian farmer. He has no superior; he is not dependent on the assistance, scarcely on the co-operation, of a single individual" (Rae 1828, p. 230). Such pride was not characteristic of all independent farmers. Rae was referring only to the Scottish farmers whose "feelings . . . are totally opposed to the principles and spirit of the Church of England." Rae claimed that the typical representative of this group "had raised himself and his family from indigence to abundance." Such people formed "a class powerful enough to govern" (ibid.).

Rae saw another class, one "weak enough to be governed" (ibid.). Their fate was somewhat different:

There are many individuals from Ireland, Scotland, and England, whose finances are exhausted, ere they reach Canada, and who are burdened with large and young families. It is impossible for these men, immediately to pursue, what has probably been their original plan, and directly push into the wilderness. They absolutely require to have previously provided some small sum for the expense of the journey, some necessary tools and utensils, and provisions for themselves and families, until they can reasonably expect to draw subsistence from the land, they had come to occupy. To obtain these indispensable, their only resource, in general, is to betake themselves to some town or village, or to its neighborhood, and then, from what they may be able to save from their wages, to collect a sum sufficient for their purpose. Years are thus inevitably consumed by the emigrant, and very often, ere he has attained his purpose, old age presses on him, or he yields to the temptations to intemperance, which new habits and foreign manners expose him to, or he sets out prematurely, and sinks under the united pressure of severe toil, want, and disease. [Ibid., p. 249]

More than any other author whom we have seen, Rae did not take a stand on self-sufficiency as such. Instead, he kept his eye on the social relations of self-sufficiency, even if this analysis was couched in religious rather than economic terms. Thus when Rae spoke out against self-sufficiency, he was not condemning it as such. Frugal independence could be the route to the development of a powerful bourgeoisie. It could also represent a stubborn resistance to capitalist social relations.

According to Rae, self-sufficiency and independence, even as it was found in Canada, was characteristic of "the most simple state of society, when art is so rude, and accumulation so little advanced, that each individual forms almost all the instruments he himself or his family exhaust" (ibid., p. 173). Thus a strong household economy, based on products that it produces for itself, rather than on purchased commodities such as pots and pans, suggested to Rae a weakness in the moral fiber of the community. Primitive accumulation thereby was given a moral sanction.

Rae clearly saw that the accumulation process would not bring material gains for the working-class commensurate with the moral progress that it promised. In an essay, which has since been lost, he explained:

> It is in the nature of this progress [of modern civilization] to convert the original simple and rude tools, first, into instruments of greater cost and efficiency, and these again into complex and difficultly constructed machines, still more costly and still more efficient. The distaff becomes a spinning wheel; and that changing its form, and wrought by other powers, is made part of a woolen factory.
>
> The rough-edged blade of the original knife is first cut into a regular saw, and wrought by one hand; it is then put into a frame, which two men operate; and this, in turn, by means of a crank and opinions, is made to go by water, and becomes a saw mill. . . .
>
> And so it is with all our implements, they are passing on to great machines. . . . And yet there was a question which might possibly have occurred to the philosophic philanthropists of that day. "Who are to be the owners of these great machines? Will the mechanics and artisans who now wield the tools own the machines, or will they be the property of a distinct class?". . . So constantly has it occurred that it may be said it has invariably happened, that the former artisans, in giving up their tools, have never become the owners of the machines which have succeeded them. These Machines . . . come to be owned by a distinct class. The operative has no property share in the industrial operation, he owns nothing but his hands and the art of using them fitly. For opportunity to use them, and for pay for their use, he depends on the owner of the machine.

> He suffers in consequence a degradation in the social scale. Formerly he was a small capitalist, now it is the characteristic of his condition to be a mere operative, destitute of capital. [cited in James 1965, p. 57–58]

To make matters worse, Rae expected that the new technology would reduce the demand for skilled labor: "As art advances from its first rude elements, the hand does less, the instrument more" (ibid., p. 353). In the course of such development, some would prosper and some would fail. Rae came close to recognizing that the probable outcome for any individual would depend upon class origins, but instead he turned to racially based explanations. Nonetheless, Rae managed to produce an extremely valuable analysis of primitive accumulation.

Why did Rae fail to win recognition for his obviously original analysis? His emphasis on personal and racial causes of poverty was congenial to classical political economy, but like Steuart, Rae favored state action to further economic development. Consequently, like Steuart, he was slighted. Take the case of Nassau Senior, whose own theory of capital owed much to the unacknowledged work of Rae. Someone put the question to Senior, how such a fine economist as Rae could oppose free trade if the case against market interference were so self-evident. Senior responded, "Oh, I never looked at that part of the book; what I am referring to is a certain chapter on the accumulation of capital, and other discussions of a like kind." As a result of this encounter, the disappointed questioner gave up on political economy:

> [He] thought that pedants who were so afraid of entangling them-selves in the labyrinth of their own science, that they would not follow a man whose genius and power they admitted a single step off the beaten road, lest they should find no end . . . were no guides for me, because it was clear that they could not have any confidence in them-selves. [Doyle 1886, cited in James 1965, pp. 167– 68]

chapter 8

Notes on Lenin and the Forging of Revolutionary Smithianism

> Consequently, in the agrarian question and the agrarian crisis the heart of the matter is not simply the removal of obstacles to the advance of agricultural technique, but *what way* these obstacles are to be removed, what class is to effect this removal and by what methods.
>
> Lenin, *The Agrarian Question in Russia at the End of the Nineteenth Century*, p. 136

Lenin on Economic Development

The strongest support for a Smithian history may be found in a most unlikely ally—Lenin. The convergence of the analysis of such disparate individuals casts considerable light on the works of both. Although Lenin wrote as an avowed antagonist of Smith, Lenin's anti-Smithian polemic was directed only at Smith's proposed resolution of value into wages and profits.

In reality, the concerns of Smith and Lenin were similar. Each found himself in a country in which a relatively rapid rate of capitalist development required the eradication of the residues of earlier social formations. Both believed that these vestiges were being dissolved naturally as a result of market forces, although Lenin was much more explicit than Smith about the relationship between capitalist development and the evolution of the social division of labor. For Lenin:

[T]he concept "market" is quite inseparable from the concept of the social division of labour—that "general basis of all commodity (and consequently, let us add, of capitalist) production" as Marx calls it. [Ibid., 1893, p. 99–100]

In one sense, Lenin parted ways with Smith, who obscured the differences between capitalist and precapitalist modes of production. Lenin was careful to maintain such distinctions. He noted:

[I]n the historical development of capitalism two features are important: 1) the transformation of the natural economy of direct producers into commodity economy, and 2) the transformation of commodity economy into capitalist economy. The first transformation is due to the appearance of the social division of labour—the specialisation of isolated (N.B.: this is an essential condition of commodity economy), separate producers in only one branch of industry. [Ibid., p. 93]

Lenin had the advantage of the historical experience of the nineteenth century, but so did all his contemporaries. Lenin, of course, is a controversial figure, revered by some, despised by others; yet a dispassionate reading of his works will reveal that whatever one may think of his methods and his goals, Lenin, more than anyone else, clearly addressed the subject of the social division of labor. He wrote:

Recently, in the United States, the woodworking factories are becoming more and more specialised, "new factories are springing up exclusively for the making of, for instance, axe handles, broom handles, or extensible tables. . . Machine building is making constant progress, new machines are being continuously invented to simplify and cheapen some side of production. . . . Every branch of furniture making, for instance, has become a trade requiring machines and special workers. . . . In carriage building, wheel rims are made in special factories (Missouri, Arkansas, Tennessee), wheel spokes are made in Indiana and Ohio, and hubs are made in special factories in Kentucky and Illinois." [Vestnik Yevropy 1893, cited by Lenin 1893, p. 101]

Listen to Lenin:

The growth of small production among the peasantry signifies the appearance of new industries, the conversion of new branches of raw material processing into independent spheres of industry, progress in the social division of labor, while the swallowing-up of small by large establishments implies a further step forward by capitalism, leading to the triumph of its higher forms. . . . [I]t is quite natural that in a more developed part of the country, or in a more developed sphere of industry, capitalism should progress by drawing small handicraftsmen into the mechanized factory, while more remote regions, or in backward branches of industry, the process of capitalist development is only in its initial stage and manifests itself in the appearance of new branches and new industries. [Lenin 1898, p. 382]

Like Smith, Lenin had an eye for the positive developments in the countryside, but without Smith's blind spot for the harsher aspects of rural development. Although he did not share the infatuation of Smith's successors for the consumption of baubles, he applauded the changing standard of living that was being adopted: "[T]he rapid development of commodity economy and capitalism in the post-Reform epoch has caused a rise in the level of requirements of the peasantry" (ibid, p. 107). Lenin was especially pleased with the cleanliness that these changes were bringing (ibid., p. 107). Even more important, Lenin, like Smith, welcomed the potential of such capitalist development to eliminate dependency, or what he termed "the Asiatic abuse of human dignity that is constantly encountered in the countryside" (Lenin 1894, p. 235).

In an extended passage based on his study of the Statistical Returns for the Moscow Gobernia, Lenin penned one of the finest descriptions of the passage from precapitalist society to capitalism in the countryside. These words are especially striking because many of the same features that Lenin cites from here from the Statistical Returns are identical to the examples earlier used by Steuart:

> As industrial occupation spreads, intercourse with the outside world
> . . . becomes more frequent. . . . They buy samovars, table crockery and
> glass, they wear "neater" clothes. Whereas at first this neatness of
> clothing takes the shape, among men, of boots in place of bast shoes,
> among the women, leather shoes and boots are the crowning
> glory . . . of neater clothing; they prefer bright, motley calicoes and
> kerchiefs, figured woolen shawls and similar charms. . . .
> In the peasant family it has been the custom "for ages" for the wife
> to clothe her husband, herself and the children [Steuart mentions that
> the same practice was common in his Scotland]. . . As long as they grew
> their own flax, less money had to be spent on the purchase of flax, less
> money had to be spent on the purchase of cloth and other materials
> required for clothing, and this money was obtained from the sale of
> poultry, eggs, mushrooms, berries, a spare skein of yarn, or a piece of
> linen. All the rest was made at home. [Lenin 1894, pp. 121]

The Report then illustrated the manner in which commercial production was ousting traditional manufactures:

> Lace was made mainly by young women of more prosperous or larger families, where it was not necessary for all the women to spin flax or weave. But cheap calico gradually began to oust linen, and to this other circumstances were added: either the flax crop had failed, or the wife wanted to make her husband a red calico shirt and herself a smarter dress, and so the custom of weaving various sorts of linen and kerchiefs at home for peasants' clothing gradually died out. . .
>
> That explains why the majority of the population do all they can to make articles for sale, and even put their children to this work. [Ibid., pp. 121–22]

Both Lenin and Smith were in complete agreement that capitalist development was "natural". Lenin differed from Smith only in his recognition of the rise of large-scale industry. Was Lenin wrong, or should I withdraw my claim that Smith's theory of development was an ideological venture?

We have already seen that the practical schemes of Wakefield had given the lie to Smithian dogma. Why would Lenin, in effect, stand as a throwback to Smith?[1] His interest in the rise of markets initially grew out of his opposition to the Narodniks, whom he held responsible for the fate of his brother, who was executed for participating in a Narodnik plot to assassinate the Tsar (Weiller 1971).

The Narodnik economists such as Vorontsov and Danielson took the position that capitalism was foreign to Russian soil. They protested against efforts of the state to implant capitalism artificially in Russia (Lenin 1894, p. 213; see also Walecki 1969). These attempts, such as the promotion of the Russian railroad system, were indeed both clumsy in execution and oppressive in effect (see von Laue 1963). Since much of the investment was imported, the net impact of this program would have been to restrict the home market, thereby stifling native Russian industry.

The distortions caused by the artificial promotion of capitalism were all

---

[1] Lenin could also find support for his position in Engels's *Anti-Duhring* (see, for example, Engels 1894, pp. 195–96); however, Engels was engaged in an attack on Duhring's ridiculous "force theory," according to which the role of forces inherent to the law of motion of capital were all but denied.

Brenner has also accused such influential theorists as A. G. Frank, E. Wallerstein, and Paul Sweezy as falling back into Smithianism. Surprisingly, Brenner then himself sounds a Smithian note by asserting that the "original pressure" for the breakdown of feudalism came from the increased demand for English cloth (Brenner 1977, pp. 76–77).

the more destructive because of the gargantuan scale of the typical Russian manufacturer. In 1914, only 17.8 percent of Russian industrial workers were employed by firms with fewer than 100 workers. In the United States, 35 percent of the industrial workers were employed by such establishments. In Russia, 41.4 percent of the industrial workers were in the pay of giant businesses with more than 1,000 workers. Around Moscow, such firms employed 57.3 percent of the workers. The comparable figure for the United States was only 17.8 percent (Trotsky 1959, p. 8).

The Russian economy suffered from the usual symptoms of a dualistic economic growth pattern. The Narodniks preferred to avoid such costs by building socialism on the basis of the traditional village economy. Lenin denounced their plans. The peasant's life was a constant round of toil. Maxim Gorky, the novelist, conveyed the sense of the Russian village in the following words: "The technically primitive labour of the countryside is incredibly heavy, the peasantry call it *strada* from the Russian verb *stradat*—to suffer" (Gorky 1922, p. 370).

Peasants were not being crushed by railroads, Lenin argued, but rather by the burdens of manual labor (Lenin 1918, p. 377). To tread the Narodnik path, Lenin charged, was to follow romantic illusions. Lenin insisted that the villages were not the bulwark of traditional social relations that the Narodniks thought them to be. Capitalism had already taken root in the countryside. He insisted:

> Russia is a capitalist country, that the power of the workers' tie with the land in Russia is so feeble and unreal, and the power of the man of property so firmly established, that one more technical advance will be necessary for the "peasant" (??) who is living by the sale of his labour-power into a worker pure and simple.
>
> [D]espite its general wretchedness, its comparatively tiny establishments and extremely low productivity of labour, its primitive technique and small number of wage-workers, peasant industry is *capitalism*. [Lenin 1894, p. 217]

In this respect, Lenin's opinion squares with that of many modern agricultural economists, who see peasants as very precise maximizers (Schultz 1964, chap. 3, and references in Hagen 1980, p. 129). Lenin extrapolated from this observation, "Free exchange and freedom of trade . . . inevitably lead to a division of commodity procedures into owners of capital and owners of labour-power" (Lenin 1921a, p. 218). In short, the Narodniks analyzed capitalism in terms of the state's success in promoting it. Lenin analyzed capitalism in terms of its spontaneous growth within the villages. In this sense,

Lenin may be termed Smithian, while the Narodniks may be credited with picking up the mantle of Steuart.

Lenin's class analysis bore some similarity to Smith's. Smith saw the progressive bourgeoisie as a spontaneous outgrowth of the village economy. The established bourgeoisie were more or less in league with the forces of mercantilism. Accordingly, Smith did not regard them highly. Lenin, too, wrote off the liberal Russian bourgeoisie as incapable of promoting development (see Kingston-Mann 1980, p. 133).

Just as Smith unfairly criticized his mercantilist rivals, Lenin may be faulted for occasionally being carried away in his polemic with the Narodniks (Weiller 1971); he may be charged with misreading some of his opponents; he may even have underestimated the potential of cottage industries "to gather up fragments of time" (see Georgescu-Roegen 1971, p. 252); nonetheless, he did provide a consistent revolutionary interpretation of the condition of Russia.[2]

The affinity of Lenin's analysis with that of Smith is obscured by the fact that Lenin identified Smith with the Narodniks. However, this identification was irrelevant to the essential problematic of Smith, who was also concerned to show the manner in which the social division of labor evolved. Lenin, too, in his most important work on the subject, *The Development of Capitalism in Russia*, began with exactly the same idea. In the first three pages, the assertion that the social division of labor was the basis of commodity production was repeated three times (Lenin 1974, pp. 37–39). The social division of labor was Lenin's central concern in one of his first known works, *On the So-Called Market Question*. In Lenin's Smithian-like analysis, "the expansion of markets is made to serve both as condition and effect of capitalist development, obscuring the manner in which capitalist relations take root and the determinants of their specific course" (Tribe 1979, p. 4; see also Crisenoy 1979, p. 20). Furthermore, like Smith, Lenin insisted that no external measures were needed to separate households from their means of production. If the peasantry were to gain access to the land "it will not abolish capitalism; on the contrary it will create a broader foundation for its development, and will hasten and intensify purely capitalist development" (Lenin 1905, p. 440).

Sounding more Smithian than Smith, Lenin contended that "in America, it was not the slave economy of the big landlords that served as the basis of capitalist agriculture, but the free economy of the free farmer working on

---

[2] After the 1905 revolution, when the peasants supported the revolution, Lenin significantly modified his stand on the role of the peasantry. This change did not represent a recantation of his economics; rather it was a revision of his estimate of the degree to which capitalism had established itself (Lenin 1907, p. 233).

free land, free from all medieval fetters, free from serfdom and feudalism" (Lenin 1974, p. 85; see also 1908, p. 140). He may well have been correct, although quantification is difficult in this sort of matter. The homesteading family often pushed itself as hard as a slave driver could push his crew. Moreover, a relatively small share of its efforts were directed toward providing itself with consumption goods. Between 1710 and 1775, for example, per capita incomes were estimated to have grown at a modest 0.4 percent per year (Lee and Pasnell 1979, p. 20). Consequently, early American farming was predominately a process of capital accumulation (Bidwell and Falconer 1941, pp. 82–83; see also Primack 1966 for a later period).

By the time of the Civil War, southern agriculture had indeed become eclipsed. Hinton Helper calculated that the combined cotton, tobacco, hay, hemp, and sugar harvest of the fifteen slave states was worth less than the hay crop of the free states (Helper 1860, p. 53). However, Helper, like Lenin, may well have overlooked the enormous contribution of earlier slave labor in the process of accumulation in the United States before the slave system ran up against the dual barriers of soil depletion and low productivity of slaves.

Based on his reading of the American experience, Lenin posed two alternative paths for Russia: First, it could distribute the land to duplicate the American conditions; second, it could give the land to large landholders who could maintain large estates such as were found in Prussia. Lenin called for the American path that "would *inevitably* withdraw the majority of these owners, whose position is hopeless in capitalist society from agriculture, and no 'right to the land' would be powerful enough to prevent this" (Lenin 1974, p. 91). Lenin judged the American path to be "the most democratic [and to cause] the masses less suffering" (Lenin 1918, p. 377). Moreover, the American path was seen as the most congenial to capitalist development (see also Lenin 1907, pp. 238–42, and 1908, pp. 40–42). Lenin confidently summed up his position, "[P]easant farming . . . *evolves in a capitalist way* and gives rise to a rural bourgoise and rural proletariat" (Lenin 1907, p. 241).

Although Lenin may have underestimated the importance of slavery to the United States economy, his imagery of the United States path was consistent with the experience of history. No matter what Wakefield said about the ease of taking up farming in this country, potential farmers faced numerous obstacles. A typical farm in the nineteenth century cost about $1,000 to establish (Danhof 1941). Competition among farmers dropped prices to disastrously low levels. Around Cincinnati, corn prices sank to six cents per bushel in some districts; in others, they fell so low that corn was burned as fuel instead of wood (Gideon 1948, p. 215; see also Marx 1968, p. 302, for a theoretical discussion of this sort of phenomenon). Credit was hard to find. The rates farmers had to pay were exorbitant, running as high as 120 percent for short-term loans (Gates 1960, p. 73). Especially in New England, where land was relatively scarce and infertile, farmers had to have recourse to debt in order to set up their children in farming (see Martineau 1837, p. 181). Competition from western grain made matters worse (Field 1978). Consequently, the distribution of wealth, which had previously remained relatively stable, began to become much more unequal after 1774 (Williamson and Lindert 1977).[3] As a result, a native-born industrial labor force was eventually generated.[4] At first, these workers were women in the Northeast, left behind by the relatively more substantial exodus of men (Wright 1978, pp. 118–19).

By the time Lenin was composing *The Development of Capitalism in Russia*, farms had become an important source of industrial labor in the United States. Between 1860 and 1900, at least twenty farmers migrated to the city for each worker who took up farming. Ten farmers' sons took up residence in the city for each one who became a farm owner (Shannon 1945, pp. 356–59; see also Goodrich and Davidson 1935). Unlike Smith, who rhapsodized about people moving to new professions by virtue of the pull of better opportunities, Lenin emphasized the push of hopelessness to explain the migration from the countryside. Although the mathematical calculations are formally identical in either case, the social chemistry is not.

The actual mechanism by which a native proletariat was created in the United States was slightly more complex than Lenin suggested. When times turned bad, people tended to move back from the city to the farm. In the course of this process, which dates back as early as the fifteenth century, the "peasantry turns up again, although in diminished number, and in a progressively worse situation" (Marx 1977, p. 912). (A. G. Frank, for example, notes that as late as the 1958 recession, the city of Detroit alone lost 50,000 workers and their families to the subsistence farms of the southern and border states: Frank 1975, p. 30.)[5] After the business cycle moved upward once again, the migration to the city could recommence on a larger scale. Consequently, the coincidence of periods of prosperity and rural exodus was consistent with the schema of Smith, who emphasized the association of the migration with

---

[3] The pressures on labor had begun long before 1774.

[4] Engels placed great hopes in this process. He wrote to Henry Demarest Lloyd, "In America, at least, I am strongly inclined to believe that the fatal hour of Capitalism will have struck as soon as a native American Working Class will have replaced a class composed in its majority by foreign immigrants" (Engels 1893; most of this letter is reprinted in Pollack 1962, pp. 83–84).

[5] Mexican immigration to the United States, for example, is highly correlated with inadequate rainfall in Mexico (Cornelius 1979).

opportunities in the city. Lenin, however, more accurately identified the underlying forces that drove the people from the countryside.

Lenin's analysis can be restated in terms of the exchange of labor power. Think back to our earlier example in which the typical household could produce all its own needs in four hours of labor (see Chapter 1). Some households will require more time; others less. Thus if the working day for a wage laborer is eight hours, an inefficient household that needs seven hours to take care of its own needs would be less likely to resist the conditions of wage labor. Under the assumption that the household would earn the same standard of living producing for itself or buying commodities for wages, the inefficient household would have less to lose from wage labor than a more efficient one that required only two or three hours to produce the same goods.[6]

What then determines the degree of inefficiency of a household? In part, the answer will depend upon purely technical phenomena. Better seed, more careful application of work, and superior equipment will all improve the efficiency of a small peasant farm. However, a family's access to the means of production is not the result of technology alone. Kautsky, whose work on agriculture won the enthusiastic praise of Lenin, demonstrated how the act of cutting off the peasant's freedom to gather firewood or hunt game increased the number of hours that a family would have to work to produce the same amount of use value (Kautsky 1899, pp. 18–19, 26). Families could cope with the resulting difficulties by curtailing their standard of living. For example, the consumption of meat seems to have fallen with the pressures put on the traditional peasant economy (Kautsky 1899, pp. 24–25).

Thus Lenin mocked the pretended efficiency of traditional producers. Yes, they could sometimes compete with modern industry, but only by lowering their standard of living to an abysmal level (Lenin 1898, pp. 400, 419).

The more productive households could overcome their difficulties, in part, by bringing more produce to market (Kautsky 1899, pp. 18–19). This approach is complicated by two factors. First, many households do not possess enough to bring a sufficient amount to market. Second, if all households were able to do so, a glut of produce would follow, such as we described in the case of the corn burnt for fuel.

In any case, the process of differentiation was set in motion. Some households, whose degree of efficiency was indistinguishable from those of their neighbors in earlier years, demonstrated an aptitude for earning profits.

---

[6] In practice, the actual process of differentiation may not be carried out with such precision (see Deere and de Janvry 1979). Nonetheless, it will conform to the broad outlines just given.

Others, who were not able to compete, lost their property to the more successful producers. Thus the surviving operations could increase their production while employing the propertyless workers to labor on their expanded holdings.

Kautsky glossed over the importance the initial pressures imposed on the traditional household economy. For the most part, he adopted the point of view that the process is understandable in terms of economies of scale and specialization. He even went so far as to advocate the efficiency of the division between mental and manual labor (Kautsky 1899, p. 97). Lenin, too, seems to have put excessive emphasis on the technical superiority of the survivors.

LeRoy Ladurie, studying an earlier period, suggests that a different sort of mechanism was also at play. He describes the activities of Guillaume Massenx, a successful French proprietor born about 1495. Here we find the acquisition of land based on usury and the reduction of costs by withholding tithes, ostensibly as an act of solidarity with the Reformation (LeRoy Ladurie 1974, pp. 127–28). This new pattern of behavior may have been socially beneficial. Certainly, it seems to be consistent with the accumulation of capital. Yet we get no indication that Massenx was necessarily more efficient in using the means of production in producing commodities—only that he was able to adjust his own circumstances more effectively to be able to profit from the new conditions.

"Men of small beginnings," the later counterparts of M. Massenx, appear to have formed the core of the emergent capitalist class (Hammond and Hammond 1819, pp. 2–3; see also Hilton 1978, and Moore 1966, pp. 9–11). Others, like his neighbors who forfeited their property in default of their debts, became the proletariat.

Smith looked upon the energy and enterprise of such successful people with favor. Indeed, they contrasted sharply with the decadent nobility. His emphasis on the role of "stock" was paralleled by Lenin's insistence that success was not the result of personal virtue; it was a consequence of the possession of capital (Lenin 1908).

For Lenin, the Russian victims of the indigenous Massenxes of his day would have no other way to turn but to the Communist Party. The faster the process proceeded, the sooner the messy work of revolution would be completed.

Implicit in this analysis is the idea that capitalist development was furthered by exactions imposed by earlier economic formations (see Brenner 1977 and Banaji 1977). As Lenin observed, "Life creates forms that unite in themselves with remarkable gradualness systems of economy whose basic features constitute opposites" (Lenin 1974, p. 199; see also Marx 1977, p. 875). Where the household economy could remain intact, the supply of labor would not be strongly forthcoming; the level of real wages would be higher. For example, Marx noted that the level of wages in agricultural districts of England varied according to the conditions under which the peasantry emerged from serfdom (Marx 1865, p. 72). Capitalist production would be impeded. What happens once the household finds itself in an environment dominated by feudal employers? Lenin agreed with the analysis of the classical political economists that under such conditions the level of paid wages would fall the more people could produce for themselves (Lenin 1908, p. 140). Lenin did not suggest, as Steuart had, that such an arrangement would substantially benefit capital. Instead, it would serve to preserve backward forms of production. Here again, the functioning of the household serves to restrict capitalist development.

Both Lenin's Russia and Smith's Britain shared the characteristic that poverty was making the life of the self-sufficient household difficult. As Smith's contemporary, the anonymous author of *American Husbandry*, observed:

> When land is difficult to be had or not good, owing to the extension
> of the settlements or to the monopolies of the country, the poor must
> be driven to other employments than those which depend on the land;
> manufacturing, commerce, fisheries, etc., must thrive in the natural
> course of things. [Anon. 1775, p. 525]

We get some indication of the pattern in which the pressures on the household economy made themselves felt from a reading of Defoe's descriptions published half a century before *Wealth of Nations*. In the remote Scottish highlands, the family retained a substantial degree of independence (Defoe 1724–26, p. 666); however, manufacturing had already taken hold in "wild, barren, poor country" such as Devonshire on Halifax, where the land was divided into small parcels (Defoe 1724–26, pp. 2, 5, and 491). Arthur Young found a similar pattern during his travels in France. Manufactures prospered where agriculture languished (Young 1794, pp. 412–38; see also Berg 1980a).

The relationship between poverty and the growth of capitalism was seen clearly by employers. Ambrose Crowley, for example, set up his works in the north rather than in the Midlands, for there "the cuntry is verry poore and populous soe workmen must of necessity increase" (cited in Pollard 1965, p. 197).

This configuration of industry and agriculture can be justified in terms of per capita resource endowments and transportation costs, but capital itself was not willing to let market forces take their apparently "natural" course. Instead, as we have seen, it devised methods to force the creation of wage labor. Had it not done so, the British peasant might well have developed the labor-intensive methods that were found in Belgium (see Slicher van Bath 1960).[7]

The course of wage labor was not merely the result of the plans of future capitalists. As we mentioned, it was also accelerated by the demands of feudalism, that tended to reduce the peasant to utter destitution. The continual narrowing of the margin of survival of the self-sufficient household provided employers with a steady flow of labor. As Longfield suggested, the conditions of these workers determined to a large extent the level of wages (see Chapter I). The fact that real wages in England between 1770 and 1800 were falling or, at best, stagnant (Deane 1957, p. 92) indicates that the pressures on these households had not subsided during the period in which the *Wealth of Nations* was published. In spite of falling wages, returns from small holdings were so low that the period 1788–1803 became known as the golden age of hand-loom weaving (see Smelser 1959, p. 138). Consequently, Smith could argue as if the contrived measures to undermine the self-sufficient household were unnecessary, only because their objectives seemed to have already been met. The deterioration of the position of the self-sufficient household continued well into the next century. We do not have to read Engels to learn of the squalor of towns such as Manchester; some people in England recognized the conditions there (see Marcus 1974, pp. 28–66, and Engels 1845b). Kay-Shuttleworth charged that in England "the aristocracy is richer and more powerful than in any other country in the world, *the poor are more oppressed, more pauperized, more numerous . . .* than the poor of any *other European nation* (Kay-Shuttleworth, cited in Smith 1853, p. 152; see also Sismondi 1971, p. 195).

This poverty was not a natural result of resource endowments, but the product of centuries of exploitation. Recall Marx's portrait of England:

> Nowhere in the world has capitalist production, since Henry VII, dealt so ruthlessly with the *traditional* relations of agriculture, adapting and subordinating the conditions to its own requirements.
>
> In this respect England is the most revolutionary country in the world. Wherever the conditions handed down by history were at variance with, or did not correspond to the conditions of capitalist production on the land, they were ruthlessly swept away; this applied not only to the position of the village communities but to the village communities themselves, not only to the habitats of the agricultural

---

[7] According to Collins, British agriculture did remain relatively labor-intensive. For example, the scythe was adopted at a relatively late date. However, the choice of technology was an appropriate adaptation to the conditions in which agricultural employers found themselves (Collins 1969).

population but to the agricultural population itself, not only to the original centres of cultivation but to cultivation itself. [Marx 1968, p. 237]

In Russia, the poverty in the traditional sector had become so extreme that Lenin saw great promise in the near term. In his mind, "[T]he rapid development of commodity economy and capitalism in the post-Reform epoch has caused a rise in the level of requirements in the 'peasantry,' too: the peasants have begun to live a 'cleaner' life (as regards clothing, housing, and so forth" (Lenin 1893, p. 107). However, Lenin also observed that the desire for cheap calico prints and the like were causing household production to die out (Lenin 1894, p. 211).

In any case, poverty, in such a setting, did not reflect a disadvantage for capitalist development; rather it was an important tool for organizing society according to its own interests. Smith, however, appeared to want capitalist society without the necessary means to create it. That position was important, not just as a plan, but also as a support for his ideological justification of capital. By the time Smith was writing, British agricultural society had already been formed, for the most part, in conformity with the needs of capital. Parts of Scotland still remained inadequately integrated into a more general social division of labor. England, however, appeared to be well ordered. For Smith, even the standard of living of the Highlanders seemed to be low enough that they, too, could soon be absorbed into the social labor process through the workings of the marketplace. Thus artificially created poverty did not seem to be necessary.

Steuart was less concerned with ideology. Too much work remained undone. For him, the world still stood in want of statesmen to carry out statesmen-like business, such as the clearing of the estates. The pace of Smithian development was too slow for him. Wakefield intended to develop this approach on a global scale. With Lenin, the outcome of the process would reach a far more advanced stage—world revolution. The only question was whether Russia would contribute to this movement more effectively by way of the Prussian or the American path to capitalism. In discussing two different forms of the two paths of capitalist development, Lenin noted:

> Both these solutions each in their own way facilitate the adoption of . . . higher technique, both are in line with agronomic progress. The only difference between them is that one bases this progress on the acceleration of the process of squeezing poor peasants out of agriculture, and the other bases it on the acceleration of the process of the labor rent system by destroying the feudal latifundia.

Consequently, Lenin believed that "the essence of the agrarian question and of the agrarian crisis is not the removal of the obstacles to raise agriculture to a higher level, but *how* these obstacles are to be removed, which class is to remove them and by what means" (Lenin 1908, p. 136).

Lenin, to his sorrow, soon learned the limits of his Smithian ideology. Although Smithianism may have been useful in his struggle against the Narodniks, it was inadequate as a basis for the Bolshevik government that he headed. He came to the recognition that "our task is to organize commodity production" (Lenin 1921b, pp. 95–96, cited in Bettleheim 1976, p. 484) and to "establish proper relations between" the working class and the peasantry (Lenin 1921a, p. 404). He learned that socialism could not be cut from whole cloth. As Steuart had observed long ago, people had to glean before they could reap. Accordingly, the New Economic Policy was constructed to foster growth within the peasant sector as a basis for future socialist development (Lenin 1921, p. 355).

The New Economic Policy was a masterpiece of practical finesse that contained a goodly number of theoretical ironies. Market relations were to be marshalled to build socialist relations. Concessions to individual incentives were to become the road toward building a broader basis of cooperation (on this, see Bettleheim 1976). In this policy, Smithian theories gave way to the statesmanlike actions implicit in Steuart.

After Stalin took over the reigns of power, the imagery of Steuart continued to echo in the Party deliberations. Stalin called for a shift in policy relative to "the bond between town and country, between the working class and the main mass of the peasantry" (Stalin 1928, p. 169). He continued Lenin's emphasis on the role of the producers' goods delivered to the peasantry rather than the consumer goods as Steuart had done. Accordingly, he recommended a "bond . . . based not only on textiles, but also metals" (ibid., p. 170). Stalin's bond, unlike Steuart's, was intended "not to preserve classes but to abolish them" (ibid., p. 170). Consequently, Stalin's program of collectivism was ironically justified in terms of cementing the bond between the town and the country (Stalin 1929, pp. 60–72). Ultimately, then, the Russian countryside was also cleared of "superfluous mouths" (Steuart 1767; 1: 58, 198).

Like the Soviets, Mao expressed a desire to establish "relations of production and exchange in accordance with socialist principles." Accordingly, he continued, "more and more appropriate forms are being sought" (Mao 1956, p. 294). China, however, had learned much from the mistakes of the Stalin era (see Mao 1955, p. 221, and 1956, p. 291). Unlike Stalin, Mao believed that the proper arrangements could not be created by fiat. However, Mao's successors, sounding almost like plagiarists of Steuart, proposed an almost entirely economic program to "link the interests of the state, collective, and individual directly so that every person in an enterprise takes it as a matter of his own *material interests* to be concerned about fulfilling the state plan and about what results the enterprise management achieves" (Hu Chiao-mu 1978, pt. 2, p. 21; emphasis added). Mao, in contrast, stressed the importance of "political work as the lifeblood of economic work" (Mao 1955a, p. 260). Mao, thus, stood for the substitution of the visible bond of politics for the invisible hand of Smith (see Wheelwright and McFarlane 1970, p. 122).

In a sense, Mao's vision may nonetheless be properly called Smithian. In spite of the best precautions, he recognized that "the spontaneous forces of capitalism have been steadily growing in the countryside" (Mao 1955, p. 201). The antidote for these Smithian forces of reaction was a patient "Smithian" program of socialist development. He insisted that economic calculations be performed on a long-term basis (Mao 1945, p. 75, 1947, p. 124). He also shared Smith's idea of a largely rural, agriculturally led development that would ultimately produce the highest possible level of industrialization. Like Smith, he favored agriculture (Mao 1956, p. 286).

The most important parallel between Smith and Mao concerns their attitudes toward people. Smith, shorn of his ideology, represented a statement of confidence in the abilities of the emergent capitalist class to bring about a progressive development of society. Mao's work also was a vigorous affirmation of the abilities of the great masses to lift society to heights previously unknown, if only they were allowed an appropriate environment in which their abilities could flourish. In this sense, socialism may be said to be the proper heir to the best of classical political economy.

Epilogue

The conclusions reached in this book should be obvious by now: In the first place, primitive accumulation has been shown to be a theoretical category that is especially valuable in analyzing the accumulation of capital in general. Second, classical political economy took an active interest in furthering policies designed to promote primitive accumulation. Finally, primitive accumulation can be understood as an aspect of the evolution in the social division of labor. Rather than discuss these results in further detail here, or even to summarize them once again, I would prefer to direct your attention to an unmentioned theme of this book that deserves further study.

In calling for the acceleration of primitive accumulation, classical political economy displayed a keen sense of the underlying forces of capital accumulation. Given the social relations of production, the small-scale producer represented an unmistakable barrier to the advance of capital.

Self-provisioning did not have to be restricted on account of its failure, but rather because of its success. Even while the Industrial Revolution was proving its enormous potential, small-scale producers displayed a remarkable tenacity. True, in many cases, they held on by lowering their standard of living, but that factor was not always a primary cause of their ability to continue. Small-scale production has its own economies, its own efficiencies. In the long run, they may not be equal to those of modern, capital-intensive production, but where capital is scarce, such technologies are particularly competitive.

The lessons that can be drawn from the the classical political economists' analysis of small-scale production may be especially useful for poor, emergent socialist states. Such societies may do well to adopt a transitional program that relies heavily on the potential of technologies similar to those used by the traditional household sector. Obviously, in working out this sort of program, classical political economy did not provide a blueprint, but then neither did Marx. Although classical political economy was originally written to aid capital in the exploitation of labor, it may, nonetheless, prove to be an important source of inspiration. Perhaps, one of the by-products of this book will be to rekindle an interest in this aspect of classical political economy.

REFERENCES

Abeille, L. P. 1768. *Principles sur le liberte du commerce des grains* (Amsterdam and Paris: Desaint).

Achenwall, Gottfried. 1767. Some observations on North America from Oral Information by Dr. Franklin, reprinted in Benjamin Franklin, *The Papers of Benjamin Franklin*, Leonard W. Larabee and William B. Wilcox, eds. (New Haven: Yale University Press, 1959–): 13: 346–77.

Adams, John. 1780. "Letter to John Luzac, 15 September 1780" in *The Works of John Adams*, Charles Frances Adams, ed. (Boston: Little, Brown, 1856): 7: 255–56.

————. 1819. "Letter to William B. Richmond, 14 December 1819," in *The Works of John Adams*, 10 vols., Charles Frances Adams, ed. (Boston: Little, Brown, 1856): 10: 384–85.

Adams, Thomas R. 1969. "The British Pamphlets of the American Revolution for 1774: A Progress Report," Proceedings of the Massachusetts Historical Society 81: 31–103.

————. 1971. "The British Look at America During the Age of Samuel Johnson" (Providence, R. I., John Carter Brown Library, typescript).

Adkins, P. J. 1977. "London's Intra-Urban Milk Supply, circa 1790–1914." Transactions of the Institute of British Geographers, n.s., vol. 2, no. 3: 383–99.

Aglietta, Michael. 1979. *A Theory of Capitalist Exploitation: The U.S. Experience*, trans. David Fernbach (London: New Left Books).

Akhtar, M. A. 1979. "An Analytical Outline of Sir James Steuart's Macroeconomic Model." *Oxford Economic Papers* 31, no. 2 (July): 283–302.

Althusser, Louis. 1970. "From Capital to Marx's Philosophy," in Louis Althusser and Etienne Balibar, eds., *Reading Capital* (London: New Left Books).

Alvord, Clarence Walworth. 1917. *The Mississippi Valley in British Politics: A Study of the Trade, Land Speculation, and Experiments in Imperialism Culminating in the American Revolution*, 2 Vols. (Cleveland: Arthur H. Clark).

Ambirajan, S. 1977. *Classical Political Economy and British Policy in India* (Cambridge: Cambridge University Press).

Ames, Fisher. 1854. *Works of Fisher Ames*, Seth Ames, ed. (Boston: Little, Brown).

Anderson, James. 1777. *Observations on National Industry* (New York: Augustus M. Kelley, 1968).

――――. 1777a. *An Inquiry into the Nature of the Corn-Laws* (Edinburgh).

Anikin, A. V. 1975. *A Science in Its Youth: Pre-Marxian Political Economy* (New York: International Publishers).

Anon. 1757. "Letter to Editor." *London Magazine* no. 26 (February): p. 87.

Anon. 1775. *American Husbandry*, H. J. Carmen, ed. (New York: Columbia University Press, 1939).

Anon. 1767. "Review of Sir James Steuart, *An Inquiry into the Principles of Political Oeconomy.*" *Monthly Review* 36 (May-June): 365–78 and 464–76; and 37 (July): 116–25.

Anon. 1767a. "Review of Sir James Steuart, *An Inquiry into the Principles of Political Oeconomy.*" *Critical Review* 23 (May-June): 321–29, and 411– 416; and 24 (July): 24–32.

Anon. 1767b. "The Reviewers Reviewed in a Letter to the Editor of the *Political Register.*" *The Political Register and Impartial Review of New Books* 1, no. 2 (June): 121–28.

Anon. 1767c. "Review of Sir James Steuart, *An Inquiry into the Principles of Political Oeconomy.*" *The Scot's Magazine* 29 (April): 199–201.

Anon. 1776. "Review of *American Husbandry.*" *Monthly Review* 54, reprinted in Anon., *American Husbandry*, H. J. Carman, ed. (New York: Columbia University Press): xvi-xxx.

Anon. 1806. "Review of Steuart's Works." *The Monthly Review; or Literary Journal, Enlarged* 50 (June): 113–21.

Anon. 1816. "The Colonial Policy of Great Britain, By a British Traveller (Philadelphia)," in Felix Flugel and Harold U. Faulkner, eds., *Readings in the Economic and Social History of the United States* (New York and London: Harper and Brothers, 1929): 61–64.

Anon. 1823. "Review of *Cottage Industry* by William Cobbett." *Edinburgh Review* 38, no. 75 (February): 105–25.

Anon. 1824. *Suggestions on the Propriety of Reintroducing British Convict Labour into British North America by a Canadian.*

Appleby, Joyce Oldham. 1976. "Ideology and Theory: The Tension Between Economic Liberalism in Seventeenth-Century England." *American Historical Review* 81, no. 3 (June): 499–515.

――――. 1978. *Economic Thought and Ideology in Seventeenth-Century England* (Princeton, N.J.: Princeton University Press).

Arbuthnot, John. 1773. *An Inquiry into the Connection Between the Present Price of Provisions and the Size of Farmers* (London).

Arnot, R. Page. 1955. *A History of the Scottish Miners from Earliest Times* (London: George Allen and Unwin).

Ashton, Trevor. 1948. *The Industrial Revolution* (London: Oxford University Press).

――――. 1972. *An Economic History of England: The 18th Century* (London: University Paperbacks).

Auden, W. H. 1956. "Introduction," *Selected Writings of Sydney Smith* (New York: Farrar, Straus and Cudahy).

Bagehot, Walter. 1880. *Economic Studies in the Works of Walter Bagehot*, 5 vols. Forrest Morgan, ed. (Hartford, Conn.: The Travelers Insurance Company, 1889): v, 237–436.

Bailyn, Bernard. 1955. *The New England Merchants in the Seventeenth Century* (New York: Harper and Row).

Banaji, Jairus. 1977. "Modes of Production in a Materialist Conception of History." *Capital and Class*, no. 3 (Autumn): 1–44.

Bancroft, George. 1854. *History of the United States, from the Discovery of the American Continent*, 10 vols. (Boston: Little, Brown).

Barber, William J. 1975. *British Economic Thought and India, 1600–1858: A Study in the History of Development Economics* (Oxford: Clarendon Press).

Bardhan, Pranab K. 1973. "Size, Productivity and Returns to Scale: Analysis of Farm-Level Data in Indian Agriculture." *Journal of Political Economy* 81, no. 3 (November–December): 45–66.

_____. 1979. "Wages and Unemployment in a Poor Agrarian Economy: A Theoretical and Empirical Analysis." *Journal of Political Economy* 87, no. 3 (June): 479–507.

Barrios de Chungra, Domitila. 1979. "Let me speak!" *Monthly Review* 30, no. 9 (February): 42–54.

Barton, John. 1817. "Observations on the Circumstances Which Influence the Condition of the Labouring Classes in Society," in John Barton, *Economic Writings*, G. Sotiroff, ed., 2 vols. (Regina, Canada: Lynn): 2: 25–112.

_____. 1833. "In Defense of The Corn Laws," in John Barton, *Economic Writings*, G. Sotiroff, ed., 2 vols. (Regina, Canada: Lynn): 2: 5–136.

Baumol, William. 1976. "Smith versus Marx on Business Morality and the Social Interest." *The American Economist* 20, no. 2 (Fall): 176.

Bearington, F. 1975. "The Development of Market Gardening in Bedfordshire, 1799–1939." *Agricultural History Review* 23: 23–47.

Becker, Gary S. 1965. "A Theory of the Allocation of Time." *The Economic Journal* 75, no. 299 (September): 493–517.

Beechy, Veronica. 1977. "Some Notes on Female Wage Labour in Capitalistic Production." *Capital and Class* no. 3 (Fall): 45–66.

Bell, John Fred. 1960. "Adam Smith: Clubman." *Scottish Journal of Political Economy* 7, no. 2 (June): 108–16.

Bellers, John. 1696. *Proposals for Raising a College of Industry, etc.* (London: T. Sonel), reprinted in Robert Owen, Appendix I. Supplement to vol. 1, *The Life of Robert Owen* (London: Effingham Wilson).

Benians, E. A. 1926. "Adam Smith's Project of an Empire." *Cambridge Historical Journal* 1: 249–83.

Benson, Lee. 1950. "Achille Loria's Influence on American Economic Thought." *Agricultural History* 24: 182–99.

Bentham, Jeremy. 1787. "Letter to Dr. Smith," reprinted in Mossner and Campbell 1977, 388–402.

_____. 1790. "Letter to Dr. Smith" reprinted in Mossner and Campbell 1977, 402–404.

_____. 1954. "The Psychology of Economic Man: Extracts Arranged by Werner Stark," in Werner Stark ed., *Jeremy Bentham's Economic Writings* (London: George Allen and Unwin): 3: 419–50.

Benyon, Erdman Doane. 1938. "The Southern White Laborer Comes to Michigan," *American Sociological Journal* 3, no. 3 (June): 333–43.

Berg, Maxine. 1980. *The Machinery Question and the Making of Political Economy, 1815–1848* (Cambridge: Cambridge University Press).

_____. 1980a. "Proto-Industry, Political Economy and the Division of Labour, 1700–1800." *Warwick Economic Research Papers* no. 170 (Conventry: University of Warwick, Department of Economics).

Berger, Peter. 1963. *Invitation to Sociology: A Humanistic Perspective* (Garden City, N. Y.: Doubleday).

Bergue, Augustin. 1976. "Alternance agricole et urbanisation au Japon." Symposium on Urban Growth in France and Japan, Toyko (30 September).

Berkeley, George. 1740. *The Querist in Berkeley's Complete Works*, 4 vols., A. C. Fraser, ed. (Oxford: Clarendon Press, 1901): 4: 415–76.

Bettelheim, Charles. 1976. *Class Struggles in the U.S.S.R.: First Period: 1917–1923* (New York: Monthly Review Press).

Bidwell, Percy Wells. 1916. "Rural Economy in New England." *Transactions of the Connecticut Academy of Arts and Sciences* 20: 251–76.

————, and John I. Falconer. 1941. *A History of Agriculture in the Northern United States, 1620–1860* (New York: Peter Smith).

Black, R. D. Collison. 1960. *Economic Thought and the Irish Question, 1817–1870* (Cambridge: Cambridge University Press).

————, and Rosamund Koenigkamp. 1972. "Biographical Introduction," in William Stanley Jevons, *Biography and Personal Journal, vol. 1. Papers and Correspondence* (London: Macmillan): 1–53.

Blackstone, William. 1775. *Commentaries on the Laws of England*, 6th ed., 4 vols. (Dublin: Company of Booksellers).

Bogard, Charles Ludlow, and Charles Manfred Thompson. 1927. *Readings in the Economic History of the United States* (New York: Longmans, Green).

Bohm-Bawerk, Eugen von. 1959. *Capital and Interest*, 3 vols. (South Holland, Ill.: Libertarian Press).

Bonwick, Colin. 1977. *English Radicals and the American Revolution* (Chapel Hill: University of North Carolina Press).

Boserup, Ester. 1965. *The Conditions of Agricultural Growth: The Economics of Agrarian Change Under Population Pressure* (Chicago: Aldine).

Boswell, James. 1799. *Boswell's Life of Johnson*, George Birkbeck Hill, ed., 6 vols. (Oxford: Oxford University Press, 1971).

Bowsher, Norman N. 1980. "The Demand for Currency. Is the Underground Economy Undermining Monetary Policy?" *Monthly Review of the Federal Reserve Bank of Kansas City* 62, no. 1 (January).

Branson, Roy. 1979. "James Madison and the Scottish Enlightenment." *Journal of the History of Ideas* 40, no. 2 (April-June): 235–50.

Braverman, Harry. 1974. *Labor and Monopoly Capital: The Degredation of Work in the Twentieth Century* (New York: Monthly Review Press).

Bray, Charles. 1841. *The Philosophy of Necessity*, 2 vols. (London: Longman, Orme, and Green).

Brenner, Robert. 1977. "Origins of Capitalist Development: A Critique of Neo-Smithian Marxism." *New Left Review* 104 (July-August): 25–92.

Brockway, Lucille. 1979. *Science and Colonial Expansion: The Role of the British Royal Botanic Gardens* (New York: Academic Press).

Bukharin, N., and E. Preobrazhenski. 1922. *The ABC of Communism: A Popular Explanation of the Program of the Communist Party of Russia* (Ann Arbor: University of Michigan Press, 1966).

Burke, Edmund. 1759. "Review of *The Theory of Moral Sentiments*." *Annual Register*, 1759, 6th ed. (London: J. Dodsley, 1777): 484–89.

Burns, Scott. 1976. *Household, Inc.* (New York: Doubleday).

————. 1979. "What Self-Reliance is Worth." *Organic Gardening* (May): 86–92.

Byington, Margaret. 1910. *Homestead: Households of a Milltown* (New York: Arno Press, 1969).

Cairncross, Alexander R. 1958. "Economic Schizophrenia." *Scottish Journal of Political Economy* 5, no. 1 (February): 15–21.

Campbell, Robert. 1953. "Sir James Steuart: A Study in the Development of Economic Thought" (Ph.D. dissertation, University of California, Berkeley).

Campbell, T. D., and I. S. Ross. 1981. "The Utilitarianism of Adam Smith's Policy Advice." *Journal of the History of Ideas* 42, no. 1 (January March): 73–92.

de Canio, Stephen, and Joel Mokyr. 1977. "Inflation and the Wage Lag During the Civil War." *Explorations in Economic History* 14, no. 2 (October): 311–36.

Cannan, Edwin. 1929. *A Review of Economic Theory* (London: P. S. King and Sons).

Cantillon, Richard. 1755. *Essai sur la nature du commerce en general*, Henry Higgs, ed. (New York: Kelley, 1964).

Carey, Lewis J. 1928. *Franklin's Economic Views* (Garden City, N.Y.: Doubleday, Doran & Co.).

Carrier, Lyman. 1918. *Journal of the American Society of Agronomy* 2: 206–11; reprinted in Anon., *American Husbandry*, H. J. Carman, ed. (New York: Columbia University Press): xii–lxi.

Carter, Ian. 1980. "The Highlands of Scotland as an Underdeveloped Region," in Frederick H. Buttel and Howard Newby, *The Rural Sociology of the Advanced Societies: Critical Perspectives* (Montclair, N.J.: Allanheld, Osmun): 353–85.

[Chalmers, George.] 1805. "Anecdotes of the Life of Sir James Steuart," in Sir James Steuart, *The Works in Political, Metaphysical, and Chronological* (New York: Kelley, 1967).

Chambers, J. D., and G. E. Mingay. 1966. *The Agricultural Revolution, 1750–1880* (New York: Schocken Books).

Chamley, Paul. 1965. *Documents Relatifs à Sir James Steuart* (Paris: Librairie Dalloz).

Chayanov, A. V. 1966. *The Theory of Peasant Economy*, Daniel Thorner, Basil Kerblay, and R. E. F. Smith, eds. (Homewood, Ill.: Richard D. Irwin).

Child, Josiah. 1751. *A New Discourse of Trade*, 5th ed. (Glasgow: Robert and Andrew Foulis).

Chinn, Dennis L. 1979. "Rural Poverty and the Structure of Farm Household Income in Developing Countries: Evidence from Taiwan." *Economic Development and Cultural Change* 27, no. 2 (January): 283–301.

Chitty, J. 1812. *A Treatise on the Game Laws and on Fisheries*, 2 vols. (London: W. Clarke and Sons).

Clarke, Richard N., and Lawrence H. Summers. 1980. "The Labour Scarcity Controversy Reconsidered." *The Economic Journal* 90, no. 357 (March): 129–39.

Coats, A. W. 1958. "Changing Attitudes Toward Labour in the Mid-Eighteenth Century." *Economic History Review* 11, n.s.: 35–51.

———. 1962. "Adam Smith: The Modern Appraisal." *Renaissance and Modern Studies* 6, 26–48.

———. 1971. "The Classical Economists and the Labourer," in his *The Classical Economists and Economic Policy* (London: Methuen): 144–79.

Cobbett, William. 1806–20. *The Parliamentary History of England*, 36 vols. (New York: Johnson Reprint Co., 1966).

———. 1830. *Rural Rides*, 2 vols. (London: J. M. Dent).

———. 1831. *Cobbett's Two-Penny Trash-Politics for the Poor*, 2 vols. (London).

Cole, Arthur Harrison, ed. 1968. *Industrial and Commercial Correspondence of Alexander Hamilton, Anticipating His Report on Manufactures* (New York: Kelley).

Collier, Frances. 1930. "An Early Factory Community." *The Economic Journal* 2 (Supple.): 117–24.

Collins, E. J. T. 1969. "Harvest Technology and Labour Supply in Britain, 1790–1870." *Economic History Review*, 2nd series, vol. 32, no. 3 (December): 453–73.

Comito, Terry. 1971. "Renaissance Gardens and the Discovery of Paradise." *Journal of the History of Ideas* 32, no. 4 (October–December): 483–506.

Colletti, Lucio. 1973. *Marxism and Hegel* (London: New Left Books).

Conner, Paul W. 1965. *Poor Richard's Politicks: Benjamin Franklin and His New American Order* (New York: Oxford University Press).

Cooke, Jacob E. 1967. "The Reports of Alexander Hamilton." in Jacob E. Cooke, ed., *Alexander Hamilton: A Profile* (New York: Hill and Wang): 64–82.

Cooper, Thomas. 1833. *A Manual of Political Economy* (Washington, D.C.: Duff Green).

Cornelius, Wayne A. 1979. "Migration to the United States: The View from Rural Mexican Communities." *Development Digest* 17, no. 4 (October): 90–101.

Cowherd, Raymond G. 1977. *Political Economists and the English Poor Laws: A Historical Study of the Influence of Classical Economics on the Formation of Social Welfare Policy* (Athens: Ohio University Press).

Coxe, Tench. 1794. *A View of the United States of America* (New York: Kelley, 1964).

de Crevecoeur, J. Hector St. John. 1782. *Letters from an American Farmer* (New York: Dutton, 1972).

de Crisenoy. 1979. "Capitalism and Agriculture." *Economy and Society* 8, no. 1 (February): 9–25.

Cunliffe, Marcus. 1979. *Chattel Slavery and Wage Slavery: The Anglo-American Context, Mercer University Lamar Memorial Lectures, no. 22* (Athens: University of Georgia Press).

Currey, Cecil B. 1965. *Road to Revolution: Benjamin Franklin in England, 1765–1775* (Garden City, N. Y.: Doubleday).

————. 1972. *Code Number 72. Ben Franklin: Patriot or Spy?* (Englewood Cliffs, N. J.: Prentice-Hall).

Danhoff, Clarence. 1941. "Farm Making Costs and the 'Safety Valve.'" *Journal of Political Economy* 49, no. 3 (June): 217–59.

Darity, William A., Jr., and Keith Hurt. 1981. "The Origins of the Doctrine of Unlimited Supplies of Labor," presented at the Annual Meeting of the History of Economics Society, East Lansing, Michigan, June 1981.

David, Paul A. 1975. *Technical Choice and Innovation in Economic Growth, Essays on American and British Experience in the Nineteenth Century* (Cambridge: Cambridge University Press).

Davis, David Brion. 1966. *The Problem of Slavery in Western Culture* (Ithaca: Cornell University Press).

Davis, John. 1803. *Travels of Four and a Half Years in the United States of America; during 1798, 1799, 1800, 1801, and 1802* (New York: H. Caritat); reprinted privately, 2 vols. (Boston: Bibliophile Society, 1910).

Deane, Phyllis. 1957. "The Industrial Revolution and Economic Growth: The Evidence of Early British National Income Estimates." *Economic Development and Cultural Change* 5, no. 1; reprinted in R. M. Hartwell, ed., *The Causes of the Industrial Revolution in England* (London: Methuen, 1967): 81–96.

————, and W. A. Coale. 1967. *British Economic Growth, 1688–1959*, 2nd ed. (Cambridge: Cambridge University Press).

Deere, Carmen Diana. 1976. "Rural Women's Subsistence Production in the Capitalist Periphery." *Review of Radical Political Economy* 8, no. 1 (Spring): 9–17.

————, and Alain de Janvry. 1979. "A Conceptual Framework for the Empirical Analysis of Peasants." *American Journal of Agricultural Economics* 61, no. 4 (November): 601–11.

Defoe, Daniel. 1724–26. *A Tour Through the Whole Island of Great Britain* (Baltimore: Penguin, 1971).

Dempsey, Bernard. 1960. *The Frontier Wage* (Chicago: Loyola University Press).

Devine, T. M. 1976. "The Colonial Trades and Industrial Investment in Scotland, c. 1700–1815." *The Economic History Review*, 2nd Series, vol. 29, no. 1 (February): 1–14.

Diamond, Daniel E., and John D. Guilfoil. 1973. *United States Economic History* (Morristown, N. J.: General Learning Press).

Dillard, Dudley. 1967. *Economic Development of the North Atlantic Community* (Englewood Cliffs, N. J.: Prentice-Hall).

Dobb, Maurice. 1963. *Studies in the Development of Capitalism* (New York: International Publishers).

Dockes, P. 1969. *L'espace dan la pensée économique du xvième siècle* (Paris: Flammarion).

Domar, Evsey. 1970. "The Causes of Slavery of Serfdom." *Journal of Economic History* 30, no. 1 (March): 18–32.

Dorfman, Joseph. 1966. *The Economic Mind in American Civilization, 1606–1865,* 2 vols. (New York: Augustus M. Kelley).

―――. 1966a. "'Piercy Ravenstone' and His Radical Tory Treatise," in *Piercy Ravenstone. 1821. A Few Doubts as to the Correctness of Some Opinions Generally Entertained on the Subjects of Population and Political Economy* (New York: Kelley, 1966).

Doyle, Sir Francis Hastings. 1886. *Reminiscences and Opinions of Sir Francis Hastings Doyle* (New York).

Draper, Hal. 1978. *The Politics of Social Classes.* Vol. 2. *Karl Marx's Theory of Revolution* (New York: Monthly Review Press).

Duckham, Baron F. 1969. "Serfdom in Eighteenth-Century Scotland." *History* 54, no. 181 (June): 178–97.

Dudden, Arthur Power. 1971. *Joseph Fels and the Single Tax Movement* (Philadelphia: Temple University Press).

Dyos, H. J., and M. Wolff. 1973. "The Way We Live Now" in idem, eds., *The Victorian City: Images and Reality,* 2 vols. (London: Routledge and Kegan Paul): 2: 893–907).

Earle, Carville, and Ronald Hoffman. 1980. "The Foundation of the Modern Economy: Agriculture and the Costs of Labor in the United States and England, 1800–1860." *American Historical Review* (December): 1055–94.

Edmonds, Thomas Rowe. 1833. *Practical, Moral, and Political Economy* (New York: Augustus M. Kelley, 1969).

Edwards, Edward. 1827. "On Agriculture and Rent." *Quarterly Review* 36, no. 51: 391–409.

Eiselen, Malcolm R. 1928. *Franklin's Political Theories* (Garden City, N. Y.: Doubleday, Doran & Co.).

Eisner, Robert. 1979. "Total Income, Total Investment and Growth," presented at the American Economic Association Annual Meetings (29 December).

Emerson, Ralph Waldo. 1940. "Ode Inscribed to W. H. Channing." *The Selected Works of Ralph Waldo Emerson,* Brooks Atkinson, ed. (New York: Modern Library).

Engels, Friedrich. 1845a. "The Agrarian Programme of the Chartists," in Marx and Engels, *Selected Works in Three Volumes* (Moscow: Foreign Languages Publishing House, 1969–73): 456–76.

―――. 1845b. "The Condition of the Working Class in England in 1844," in Marx and Engels, *Marx and Engels: 1844–1845. Collected Works* (New York: International Publishers): 4: 295–584.

―――. 1881. "The Peasant Question in France and Germany," in Marx and Engels, *Marx and Engels, 1845–1848. Collected Works* (New York International Publishers, 1976): 6: 456–76.

―――. 1887. "The Housing Question," in Karl Marx and Frederick Engels, *Selected Works in Three Volumes* (Moscow: Progress Publishers, 1969–73): 2: 295–375.

―――. 1891. "The Origin of the Family, Private Property and the State," in Marx and Engels, *Selected Works in Three Volumes* (Moscow: Progress Publishers, 1969–1973).

―――. 1893. "Letter to Henry Demarest Lloyd, May 27, 1893," in Henry Demarest Lloyd, *The Correspondence of Henry Demarest Lloyd, January 6, 1891 to August 31, 1893.* Reel 4. *Henry Demarest Papers* (Microfilm edition) Madison: State Historical Society of Wisconsin, 1970.

————. 1894. *Anti-Duhring: Herr Eugen Duhring's Revolution in Science* (Moscow: Progress Publishers, 1969).

————. 1954. *Dialetics of Nature* (Moscow: Foreign Languages Publishing House).

Ensor, George. 1818. *Inquiry Concerning the Population of Nations* (New York: Augustus M. Kelley, 1967).

Escher, Hans Caspar. 1814. "Letters from England," in W. O. Henderson, ed., *Britain Under the Regency, The Diaries of Escher, Bodmer, May and Gallois, 1814–1818* (New York: Augustus M. Kelley, 1968).

Ewen, Stuart. 1976. *Captains of Consciousness: Advertising and the Social Roots of Consumer Culture* (New York: McGraw-Hill).

Fage, Anita. 1952. "La vie et l'oevrre de Richard Cantillon (1697–1734)," in Institut National d'etudes demographique, *Richard Cantillon: Essai du Commerce en General* (Paris: INED, 1952): xxiii–xlii.

Fay, C. R. 1932. *The Corn Laws and Social England* (Cambridge: Cambridge University Press).

————. 1956. *Adam Smith and the Scotland of His Day* (Cambridge: Cambridge University Press).

Fetter, Frank Whitson. 1943. "The Early History of Political Economy in the United States." *Proceedings of the American Philosophical Society* 87, pp. 51–60; reprinted in James A. Gherity, *Economic Thought: A Historical Anthology* (New York: Random House, 1965): 472–90.

————. 1953. "The Authorship of Articles in the *Edinburgh Review*, 1807–1847." *Journal of Political Economy* 61, no. 3 (June): 232–59.

————. 1957. "Introduction." *The Economic Writings of Francis Horner in the* Edinburgh Review, Frank Whitson Fetter, ed. (New York: Kelley and Milman): 1–27.

————. 1980. *The Economist in Parliament: 1780–1868* (Durham: Duke University Press).

Field, Alexander. 1978. "Sectoral Shift in Antebellum Massachusetts." *Explorations in Economic History* 15, no. 2 (April): 146–71.

Fite, Gilbert C., and Jim E. Reese. 1965. *An Economic History of the United States,* 2nd ed. (Boston: Houghton Mifflin).

Fleisig, Heywood. 1976. "Slavery, the Supply of Agricultural Labor, and the Industrialization of the South." *Journal of Economic History* 36, no. 3 (September): 572–97.

Flink, James J. 1975. *The Car Culture* (Cambridge, Mass.: MIT Press).

Fobre, Nancy. 1980. "Patriarchy in Colonial New England." *Review of Radical Political Economy* 12, no. 2 (Summer): 4–13.

Fogel, Robert William, and Stanley Engerman. 1974. *Time on the Cross: The Economics of American Negro Slavery* (Boston: Little, Brown).

Foner, Philip S. 1975. *From Colonial Times to the Founding of the American Federation of Labor. Volume 1. History of the Labor Movement in the United States* (New York: International Publishers).

Forster, N. 1767. *An Inquiry into the Causes of the Present High Price of Provisions* (London).

Foster-Carter, Aidan. 1978. "Can We Articulate 'Articulation?'" in John Clammer, ed. *The New Economic Anthropology* (New York: St. Martin's Press).

Foucalt, Michel. 1965. *Madness and Civilization: A History of Insanity in the Age of Reason* (New York: Harper Torchback).

Fox-Genovese, Elizabeth. 1976. *The Origins of Physiocracy: Economic Revolution and Social Order in Eighteenth-Century France* (Ithaca, N.Y.: Cornell University Press).

Fraginals, Manuel Moreno. 1978. *El Ingenio,* 3 vols. (Havana: Editorial de Ciencias Sociales).

Frank, André Gunder. 1975. *On Capitalist Underdevelopment* (Bombay: Oxford University Press).

_____. 1978. *World Accumulation, 1492–1789* (New York: Monthly Review Press).

Franklin, Benjamin. 1905–07. *The Writings of Benjamin Franklin*, 10 vols. Albert Henry Smyth, ed. (New York: Macmillan).

_____. 1959– . *The Papers of Benjamin Franklin*, Leonard W. Larabee and William B. Wilcox, eds. (New Haven: Yale University Press).

_____. 1964. *The Autobiography of Benjamin Franklin* (New Haven: Yale University Press).

Furniss, Edgar. 1965. *The Position of the Laborer in a System of Nationalism* (New York: Augustus M. Kelley).

Garnett, R. G. 1971. "Robert Owen and Community Experiments," in Sidney Pollard and John Salt, eds., *Robert Owen, Prophet of the Poor; Essays in Honour of the Two-Hundredth Anniversary of His Birth* (Lewisburg, Pa.: Bucknell University Press).

Gates, Paul. 1960. *The Farmers' Age: Agriculture 1815–1860* (New York: Harper and Row).

George, M. Dorothy. 1953. *England in Transition* (Baltimore: Penguin Books).

_____. 1964. *London Life in the Eighteenth Century* (New York: Harper and Row).

Georgescu-Roegen, Nicholas. 1971. *The Entropy Law Hand Economic Process* (Cambridge: Harvard University Press).

Gideon, Siegfried. 1948. *Mechanization Takes Command* (New York: Oxford University Press).

Gilbert, Geoffrey. 1980. "Economic Growth and the Poor in Malthus' Essay on Population." *History of Political Economy* 12, no. 1 (Spring 1980): 83–96.

Goodrich, Carter, and Sol Davison. 1935. "The Wage Earner in the Westward Movement, Part 1." *Political Science Quarterly* 50, no. 2 (June): 161–85.

Goodwin, Craufurd D. W. 1961. *Canadian Economic Thought: The Political Economy of a Developing Nation, 1814–1914* (Durham, N.C.: Duke University Press).

Gordon, Barry. 1976. *Political Economy in Parliament, 1819–1823* (New York: Barnes and Noble).

Gorky, Maxim. 1922. "On the Russian Peasantry," reprinted in Teodor Shanin, *Peasants and Peasant Societies: Selected Writings* (Baltimore: Penguin Books): 369–71.

Gorz, André. 1968. *Strategy for Labor* (Boston: Beacon Press).

Gourne, Edward G. 1894. "Alexander Hamilton and Adam Smith." *Quarterly Journal of Economics* 7, no. 2 (April): 328–44.

Graham, H. Grey. 1937. *The Social Life of Scotland in the Eighteenth Century* (London: A. C. Black).

Grampp, William. 1960. *The Manchester School of Economics* (Stanford, Calif.: Stanford University Press).

_____. 1979. "Adam Smith and the American Revolutionists." *History of Political Economy* 11, no. 2 (Summer): 179–191.

_____. 1965. *Economic Liberalism*, 2 vols. (New York: Random House).

Gray, Malcolm. 1951. "The Kelp Industry in the Highlands and Islands." *The Economic History Review*, 2nd series, vol. 4, no. 2 (May): 197–209.

Greer, Edward. 1979. *Big Steel: Black Politics and Corporate Power in Gary, Indiana* (New York: Monthly Review Press).

Grigg, D. B. 1974. *The Agricultural Systems of the World: An Evolutionary Approach* (Cambridge: Cambridge University Press).

Groenwegen, P. D. "Turgot and Adam Smith." *Scottish Journal of Political Economy* 16, no. 3 (November): 271–87.

Guest, R. 1823. *A Compendius History of the Cotton Manufacture* (Manchester: Joseph Pratt).

Habbakuk, H. J. 1967. *American and British Technology in the Nineteenth Century: The Search for Labour-Saving Inventions* (Cambridge: Cambridge University Press).

Hagen, Everett E. 1980. *The Economics of Development*, 3rd ed. (Homewood, Ill.: Richard D. Irwin).

Halevy, Elie. 1961. *A History of the English People in the Nineteenth Century. Vol. 2, The Liberal Awakening (1815–1830)* (New York: Barnes and Noble).

Hall, Charles. 1805. *The Effects of Civilization on the People in European States* (New York: Augustus M. Kelley, 1965).

Halsband, Robert. 1956. *The Life of Lady Mary Wortley Montagu* (Oxford: Clarendon Press).

Hamilton, Alexander. 1961. *The Papers of Alexander Hamilton,* Harold C. Syrett, ed. (New York: Columbia University Press).

Hamilton, James C. 1879. *Life of Alexander Hamilton: A History of the Republic of the United States of America* (Boston).

Hammond, J. L., and Barbara. 1919. *The Skilled Labourer, 1760–1832* (New York: Harper and Row, 1970).

Hansard's Parliamentary History. 1830. 3rd series, vol. I (October 26–December 30).

Hariot, Thomas. 1588. *A Briefe and True Report of the New Found Land of Virginia,* in David Beers Quinn, ed., *The Roanoke Voyages, 1584–1590,* 2 vols. (London: The Hakluyt Society): 317–87.

Harris, Marshall. 1953. *Origin of the Land Tenure System in the United States* (Ames: Iowa State University Press).

Hartman, Heidi. 1976. "Women's Work in the United States," *Current History* 70, no. 416 (May): 215–19.

Hartwell, Ronald Max. 1978. "Adam Smith and the Industrial Revolution," in Fred R. Glahe, *Adam Smith and the Wealth of Nations, 1776–1976* (Boulder, Colo.: Associated University Press).

Harvey, David. 1976. "Labor, Capital and Class Struggle Around the Built Environment in Advanced Capitalist Societies." *Politics and Society* 6, no. 3: 265–97.

Hayek, Friedrich A. 1932. *Prices and Production* (New York: Macmillan).

Hegel, Georg Wilhelm Friedrich. 1821–22. *Lectures on the Philosophy of World History* (Cambridge at the University Press).

Helper, Hinton. 1860. *The Impending Crisis of the South: How to Meet It* (New York: A. B. Burdick).

Henneau-Depooter. 1959. *Miseres et luttes sociales Jans le Haunaut, 1860–1890* (Bruxelles: Universite libre de Bruxelles).

Herrick, Cheesman A. 1926. *White Servitude in Pennsylvania: Indentured and Redemption Labor in Colony and Commonwealth* (Freeport, N.Y.: Books for Libraries Press, 1970).

Higgs, Henry. 1931. "The Life and Work of Richard Cantillon," in Richard Cantillon, *Essai sur la nature du commerce en general,* Henry Higgs, ed (New York: Augustus M. Kelley, 1964): 363–89.

Hill, Christopher. 1964. *Puritanism and Revolution: The English Revolution of the 17th Century* (New York: Schocken Books).

———. 1967. *Society and Puritanism* (New York: Schocken Books).

Hilton, Boyd. 1977. *Corn, Cash, Commerce: The Economic Policies of the Tory Governments, 1815–1830* (New York: Oxford University Press).

Hilton, Rodney. 1978. "Reasons for Inequality Among Medieval Peasants." *Journal of Peasant Studies* 5, no. 3 (April): 271–84.

Hobbes, Thomas. 1651. *Leviathan* (Baltimore: Penguin, 1968).

Hobsbawm, E. J., and George Rude. 1968. *Captain Swing* (New York: Pantheon).

———. 1974. "Custom Wages and Workload in Nineteenth-Century Industry," in Peter N. Stearns and Daniel J. Walkowitz, eds., *Workers in the Industrial Revolution* (New Brunswick, N.J.: Transaction Books, 1964): 232–54.

Hollander, Samuel. 1971. "The Development of Ricardo's Position on Machinery." *History of Political Economy* 3, no. 1 (Spring): 105–35.

_____. 1979. *The Economics of David Ricardo* (Toronto: University of Toronto Press).

Hollis, Patricia. 1973. *Class and Conflict in Nineteenth-Century England* (London: Routledge and Kegan Paul).

Hopkins, A. G. 1966. "The Lagos Strike of 1897: An Exploration in Nigerian Labour History," *Past and Present* 35 (December); reprinted in Robin Cohen, Peter C. W. Gutkind, and Phyllis Brazier, eds., *Peasants and Proletarians: The Struggles of Third World Workers* (New York: Monthly Review Press): 87–106.

Horn, Pamela. 1980. *The Rural World, 1750: Social Change in the English Countryside* (New York: St. Martin's Press).

Horner, Francis, M. P. 1843. *Memories and Correspondence of Francis Horner, M. P.*, Leonard Horner, ed., 2 vols. (London: John Murray).

Hu Chiao-mu. 1978. "Observe Economic Laws, Speed Up the Four Modernizations." 3 pts., *Peking Review* 45–47 (November 10, 17, and 24).

Hughes, J. R. T. 1976. *Social Control in the Colonial Economy* (Charlottesville: University Press of Virginia).

Hume, David. 1751. "An Inquiry Concerning the Principles of Morals," *The Philosophical Works of David Hume*, 4 vols., T. H. Green and T. H. Gross, eds. (Aalen: Scientia Verlag, 1964): 4: 167–287.

1752. "On Commerce," in David Hume, *Writings on Economics*, Eugene Rotwein, ed. (Madison: University of Wisconsin Press, 1955).

_____. 1752a. "Of the Original Contract," *The Philosophical Works of David Hume*, 3: 443–60.

_____. 1752b. "On the Populousness of Ancient Nations," in Eugene Rotwein, ed., *David Hume: Writings on Economics*, pp.: 108–83.

_____. 1752c. "Of Taxes," in *The Philosophical Works of David Hume*, 3: 356–60.

Humphries, Jane. 1976. "Women: Scapegoats and Safety Valves in the Great Depression." *Review of Radical Political Economy* 8 no. 1 (Spring): 98–121.

_____. 1977. "The Working Class Family, Women's Liberation, and Class Struggle: The Case of Nineteenth Century British History." *Review of Radical Political Economy* 9, no. 3 (Fall): 25–41.

Hutcheson, Francis. 1749. *A Short Introduction to Moral Philosophy*, 5th ed. (Philadelphia: Joseph Cruckshank, 1788).

_____. 1755. *A System of Moral Philosophy*, 2 vols. in 1 (New York: Augustus M. Kelley, 1968).

Hyse, Richard. 1971. "Richard Cantillon, Financier to Amsterdam, July to November 1720." *Economic Journal* 81, no. 324 (December): 812–25.

Ignatieff, Michael. 1978. *A Just Measure of Pain: The Penitentiary in the Industrial Revolution, 1750–1850* (New York: Pantheon).

Inglis, Brian. 1971. *Poverty and the Industrial Revolution* (London: Hodder and Stoughton).

Institut National d'Etudes Demographiques. 1966. *Pierre de Boisguilbert ou la naissance de l'economie politique*, 2 vols. (Paris: INED).

International Bank for Reconstruction and Redevelopment. 1977. *Papua New Guinea: Its Economic Situation and Prospects for Development* (Washington, D.C.: The World Bank).

James, Patricia. 1979. *Population Malthus: His Life and Times* (London: Routledge and Kegan Paul).

James, R. Warren. 1965. *Introduction to John Rae, Political Economist: An Account of His Life and a Compilation of His Main Writings*, 2 vols. (Toronto: University of Toronto Press).

Jefferson, Thomas. 1787. "Notes on Virginia," extracted in Henry William Spiegel, ed., *The Rise of American Economic Thought* (New York and Philadelphia: Chilton, 1960): 42–43.

_____. "Letter to Thomas Diggs, 19 June 1788," in *The Papers of Thomas Jefferson*. Vol.

13, March - 7 October 1788. Julian P. Boyd, ed. (Princeton, N.J.: Princeton University Press): 260.

————. 1817. "Forward," in *A Treatise on Political Economy* (Detroit: Center for Health Education, 1973).

————. 1950– . *The Papers of Thomas Jefferson*, Vol. 8, 25 February to 31 October 1785, Julian P. Boyd, ed. (Princeton, N.J.: Princeton University Press).

Jensen, Joan M. 1980. "Cloth, Butter and Boarders." *Review of Radical Political Economy* 12, no. 2 (Summer): 14–24.

Jevons, William Stanley. 1875–76. *Lectures on Political Economy. Vol. 6. Papers and Correspondence of William Stanley Jevons*, R. D. Collison Black, ed. (New York: Augustus M. Kelley).

————. 1972. *Biography and Personal Journal. Vol. 1 Papers and Correspondence*, R. D. Collison Black and Rosamund Koenigkamp, eds. (London: Macmillan).

Johnson, Arthur. 1909. *The Disappearance of the Small Landowner* (London: Oxford University Press, 1963).

Johnson, Samuel. 1774. "A Journey to the Western Islands of Scotland," in Mary Lascelles, ed., vol. 9, *The Works of Samuel Johnson* (New Haven, Conn.: Yale University Press, 1971).

Kalm, Per. 1770–71. *Travels in North America (1748–1750)*, 3 vols., J. R. Forster, Jr., ed. (London: Warrington).

Kautsky, Karl. 1899. *Die Agrarfrage: Eine Ubersicht uber die Tendenzen der modernen Landwirtschaft und der Agrarpolitik der Socialdemokratie* (Stuttgart: Dietz).

Kelley, Florence Finch. 1906. "An Undertow to the Land: Successful Efforts to Make Possible a Flow of the City Population Countryward." *The Craftsman* 11 (December): 294–310.

Kemp-Ashraf, P. M. 1966. "Introduction to the Selected Writings of Thomas Spence," in *Life in Literature of the Working Class, Essays in Honor of William Gallagher*, P. M. Kemp-Ashraf and Jack Mitchell, eds. (Berlin, German Democratic Republic: Humboldt-Universitat): 271–91.

Ketton-Cremer, R. W. 1965. "Johnson and the Countryside." in Mary Lascelles et al., *Johnson, Boswell and Their Circle: Essays Presented to Lawrence Fitzroy Powell* (Oxford: Clarendon Press): 65–75.

Keynes, J. M. 1938. "Adam Smith as Student and Professor." *Review of Economic History* 3 (February): 33–46.

————. 1963. *Essays in Biography* (New York: W. W. Norton).

Kindleberger, Charles. 1976. "This Historical Background: Adam Smith and the Industrial Revolution," in Thomas Wilson and Andres S. Skinner, eds., *The Market and the State. Essays in Honour of Adam Smith* (Oxford: Clarendon Press): 1–25.

King, John. 1981. "Utopian or Scientific? A Reconsideration of the Ricardian Socialists" (University of Lancaster, typescript).

Kingston-Mann, Esther. 1980. "A Strategy for Marxist Bourgeois Revolution: Lenin and the Peasantry, 1907–1916." *Journal of Peasant Studies* 7, no. 2 (January): 131–57.

Kippis, Dr. Andrew. 1842. *The Life of Sir James Steuart Denham of Coltness and Westshield* (Edinburgh: Maitland Club).

Knox, William. 1769. *Controversy Between Great Britain and Her Colonies, Reviewed* (London: J. Almon).

Koebner, R. 1959. "Adam Smith and the Industrial Revolution." *Economic History Review*, 2nd series, vol. 11, no. 3: 381–91.

Kolko, Gabriel. 1978. "Working Wives: Their Effects on the Structure of the Working Class." *Science and Society* 42, no. 3 (Fall): 257–77.

Kroos, Herman E., and Charles Gilbert. 1972. *American Business History* (Englewood Cliffs, N.J.: Prentice-Hall).

Kropotkin, Peter. 1898. *Fields, Factories and Workshops* (New York: Greenwood Press, 1968).

——. 1906. *The Conquest of Bread* (New York: New York University Press, 1972).

Kuczynski, Jurgen. 1967. *The Rise of the Working Class* (New York: McGraw-Hill World University Library).

Kuznets, Simon. 1965. *Economic Growth and Structure* (New York: W. W. Norton).

Lancaster, Kelvin John. 1966. "A New Approach to Consumer Theory." *Journal of Political Economy* 74, no. 2 (April): 132–57.

Lascelles, Mary. 1971. Introduction to Samuel Johnson, *A Journey to the Western Islands of Scotland. Vol. 9. The Works of Samuel Johnson* (New Haven: Yale University Press): pp. xiii–xxxvii.

Laslett, Peter. 1971. *The World We Have Lost: England Before the Industrial Age* (New York: Scribners).

von Laue, Theodore H. 1963. *Serge Witte and the Industrialization of Russia* (New York: Atheneum).

Lazonick, William. 1978. "The Subjugation of Labor to Capital: The Rise of the Capitalist System." *Review of Radical Political Economy* 10, no. 1 (Spring): 1–31.

Lee, Sidney, ed. 1879. *Dictionary of National Biography* (London: Smith Elder & Co.).

Lee, Susan Previant, and Peter Passell. 1979. *A New Economic View of American History* (New York and London: W. W. Norton).

Lemon, James T. 1967. "Household Consumption in Eighteenth-Century America and Its Relationship to Production and Trade: The Situation Among Farmers in Southeastern Pennsylvania." *Agricultural History* 41, no. 1 (January): 58–70.

Lenin, V. I. 1893. "On the So-Called Market Question," in V. I. Lenin, *Collected Works*, 45 vols. (Moscow: Foreign Languages Publishing House): 1: 79–125.

——. 1894. "What 'The Friends of the People' Are and How They Fight the Social Democrats," in *Collected Works*, 1: 129–332.

——. 1898. "The Handicraft Census of 1894–1895 in Perm Gubernia and General Problems of the 'Handicraft Industry,'" in *Collected Works*, 2: 355–458.

——. 1905. "Petty-Bourgeois and Proletarian Socialism," in *Collected Works*, 9: 438–46.

——. 1907. "The Agrarian Program of Social Democracy in the First Russian Revolution, 1905–1907," in *Collected Works*, 13: 217–429.

——. 1908. "The Agrarian Question in Russia at the End of the Nineteenth Century," in *Collected Works*, 15: 69–147.

——. 1913. "The Land Question and the Rural Poor," in *Collected Works*, 19: 376–78.

——. 1921a. "Report on the Substitution of a Tax in Kind for the Surplus Grain Appropriation, March 15," in *Collected Works*, 32: 214–38.

——. 1921b. "Report of the Moscow Gubernia Conference of the Russian Communist Party," in *Collected Works*, 33: 81–108.

——. 1921c. "The Tax in Kind: The Significance of the New Policy and Its Conditions," in *Collected Works*, 32: 329–65.

——. 1974. *The Development of Capitalism in Russia* (Moscow: Progress Publishers).

LeRoy Ladurie, Emmanuel. 1974. *The Peasants of Languedoc*, trans. John Day (Urbana: University of Illinois Press).

Leslie, T. Cliffe. 1888. *Essays in Political Economy* (New York: Augustus M. Kelley, 1969).

Levy, Hermann. 1966. *Large and Small Holdings*, trans. Ruth Kenyon (New York: Augustus M. Kelley).

Levy, S. Leon. 1970. *Nassau W. Senior, 1790–1864* (Kelley: New York).

Lewis, William Arthur. 1954. "Economic Development with Unlimited Supplies of Labour." *Manchester School* 22, no. 2 (May): 139–91.

———. 1958. "Unlimited Labour: Further Notes." *Manchester School* 26, no. 1 (January): 1–32.

———. 1976. "The Diffusion of Development," in Thomas Wilson and Andrew S. Skinner, eds., *The Market and the State: Essays in Honour of Adam Smith* (Oxford: Clarendon Press): 135–56.

List, Friederich. 1841. *Das Nationale System der Politischen Oekonomie* (Jena: Gustav Fischer, 1950).

Locke, John. 1698. *Two Treatises on Government*, 2nd ed., Peter Laslett, ed. (Cambridge: Cambridge University Press, 1967).

Longfield, Mountifort. 1834. *Lectures on Political Economy Delivered in Trinity and Michaelmas Terms, 1833* (Dublin: Richard Millikan and Sons), reprinted in *The Economic Writings of Mountifort Longfield*, R. C. D. Black, ed. (New York: Augustus M. Kelley, 1971).

Lowe, Joseph. 1823. *The Present State of England in Regard to Agriculture, Trade, and Finance* (London: Longmans, Hurst, Rees, Orme, and Brown).

Luxemburg, Rosa. 1968. *The Accumulation of Capital* (New York: Monthly Review Press).

McCoy, Drew R. 1980. *The Elusive Republic: Political Economy in Jeffersonian America* (Chapel Hill: University of North Carolina Press).

McCulloch. John R. 1824. "Political Economy." *Encyclopedia Britannica*, 4th ed. supplement, reprinted as John McVickar, *Outlines of Political Economy* (New York: Augustus M. Kelley, 1966).

———. 1825. *Outlines of Political Economy*, Rev. John M'Vickar, ed. (New York: Augustus M. Kelley, 1966).

———. 1825a. "Evidence Given Before the Select Committee on Ireland." *British Parliamentary Papers*, 8: 811–35.

———. 1841. *Statements, Illustrative of the Policy and Probable Consequences of the Proposed Repeal of the Corn Laws* (Edinburgh).

———. 1845. *The Literature of Political Economy: A Classified Catalogue of Select Publications* (New York: Augustus M. Kelley, 1964).

———. 1854. *A Treatise on the Circumstances Which Determine the Rate of Wages and the Condition of the Labouring Classes* (New York: Kelley, 1967).

Macfie, A. L. 1971. "The Invisible Hand of Jupiter." *Journal of the History of Ideas* 32 no. 4 (October-December): 595–99.

McKendrick, Neil. 1961. "Josiah Adams and Factory Discipline," in *The Historical Journal* 4, no. 1: 30–55.

Macpherson, C. B. 1962. *The Political Theory of Possessive Individualism: Hobbes to Locke* (London: Oxford University Press).

Madison, James. 1787. "Appointment of Representatives in the Legislature," in Madison 1962– : 10: 98–100.

———. 1962– . *The Papers of James Madison*, William Hutchinson and William Rachal, eds. (Chicago: University of Chicago Press).

Magubane, Bernard Makhosezwe. 1979. *The Political Economy of Race and Class in South Africa* (New York: Monthly Review Press).

Main, Jackson Turner. 1965. *The Social Structure in Revolutionary America* (Princeton, N. J.: Princeton University Press).

Maital, Schlomo, and Patricia Haswell. 1977. "Why Did Ricardo (Not) Change His Mind? On Money and Machinery." *Economics* 44, no. 176 (November): 359–68.

Maitland, James, Eighth Earl of Lauderdale. 1804. *An Inquiry into the Nature and Origin of Public Wealth* (New York: Augustus M. Kelley, 1966).

Malthus, Thomas Robert. 1820. *Principles of Political Economy*, 1st. ed. (London: John

Murray, reprinted in part in David Ricardo, *Notes on Malthus. Vol. 2. The Works and Correspondence of David Ricardo*, Piero Sraffa, ed. (Cambridge: Cambridge University Press, 1951).

———. 1826. *Essay on the Principle of Population*, 7th ed. 2 vols. (London: J. M. Dent, 1958).

———. 1836. *Principles of Political Economy, Considered with a View of Their Practical Application* (New York: Augustus M. Kelley, 1951).

———. 1966. *The Travel Diaries of T. R. Malthus*, Patricia Jones, ed. (Cambridge: Cambridge University Press).

———. 1976. *An Essay on the Principle of Population: Text, Sources and Background Criticism*, Philip Appleman, ed. (New York: W. W. Norton).

Mandeville, Bernard. 1723. *The Fable of the Bees*, F. B. Kaye, ed. (Oxford: Clarendon Press, 1954).

Mantoux, Paul. 1961. *The Industrial Revolution in the Eighteenth Century: An Outline of the Beginnings of the Modern Factory System in England* (New York: Harper and Row).

Mao Tse-Tung. 1945. "Policy Work for Liberated Areas," in *Selected Works*, 5 vols. (Peking: Foreign Languages Press, 1965–77): 4: 75–79.

———. 1947. "Greet the New High Tide of the Chinese Revolution," in *Selected Works*, 4: 119–27.

———. 1955. "The Debate on the Co-Operative Transformation of Agriculture and the Current Class Struggle," in *Selected Works*, 5: 211–34.

———. 1955a. "Editor's Notes from Socialist Upsurge in China's Countryside," in *Selected Works*, 5: 242–76.

———. 1956. "On the Ten Great Relationships," in Mao Tse-Tung, *Selected Works*, 5: 284–307.

Marcus, Steven. 1974. *Engels, Manchester, and the Working Class* (New York: Vintage).

Marshall, Alfred. 1927. *Principles of Economics: An Introductory Volume*, 8th ed. (London: Macmillan & Co.).

Martineau, Harriet. 1837. *Society in America* (New York), extracted in Felix Flugel and Harold Faulkner, eds. *Readings in the Economic and Social History of the United States* (New York and London: Harper and Brothers): 179–83.

Marx, Karl. 1842. "Proceedings of the Sixth Rhine Province Assembly. Third Article. Debates on the Law on Thefts of Wood," Karl Marx and Frederick Engels, *Marx, 1835–1843. Vol. 1 Collected Works* (New York: International Publishers, 1975): 224–63.

———. 1845. "On Friedrich List's Book, *Das Nationale System der Politischen Oekonomie*," in Marx and Engels, *Collected Works*. Vol 5. Marx and Engels, 1844–1845 (New York: International Publishers, 1975): 265–94.

———. 1847. *The Poverty of Philosophy* (New York: International Publishers).

———. 1852. "The Eighteenth Brumaire of Louis Bonaparte," in Karl Marx and Frederick Engels, *Selected Works in Three Volumes* (Moscow: Foreign Languages Publishing House, 1969–73): 1: 394–487.

———. 1853. "The Future Results of British Rule in India," in Marx and Engels, *Selected Works in Three Volumes*, 1: 494–99.

———. 1853a. "Elections—Financial Clouds—The Dutchess of Sutherland and Slavery," in Marx and Engels, *Collected Works. Vol. 2. Marx and Engels, 1851–1853*: 486–94.

———. 1858. "The Chinese Trade Figures," in Schlomo Avineri, *Karl Marx on Colonialism and Modernization* (Garden City, N.Y.: Doubleday, 1968): 333–38.

———. 1859. *A Contribution to the Critique of Political Economy* (New York: International Publishers, 1970).

———. 1865. "Wages, Price and Profit," in Marx and Engels, *Selected Works in Three Volumes*, 2: 31–76.

———. 1963, 1968, and 1971. *Theories of Surplus Value* (Moscow: Progress Publishers).

――――. 1965. *Precapitalistic Economics Formations* (New York: International Publishers).

――――. 1967. *Capital*, vols. 2 and 3 (New York: International Publishers).

――――. 1970. *Critique of Political Economy* (New York: International Publishers).

――――. 1974. *Grundrisse* (New York: Vintage).

――――. 1977. *Capital*, volume 1 (New York: Vintage).

――――, and Frederick Engels. 1846. "Feuerbach, Opposition of Materialist and Idealist Outlook," in Karl Marx and Frederick Engels, *Selected Works in Three Volumes* (Moscow: Progress Publishers, 1969–1973): 1: 16–80.

――――. 1846a. *The German Ideology*, in Karl Marx and Friedrich Engels, *Collected Works. Vol 5. Marx and Engels: 1845–1847* (New York: International Publishers, 1976): 19–540.

――――. 1942. *Selected Correspondence* (New York: International Publishers).

――――. 1973. *Marx/Engels Werke* (Berlin: Dietz).

――――. 1975. *Selected Correspondence* (Moscow: Progress Publishers).

Marx, Leo. 1964. *The Machine in the Garden: Technology and the Pastoral Ideal in America* (New York: Oxford University Press).

Matsukawa, Shichiro. 1965. "An Essay on the Historical Uniqueness of Petty's Labor Theory of Value." *Hitotshubashi Journal of Economics*, 5, no. 2 (January): 1–11.

Mayer, Margit, and Margaret A. Fay. 1977. "The Formation of the American Nation-State." *Kapitalstate* no. 6 (Fall): 39–90.

Meek, Ronald L. 1963. *The Economics of Physiocracy* (Cambridge: Harvard University Press).

――――. 1976. *Social Science and the Ignoble Savage* (Cambridge: Cambridge University Press).

――――. 1977a. "New Light on Adam Smith's Glasgow Lectures on Jurisprudence," in *Smith, Marx, and After: Ten Essays in the Development of Economic Thought* (London: Chapman and Hall): 57–91.

――――. 1977b. "Smith, Turgot, and the Four Stages Theory," *Smith, Marx, and After*, pp. 18–32.

――――. 1977c. "Smith and Marx," *Smith, Marx, and After*, pp. 1–17.

――――. 1977d. "The Development of Adam Smith's Ideas on the Division of Labour," in *Smith, Marx, and After*, pp. 33–56.

Meillasoux, Claude. 1972. "From Reproduction to Production: A Marxist Approach to Economic Anthropology." *Economy and Society* 1, no. 1 (February): 93–105.

Melotti, Umberto. 1977. *Marx and the Third World* (London: MacMillan).

Mendels, Franklin F. 1972. "Proto-Industrialization: The First Phase of the Process of Industrialization." *Journal of Economic History* 32, no. 1 (March): 241–61.

――――. 1975. "Agriculture and Peasant Industry in Eighteenth Century Flanders," in William N. Parker and Eric L. Jones, eds., *European Peasants and Their Markets* (Princeton, N. J.: Princeton University Press).

Merivale, Herman. 1841. *Lectures on Colonization and Colonies—Delivered Before the University of Oxford, 1839, 1840, and 1841* (London: Longman, Orme, Brown, Green and Longmans).

Merrington, John. 1976. "Town and Country in the Transition to Capitalism," in Rodney Hilton, ed., *The Transition from Feudalism to Capitalism* (London: New Left Books): 170–95.

Mill, James. 1826. *Elements of Political Economy*, in Donald Winch, ed., *James Mill: Selected Economic Writings* (Chicago: University of Chicago Press, 1966): 203–366.

Mill, John Stuart. 1848. *Principles of Political Economy with Some of Their Applications to Social Philosophy. Vols 2–3. Collected Works*, J. M. Robson, ed. (Toronto: University of Toronto Press, 1965).

Millar, John. 1806. *The Origin of the Distinction of Ranks; or An Inquiry into the Circumstances*

Which Give Rise to Influence and Authority in the Different Members of Society, 4th ed. (Edinburgh: Blackwood).

Mills, Richard Charles. 1915. *The Colonization of Australia (1829–42): The Wakefield Experiment in Empire Building* (London: Sidgwick and Jackson).

Mirabeau, Marquis de. 1756. *L'Ami des Hommes* (Paris).

Mitchell, Broadus. 1957–62. *Alexander Hamilton*, 2 vols. (New York: Macmillan & Co.).

Montagu, Lady Mary Wortley. 1966–67. *The Complete Letters of Lady Mary Wortley Montagu*, 3 vols. (Oxford: Clarendon Press).

Montgomery, David. 1979. *Workers' Control in America: Studies in the History of Work, Technology, and Labor Struggles* (Cambridge: Cambridge University Press).

Moore, Barrington, Jr. 1966. *Social Origins of Dictatorship and Democracy: Lord and Peasant in the Making of the Modern World* (Boston: Beacon Press).

Moore, Wilbur. 1951. *Industrialization and Labor* (Ithaca, N.Y.: Cornell University Press).

———. 1955. "Labor Attitudes Toward Industrialization in Underdeveloped Countries." *American Economic Review* 45, no. 2 (May): 156–65.

Morely, Derek Wragge. 1954. *The Evolution of an Insect Society* (London: Allen and Unwin).

Morgan, Edmund. 1975. *American Slavery, American Freedom: The Ordeal of Colonial Virginia* (New York: W. W. Norton).

———. 1976. *The Challenge of the American Revolution* (New York: W. W. Norton).

Moser, Arthur. 1966. *Getting Agriculture Moving: Essentials for Development and Modernization* (New York: Frederick A. Praeger).

Mossner, Ernest Campbell, and Ian Simpson Ross, eds. 1977. *The Correspondence of Adam Smith* (Oxford: Clarendon Press).

Munsche, P. B. 1980. *Gentlemen and Poachers: The English Game Laws 1671–1831* (Cambridge: Cambridge University Press).

Myers, Ramon H. 1980. *The Chinese Economy: Past and Present* (Belmont, Calif.: Wadsworth).

Nallet, Henri, and Clause Servolin. January 1978. *Le paysan et le droit* (Paris: Institut national de la recherche agronomique, Economie et sociologie rurales).

Needham, Joseph. 1969. *The Grand Titration: Science and Society in East and West* (Toronto: University of Toronto Press).

Nelson, Frederick J., and Willard W. Cochrane. 1976. "Economic Consequences of Federal Commodity Programs." *Agricultural Economics Research* 28, no. 2 (April): 52–64.

Nordhaus, William, and James Tobin. 1972. "Is Growth Obsolete?" in Milton Moss, ed., *The Measurement of Economic and Social Performance, National Bureau of Economic Research Studies in Income and Wealth*, no. 38 (New York: Columbia University Press).

North, Douglass C. 1966. *The Economic Growth of the United States, 1790–1860* (New York: W. W. Norton).

Nurske, R. 1953. *Problems of Capital Formation in Underdeveloped Countries* (Oxford: Basil Blackwell).

Nutter, G. Warren. 1976. "Adam Smith and the American Revolution" (Washington, D.C.: American Enterprise Institute, Reprint no. 54).

O'Brien, D. P., and A. C. Darnell. 1978. "Torrens, McCulloch, and the 'Digression on Sismondi': Whose Digression?" University of Durham, Department of Economics, Working Paper no. 22 (September).

O'Connor, Feargus. 1845. "The Land Plan . . . . ," reprinted in Patricia Hollis, ed. *Class and Conflict in Nineteenth-Century England* (London: Routledge and Kegan Paul, 1973): 307–8.

———. 1848. "Free Trade and the Land Plan," in Hollis, ed. *Class and Conflict in Nineteenth-Century England*, p. 309.

———. 1848. "A Treatise on the Small Farm System and the Banking System." *The Labourer* 3: 54–100.

O'Connor, Michael J. L. 1944. *Origins of Academic Economics in the United States* (New York: Garland, 1974).

Ogg, F. A., ed. 1906. *Personal Narratives of Travel in Virginia, Maryland, Ohio, Indiana, Kentucky, and of a Residence in the Illinois Territory (1817–1818)* (Cleveland).

Olwig, Karen Fog, and Kenneth Olwig. 1979. "Underdevelopment and the Development of the 'Natural' Park Ideology." *Antipode* 11, no. 2: 16–25.

Owen, Robert. 1813. "Second Essay on the Formation of Character," in *A New View of Society and Other Writings*, G. D. H. Cole, ed. (London: Dent, 1949): 22–38.

———. 1857. *The Life of Robert Owen* (London: Effingham Wilson).

Peffer, William. 1891. *The Farmer's Side. His Troubles and Their Remedy* (New York).

Pennant, Thomas. 1771. *A Tour in Scotland* (Chester).

———. 1772. *A Tour in Scotland*, 2nd ed. (London: B. White).

———. 1774. *A Tour in Scotland*, 3rd ed., ii, *A Tour in Scotland and Voyage to the Herbrides* (Chester).

Perelman, Michael. 1977. *Farming for Profit in a Hungry World: Capital and the Crisis in Agriculture* (Montclair, N.J.: Allanheld, Osmun).

———. 1981. "The Social Division of Labor, Agricultural Technology, and the Organization of Production in the United States." Unpublished ms.

———. 1981a. "Constant Capital and the Social Division of Labor." *The Review of Radical Political Economics* 13, no. 3 (Fall): 43–53.

Pessen, Edward. 1973. *Riches, Class and Power Before the Civil War* (Lexington, Mass.: D. C. Heath).

Pettengill, John. 1981. "Firearms and the Distribution of Income: A Neo Classical Model." *The Review of Radical Political Economics* 13, no. 2 (Summer): 1–10.

Petty, Sir William. 1662. "Treatise of Taxes and Contributions," in *The Writings of Sir William Petty*, 2 vols., C. H. Hull, ed. (Cambridge: Cambridge University Press): 1: 1–97.

———. 1683. "Another Essay on Political Arithmetick," in *Writings of William Petty*, 1: 453–76.

———. 1687. "A Treatise of Ireland," in *The Writings of William Petty*, 2: 545–621.

———. 1690. "Political Arithmetick, 1690," in *Writings of William Petty*, 1: 237–312.

———. 1691. "Verbum Sapienti," in *Writings of William Petty*, 1: 99–120.

———. 1927. *The Petty Papers: Some Unpublished Papers of Sir William Petty*, The Marquis of Lansdowne, ed., 2 vols. (London: Constable).

Philipponeau, Michel. 1956. *La vie rurale de la Banlieu Parisienne: Etude de geographie humaine* (Paris: Librairie Armand Colin).

Plath, Raymond Arthur. 1939. "British Mercantilism and the British Colonial Land Policy in the Eighteenth Century," Ph.D. Dissertation, University of Wisconsin.

Platteau, Jean-Philippe. 1978. *Les economistes classiques et le sous-developement*, 2 vols. (Namur, Belgium: Presses Universitaires de Namur).

Pollack, Norman. 1962. *The Populist Response to Industrial America* (Cambridge: Harvard University Press).

Pollard, Sidney. 1965. *The Genesis of Modern Management* (Cambridge: Harvard University Press).

———. 1978. *The Cambridge Economic History of Europe. Vol, 7. The Industrial Economies, Part 1: Britain, France, Germany, and Scandinavia*, Peter Mathias and M. M. Postan, eds. (Cambridge: Cambridge University Press): 97–179, 648–64.

Ponce, I. 1870. *Traite d'agriculture pratique et d'economie rurale* (Paris: Librairie Agricole de la Maison Rustique).

Postan, M. M. 1966. "England," in *The Cambridge Economic History of Europe, Volume 1, The Agrarian Life of the Middle Ages*, M. M. Postan, ed. (Cambridge: Cambridge University Press): 549–632.

Postlethwayt, Malachy. 1751. *The Universal Dictionary of Trade and Commerce, Translated from the French of the Celebrated Monsieur Savary* (London).

Pownall, Governor. 1776. *A Letter from Governor Pownall to Adam Smith, L.L.D. F.R.S., Being an Examination of Several Points of Doctrine, Laid Down in His Inquiry into the Nature and Causes of the* Wealth of Nations (London), reprinted in Ernest Campbell Mossner and Ian Simpson Ross, eds., *The Correspondence of Adam Smith* (Oxford: Clarendon Press, 1977): 337–76.

Price, Richard. 1783. *Observations on the Importance of the American Revolution and the Means of Making It a Benefit to the World* (London).

Primack, Martin. 1966. "Farm Capital Formation as a Use of Farm Labor in the United States, 1850–1910." *Journal of Economic History* 26, no. 3 (September): 348–62.

Prothero, Iorwerth. 1969. "Chartism in London." *Past and Present* no. 44 (August): 76–105.

Puckle, James. 1700. "England's Path to Wealth and Honour," in Walter Scott, *A Collection of Scarce and Valuable Tracts* (London, 1814).

Quesnay, Francois. 1758. "Tableau economique," in Marguerite Kuczynski and Ronald Meek, eds., *Quesnay's Tableau Economique* (New York: Augustus M. Kelley, 1972).

Rabbeno, Ugo. 1895. *American Commercial Policy* (New York and London: Macmillan).

Rae, John. 1895. *The Life of Adam Smith* (New York: Augustus M. Kelley, 1965).

———. 1825. "Sketches of the Origin and Progress of Manufactures and of the Policy Which Has Regulated their Legislative Encouragement in Great Britain and in Other Countries." *Canadian Review and Literary Journal* 3 (March), reprinted in R. Warren James, ed. *John Rae, Political Economist: An Account of His Life and a Compilation of His Main Writings*, 2 vols. (Toronto: University of Toronto Press 1965.): 1:195–206.

———. 1828. "Letter the Honourable Mr. Stanley, on the Relative Claims of the English and Scotch Churches in Canada." *Religious, Literary, and Statistical Intelligencer* (August), reprinted in James, ed. 1965. *John Rae, Political Economist*, 1: 221–57.

———. 1834. *Statement of Some New Principles on the Subject of Political Economy* (Boston), reprinted as vol. 2 of James, ed., *John Rae, Political Economist*.

———. 1862. "Letter to R. C. Wyllie, March 1862," reprinted in James, ed., *John Rae, Political Economist*, 1: 368–99.

Ransom, Roger, and Richard Sutch. 1977. *One Kind of Freedom: The Economic Consequences of Emancipation* (Cambridge: Cambridge University Press).

Rattner, Sidney, James Soltow, and Richard Sylla. 1979. *The Evaluation of the American Economy* (New York: Basic Books).

Ravenstone, Piercy. 1824. *Thoughts on the Funding System and Its Effects* (London: J. Andrews, repr. Kelley, 1966).

Raymond, Daniel. 1823. *Elements of Political Economy*, 2nd ed. (Baltimore: F. Lucas, Jr., and E. J. Coale).

Redford, Arthur. 1926. *Labour Migration in England, 1800–1850* (Manchester: Manchester University Press).

Reid, Douglas A. 1976. "The Decline of St. Monday." *Past and Present* 71 (May): 76–101.

Rendall, Jane. 1978. *The Origins of the Scottish Enlightenment* (New York: St. Martin's Press).

Ricardo, David. 1951–73. *The Works and Correspondence of David Ricardo*, 11 vols., Piero Sraffa, ed. (Cambridge: Cambridge University Press).

Rich, E. E. 1967. "Colonial Settlement and Its Labour Problems." in E. E. Rich and C. H. Wilson, eds., *The Cambridge History of Europe. 4. The Economy of Expanding Europe in the Sixteenth and Seventeenth Centuries* (Cambridge: Cambridge University Press): 308–73.

Robbins, Lionel. 1958. *Robert Torrens and the Evolution of Classical Economics* (London: Macmillan & Co.).

Robertson, A. J. 1971. "Robert Owen, Cotton Spinner: New Lanark," in Sidney Pollard and John Salt, eds., *Robert Owen, Prophet of the Poor: Essays in Honour of the Two-Hundredth Anniversary of His Birth* (Lewisburg, Pa.: Bucknell University Press): 145–65.

Robertson, William. 1769. "A View of the Progress of Society in Europe, From the Subversion of the Roman Empire, to the Beginning of the Sixteenth Century," reprinted in *The Works of William Robertson*, 12 vols. (London: 1817).

————. 1769a. *The History of the Reign of the Emperor Charles the Fifth*, 3 vols. (Philadelphia: J. B. Lippincott Co., 1884).

————. 1777. *The History of America*, reprinted in *The Works of William Robertson, D.D.*, 12 vols. (London, 1817).

————. 1781. *The History of Scotland*, 2 vols. (London: T. Caddell).

Robinson, Harriet H. 1898. *Loom and Spindle, or Life Among the Early Mill Girls* (Kailua, Hawaii: Pacifica Press, 1976).

Robinson, Joan. 1960. "The Philosophy of Prices," reprinted in J. Robinson, *Collected Works*, Vol. 2. (Oxford: Basil Blackwell, 1964): 27–48.

Rodbertus-Jagetzow, Carl. 1899. *Das Kapital*; reprinted as Vol. 2. Aus den Literaschen Nachlass von Carl Rodgertus-Jagetzow H. Schumacher Zarchlin, A. Wagner, and T. Kozak, eds., (Berlin: Puttkammer und Muhlbrecht).

Rodney, Walter. 1974. *How Europe Underdeveloped Africa* (Washington, D. C.: Howard University Press).

Rosenstein-Rodan, Paul. 1943. "Problems of Industrialization of Eastern and South-Eastern Europe." *Economic Journal* 53, nos. 210–211 (June–September): 202–11.

Ross, Eric. 1973. *The Leviathan of Wealth: The Sutherland Fortune in the Industrial Revolution* (London: Routledge and Kegan Paul).

Rotwein, Eugene, ed. 1955. *David Hume: Writings on Economics* (Madison: University of Wisconsin Press).

Rude, George. 1980. *Ideology and Popular Protest* (New York: Pantheon Books).

Rudkin, Olive D. 1966. *Thomas Spence and His Connections* (New York: Kelley).

Rumford, Count. 1795. "Of Food: And Particularly the Feeding of the Poor," in *Collected Works of Count Rumford*, Sanborn C. Brown, ed., 5 vols. (Cambridge: Harvard University Press, 1968–70): 5: 169–262.

Ruskin, John. 1866. *Crown of Wild Olives*, reprinted in *Vol. 1. Works of John Ruskin* (New York: Library Edition, 18??): 1–94.

Sabel, Charles. 1982. *Work and Politics: The Division of Labor in Industry* (New York: Cambridge University Press).

Sachs, William S. 1953. "Agricultural Conditions in the Northern Colonies Before the Revolution." *Journal of Economic History* 13, no. 3 (Summer): 274–90.

Samuel, Raphael. 1973. "Comers and Goers," in H. J. Dyos and Michael Wolff, eds., *The Victorian City*, 2 vols. (London: Routledge and Kegan Paul): 1: 123–63.

Samuels, Warren. 1966. *The Classical Theory of Economic Policy* (Cleveland, Ohio: World Publishing).

————. 1973. "Adam Smith and the Economy As a System of Power." *Review of Social Economy* 31, no. 2 (October): 123–37.

Say, Jean-Baptiste. 1821. *Letters to Malthus on Several Subjects of Political Economy and the Cause of the Stagnation of Commerce*, trans. John Richter (New York: Augustus M. Kelley, 1967).

————. 1843. *Cours Complet d'economie politique* (Brussels: Societe Typographique Belge).

Say, J. B. 1880. *Treatise on Political Economy*, 4th ed., C. R. Princep, trans. (New York: Augustus M. Kelley, 1964).

Schlesinger, Arthur. 1945. *The Age of Jackson* (New York: Book Find Club).

Schultz, Theordore. 1964. *Transforming Traditional Agriculture* (New Haven: Yale University Press).

_____. 1968. "Institutions and the Rising Value of Man." *American Journal of Agricultural Economics* 50, no. 5 (December): 1113–22.

Schumpeter, Joseph A. 1954. *History of Economic Analysis* (New York: Oxford University Press).

Schuyler, Robert Livingston, ed. 1931. *Josiah Tucker: A Selection from His Economic and Political Writings with an Introduction by Robert Livingston Schuyler* (New York: Columbia University Press).

Scitovsky, Tibor. 1976. *The Joyless Economy: An Inquiry into Human Satisfaction* (New York: Oxford University Press).

Scott, William R. 1934. "Adam Smith and the Glasgow Merchants." *Economic Journal* 44: 506–508.

_____. 1965. *Adam Smith as Student and Professor* (New York: Kelley).

Seligman, E. R. A. ed. 1910. Introduction to Adam Smith, *An Inquiry into the Nature and Causes of the Wealth of Nations* (London: Everyman's Edition).

Semmel, Bernard. 1970. *The Rise of Free Trade Imperialism* (Cambridge: Cambridge University Press).

Sen, S. R. 1957. *The Economics of Sir James Steuart* (Cambridge: Harvard University Press).

Senior, Nassau. 1831. *Three Lectures on the Rate of Wages with a Preface on the Causes and Remedies of the Present Crisis* (New York: Augustus M. Kelley, 1959).

_____. 1832. *A Letter to Lord Howick on a Legal Provision for the Irish Poor*, 3rd ed. (London: John Murray).

_____. 1836. *An Outline of the Science of Political Economy* (New York: Augustus M. Kelley, 1938).

_____. 1841. "Grounds and Objects of the Budget." *Edinburgh Review* 73 (July): 503–59.

_____. 1868. *Journals, Conversations and Essays Relating to Ireland*, 2 vols., 2nd ed. (London: Longmans, Green & Co.).

_____. 1871. *Journals Kept in France and Italy*, 2 vols., 2nd ed. (London: Henry S. King).

_____. 1928. *Industrial Efficiency and Social Economy*, 2 vols., S. Leon Levy, ed. (New York: Holt).

Shannon, Fred. 1945. "A Post Mortem on the Labor Safety-Valve Theory." *Agricultural History* 19, no. 1 (January): 31–37.

Shireff, Patrick. 1835. "A Tour Through North America," extracted in E. L. Bogard and C. M. Thompson, eds. *Readings in the Economic History of the United States* (New York: Longmans and Green, 1927): pp. 464–67.

Sinclair, Sir John. 1803. "Observations on the Means of Enabling a Cottager to Keep a Cow by the Produce of a Small Portion of Arable Land," in *Essays in Miscellaneous Subjects*, reprinted in *The Annual Register* 45 (1805): 850–57.

Sismondi, J.-C.-L. de Simonde. 1827. *Nouveaux principles d'economie politique* (Paris: Calman-Levy, 1971).

Skinner, Andrew S. 1966. *Introduction to Sir James Steuart, An Inquiry into the Principles of Political Economy*, 2 vols. (Chicago: University of Chicago Press).

_____. 1976. "Adam Smith and the American Economic Community: An Essay in Applied Economics." *Journal of the History of Ideas* 37, no. 1 (January-March): 59–78.

Slicher van Bath. 1960. "The Rise of Intensive Husbandry in the Low Countries," in J. S. Bromley and E. H. Kossman, eds. *Britain and the Netherlands: Papers Delivered at the Oxford-Netherlands Historical Conference, 1959* (London: Chatto and Windus): 130–53.

Smelser, Neil J. 1959. *Social Change in the Industrial Revolution: An Application of Theory to the British Cotton Industry* (Chicago: University of Chicago Press).

Smith, Abbot Emerson. 1927. *Colonists in Bondage: White Servitude and Convict Labor in America, 1607–1776* (Chapel Hill: University of North Carolina Press).

Smith, Adam. 1755–56. "Letters to the Editor of the *Edinburgh Review*." Reprinted in *Adam Smith, Essays on Philosophical Subjects*, W. P. D. Wightman and J. C. Bryce, eds. (Oxford: Clarendon Press, 1980): 242–56.

————. 1759. *The Theory of Moral Sentiments*, D. D. Raphael and A. L. Macfie, eds. (Oxford: Clarendon Press, 1976).

————. 1762–63. *Lectures on Rhetoric and Belles Lettres*, John M. Lothian, ed. (London: Thomas Nelson, 1963).

————. 1763. *Lectures on Police, Justice, Revenue and Arms* (New York: Kelley, 1964).

————. 1763a. "An Early Draft of Part of the *Wealth of Nations*," in William Robert Scott, *Adam Smith as Student and Professor* (New York: Kelley, 1965): 322–56.

————. 1790. "The Principles Which Lead and Direct Philosophical Enquiries; Illustrated by the History of Astronomy," in Adam Smith, *Essays on Philosphical Subjects*, W. P. D. Wightman and J. C. Bryce, eds. (Oxford: Clarendon Press, 1980): pp. 31–106.

————. 1790a. "Of the Nature of that Imitation which takes place in what are called the Imitative Arts," In Adam Smith, *Essays on Philosophical Subjects*, W. P. D. Wightman and J. C. Bryce, eds. (Oxford: Clarendon Press, 1980): pp. 176–209.

————. 1937. *An Inquiry into the Nature and Causes of the* Wealth of Nations (New York: Modern Library).

————. 1976. *An Inquiry into the Nature and Causes of the* Wealth of Nations, R. H. Campbell and A. S. Skinner, eds. (New York: Oxford University Press).

————. 1977. *The Correspondence of Adam Smith*, Mossner and Ross, eds. (Oxford: Clarendon Press).

————. 1978. *Lectures on Jurisprudence*, R. L. Meek, D. D. Raphael, and P. G. Stein, eds. (Oxford: Clarendon University Press).

Smith, E. Peshine. 1853. *A Manual of Political Economy* (New York: Garland, 1974).

Smith, Captain John. 1616. "A Description of New England," reprinted in *Captain John Smith, Works, 1608–1631*, vols. 4 and 5 of Edward Arber, ed., *The English Scholars' Library* (Birmingham, England, 1884).

Smith, J. Russell. 1925. *Industrial and Commercial Geography*, 2nd ed. (New York: Henry Holt).

Smith, Sydney. 1819. "Game Laws." *Edinburgh Review* 31, no. 62 (March): 295–309.

————. 1821. "Spring Guns and Man Traps." *Edinburgh Review* 35, no. 69 (March): 213–34.

Smith, Thomas C. 1966. *The Agrarian Origins of Modern Japan* (New York: Atheneum).

Smout, T. C. 1969. *A History of the Scottish People, 1560–1830* (New York: Charles Scribner's Sons).

Smuts, Robert W. 1959. *Women and Work in America* (New York: Columbia University Press).

Sohn-Rethel, Alfred. 1978. *Intellectual and Manual Labour: A Critique of Epistemology* (London: Macmillan).

Soltow, J. H. 1959. "Scottish Traders in Virginia, 1750–1775." *Economic History Review*, 2nd series, vol. 12, no. 1 (August): 83–98.

Spence, Thomas. 1807. *The Restorer of Society to Its Natural State*, 2nd ed. (London).

Spengler, Joseph J. 1968. "The Political Economy of Jefferson, Madison and Adams." in David Kelley Jackson, ed., *American Studies in Honor of William Kenneth Boyd* (Freeport, N.Y.: Books for Libraries Press).

Spenser, Edmund. 1591. "Complaints. Mother Hubbard's Tale," in Edwin Greenlaw et al., eds., *The Works of Edmund Spenser: A Variorum Edition*, 9 vols. (Baltimore: John Hopkins Press): 7, pt. 2: 104–40.

Spiegel, Henry William. 1960. *The Rise of American Economic Thought* (Philadelphia: Chilton).

Stalin, Josef. 1928. "Industrialization and the Grain Problem: Speech, 9 July 1928," in *Works. 11. 1928–March 1929* (Moscow: Foreign Languages Publishing House, 1954).

———. 1929. "The Right Deviation in the C.P.S.U. (B); Speech delivered at the Central Committee and the Control Commission of the C.P.S.U. (B) in April 1929," in *Works. Vol. 12. April 1929–June 1930* (Moscow: Foreign Languages Publishing House, 1954).

Stark, Werner. 1944. *The History of Economics in Relation to Social Development* (London: Kegan Paul).

Stearns, Peter N. 1974. "Working-Class Women in Britain, 1890–1914," in Peter N. Stearns and Daniel J. Walkowitz, eds., *Workers in the Industrial Revolution: Recent Studies of Labor in the United States and Europe* (New Brunswick, N.J.: Transaction Books): 401–24.

———. 1974a. "National Character and European Labor History," in Peter N. Stearns and Daniel J. Walkowitz, eds., *Workers in the Industrial Revolution: Recent Studies of Labor in the United States and Europe* (New Brunswick, N.J.: Transaction Books): 13–33.

Steuart, Sir James. 1767. *An Inquiry into the Principles of Political Economy, Being an Essay on the Science of Domestic Policy in Free Nations*, Vols. 1–4, in *Sir James Steuart, The Works: Political, Metaphysical and Chronological*, 6 vols. (New York: Augustus M. Kelley, 1967).

———. 1769. "Considerations on the Interest of Lanark," in *Sir James Steuart, The Works*, 5: 286–306.

———. 1772. *The Principles of Money Applied to the Present Sate of Bengal*, in *Sir James Steuart, The Works*, 5: 1–120.

———. 1966. *An Inquiry into the Principles of Political Economy*, 2 volumes, Andrew S. Skinner, ed. (Chicago: University of Chicago Press).

Stevens, David. 1975. "Adam Smith and the Colonial Disturbances," Thomas Wilson and Andrew Skinner, eds., *Essays on Adam Smith* (Clarendon: Oxford University Press): 202–17.

Stewart, Dugald. 1811. "Account of the Life and Writings of Adam Smith, L.L.D.," in *The Works of Adam Smith*, 5 vols. (London: T. Caddell and W. Davies): 5: 400–552.; reprinted in Adam Smith, *Essays on Philosophical Subjects*, W. P. D.Wightman and J. C. Bryce, eds. (Oxford: Clarendon Press, 1980): pp. 269–352.

———. 1855. *Lectures on Political Economy*, 2 vols., Sir W. Hamilton, ed. (New York: Augustus M. Kelley, 1968).

Stigler, George. 1951. "The Division of Labor Is Limited by the Extent of the Market." *Journal of Political Economy* 59, no. 3 (June): 185–93.

Strauss, E. 1954. *Sir William Petty, Portrait of a Genius* (Glencoe, Ill.: The Free Press).

Suffield, Edward, 3d Baron. 1825. *Considerations on the Game Laws* (London).

Sward, Keith. 1972. *The Legend of Henry Ford* (New York: Atheneum).

Sweezy, Paul. 1980. "Japan in Perspective." *Monthly Review* 31, no. 9 (February): 1–14.

Swift, Jonathan. 1723–24. "The Drapier's Letters," reprinted in *Jonathan Swift, "The Drapier's Letters" and Other Works* (Oxford: Basil Blackwell, 1959): 1–152.

———. 1726. *Gulliver's Travels*, vol. ll. *Collected Works*, Herbert Davis, ed. (Oxford: Basil Blackwell, 1959).

———. 1729. "A Modest Proposal for Preventing the Children of Poor People in Ireland from Being a Burden to Their Parents or Country; and for Making Them Beneficial to the Publick," in *Irish Tracts, 1728–1733*, vol. 12 of his *Collected Works*, Herbert Davis, ed. (Oxford: Basil Blackwell, 1964): 107–18.

_____. 1731. "The Answer to the Craftsman," reprinted in *Jonathan Swift, Irish Tracts, 1728–1733*, Herbert Davis, ed. (Oxford: Basil Blackwell, 1964).

Taper, Bernard. 1979. "Minaturizing Agriculture." *Science 80*, 1, no. 1 (November).

Taussig, Michael. 1979. "Black Religion and Resistance in Columbia." *Marxist Perspectives* 2, no. 2 (Summer): 84–117.

Tawney, R. H. 1926. *Religion and the Rise of Capitalism: A Historical Study* (New York: New American Library, 1947).

Taylor, Paul S. 1972. *Georgia Plan: 1732–1752* (Berkeley: University of California Institute for Business and Economic Research).

Temin, Peter. 1971. "Labor Scarcity in America." *Journal of Interdisci plinary History* 1, no. 2 (Winter): 251–64.

Temperley, Howard. 1977. "Capitalism, Slavery, and Ideology." *Past and Present* no. 75 (May): 94–118.

Therborn, Goran. 1980. *Science, Class, and Society* (New Left Books: London).

Thirsk, Joan. 1978. *Economic Policy and Projects: The Development of a Consumer Society in Early Modern England* (Oxford: Clarendon Press).

Thomas, Brinley. 1980. "Towards an Energy Interpretation of the Industrial Revolution." *Atlantic Economic Journal* 8, no. 1 (March): 1–15.

Thomas, Gabriel. 1698. *An Historical and Geographical Account of Pennsylvania and of West New Jersey* (Harrisburgh, Pa.: Aurand Press, 1938).

Thomas, Keith. 1964. "Work and Leisure." *Past and Present* no. 29 (December): 50–66.

Thompson, E. P. 1963. *The Making of the English Working Class* (New York: Vintage).

_____. 1975. *Whigs and Hunters: The Origin of the Black Act* (New York: Pantheon).

Thompson, Noel. 1977. "Ricardian Socialists/Smithian Socialists: What's in a Name?" Research Paper (University of Cambridge: Faculty of Economics and Politics).

Thompson, T. Perronet. 1808. "Letter to Miss Baker, June 6." reprinted in L. G. Johnson, *General T. Perronet Thompson, 1783–1869* (London: George Allen and Unwin, 1957): p. 33.

Thweatt, William O. 1974. "The Digression of Sismondi: by Torrens or Mcculloch?" *History of Political Economy* 6, no. 4 (Winter): 435–53.

Tobias, J. J. 1967. *Crime and Industrial Society in the Nineteenth Century* (New York: Schocken Books).

Tocqueville, Alexis de. 1848. *Democracy in America* (New York: Doubleday, 1966).

Torrens, Robert. 1808. *The Economists Refuted* (London: S. A. and H. Oddy).

_____. 1817. "A Paper on the Means of Reducing the Poors Rates and of Affording Effectual and Permanent Relief to the Labouring Classes," printed as an Appendix to *Colonization of South Australia* (London, 1935).

_____. 1828. Substance of a Speech Delivered by Colonel Torrens in the House of Commons . . . (London: Longmans, Rees, Orme, Brown and Green).

_____. 1833. *Letters on Commercial Policy* (London: London School of Economics and Political Science, 1958).

_____. 1835. *Colonization of South Australia* (London: Longman, Rees, Orme, Brown, Green, and Longman).

Townsend, Joseph. 1786. "A Dissertation on the Poor Laws by a Well Wisher to Mankind," reprinted in John R. McCulloch, *A Select Collection of Scarce and Valuable Economic Tracts* (New York: Augustus M. Kelley, 1966): 395–450.

Tribe, Keith. 1978. *Land, Labour, and Economic Discourse* (London: Routledge and Kegan Paul).

_____. 1979. "Introduction to de Crisenoy." *Economy and Society* 8, no. 1 (February): 1–8.

Triffen, Robert. 1940. *Monopolistic Competition and General Equilibrium Theory* (Cambridge: Harvard University Press).

Trotsky, Leon. 1932. *The Russian Revolution: The Overthrow of Tzarism and the Triumph of the Soviets.* F. W. Dupee, ed. (New York: Doubleday).

Tsuzuki, Chushichi. 1971. "Robert Owen and Revolutionary Politics," in Sidney Pollard and John Salt, eds., *Robert Owen, Prophet of the Poor: Essays in Honour of the Two-Hundredth Anniversary of His Birth* (Lewisburg, Pa.: Bucknell University Press): 13–39.

Tucker, Josiah. 1776. *A Series of Answers to Certain Objections Against Separation from the Rebellious Colonies* (Glouster).

Tully, Alan. 1973. "Patterns of Slaveholding in Colonial Pennsylvania: Chester and Lancaster Counties, 1728–1758." *Journal of Social History* 6, no. 3 (Spring): 284–305.

Turgot, M. 1766. "Reflections on the Formation and Distribution of Wealth," reprinted in John R. McCulloch, ed., *A Select Collection of Scarce and Valuable Tracts* (New York: Augustus M. Kelley, 1966).

Tuttle, William N., Jr. 1967. "Forerunners of Frederick Jackson Turner: Nineteenth-Century British Conservatives and the Frontier Thesis." *Agricultural History* 41, no. 3 (July): 219–27.

Tyron, Rolla Milton. 1917. *Household Manufacturers in the United States, 1640–1860* (New York: Augustus M. Kelley, 1966).

United States Department of Agriculture, Agricultural Statistics, 1979 (Washington, D.C.: U.S. Government Printing Office).

United States House of Representatives. 1961. *Manpower Utilization and Training, Committee Hearings*, 87th Congress (Washington, D.C.: U.S. Government Printing Office).

Vicker, Ray. 1981. "Portable Workplaces: Computer Terminals Allow More People to Work at Home Instead of Commuting." *Wall Street Journal* (4 August): p. 46.

Viner, Jacob. 1927. "Adam Smith and Laissez Faire," reprinted in Viner, *The Long View and the Short* (Glencoe, Ill.: The Free Press, 1958): 198–232.

———. 1965. "Guide to John Rae's Life of Adam Smith," in *John Rae, The Life of Adam Smith* (New York: Augustus M. Kelley).

———. 1968. "Man's Economic Status," in James L. Clifford, ed., *Man Versus Society in 18th Century Britain: Six Points of View* (Cambridge: Cambridge University Press: 22–53.

Wakefield, Daniel. 1804. *An Essay on Political Economy*, 2nd ed. (London: F. C. and J. Rivington).

Wakefield, Edward Gibbon. 1829. "Letter from Sydney: The Principle Town of Australasia," in M. F. Lloyd Pritchard, ed., *The Collected Works of Edward Gibbon Wakefield* (Glasgow and London: Collins, 1968): pp. 93–186.

———. 1831a. "Letter from P_____ to Lord Howick, No. iii," *Spectator* (8 January).

———. 1831. "Facts Relating to the Punishment of Death in the Metropolis," reprinted in *Collected Works*, pp. 184–267.

———. 1834. *England and America* (Boston: Harper and Row).

———. 1835. "Commentary," in *Adam Smith, An Inquiry into the Nature and Causes of the Wealth of Nations*, 6 vols. (London: Charles Knight).

———. 1836. "Response to Question 610," in *The Report of The Select Committee on the Disposal of Public Lands in British Colonies, British Parliamentary Papers*.

———. 1841. "Letter to the Colonization Commissioners June 2, 1835," printed in Appendix to *The Report on the Select Committee on South Australia, Parliamentary Papers*.

———. 1849. *A View of the Art of Colonization in Letters Between a Statesman and a Colonist* (Clarendon: Oxford University Press, 1914).

Walecki, A. 1969. *The Controversy over Capitalism* (New York: Oxford University Press).

Walker, Katheryn E., and Margaret E. Woods. 1976. *Time Use: A Measure of Household Production of Family Goods and Services* (Washington, D.C.: Center for the Family of the American Home Economics Association).

Wallace, Robert. 1809. *A Dissertation the Numbers of Mankind in Ancient and Modern Times* (Edinburgh: Archibald Constable).

Wallas, Graham. 1919. *The Life of Francis Place,* 3rd ed. (New York: A. A. Knopf).

Walpole, Horace. 1937–74. *The Yale Edition of Horace Walpole's Correspondence,* 38 vols., W. S. Lewis, ed., Vol. 34. *Horace Walpole's Correspondence with the Countess of Upper Ossory. pt. 3. 1788–1797* (New Haven: Yale University Press).

Walsh, Vivian, and Harvey Gram. 1980. *Classical and Neoclassical Theories of General Equilibrium: Historical Origins and Mathematical Structure* (New York: Oxford University Press).

Ware, Norman Joseph. 1924. *The Industrial Worker, 1840–1860* (Boston: Houghton-Mifflin).

———. 1931. "The Physiocrats: A Study in Economic Rationalization." *American Economic Review* 21, no. 5 (December): 607–19.

Weber, Max. 1923. *General Economic History,* Frank Knight, trans. (New York: Collier Books, 1961).

Webster, Daniel. 1879. "First Settlement of New England, A Discourse Delivered at Plymouth on the 22nd December 1820," in *Daniel Webster, The Great Speeches and Orations of Daniel Webster, with an Essay on Daniel Webster as a Master of English Style,* Edwin P. Whipple, ed. (London: Sampson, Low, Marston, Searle and Rivington): 25–54.

Weiller, Jean. 1971. Preface to J. C. L. Simonde de Sismondi, *Nouveaux principles d'economie politique* (Paris: Calman-Levy).

Weld, Isaac, Jr. 1800. *Travels Through the States of North America, and the Provinces of Upper and Lower Canada, during the Years 1795, 1796, and 1797,* 4th ed., 2 vols. (New York: Johnson Reprint Co., 1968).

Wells, Roger A. E. 1979. "The Development of the English Rural Proletariat and Social Protest, 1700–1850." *Journal of Peasant Studies* 6, no. 2 (January): 115–39.

Wermel, Michael. 1939. *The Evolution of Classical Wage Theory* (New York: Columbia University Press).

Western, J. R. 1965. *The English Militia int he Eighteenth Century: The Story of a Political Issue: 1660–1802* (London: Routledge and Kegan Paul).

Wetzel, W. A. 1895. "Benjamin Franklin as an Economist." Johns Hopkins University Studies in Historical and Political Science (September).

Weulersse, Georges. 1910. *Le Mouvement Physiocratique en France (de 1756 a 1770),* 2 vols. (Paris: Felix Alcan; reprinted by Johnson Reprint Co., New York, 1968).

———. 1959. *La Physiocratie a la fin du Regne de Louis XV (1770–1774)* (Paris: Press Universitaire de France).

Wheelwright, E. L., and Bruce McFarlane. 1970. *The Chinese Road to Socialism: Economics of the Cultural Revolution* (New York: Monthly Review Press).

Whitney, Lois. 1924. "Primitivistic Theories of Epic Origins." *Modern Philology* 21, no. 4 (May): 337–78.

Wicksteed, Philip H. 1910. "The Common Sense of Political Economy," reprinted in *The Common Sense of Political Economy and Selected Papers and Reviews on Economic Theory,* 2 vols., Lionel Robbins, ed. (London: Routledge and Kegan Paul, 1933).

von Wieser, Friedrich. 1922. *Social Economics,* trans. A. Ford Hinrichs (New York: Augustus M. Kelley, 1967).

Wight, Andrew. 1778–84. *Present State of Husbandry Extracted from Reports to the Commissioners of the Annexed Estates,* 4 vols. (Edinburgh: T. Caddell).

Wiles, Richard C. 1968. "The Theory of Wages in Later English Mercantilism." *Economic History Review,* 2nd series, vol. 31, no. 2 (April): 113–26.

Wilkinson, Olga. 1964. *The Agricultural Revolution in the East Riding of Yorkshire* (York: East Yorkshire Local History Society).

Williams, Samuel. 1809. *Natural and Civil History of Vermont,* 2nd ed., 2 vols. (Burlington).

Williams, William Appleman. 1966. *The Contours of American Economic History* (New York: Quadrangle).

Williamson, Jeffrey G., and Peter H. Lindert. 1977. "Long-Term Trends in Wealth Inequality" (Madison, Wis: Institute for Research on Poverty, Discussion Paper No. 472–77, December).

Willis, Karl. 1979. "The Role in Parliament of the Economic Ideas of Adam Smith, 1776–1800." *History of Political Economy* 11, no. 4 (Summer): 505–44.

Wilson, Thomas, and Andrew Skinner, eds. 1976. *The Market and the State: Essays in Honour of Adam Smith* (Oxford: The Clarendon Press).

Winch, Donald. 1975. *Classical Political Economy and Colonies* (Cambridge: Harvard University Press).

———. 1978. *Adam Smith's Politics: An Essay in Histographical Revision* (Cambridge: Cambridge University Press).

Wittkowsky, Georgy. 1943. "Swift's Modest Proposal: The Biography of an Early Georgian Pamphlet." *Journal of the History of Ideas* 4 (June–October): 75–104.

Wolfstetter, Elmar. June 1973. "Surplus Labour, Synchronized Labour Costs and Marx's Labour Theory of Value." *The Economic Journal* 83, no. 331: 787–809.

Wordie, J. R. 1974. "Social Change on the Levenson-Gower Estates, 1714–1832," *The Economic History Review*, 2nd series, vol. 27, no. 4 (November): 593–605.

Wordsworth, William. 1802. "Preface to the Second Edition of Lyrical Ballads," in *The Poetical Works of William Wordsworth*, E. de Selincourt, ed., 5 vols. (Oxford: Clarendon Press, 1944): 2: 384–404.

Wright, Gavin. 1978. *The Political Economy of the Cotton South: Households, Markets and Wealth in the Nineteenth Century* (New York: W. W. Norton).

Wynne-Edwards, V. C. 1962. *Animal Dispersion in Relation to Human Behavior* (New York: Hafner).

Young, Arthur. 1774. *Political Arithmetic*, Part I (London).

———. 1794. *Travels in France During the Years 1787–1788–1789* (Garden City, N.Y.: Anchor Books, 1969).

Zahler, Helene Sarah. 1941. *Eastern Working Men and National Land Policy* (New York: Greenwood Publishers, 1969).

Index